THE
VISION
OF THE
SOUL

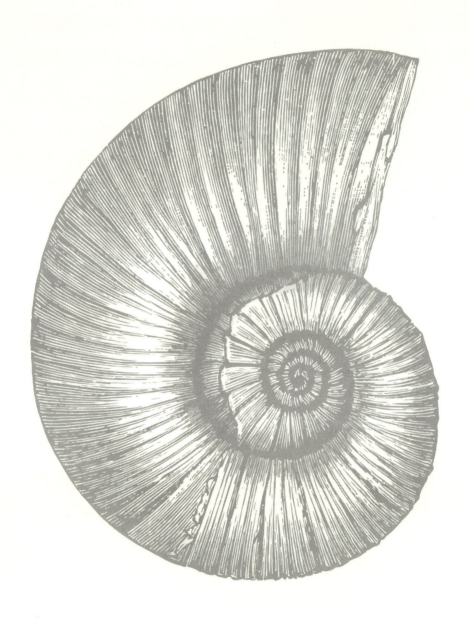

THE
VISION
OF THE
SOUL

TRUTH, GOODNESS,
AND BEAUTY
IN THE WESTERN
TRADITION

James Matthew Wilson

The Catholic University of America Press
Washington, D.C.

The paper used in this publication meets the minimum
requirements of American National Standards for Information
Science—Permanence of Paper for Printed Library Materials,
ANSI Z39.48-1984.

∞

Library of Congress Cataloging-in-Publication Data
Names: Wilson, James Matthew, author.
Title: The vision of the soul : truth, goodness, and beauty in the
western tradition / James Matthew Wilson.
Description: Washington, D.C. : The Catholic University of
America Press, 2017. | Includes bibliographical references and index.
Identifiers: LCCN 2016053715 | ISBN 9780813229287
(pbk. : alk. paper)
Subjects: LCSH: Aesthetics. | Art—Philosophy. |
Conservatism. | Conservatism and literature. | Burke, Edmund,
1729–1797. | Maritain, Jacques, 1882–1973. |
Christianity—Philosophy. | Platonists.
Classification: LCC BH39 .W555 2017 | DDC 111/.85—dc23
LC record available at https://lccn.loc.gov/2016053715

The mind has, as it were, eyes of its own, analogous to the soul's senses. The certain truths of the sciences are analogous to the objects which the sun's rays make visible, such as the earth and earthly things. And it is God himself who illumines all. I, Reason, am in minds as the power of looking is in the eyes.

ST. AUGUSTINE

If I … am a Thomist, it is in the last analysis because I have understood that the intellect sees.

JACQUES MARITAIN

CONTENTS

Part III. Reason, Narrative, and Truth

PREFACE

Most writers, I imagine, carry a sense of their life's work about with them, awaiting only the occasions of free time, editors' requests, or generous commission to get that work written. Since I first began to think seriously about the nature of the intellectual life, the purpose of education, and the function of art in my student years, I have fumbled toward a conception of these things that could make sense of them to me and that could be sufficiently comprehensive to serve as a guide to others. This was made all the more necessary and all the more challenging on account of my dogged connatural sense that the quest for truth, the reality of beauty, and the ordering of all things by a Good that transcends them, were three formative principles that lent human life its particularly and inescapably dramatic character. For, when I turned to the great quadrangles of the public university or the smaller cubes of the college classroom, I for the most part encountered persons who not only claimed not to possess such a sense, but who were committed to a reformation of the human spirit and civilization on principles that explicitly denied it. For most persons in our age, beauty is a subjective velleity, a term that names an incidental taste rather than a real thing: one that should be left to waste outside the threshold of serious discussion. Similarly, the truth of reason is taken for either the narrow province of empirical or quantifiable observation and repeatability, the ideology of imperialists intended to marginalize the marginalized, or the critical thinking of the dispossessed, for whom education becomes a mere drawing out of the inner confidence-man.

While I was stout in debate with my friends and antagonists on these matters, I never believed I would have opportunity to lay my case before the general public. I was not only mistaken on that point, but have been given several opportunities to give new voice to old, but unjustly discarded, arguments for the normative goodness of creation, for the ordered beauty of being, and for the light of truth as the natural and highest end of human life. I have, therefore, many persons to thank for occasioning these chapters and, in the process, for giving me time and place to work through the problem of the status of the three great transcendental properties of being in the context of a modernity too jaded to believe its own eyes about them. I would never have presumed to deserve an editor's, not to mention the reader's, attention on this subject had not my various editors and hosts given it without the asking.

"The Drama of Cultural Conservatism" first appeared in *The Point* magazine, and revisions of it were delivered as lectures at Yale University and Christendom College. "The Hunger for Reality" and "What Is the Western Tradition?" both began as lectures delivered to the students and faculty (respectively) of the Great Hearts Academies of Phoenix, Arizona. I owe many thanks to Erik Twist, David Williams, and Dan Scoggin for their generous invitation and gracious hospitality. I should also thank the various students and faculty of the Academies, who in a little more than a decade have become the standard bearers for truth, goodness, and beauty in contemporary education; their academies are among the few to be justly so named in our day.

The whole of Part II originally appeared as installments in my monthly essay series, *The Treasonous Clerk*, published in the Intercollegiate Studies Institute's *First Principles* web journal. "Reasoning about Stories" and "Novel, Myth, Reality" appeared in *Front Porch Republic*. *American Arts Quarterly* published a shorter version of "Mnemosyne: Mother of the Arts" as "Unleashed from the Exemplar." Versions of "Retelling the Story of Reason" and "The Consequences of Our Forgetting" were first delivered as a single lecture at Virginia Tech University, sponsored by the Intercollegiate Studies Institute, and subsequently appeared in the print and web editions of *Anamnesis* (respectively). "Still Interested in the Truth" first appeared in *Big Questions Online*.

I must thank the Intercollegiate Studies Institute for its great generosity, and especially Jed Donahue, who encouraged me to persist in the essays on beauty even as they swelled beyond the intended span and scope. I thank Sandra Sanderson, Peter Howarth, and Rod Dreher, for finding room for my essays in their publications. Jeremy Beer and Mark Mitchell provided me a place in the masthead of *Front Porch Republic*, and that is only the most concrete of their many kindnesses and encouragements to me over these last few years—for which I am most thankful. Beyond these particular and great helps, I must also extend my gratitude to Annette Kirk of the Russell Kirk Center for Cultural Renewal, who provided me peace, quiet, and time in the Kirk library to plug away at some of these pages.

I have the privilege of serving in a rare academic department at Villanova University where my colleagues are committed to the life of truth and beauty with a depth and seriousness that can only inspire my awe and admiration. If the intellectual life as I understand it is under assault in the academy as a whole, my colleagues nonetheless have provided an environment where it may flourish, and which would have been the envy of medieval Paris. In particular, I must thank David C. Schindler, whose intellectual fingerprints may be found all over this book. I also thank my research assistant, Megan Malamood, for helping me complete the revisions of this book, and all those students in the Department of Humanities whose dialectic has given me a chance to journey a bit deeper into the mystery of being. Finally, I would like to thank Trevor Lipscombe, Theresa Walker, and Anne Needham, at the Catholic University of America Press, who did so much to bring this long germinating book into print.

The world is a basilica, the cosmos a liturgy—so the Catholic tradition reveals to us. But nothing has given me a firmer sense of the beautiful pageant of life or the manifestation of the truth that penetrates and saturates all things than I have in the company of my wife and in the union of our love made visible in our children. To them I offer my deepest thanks, for they are each great goods in themselves and revelations of the one Good.

Needless to say, if many persons have given me inspiration or occasion to write these pages, it is I, a hopeful, zealous, but undeserving amateur, who must take responsibility for any errors of text or theory in them.

THE
VISION
OF THE
SOUL

The Drama of Cultural Conservatism

The Man Who Discovered England

The reflections with which I begin these pages may seem, at moments, to indulge in the barbed and the bitter, and the reader unfamiliar with my subject and with my own work, and otherwise disinclined to assertive denunciation, may be tempted to let the book slip back quietly to the shelf. But what I have to say on the matter of conservatism and culture emerges from my own life experience and comes in answer to questions salient to my own search for self-knowledge as well as to questions of a more obviously public nature regarding the goods of political and intellectual life. I think they will prove of some interest not only to those who bristle at the word "conservative," but to those who would normally greet the term with indifference.

Without ever having encountered any sustained articulation of conservative ideas, without having ever sought them out, I discovered in the middle of my undergraduate years that I had become a conservative—or rather, had become one again after a curious childhood adoration of Ronald Reagan. It suddenly appeared that the term "conservative" was one that described a disposition and set of beliefs I had almost inadvertently acquired in response to my encounters with fellow students and the professoriate at the University of Michigan; in bewilderment before the po-

INTRODUCTION

ems of W. B. Yeats, Yvor Winters, T. S. Eliot, and Dante, and in fear of the novels of Dostoyevsky and William Faulkner; through my reencounter with the Catholicism of my youth that I had set out with the fine intention of forgetting; and, behind all the above, in repugnance before the many-splendored grotesquerie of contemporary society, which seemed to have long since taken for granted that the highest achievement possible in human life was the technocratic easement of pain and the only happiness the forgetful pleasantries of the hour.[1]

G. K. Chesterton begins his great book, *Orthodoxy* (first published in 1908), with the story of an English yachtsman who sets out on an ocean journey in hope of exploring new lands.[2] But, the yachtsman having lost his bearings, his sailboat leaves him on a strange shore that, it just so happens, is nothing other than his native land. There, he discovers for the first time that which he has always known and—relieved of the prejudice and scorn familiarity sometimes breeds—he finds it good. So did I find myself staring upon a flat Midwestern landscape figured with artifacts I had once not even found arcane but now saw to be beacons of truth, goodness, and beauty. When I asked myself what accounted for this change of perception, I had chiefly to turn to the books I had been reading, the Renaissance paintings I had been visiting in the university museum almost ritualistically, and the orchestral music to which I listened while studying—initially only because, lacking lyrics, it did not distract me. Having never ingested a polemical screed or jeremiad from the right, I found myself already accepting what Russell Kirk would call the "canons of conservatism."

It was poetry that helped me find words to order these awakened sympathies. Literature's narrative dimensions suggested to me that there was something invaluable about the past: it was a source of life and a seat of wisdom, a mystery with which one lived, rather than a corpse whose frozen grip we feel tugging at our ankles. Moreover, the backward journey of narrative into the past appeared as just one particularly cogent form of the reflective journey any person undertakes when asking the fundamental questions about his existence. And I saw that that journey could not

1. I recall the figures in some of these encounters in "Conservative Critics of the Bourgeoisie" in *Modern Age* 55, no. 3 (Summer 2013): 14–26.
2. G. K. Chesterton, *Collected Works* (San Francisco: Ignatius, 1986), 1:211–13.

end with the superficies of everyday life, but rather ascended to enduring truths that only flash and figure in our life of appearances.

I soon discovered that not all art provoked one to peer through, behind, and above the present moment, and indeed that the works I had tended to pick up only to put down again half-read were those that conceived of that art of story-telling simply as an account of the emergence from ignorance, oppression, and superstition into the clean light of a free man's rational worship of himself. But once I had sifted out the Zolas and the Karen Finlays, the Kushners, the indy rockers, the Brechts, and the George Eliots, I found the grain that was left had grown up in a long and fertile tradition—one that another Michigander, Russell Kirk, in *The Conservative Mind: From Burke to Eliot* (first published in 1953), had at least begun to catalogue and distill almost half a century earlier. I had come upon conservatism by way of the literary precisely because conservatism, in a fundamental way that testifies to its veracity rather than its fictitiousness, is a literary movement.[3] And so, to understand the nature of conservatism requires undoing a number of misapprehensions that have passed into the realm of common knowledge regarding both conservatism's nature and the nature of art.

The *Bien-Pensants* of the Liberal Order

The reader may be forgiven if he presumes the use of the term of "cultural conservatism" to test the limits of the plausible. We have come to associate this oft-spoken phrase primarily with others—such as the "moral" or "silent majority," and "traditional" or "family values"—that bespeak, in some minds at least, not a notion of culture as cultivation, as lively growth within a fertile field, but only culture as *cult*, a static and received, putatively sacred, order before which life must kneel and growth must stultify.

---

3. A similarly literary initiation into the tradition a conservative reveres occurred for Russell Kirk about seventeen miles from Ann Arbor, where mine took place. The opening pages of his memoir, *The Sword of Imagination* (Grand Rapids, Mich.: William B. Eerdmans Publishing Company, 1995), are speckled with literary allusions, building up to the deliverance of a gift from his grandmother, Eva Pierce, who gave him a "lively history of the descendants of [his ancestor] Abraham Pierce of the Old Colony" (4–5). Kirk then associates this history with another book, an ancestral copy of Hawthorne's *Grandfather's Chair*. Old books handed down as a fragile inheritance are the adequate symbols of conservatism, Kirk suggests.

We typically maintain such associations, which amount to a presumption to *disassociate* culture and conservatism, alongside another set that joins liberalism to cultivation, sophistication, intelligence, and creativity.

I have generally found these presumptions contrary to the reality of things, and yet have not had to search long to apprehend the reasoning behind them. In our time, after all, to be "cultured"—that is, to make even pretenses of having cultivated one's spirit, mind, or sensibility above the level of a clever ape, a utilitarian hedonist—usually entails only a small number of perfunctory gestures that accompany a description of oneself as "liberal." One reads a newspaper or magazine; one has National Public Radio as a preset for one's listening pleasure on the long commute to a cubicle in the city; one has ground one's way through the latest memoir by some young author who has managed to narrate her compounded victimhood—suffering demographic oppression because of her race or sex and the benighted violence endemic to her family's "ethnic" traditions, as well as her exodus through such traumas to the gleaming liberation that only the late-modern American city makes possible. One reads book reviews and even new novels with some regularity, and, while others fail even to think of poetry, one sometimes mentions it with a succulent sigh and faraway look: "Ah, yes, poetry," it implies, "I dare not say more."

The disenchanted elite among such claimants to culture may combine an interest in installation art with "indy" rock or, if a bit more comfortable within the established order, they attend orchestral performances they lack the basic training to tell apart, or the occasional play whose only interest is its scintilla of sexuality feeding into political topicality. The culture of liberal America tends to the self-congratulatory rather than to the discerning, to the dutiful observation of refinement and right-thinking rather than to good art and actual enjoyment. Such gestures merely embroider a series of thickly-knit clichés about sexual liberation, social justice, and free expression within the limits of the politically correct.

What I wish to propound by this sardonic brief is that there is nothing especially lively about liberal culture; on the contrary, it is moribund in its conventions largely because it serves, again, to ornament a conception of human life whose end is everlasting freedom of choice, what James Kalb has defined as the imperative to "equal freedom."[4] Such cultural

4. See James Kalb, *The Tyranny of Liberalism* (Wilmington, Del.: ISI Books, 2008).

manifestations serve mainly to iterate and reiterate that every habit or idea received from the past or from any source outside one's "identity" is oppressive and that, therefore, a harmless self-expression "transgressive" of previously established goods is the highest end to which a person may aspire. Art's allure is its transgression of the marketplace, but it transgresses the marketplace in the eyes of its liberal consumers only because it appears to them as useless and obscure.

The pursuit of culture-as-transgression thus leads not only to a cult of opacity, but to something like its opposite as well: the familiar path of degradation that everyone recognizes though only a few will condemn. First, we admit strains of the pornographic into supposedly high art; then we demystify the idea of "high art" altogether; ultimately, the pornographic itself, having been declared "equal," becomes the only kind of art we have left. When the sexually explicit can be entangled with some complex or at least impenetrable theoretical scaffolding—then one has a recipe for success. All of this is accompanied, of course, by sneers at the prudery of the ignorant, who used simply not to "get" the beauty of banal abstract canvases, but now are ridiculed for being so ingenuous as to think there should be such a thing as "beauty" to get.

Liberalism identifies equality and freedom as the Good: its society proposes as an ideal nothing more specific than the sloughing off of received habits and beliefs and the dissolving of all apparent social hierarchies. Once this has been obtained, liberalism has nothing more to say: it has no positive content, its goods being mere negations. In practice, this has led to the assumption that to be free means to refuse all form; to be intelligent means not to believe in anything; to be well cultured means to see all cultural judgments as, at best, "merely subjective," and, at worst, as expressions of power and ideology. In the contemporary academy, these conclusions tend to take on an evangelical sincerity, a zeal to debunk and degrade; but for most of us, the loss of substantive beliefs and standards leaves the world feeling, often, incredibly convenient and entertaining, but sometimes, unbearably light and empty. While it will be the burden of my second chapter to call into question this experience of reality, for my present purpose I wish only to suggest how counter-intuitive it is to associate this cultural vision with either vitality or refinement. A peculiarly nauseating species of repetition and a relentless commitment to the indifference and, therefore, meaningless equality of things—save the fetish of the new—seems a more accurate diagnosis.

The "Stupid Party's" Revolution

And yet, for decades, indeed since the constitution of "conservative" and "liberal" as meaningful terms in the wake of the French Revolution, liberalism in particular and the left in general have been associated with intellect and culture while conservatism has been dismissed, in John Stuart Mill's phrase, as "the stupid party." How can this be? And why did I begin by allowing this misperception as excusable?

Conservatives have traditionally spoken of themselves as the voices of truth, goodness, and beauty drowned by the tide of modern revolution. They have been by nature pessimistic, at least regarding the probable fortunes of the proliferating, utopian schemes for the perfection of a dual-natured man—one who may be neither beast nor angel but becomes most bestial when he aspires to remake himself, by "positive thinking" or advanced technology, in the form of the angelic. But they have above all been hopeful, affirming the sound intelligence that reveres received traditions and practical wisdom as the foundation of all knowledge. They have stood in defense of a complex network of intermediate institutions and bonds of love and friendship as the natural alternative to individual loneliness and state tyranny. And they have affirmed in faith the human intellect as incapable of reducing itself to a crudely rational instrument for material security, precisely because its true happiness and sole peace is to be found in the contemplation of the Good—which it can never harness for its own use and domination, but which it may serve in joy.

If they have believed in these things, they have also believed that they were on the losing side of history: tradition, community, order, intellect, and the sacred were destined, in the short run at least, to be trampled. The liberal rush to establish a rationalized order relieved of all inherited burdens and committed to the perpetual acquisition of power and control over human life would uproot these goods from the heart of society. And the Marxist and fascist deluge that sought to surpass liberalism and to stretch human ideological and technological might to ends even beyond the dreams of perpetual acquisition—to the totalizing reign of the

State or the dictatorship of workers—these movements would extinguish even those residual goods conservatives might otherwise protect at society's margins and backwaters.

Once again, I readily excuse the reader who has not found much reverence for these things in the policies and practices of mainstream conservative politicians during the last thirty or more years. And yet, one hears—or at least heard—paeans to them in conservative rhetoric; indeed, Ronald Reagan was capable of ringing the church bells of national and sacred tradition with a resonance that almost survived his combining it with the sorts of utopian, progressivist language proper to his hero, the classical liberal Thomas Paine, and with a confidence in economic ambition, growth, and markets that nearly surpassed the brazen "scientific" materialism of Marx. In just such a combination, a grafting of leftist utopian root stock onto the tendrils of conservative rhetorical reverence, a silent revolution occurred.

We can define that revolution in two ways. First, it involved the mutation of conservative beliefs in the necessity of private property, the family economy, the robust life of non-state institutions including the Church and the market, and of frugality and modesty in all cooperative and political schemes. These beliefs were quietly funneled into the ideologies of "supply-side economics," which promised all these things could be not only preserved but strengthened through a commitment to breathless, state-manipulated economic growth. But if we dilate more widely, we may justly say, also, that conservatism's natural practice of standing on principle athwart the march of "progress," and its taking its "stand" therefore in intellectual and literary—that is, cultural—forms, were both transformed from within until they became unrecognizable. Party politics supplanted cultural conservation.

Suddenly, the march of progress was on the side of *soi-disant* conservatives; by 1994, Newt Gingrich could declare himself a "conservative futurist" and no one seemed to think that an oxymoron, although, by 2006, most clearly thought that intelligent, modest, or domestically-oriented conservatism certainly was. Conservatism went from being the resonant minority, literary voice declaiming the goodness, truth, and beauty our ancestors had made possible, and which the present was dismantling, to being the voice of an expansive, institutional politics of economic, foreign-policy, and, often, cultural liberalism. Growth and markets, free-dom and power, new world orders and the inception of a new American century, were now the credo of Reagan Republicans as much as they had been of Wilsonian Democrats—or even of French Jacobins two centuries before.

Conservatism as Literary Movement

In an amusing lecture delivered to the London Conservative Union in 1955, T. S. Eliot sought to describe the "Literature of Politics," and partic-ularly to name the classic texts from the literature of conservatism. "There are four names which we could all, without any prompting, repeat in chorus," he observes, and they are, "of course, the names of Bolingbroke, Burke, Coleridge, and Disraeli."[5] If one attends to the middle names alone, something comes into focus: the two most influential philosophi-cal voices in Anglophone Romanticism, they who gave birth to a set of categories and standards through which art and politics, states and feel-ings, revelation and the Church, would be conceived for more than a cen-tury, were the old fathers of modern conservatism. Crucially, it is Eliot who recites these names, though he protests anyone could do so: Eliot, perhaps the greatest, certainly the most influential, poet and man of let-ters of the twentieth century. We might go so far as to say that the chief difference between Eliot and Burke and Coleridge is that Eliot lived in a period where the label "conservative" could be explicitly applied to them all. And so, the defining figures of two centuries of Anglo-American cul-ture—the first romantics and the don of modern poetry—also happen to be, respectively, the antecedents and consummation of conservatism.

Let us stick with that list for a moment longer. Eliot's prose by nature tended to the formation of lists. Having given up philosophy in 1915, af-ter arguing himself out of the capacity for any serious belief, Eliot elected for a vocation as poet and literary critic.[6] And, as critic and poet alike, he preferred to cite, quote, and list others whenever possible. In his younger

---

5. T. S. Eliot, *To Criticize the Critic and Other Writings* (New York: Farrar, Straus and Gir-oux, 1965), 137–38.

6. T. S. Eliot, *The Letters*, rev. ed., ed. Valerie Eliot and Hugh Haughton (London: Faber and Faber, 2009), 1:87.

years, this allowed him to introduce ideas in clouds, affirming general beliefs or "tendencies" by way of citing various concurrent voices, even as he acknowledged them mere convenient impositions on a reality that could never be known or precisely described. Knowledge "imposes a pattern, and falsifies," he would write much later in "East Coker," reprising even as revising and overcoming the philosophical skepticism of his youth.[7]

Even after his conversion to Anglo-Catholicism in 1927, Eliot kept listing and quoting, having accepted his position as critic and poet—as the voice and analyst of thoughts that belong to others or to everyone. This sense of deference to tradition, whether grounded in the necessary imprecision of the "knowledge of experience" and the vague genius of commonplaces, or, as it very early became, in hopes of evoking an eternal ideal order of which individual persons were particular expressions, suggests Eliot's conservatism in tendency long before he visited the London Conservative Union. But there, he at last made explicit what readers of Eliot—and, indeed, of much modern poetry—have always known: for all the appearance of anarchy and novelty, much of modern art remains opaque if one does not have a sense of how right-wing politics and sacramental Catholicism inform it. Modernist art nearly always appears as an eruption. What is erupting? The "permanent things," in the form of tradition, into a disconnected and confused present.[8] How does one describe the eruption? As a symbol, in Coleridge's use of that word: the manifestation-in-identity of a literal thing and a figural reality beyond it, a part iconic of a greater whole—in a word, a sacrament.[9]

But here begins an avenue we cannot take. My ambition is not to prove that modern art requires a conservative exegesis, but that conservatism is—contemporary movement conservatism not withstanding—literary in nature. And so, let us return to Eliot's list. If we acknowledge it is not unusual to find him listing names rather than presenting ideas, we should also

7. T. S. Eliot, *Complete Poems and Plays 1909–1950* (New York: Harcourt, Brace and Company, 1980), 125.

8. T. S. Eliot, *Christianity and Culture* (San Diego: Harcourt, Brace and Company, 1976), 76.

9. Samuel Taylor Coleridge, *The Major Works* (Oxford: Oxford University Press, 1985), 672. Mary Rahme summarizes Coleridge's theory pithily as "a part of that unity which it represents," "a concrete, special, and temporal object through which the universal and eternal can be glimpsed" (619). From "Coleridge's Concept of Symbolism," *Studies in English Literature, 1500–1900* 9, no. 4. (Autumn 1969): 619–32.

observe that, in 1955, Eliot had particular reason to be reflecting on the conservative literary tradition. In 1953, in his office as an editor for Faber and Faber, he had published the British edition of a book by a young admirer of his; Russell's Kirk's *The Conservative Mind*, which was then subtitled *From Burke to Santayana*, would provide Eliot a rich literary and historical genealogy of conservative thinkers—what Kirk called "scholars" to differentiate them from leftist "intellectuals": Edmund Burke, John Adams, Sir Walter Scott, Samuel Taylor Coleridge, John Calhoun, Alexis de Tocqueville, Orestes Brownson, Benjamin Disraeli, John Henry Newman, Henry Adams ... the list goes on.[10] In the first edition, it ended with three figures, two of whom had taught Eliot at Harvard, and the other of whom was a friend with whose mind Eliot profoundly identified: the new humanists, Irving Babbitt and Paul Elmer More, and the "aesthetic Catholic" materialist, George Santayana. In Kirk's book, the re-description of these figures builds up a constellation of conservative dispositions whose first exemplar is Edmund Burke and whose loosely shared beliefs Kirk would list as six "canons of conservatism":

1. "Belief in a transcendent order, or body of natural law, which rules society as well as conscience."

2. "Affection for the proliferating variety and mystery of human existence."

3. "Conviction that civilized society requires orders and classes."

4. "Persuasion that freedom and property are closely linked."

5. "Faith in prescription and distrust of 'sophisters, calculators, and economists' who would reconstruct society upon abstract designs."

6. "Recognition that change may not be salutary reform."[11]

Was Eliot recalling Kirk's hard study as he stood before the lunching conservatives of London? We know he was: Eliot cites an essay of Kirk's in his remarks and indicates Kirk as his source for knowledge of conservatism's history as well as its present fortunes.[12] Almost two decades later, Kirk would discuss the citation in his wonderful biography of Eliot, *El-*

---

10. Russell Kirk, *The Conservative Mind: From Burke to Eliot*, 7th ed. (Washington, D.C.: Regnery Publishing, 2001), 479.

11. Kirk, *The Conservative Mind*, 8–9.

12. Eliot, *To Criticize the Critic*, 141.

iot and His Age.[13] Between the two of them, Eliot and Kirk rearticulated what Burke and Coleridge had initiated: the idea of culture was *the* quintessentially conservative phenomenon. That is, as the Marxist social theorist Raymond Williams suggests in *Culture and Society*, the idea of "culture" derives from the tradition of thought begun in the writings of Burke—a tradition that is explicable in its philosophical dimensions by the canons Kirk enumerates, but not reducible to them, and that developed mainly through the writers Kirk discusses in his seminal volume.[14]

Political Aesthetics

The conservatism of Burke and Coleridge sought to remind modern man, in an age of revolutionary upheaval, that politics was an activity built of art, meaning, representation, and community. The lives of peoples and governments, consequently, must be understood in terms of beauty. Burke's *Reflections on the Revolution in France* (first published in 1790) contended this in multiple ways, the three most influential of which may be summarized under the rubrics of society as artwork, moral truth as dramatic, and, following from these, politics as aesthetic.

For much of *Reflections*, Burke was concerned to establish the unbridgeable intellectual chasm that divided the Glorious Revolution of 1688 and British constitutionalism from the French Revolution of 1789 and Jacobin republicanism. The latter established legitimate government on a basis of abstract principles enumerated in the language of natural rights; the former, in contrast, legitimated polity and state alike in terms of a precious inheritance. The Constitution prescribed no natural or permanent formula for legitimate government, but was itself merely the work of generations, who conserved and corrected in fear and trembling.[15] This Constitution indicated a birthright, an heirloom, handed down through generations, at once giving voice to the claims of the past on the present and to the promise that the ultimate end of government is the service of

13. Russell Kirk, *Eliot and His Age* (Wilmington, Del.: ISI Books, 2008), 328. First published 1971.

14. Raymond Williams, *Culture and Society* (New York: Harper and Row, 1966). First published 1958.

15. Edmund Burke, *Reflections on the Revolution in France*, ed. J. C. D. Clark (Stanford, Calif.: Stanford University Press, 2001), 170.

the perfection of man as a creature made for eternal life in God—an end that transcends temporal society and government but toward which their steps are directed.[16] In fine, there is no necessary original or intermediary form of the state, and so the present is especially obliged to past generations, because past precedent is the only guide to how one should proceed into the future; at the same time, the ultimate purpose of the state transcends such haphazard, muddling, and prudential limits, thus endowing the political realm at once with an aureole of the fragile and the sacred.

Society and statecraft thus take on the character of works of art: hewn by the human intellect out of the recalcitrant rock of human nature, but ordained by God to a particular end beyond the capacities of the human mind to achieve. One cannot know in advance what the rules of such things are, but no one can doubt that there are laws inherent to them. Such notions are typically described in terms of "organic" society or culture, and this is an appropriate term insofar as it distinguishes Burke's conception of society from those ethereal and mathematical theorizations advanced by the French revolutionaries and their English Nonconformist fellow travelers. English society and its Constitution are organic, he argues, because they grow and develop like a tree: slowly and with much care. Any serious turn would uproot and kill. On the whole, however, conceiving of society as an artwork better expresses the intricacies of Burke's thought, so long as one keeps in mind two related, but in our age often separated, notions. One must think of an artisan's prudential care, reliance on the practices of past masters, and deference to his purpose— the well-made, useful thing—but one must also think of the deference of those who inherit or receive an artwork to the unrepeatable genius of the artist. Inherited convention and reverent reception make an artwork possible, though no necessary law can guarantee its success or persistence.

In the most fevered and potent passages of *Reflections*, Burke provides us with a complementary theory of morality that builds upon this view of society as artwork: truth is known by means of sensibility situated in a dramatic form rather than by abstraction and logic. The manifestation (rather than the abstract deliverance) of this theory is Burke's account of the infamous arrest of the royal family—Louis XVI, Marie Antoinette, and children—as they fled in the immediate aftermath of the Revolution

---

16. Burke, *Reflections on the Revolution in France*, 181–83, 262.

in October 1789. They were forced to march on foot back to the Tuileries Palace in Paris, surrounded on either side by a shouting and scowling mob. As Burke describes the sanguinary and pathetic episode, he contrasts the events themselves with the commentary the Revolutionaries and English Nonconformists give to it. *They* call it a beautiful day. *They* call it a triumph of reason and right. *They* look upon the spectacle of a fallen king, like it, and clamor also for the stringing up of the Bishops of France. To which Burke replies: after the royal family

had been made to taste, drop by drop, more than the bitterness of death, in the slow torture of a journey of twelve miles, protracted to six hours, they were, under a guard, composed of those very soldiers who had thus conducted them through this famous triumph, lodged in one of the old palaces of Paris, now converted into a Bastille for kings.

Is this a triumph to be consecrated at altars? to be commemorated with grateful thanksgiving? to be offered to the divine humanity with fervent prayer and enthusiastick ejaculation? ...

At first I was at a loss to account for this fit of unguarded transport. I knew, indeed, that the sufferings of monarchs make a delicious repast to some sorts of palates.[17]

The depiction swells still further with dramatic intensity. As he recalls the Queen's wretched state, he is taken back in thought to his own encounter with her:

It is now sixteen or seventeen years since I saw the queen of France, then the dauphiness, at Versailles; and surely never lighted on this orb, which she hardly seemed to touch, a more delightful vision. I saw her just above the horizon, decorating and cheering the elevated sphere she just began to move in, —glittering like the morning-star, full of life, and splendor, and joy. Oh! what a revolution! and what an heart must I have, to contemplate without emotion that elevation and that fall! ... little did I dream that I should have lived to see such disasters fallen upon her in a nation of gallant men, in a nation of men of honour and of cavaliers. I thought ten thousand swords must have leaped from their scabbards to avenge even a look that threatened her with insult.—But the age of chivalry is gone.— That of sophisters, oeconomists, and calculators, has succeeded; and the glory of Europe is extinguished for ever.[18]

---

17. Burke, *Reflections on the Revolution in France*, 234–45.
18. Burke, *Reflections on the Revolution in France*, 237–38.

The pitched language excites the reader's emotions, seduces his moral sensibility to pity the Queen and lament the calamity, even if he is unsure what lesson for justice might be abstracted from the events in France by more impartial means. We may be tempted to ask Burke to lay down his rhetoric before reasoning, as one of his gallants might lay down his sword before entering a court of justice, but this misses the theory behind such language. Burke has little faith in ethereal argumentation; one cannot set aside the particular to pick up the truth, for they are congealed in the same object. The place of moral judgment lies in experience, in history, and history is a dramatic stage. In accounting for why he feels so differently about these events than the Nonconformist Reverend Dr. Price, Burke explains,

> because it is *natural* I should; because we are so made as to be affected at such spectacles with melancholy sentiments upon the unstable condition of mortal prosperity, and the tremendous uncertainty of human greatness … We are alarmed into reflexion; our minds (as it has long since been observed) are purified by terror and pity … Some tears might be drawn from me, if such a spectacle were exhibited on the stage.[19]

We know from contemporary accounts that Burke was frequently moved to tears when discussing the Revolution. And so, he does not indulge in histrionics when he proposes that "the theatre is a better school of moral sentiments than churches."[20] Moral truth, perhaps all truth, must be encountered and weighed on the balance of drama, the scales of the comic and the tragic. It may not, therefore, be arrived at by a "metaphysical" *a priori*, by abstract laws outside of the drama of social life.

Having conceived society as an artwork and moral truth as dramatic, Burke concludes that politics is a kind of aesthetics. Thus, he says that a good state should be like a good poem.[21] A poem, as artwork, must be objectively lovely, that is, well formed; a poem, as dramatic experience, should be subjectively potent, that it may work upon the affections of its audience, society, to remind it of the truths of human nature. And so, Burke concludes that the entire realm of the political operates according to principles

19. Burke, *Reflections on the Revolution in France*, 243.
20. Burke, *Reflections on the Revolution in France*, 244.
21. Burke, *Reflections on the Revolution in France*, 241.

of beauty and love—that which pleases when seen, as St. Thomas Aquinas phrased it.[22]

Provoked into existence by the outrages of classical liberalism's revolution against the hard-earned integrity of modern society, Burke's theory of political aesthetics is the cornerstone of the conservative tradition. The French revolutionaries proposed that reason and political right were reducible to a few abstract principles in the realization of which the world may be justly set aflame. Burke insisted, to the contrary, that social life is fragile and intricate, woven by threads often invisibly fine and requiring the mind and heart to operate in concert if they are to be properly understood and acted upon. His was in fact the consummate modern and historical critique of ahistorical innovators; it has since come to appear as the consummate anti-modern critique.

Modern persons generally insist that reason and reason's truth must be self-grounding and self-demonstrating—they must rely upon nothing outside of reason's methods and culminate in nothing less than a mathematical certainty. They insist that goodness—morality and ethics—must derive from similarly absolute and *a priori* laws, if it is to have any rational claim upon us. To this, Burke replies that truth and goodness alike are reconciled in, and graspable in terms of, beauty. The realm of the aesthetic is where truth and goodness become manifest to us. As such, there can be no *a priori* method of ascertaining truth or of discerning moral law; these things are discovered in the dramatic story of human life, they unfold within a plot rather than revealing themselves above and beyond the historical world. The beautiful lies before us as a fulfillment still to come, and so does not squat behind us, like a jockey on a racehorse beating its sides with the crop of fixed rules or "categorical imperatives."

Without being anti-intellectual, Burke contends that the rarified intellect cannot ascertain truth; without being relativist, he insists that moral and positive law alike are only gradual discoveries and precious heirlooms inextricable from life in a particular community, which itself forms part of an "eternal society" of the dead, the living, and the still to be born.[23] Finally, without reducing judgment to sensibility, he suggests that

---

22. Thomas Aquinas, *Summa Theologica*, trans. Fathers of the English Dominican Province (Allen, Tex.: Christian Classics, 1981), I.5.4.

23. Burke, *Reflections on the Revolution in France*, 261.

the affections play a largely determinate role in the life of human societies. True wisdom arises from the essential unity of the acts of reason and will. It does not separate them.

Burke's conservatism teaches that politics is aesthetics; life as a whole is aesthetic; and therefore the arts of the beautiful play a role in human life quite other than that of gratuitous ornamentation. Rather, they are epistemic—artistic form is in some sense the ground of our knowing. Hence, the advent of the word "culture," which Raymond Williams justly defines as the "whole way of life of a people."[24] A culture is the artwork of generations, a concrete form, a shared habit of being. As Aristotle and Aquinas tell us, something exists only to the extent that it has form, and we may know something fully only in terms of its form.[25] Such is the first lesson of their metaphysics—adducing the implications of which will guide the subsequent chapters of this study. To see the form of an artwork, a culture, or the whole of reality is an activity grounded in beauty and being alike. The most enduring definition of beauty, after all, is *the splendor of form*: an appearance of beings that opens onto the depths of Being.[26]

The Conservative Font of Christian Platonism

It was Burke's genius to recognize in the modern context this fundamental unity of being and beauty, reality and aesthetics, which partially explains what he intended in coining the phrase "the moral imagination."[27] He did not always do so with perfect clarity. His early *Philosophical Enquiry into the Origin of Our Ideas of the Sublime and Beautiful* (first published 1757)[28] offers an impoverished, even frivolous, understanding of the aesthetic dimensions of reality and human life—one to which we shall return below. And yet, it sufficed as a foundation upon which

24. Williams, *Culture and Society*, xvi.

25. Aquinas, *Summa Theologica*, I.5.2, I.5.4.

26. Jacques Maritain, *Art and Scholasticism and the Frontiers of Poetry*, trans. Joseph W. Evans (Notre Dame, Ind.: University of Notre Dame Press, 1962), 24–25.See also Hans Urs von Balthasar, *The Glory of the Lord: A Theological Aesthetics*, trans. Erasmo Leiva-Merikakis (San Francisco: Ignatius Press, 1982), 1:118–19.

27. Burke, *Reflections on the Revolution in France*, 239–240.

28. Currently available in Edmund Burke, *A Philosophical Enquiry into the Sublime and the Beautiful and Other Pre-Revolutionary Writings*, ed. David Womersley (London: Penguin Books, 1998), 49–200.

to build. In the crisis of the French Revolution, he was made to see the modern world coming into being along simpler lines—a mechanical rationalism, a utilitarian morality, a "procedural" aesthetics that valued only the force of defiant genius, neglecting custom, ritual, and all other accouterments of received traditions. The conservative tradition has itself constituted the punctuated, uneven development of Burke's own uneven insights in the face of liberal modernity's continuous march toward a society without a past, a rational order disencumbered of all inheritance, a rationalism that knows nothing of the heart's much less of the intellect's higher aspirations. Burke, thus, *gave* us "culture," a concept by which modernity could be critiqued for its refusal of the sacred *cultus* of the past, and for its neglect in *cultivating* with care the legacy of past and present in hopes of securing it for future generations. While every people has its culture, it is the conservative who truly understands what "culture" means.[29]

This recognition of the "oneness" of being and beauty accounts for the principle behind Kirk's six canons of conservatism and also hints at the historical font of traditional conservatism. Taken by themselves, it would be plausible to describe the six canons as a mere suspicion of change and codified deference to the prescriptions of the past—and, of course, these are evident qualities of conservatism. But mere skepticism before innovation does not a conservative make. Rather, we see the compelling nature of the six canons best in light of reality's constitution as ontologically beautiful.

The "belief in a transcendent order, or body of natural law," indicates that reality in general and cultures in particular possess an architectonic: formal principles, constitutive laws, give a culture being, coherence, and purpose. They not only indicate how it may develop but essentially orient that development. Natural law primarily directs creation, including society, to its end, while it only secondarily serves as a boundary or restraint. Once again, the idea of an "organic" culture or society presents itself: no matter how obscure the appearance of a seed, it can grow into only one particular species of plant, and yet, though the acorn may grow into only the oak, the varieties of growth within that limit are immense and largely unpredictable.

---

29. Russell Kirk, *Redeeming the Time* (Wilmington, Del.: ISI Books, 1999), 12.

Hence, the conservative "affection for the proliferating variety and mystery of human existence," confesses *not* an uncritical love of what is now often called "diversity." This liberal concept suggests merely that change and difference are goods in themselves, and incoherence is preferable to integrity, because one cannot determine publically, or perhaps even privately, what constitutes the good of human society, the good life for the human person, or the goodness of a community's form. The liberal loves difference insofar as it undermines coherence and conclusion, and loves change, because it alone can indicate a condition of freedom—a reserve of potency never to be determined by form, an evasion of every bond, net, or root. But conservatives recognize that variety within the organic architectonic of a culture accounts for much of the beauty, goodness, and freedom of human life precisely because it contributes in practical ways toward the discovery, achievement, and reflection in the social order, of a definite and transcendent end, the Good Itself. Individual variations suggest the nobility and the imperfection of man, whose historical drama speaks of contestation of, advances toward, and retreats from, an end that transcends the particulars of any culture and that would remain even if civilization itself should falter: the telos, the fulfillment, the true happiness, the one and only heaven, possible for human life. Cultures grow in diverse ways because humans begin in very various conditions and come to understand themselves in uneven fashions, all the while seeking the same ultimate end.

Traditions are precisely these uneven, sometimes retreating or decaying, practical developments through which human beings seek to understand and live in the truth of what is unconditionally good. This sense of culture as organically various, but founded on intelligible principles and leading toward some definite end, distinguishes conservatism from liberalism, because conservatism judges the particulars of human life as good in terms of a transcendent form. Critics of conservatism often decry its bows to Christianity as an insincere, effectively utilitarian, recognition of the social and moral discipline of religion; without some binding divine-sanctioned ethic, anarchy would be loosed upon the world.[30] Surely the conservative does indeed recognize this usefulness, this *social*

---

30. They think of conservatives as Hobbesian, perhaps only because liberals tend to think in Hobbesian terms even though they dislike Hobbesian outcomes. See Russell Kirk, *Redeeming the Time*, 10–11.

function of religion, but at root this belief in a transcendent order bespeaks a confidence in the *rational* function of religion. The human intellect can imperfectly but really grasp the True, the Good, and the Beautiful—some of the Divine Names Dionysius the Aeropagite enumerated in his Christian Platonist theology.[31] Thus, our reasonings and our aesthetic judgments are based on a certain foundation even if we do not possess with certain knowledge the full vision of that foundation. Kirk's canons regarding the need for orders and classes, and for private property, indicate that a culture, in being ordered to some good or beauty beyond itself, also participates in the Good and the Beautiful. It therefore should have a particular form, a beautiful structure, reflective of both the goodness of things in particular and the order of justice as a whole, and recognizable in those terms. It must contain ordered differences composing both hierarchy and harmony. We repeat, with Burke and Cicero: a country, like a poem, should be lovely.

As for the last two canons—faith in prescription and suspicion of change—these do not instance an enervating doubt about the benefits of human innovation. They are consequences of a conviction that the architectonic principles of a culture are slow to discover, are generally not subject to our control or domination, and—because ordered to a sacred end and indeed interpretive of it—participate in the sacred. They must be altered only with caution and reverence.

What should become clear from this account of the canons is that within them lies a theory of being, truth, goodness, and beauty as one; this theory, historically, has been most fully expressed in the central tradition of western thought, that of Christian Platonism. We shall provide a detailed account of that tradition in the next two chapters, but it is worth offering a preliminary sketch of conservatism as Christian Platonism in the terms George Santayana gave in his *The Genteel Tradition at Bay*, which is one of the classic critical accounts of American conservatism's position in the modern West. In the second part of his essay, Santayana begins by painting a satirical picture of the materialist ("romantic") metaphysics that underwrites the liberal obsession with indeterminacy-as-freedom. These devotees of "a liquid chaos" would "detest to be caged even

---

31. Pseudo-Dionysius, *The Complete Works*, trans. Colm Luibheid (New York: Paulist Press, 1987), 71–77, 110.

in an infinite world, if there is any order in it. Indetermination seems to them liberty; they feel that idiocy and accident are far more deeply rooted than method in their own being, and they think it must be so also in the world at large."[32]

A devoted student himself of Christian Platonism, though also a philosophical materialist after his private fashion, Santayana underscored that the Christian Platonic view of things provided an answer to liberalism specifically by insisting that beyond any reified moral laws—such as Kirk's canons—must rest a vision of the Good and the good life for man. Beyond the chaos of everyday experience, Santayana proposes, exists a

supernatural sphere—a sphere and not a medley—to which morality and religion may be tempted to appeal. As the Indian, Platonic, and Christian imagination has conceived it, the supernatural has an eternal nature and a sublime order of its own. It forms an elder cosmos surrounding our nether world and destined to survive it. In that cosmos a hierarchy of spirits continually descends and ascends all the steps of moral decline and exaltation; and there the inexplicable burdens and tantalizing glories of this life find their origin and their fulfillment.[33]

The conservative embraces this "Christian Platonism" as providing a normative account of the cosmos and of moral life founded in the contemplative vision of the supernatural Good. Because it is understood in terms of intellectual *vision*, not as a mere set of propositions or a slaking of appetite, the Good must also be called the Beautiful.[34]

Although modern conservatism has often found speech in what it refuses or condemns, or in the language of the natural law to which it defers, such things are but reflections of a greater light. That greater light is the Beauty for which man, the rational and political animal, is ultimately destined; its source is God, and its condition we call "happiness." Conservatism is the modern offspring of a perennial Christian Platonist tradition. It inevitably plays and replays, upon the stage of history, Plato's great drama in the *Symposium*, where Socrates tells us beauty is the foundation

32. George Santayana, *The Essential Santayana*, ed. Martin A. Coleman (Bloomington: Indiana University Press, 2009), 564.

33. Santayana, *The Essential Santayana*, 564.

34. Santayana, in his own formulation of the Christian Platonist tradition on a naturalistic foundation, notes that "the fruition of happiness is intellectual (or as perhaps we should now call it, esthetic)" (*The Essential Santayana*, 575).

and cause of all discipline, and where that wild liberal, Alcibiades, would jealously destroy beauty and discipline alike.

Romanticism and Anti-Modernism

The intellectual historian may hear this analysis and observe, "What you are describing is not conservatism—it is romanticism." Or he might say, "conservatism is modern, while the Christian Platonism you describe is something other and far more ancient." He would be partly right on both counts. Apart from its ancient theological roots, conservatism marks a pivotal moment within the wider historical phenomenon of the modern romantic revival, and both may be understood in terms of a becoming-visible of certain dimensions of premodern or traditional ways of life under siege by the various forces of modernity.[35] Romanticism comprises a series of diverse responses to modernity, many of which are at home with such innovations as the "disenchantment" of the world, the fetish of "progress," and the rise of "equal freedom" as the highest good for the human being. Hence, many ideas from the romantic period evidently derive from Immanuel Kant, the quintessential philosopher of modernity; but the romantics also constituted a revival of Platonist and Christian Platonist conceptions of reality.[36] As we shall note in chapter three, even Kant's theories often seem mere subjective distortions of the realism of that tradition.

Conservatism describes a narrower strain within romanticism that is more wholly continuous with the Christian Platonic tradition, or rather is a specifically modern attempt to retrieve and preserve that tradition, however partially. The conservative sees and affirms, under the pressures of radical social disruptions, reality as having aesthetic form and, in consequence, prescribes culture—the whole way of life of a people, the aesthetic form that gives their lives shape—as the necessary criterion of every judgment. This sense of life and culture as an art of the beautiful has not always led to conservatives' practicing or prioritizing the fine arts,

35. Romanticism is in this sense an attempt to revive the essentially Roman form of western civilization, as argued in Rémi Brague, *Eccentric Culture* (South Bend, Ind.: St. Augustine's Press, 2002), 101.

36. See M. H. Abrams, *The Mirror and the Lamp* (Oxford: Oxford University Press, 1953), 58–59.

although it often has. From Burke, Wordsworth, and Coleridge, to Newman and the Oxford Movement; from Santayana, More, and Babbitt to
Allen Tate, Flannery O'Connor, Robert Frost, T. S. Eliot, Yvor Winters,
and Walker Percy—we see that the majority tradition in Anglo-American
writing since the French Revolution has been in some sense conservative.
I have given a very narrow list, here, citing only those figures who have
been of most immediate influence on me. Each of them displays attributes
that are unmistakably modern, but each of them also endeavored to resur-
rect or renovate premodern traditions rooted in the Christian Platonic
inheritance. Sometimes they do so explicitly and comprehensively, sometimes eccentrically or only fragmentarily. In this, as we already noted,
Burke is a paradigm.

If we were to formulate a list of the minority liberal tradition in
Anglo-American letters we would discover something curious. From
Blake and Shelley to Walt Whitman and Hart Crane, the liberal literary
tradition drinks at its source from the conservative; it has no independent life and would prove a *hortus siccus* rather than a creative flowering
did it not appropriate, adapt, and fundamentally pirate the conservative
tradition of maintaining the sense and sensibility of the past and standing
athwart the reductive excesses of modernity. Freedom and equality are so
far from being manifested in particular forms as to serve as the political
equivalent of a vacuum. In their liberal variety, they are purely negative
in character. In contrast, and this is a point to which we shall return in
Part II, conservatism is not chiefly a political movement—it is a literary
one, and in at least three senses. Its representative figures have been great
writers; it emphasizes what Kirk called the imaginative nature of reality
and moral judgment; and so it ultimately reconciles reason and morality
within the field of the dramatic, the poetic—the Beautiful.

The conservative tradition is thus an anti-modern product of modernity, an often untraditional defense of tradition. Eliot observes in his address that conservatism came into being through "a fusion of Tory and
Whig elements, due largely to the effect of the French Revolution upon
the mind of Burke."[37] And that origin has proven consistently to be both
a benefit and a liability. Through much of the last two centuries, the in-

---

37. Eliot, *To Criticize the Critic*, 138.

tegrity of conservatism as a vision of culture relegated it to the literary and academic realm; John Crowe Ransom and the other Agrarians of the 1930s, with their insurrectionist rhetoric leading mostly to the production of literary criticism, testify to this.

Had conservatism not been, in this sense, literary in genus, it no doubt would have been fully rooted out by the ascendant liberal forces of western culture. Conservative thought in its purity was preserved within the depths of the liberal establishment as a source of life and fertility whose full power was forestalled by accusations of nostalgia and sentiment. Because it synthesized older "Tory" ideas with "Whig" ones, conservatism could persist even as it carried anti-modern principles into the heart of the modern world. Always alongside these literary conservatives, however, were others more expressly political; the Old Right's resistance to American economic-imperial ambitions and the New Deal provides but one instance of conservatism coalescing into a political movement during a particular historical moment. At such times, conservatism's refusal to be "reconciled" to modernity shows forth as an alternative program to liberal society, and so it is appropriately declared—in praise and condemnation alike—as "reaction."

In more recent decades, the major figures of conservatism turned with greater frequency to law and political theory rather than to more deliberately cultural enterprises—and, finally, to institutional politics. In itself, this betrayed nothing. Russell Kirk, who authored several novels and short stories, in his political and historical writings plowed the field for just such an unexpected development without himself succumbing to it. He sharpened a conservative political vision even as he refused to reduce it to a platform. But just as Marxists cease preaching the "withering of the state" as soon as they have captured it, so modern conservatives after the 1950s increasingly went from viewing the centralization of state power as a temporary expedient forced upon us by the Cold War to seeing it as a means of cementing political power. Many conservatives came to embrace the modern state, which was itself a child of liberalism, until, with the arrival of neo-conservatism to power as a faction within the Reagan administration, mainstream conservatives were no longer easy to distinguish from the calculating, imperialist, statist liberals it had been their vocation to oppose. Kirk and Patrick J. Buchanan both admired Reagan, even though within his otherwise conservative disposition was rooted the belief of Thomas Paine that human beings have it in their power to remake the world according to the pattern of their will. This radical strain in Reagan was all too susceptible to the whisperings of the neo-conservatism that has come into broad public suspicion since the 2003 invasion of Iraq.

Amid this "conservative" ascendency, traditional conservatism was slowly relegated to the familiar margins—represented by such periodicals as *Modern Age*, *Chronicles*, and *The American Conservative*. It could claim few widely known intellectual and cultural figures for much the same reason the far left can claim few: both have been easily excluded from the consensus mode of liberalism found on the television news channels and in the major news organizations. Both appear almost incomprehensible to the average American, who has come to think of society as little more than the aggregate of weak and isolated individuals, whose relations are chiefly mediated by the mechanisms of market and consumption, and whose sense of communal responsibility and common good is almost entirely absorbed within the omnicompetent "good will" of the state.

I am sorry to say that the far left, marginal though it be, is probably *more* intelligible to most Americans in our day. Having prized equal freedom as the sole incontrovertible good for so long, they understand revolutionary leftism as at least intending to bring an apotheosis of equal freedom that the "creative destruction" of state and corporate capitalism cannot attain. Often, the far left speaks aloud the bad conscience of an adolescent middle class and resonates especially profoundly with young people educated into our contemporary politics of guilt.

Traditional conservatism, in contrast, strikes the contemporary breast only in those brief moments when the loneliness of the modern individual breaks forth and leads him to question the normally unquestioned good of technological and media-saturation; when he sees for a moment that the material ugliness of our civilization cannot be solved by "green" technology but only by a fundamental readjustment of the human person's attitude toward creation and acquisition to antique standards; when, ever more rarely, he reads a book that stirs in him an image of genuine heroism unmotivated by mere trauma and realized in a form more lasting than the bloody phantasmagorias of contemporary Hollywood; or when he senses that the heart's deepest longing is for a permanent happiness, and that happiness is possible only in an extended natural community with ties that bind but ties that uphold as well.

At these margins, and in these fugitive moments, can some restored literary conservatism be revived? Does our age have within it a Burke, a Coleridge, an Eliot? The historical record does not give us cause for optimism, and the present age of relativist skepticism and consumer spectacle, of pornographic anti-culture and enthralled senses, gives us positive grounds for doubt. But the chapters that follow are founded on hope: hope that the defense they make of a culture of truth, goodness, and beauty—and indeed, of the reality of that trinity as ordering reality as such—will resonate with the sensibility of its readers and help them on their sundry roads to living well in the world; hope that its arguments will be sufficiently compelling to cause a few souls to rethink our present cultural regime; and hope, finally, that its resources may help the conservative voices of today and tomorrow to find a language adequate to express the passions of their breast.

The Vision of This Book

After such an extensive introductory argument, it would be well to draw together the most significant claims I have made, and to gesture toward how they will guide us through the following chapters. I began by indicating that, despite certain popular conceptions, the liberal imagination is intrinsically sterile, has been largely parasitic, and ultimately has little to share with us about the human condition or the nature of reality besides one unsatisfactory insight: the word "freedom" lures us, no matter its content or absence thereof. The liberal imagination melds the human values of freedom and equality with the ontological quality of indeterminacy, so that it may initially seduce one with the promise of liberation, but finally settles into either bored silence or even the peculiar wish for self-annihilation in which the human being feels every inheritance, including that of the body and its limitations, as an unforgivable injustice.[38]

I proposed that, in contrast to this unhappy vision, conservatism, rooted in the twin principles of *cult* and cultivation, provides a more

---

38. Russell Kirk, *Prospects for Conservatives* (n.p.: Imaginative Conservative Books, 2013), 75–105.

compelling and adequate account of culture as the whole way of life of a people and as the expression of a given people's slow pursuit of the Good. The writings of Burke provide a specifically modern vocabulary for understanding this: human life is dramatic, and culture is an "organic" work of art. True politics will always be in a fundamental sense aesthetic, concerned with the formation, the journey toward realized form, of a community. Beauty comes to appear as its guiding principle. Among Burke's many distinctions is his finding a vocabulary to make the ordering of culture and politics to beauty visible, and I contended that this is what situates him specifically as a romantic and conservatism more generally as a "literary" movement.

But Burke as conservative did not invent this political and cultural aesthetics. Rather, he made it visible as best as he was able for a modern age otherwise given over to what Kirk would call a "defecated reason," a rationalism that attempts to reject past and future in favor of a mechanistic and ahistorical vision of politics and human life. Burke's was a rear-guard defense of an ancient and venerable understanding of beauty as convertible with, as bound to, truth and goodness. In response to the atrocities of the French Revolution, he spoke in defense of tradition in general, of the English constitutional tradition, but above all of the great tradition that gives form to and nourishes western civilization. This I have called, following Santayana, the Christian Platonist tradition. When we ask, what is it that conservatives wish to conserve, Burke and his descendants tell us, above all, they wish to conserve the riches that have been given into our possession by way of the long, uneven assimilation of the genius of Athens with that of Jerusalem. Thus, in turning to Kirk's six canons of conservatism, I offered an account of them in which they appear as the desideration of the Christian Platonist outlook. Like Burke before him, Kirk sought to voice principles of permanent authority in response to the peculiar challenges modern liberalism and rationalism posed. And while it has been all too easy for Kirk's readers to understand his canons as nothing other than a loosely defined objection to liberal modernity, it is nonetheless true that they are rooted in a far more enduring and positive vision of reality.

Bringing to the fore the fundamental identity of conservatism and romanticism with the legacy of Christian Platonism does more than simply deepen our understanding of Kirk's writings. Rather, it explains why the minds of Kirk and Burke are fundamentally conservative. For, the foundational insight of Christian Platonism is precisely that reality is ordered to beauty. Truth presents itself as form—as a kind of vision. Wisdom therefore may be understood as the soul's vision of the beautiful shape of things in themselves and all their relations. We arrive at the fulfillment of our intellectual natures at just that point where we behold the splendorous form of truth, where we perceive all things as goods ordered, structured or bestowed with form, by the Good. Conservatism is the acceptance of this order. The conservative wishes to preserve the conditions that make it possible for human beings to perceive the reality of truth and goodness, and—above all, holding these things together—beauty.

Christian Platonism is the tradition of the West. Western civilization is founded on an anthropology that teaches that man has an intellect that, at its best, sees, and on a metaphysics that tells us that the reality seen is the beauty of being. Though it may surprise to hear this in such a frank formulation, this is hardly news. When someone speaks to us about a difficult matter with inadequate or garbled words, we often reply, "I'm not sure I followed all that, but I *see what you mean.*" Like Chesterton's man who discovered England, when we examine these traditional teachings of the West, we find that, in fact, we are recovering what we already knew. It should be no surprise, then, that previous efforts to recall the riches of the western tradition for a new generation have found their center in the idea of intellectual vision.

In the aftermath of the Second World War, Joseph Pieper sought to heal the wounds of the West by reminding it of its conception of leisure. Play, study, and prayer all converge at their highest realization; human beings, at their best, may experience a pure joy in the perception of truth, the only response to which is an overflowing of the lips in praise. He defended leisure as the basis of such contemplation; but for his defense to cohere, Pieper saw that he must distinguish the grinding factory of discursive reason, *ratio*, from its fulfillment in the peaceful contemplation of the intellect, *intellectus*. Reasoning works, but *intellectus* is a "purely receptive 'looking,'" the ability of the mind to be "simply looking."[39] So also,

---

39. Joseph Pieper, *Leisure, the Basis of Culture*, trans. Gerald Malsbary (South Bend, Ind.: St. Augustine's Press, 1998), 11.

in the aftermath of the efforts of the '60s generation to cast off the whole of the western tradition along with the regimes of western imperialism, E. F. Schumacher subtly yet provocatively sought to restore that wisdom to its proper place by recasting it in the language of the culture of narcissism. Plato and St. Thomas Aquinas take on a certain therapeutic overtone in Schumacher's hands, but one can only marvel at how skillful he was in conveying the Christian Platonist tradition with its integrity intact even as he appealed to the prejudices of a readership that held the West in contempt, dabbled in New Age babble, and was stimulated by all manners of Oriental bric-a-brac and therapeutic impoverishments of spirit. What is most remarkable, however, is Schumacher's emphasis that the wisdom he has to share, which, again, is above all the wisdom of the tradition of the West, finds its center in the idea of intellectual vision. "With the light of the intellect," he writes, "we can see things which are invisible to our bodily senses ... beyond this seeing there is neither the possibility of nor the need for any further proof."[40] We experience the full knowledge of anything as a kind of seeing: the truth is there before us, subject entirely, from all sides as it were, to our gaze. We sense the finality of such knowledge precisely because we *see* its form: this or that truth has revealed its secrets to us and, at last, our minds may rest in that truth rather than hurry on, in anxiety or disappointment, in search of the next curiosity.

This brings us to the specific argument of this book. It will draw upon the understanding of conservatism described above and the insights it affords in order to offer a new defense of some ancient ideas. When Kirk published *The Conservative Mind* in 1953, his history of ideas and his own methods as a literary biographer and philosophical historian were well suited to the needs of his times. *The Conservative Mind* provided a penetrating critical history of the developments and decline of conservative thought from Burke to the present. But, perhaps more importantly, along the way it provided portraits of great figures. Following Burke, Kirk understood that scenes from the drama of history, sketches of the great figures who acted in history, would provide models for his day. While Kirk thought the contemporary world to be far gone in decadence, he also maintained a belief—one he shared with Chesterton—that the basic

---

40. E. F. Schumacher, *A Guide for the Perplexed* (New York: HarperCollins, 1977), 46.

goodness and order of the Christian Platonist tradition was still intact in the customs and natural dispositions of his fellow men.

Kirk was not wrong in that belief. In his day, as in ours, readers still respond powerfully to his many books and are stirred to emulate the portraits they contain. But the decadence has not been reversed; as my opening pages suggest, it has, if anything, continued: the march of liberalism has not slowed even as it has arrived ever closer to the ghastly abyss of nihilism and a self-annihilating version of epicureanism. Further, the conservative movement in America that Kirk helped to found has been, as one might expect of any human endeavor, all too easily co-opted by the spirit of the times. Rather than, as William F. Buckley famously said, standing athwart history, saying "stop," neo-conservative advocates of a "new American century" and enthusiasts for the creative destruction of "capitalism" have proven quite willing to march under the banner of "progress," and to participate in the uprooting and destruction of that culture conservatives were meant to protect.

I should repeat, every human endeavor will miscarry eventually, and Kirk gave us little reason to believe that "movement conservatism" would be the exception. One possible response to the perversion of conservatism in our day would be to abandon the word altogether. Based on the account I have given in this chapter, we should understand conservatism as a response to the events of a particular historical period: the political modernity inaugurated by the French Revolution. Since we may well be in a moment of political postmodernity, in which many of the haunting possibilities prophesied in modern dystopian novels have not only come to pass but have become a feature of everyday life, should we not consign "conservatism" to the archives and formulate from scratch a wholly new response to present threats to human happiness and the tattered robes of humane culture?

For my part, I do not think so. Rather, we should preserve what we can of an authentic conservatism, recognizing that the long line of great conservative thinkers from Burke and Coleridge to Eliot and Kirk still have much to teach us. But I do think, as the times are more desperate, it will no longer suffice to rally around the inspiring portraits of such figures. Our culture has too much lost the first principles of perception that would allow us to interpret such portraits properly, to see their forms as intelligible wholes. We must, therefore, do what we can to return to and rearticulate those first principles themselves. That is the mission of this book: to provide a compelling account of truth, goodness, and beauty that will make the reality of these transcendental properties of being visible, comprehensible, and defensible for a new generation.

Like Pieper and Schumacher before me, I am convinced that the principle of principles, what can never be lost absolutely because it is true, and what must not be lost for our age if it is to know anything of order, purpose, and happiness, is that of intellectual vision. If the intellect sees, then that will have implications for every aspect of human life. We shall have to rethink what the Good and the good life for man are with reference to the intellect's desire for vision. Truth, if truth is a reality that appears, will also take on new aspects. And, at the heart of this book and woven throughout it, the nature of beauty as a property of being, as the definitive attribute of form itself, will reassume the primacy that the western tradition has generally afforded it.

Christian Platonism proclaims that man is a creature who sees with his intellect. Conservatism seeks to defend this anthropology against the assaults of the age of liberalism, an age that would reduce man to his body, reason to technological innovation, and would impoverish the reality in which he lives by exiling truth, goodness, and beauty from its intrinsic structure. This book in particular speaks in defense of these things, calling its readers to a renewed vision of truth, goodness, and beauty as realities to be seen, as the lights in the darkness after which our minds by their very natures are made to seek.

In Part I, "The Real, the West, and the Good," I begin with the problem of goodness that all persons must face. We all desire some *good*, but what basis do we have to select from among the wide array of *goods* available to us? Does this buffet of desirable things not in itself testify that there is no particular good at which all human beings should aim simply in virtue of their being persons? I take a selective survey of modern thinkers who have been responsible for causing that question to seem either intractable or deserving of a negative answer. And then, I turn to Aristotle and provide a phenomenological reflection in favor of the reality of truth, goodness, and beauty and, further, in favor of the pursuit of these realities as the aim of human desire. We are by nature hungry for reality and, it may surprise the modern person to discover, reality is rich enough to satisfy our hunger. This Christian Platonic anthropology established, I seek to answer two questions. What is the good that conservatives wish to protect? That is, what is the western tradition? In providing an account of that tradition I naturally sketch a deeper account of the reality that, in the previous chapter, I had argued we are just in seeking as the final cause of all our appetites. I look into the foundations of western civilization in order to uncover six insights that guide all characteristically western thinking. Just as Kirk proposed six canons in his day, my effort to return more systematically, or theoretically, to first principles yields these six insights of the Christian Platonist tradition, the fulcrum of which is the word to which we have already adverted many times: Beauty.

Precisely because beauty is central to the Christian Platonist tradition, it constitutes the subject of Part II, "Art, Being, and Beauty." There, we return to the scene of present-day and aboriginal conservatism, in order to confront the failures of the present and to recover the genius of conservative thinkers as part of a "literary movement." Conservatives have a responsibility to beauty not chiefly in terms of its political "uses," but as the property of being that holds all things together. I then offer three discussions of the beautiful that may be of contemporary interest. I offer a "Dantesque" one, in which the beauty of art serves as a kind of prelude to philosophical wisdom, opening the mind to new possibilities by way of the imagination; this I take to be a plausible, but not satisfactory, account of the romantic theory of the imagination often attributed to Burke and Kirk as the "moral imagination." I then turn to the Frankfurt school theorist, Theodor W. Adorno, and consider his penetrating anti-metaphysical account of beauty. Perhaps some common ground may be discovered between the modern left and right in such a moving account of the role of beauty in a benighted modern age. At the least, Adorno shows us how crucial beauty is for the perception of truth. Finally, I turn to St. Thomas Aquinas by way of the French philosopher, Jacques Maritain. In Maritain's *Art and Scholasticism*, we find the blueprint for recovering a robust understanding of beauty as the ordering principle of all reality; we find also a renewed appreciation, not adequately realized in the previous discussions of beauty, for why the fine arts do—and should—play a central role in human life. An aesthetic education, as Maritain suggests, is an initiation into the perception of reality. It prepares us to see the form of things, to exercise the vision of our souls that is the fulfillment of the human vocation. For the sake of our culture, it follows, we must also recover a conception of the fine arts that is ordered to beauty, not because a good culture will be one that is nicely ornamented, but because the fine arts are one important way in which we fulfill our natures, perceive the truth, and move toward the good. The way of beauty is not, however, primarily a moral path. It is epistemic; it is a way of knowing rooted in the seeing of the form of things.

The linkage I have just proposed between beauty, artistic form, the form of a well-lived human life, and truth-as-form, guides the inquiry of Part III, "Reason, Narrative, and Truth." As I have already suggested, the act of storytelling is largely—though not *necessarily*—a conservative act. There are, of course, liberal narratives; there are stories whose chief intent is to encourage us to leave the past behind and to dwell, if anywhere, only in a present whose chief virtue is its overcoming of the past. But even such stories bear within them the imprint of the past as a lesson in truth. A conservative understanding of stories, as Kirk's historical writings imply, is one that views the connection between story-telling and reason as an intimate one. The stories we tell may possess several kinds of rational and moral authority, some of which I review in "Reasoning about Stories." I conclude by suggesting that this may be precisely because the exercise of reasoning and the exercise of story-telling are in some sense one. In "Mnemosyne: Mother of the Arts," I follow one important implication of that argument to suggest that narrative is also foundational to the fine arts in general; Mnemosyne—Memory—is the mother of the muses. And so, a proper understanding of the arts—including the ontological one, where art is ordered to beauty, as I proposed in Part II—will have to account for the way in which all art derives from the vault of memory, where stories dwell. In "Novel, Myth, Reality: An Anatomy of Make-Believe," I respond to some of the theories of story-telling that have emerged in response to the foundational character of narrative to the arts. Figures such as Northrop Frye and Joseph Campbell suggest that narrative is foundational to the human experience of reality because we operate within something like a collective unconsciousness of archetypes that give form to stories and our perception of our lives as stories. But I believe this does not go far enough. As in earlier chapters, here I push our thinking beyond mythical archetypes to ontological form—to an encounter with being.

These preliminary reflections prime us for the central argument of Part III, which is the "retelling" of the story of reason. In defense of a rich understanding of truth as the "good of the intellect," I begin with a review of the typical modern understanding of the relation of *mythos* and *logos*, which tends to dismiss stories in favor of an ahistorical analytic rationality. In response to this modern "myth" about reason, I set forth three arguments that encourage us to rethink the connection between narrativity and rationality. *Mythos* and *logos* are naturally bound up with each other, often interwoven together, and—finally—we must understand that human reason always operates in a narrative context. When it does not, it ceases to be rational. Further, narrative always operates in a rational context, its form manifesting a kind of truth. This leads to a concluding argument that revisits one of the themes from the first and second chapters: might not the modern practice of severing *mythos* from *logos* be responsible for many of the unfortunate features of the modern world—including the disenchantment with the intellectual life, which should be thought of as the human person's highest and happiest end? Truth is the destination of a pilgrimage, the ordering principle of the properly human way of life, but it cannot appear as such if we think our life-stories are obstacles to the arrival of truth, or that our shared histories serve merely to dissolve truth within an ever-receding horizon of relativism.

In sum, this volume provides arguments in defense of the Christian Platonist conception of the well-lived human life as the pursuit of the Good; arguments for a rich metaphysics of beauty that helps explain the important role of the arts in the sustenance of human culture and above all the role of beauty, as a property of being, in our capacity to know the world; and, finally, for a renewed confidence in truth also as a property of being, but one which, for human beings at least, can be sustained only if we understand the close relationship between narrative form and ontological form. I close with a short reflection on how, in our present circumstances, we may take up these insights and work for the conservation of the tradition of the West and the renewal of our impoverished but still Christian Platonist civilization.

PART I

THE

REAL,

THE

WEST,

AND THE

GOOD

ONE

The Hunger for Reality

Phantasmagorias of Desire

When we look at the world around us, we see it positively teeming with desires: squirrels foraging for food to fill their bellies, dogs on the prowl for a mate, flowers craning their heads upward to drink in the sun. Indeed, desire is not limited to living things, as all material objects tenaciously cling and conform to the laws of nature, though not by a will of their own.[1] Human beings offer the most varied spectacle of desire, not only seeking a wide range of objects to slake their hungers, but also seeming to be moved by desires that are idiosyncratic and peculiar, so that we can understand that they want *something*, but perhaps not what; or, having figured that out, we find ourselves at a loss as to *why* anyone would want it.

We may well, at first, be wonder-struck at this panorama of hungers and desires, but so completely can it overwhelm that we are sometimes led into dismay, cynicism, and, at last, indifference, as if the whole of nature were just an endless show of meaningless appetites frustrated, or attained and forever renewed: as if it were desire itself, not some particular object of desire, that drove the roving cosmos. The Irish poet Thomas Kinsella described this view of things many years ago, and did so with chilling brevity, in a sketch of a barn owl. He imagines the owl's hungry, circling

---

1. Thomas Aquinas, *Summa Theologica*, I-II.26.1

flight in search of prey. Her return, fed and full, to the rafters. There, she will wait for that same hunger to come back and the circle to recommence. He writes of

> the drop with deadened wing-beats; some creature
> torn and swallowed; her brain, afterward,
> staring among the rafters in the dark
> until hunger returns.[2]

Can there be any end to such desires? Can the owl's iterated hungers cease in any way but death? Is the owl herself anything more than a brain that stares, hungers, flies, and devours? Finally, is there any difference between the owl's life and that of any other creatures? Kinsella, elsewhere, suggests no, that "life is hunger, hunger is for order, / And hunger satisfied brings on new hunger // Till there's nothing to come …"[3]

The conservative and Christian Platonist tradition proposes that such questions need not lapse into interminable despair, but may receive a positive answer. Nearly twenty-four hundred years ago, the Greek philosopher Plato argued in his dialogue, the *Symposium*, that every action seeks some end; every desire has an object of one sort or another.[4] In the same way we can identify the desire for food and the desire for sunlight as both being *desires*, so too, he argued, can we settle upon a common term for those myriad things we seek. They are goods: to be a good means simply to be an object that is desirable. Plato then asks, given that all human beings are seeking goods—as he puts it, that they love what is good—what happens to them when they get the good they want the most? They become happy. To be simply happy—permanently, and not just for a moment's feeling—means, he tells us, to possess the good *forever*.

After Plato establishes that we desire goods, and to possess what we desire forever is to be happy, a leading character in his dialogue, the priestess Diotima, voices a striking conclusion. She says,

---

2. Thomas Kinsella, *Collected Poems* (Winston-Salem, N.C.: Wake Forest University Press, 2006), 114.

3. Kinsella, *Collected Poems*, 90.

4. Plato, *Symposium*, 200a3. Unless otherwise noted, all quotations from Plato are taken from *Complete Works*, ed. John M. Cooper (Indianapolis: Hackett Publishing Company, 1997).

That's what makes happy people happy, isn't it—possessing good things. There's no need to ask further, "What's the point of wanting happiness?" The answer you gave seems to be final.[5]

Consider for a moment the question she tells us we need not ask. We can ask a person who goes into a store to buy a bag of nails, "What do you want those nails for?" We can even ask, "Why did you buy that hamburger?" and receive a meaningful, if obvious, answer. But if happiness really means to possess forever the good we desire, then it would seem both superfluous and hopeless to ask, "Why do you want to be happy?" You could hardly desire anything else. For, Plato's definition of happiness as *the possession of the good forever* seems to have anticipated all possible objections. Even those people who seek out things sorrowful or depressing are seeking such things *as goods*; they merely illustrate the paradox that some people search for happiness in feelings of sorrow. We may be disturbed by those who find great joy in horror films, dirge-like rock music, or weepy romance novels, but we nonetheless understand the economy of happiness in which such things can play a role. While our disturbance should prompt us to ask whether such things can really make one happy, it is nonetheless true that the query *why* one would wish to be happy is unanswerable. There is nothing to ask *beyond* happiness, because there is, by definition, nothing qualitatively better than that which is most good and nothing quantitatively beyond *forever*.

Here is my point. Most of us are aware of the omnipresence of desire in our world: it is everywhere, and if that were all we could be certain of, it would make for a grim if dynamic spectacle. Many of us look about us and feel the nausea conveyed by Kinsella's poem. But we can also be certain that everywhere desire is present, so too is a conception of goodness and a view of happiness. What seems so unsettled in our day is not that everyone wants to be happy, but that so many persons seek happiness in such irreconcilable and erratic ways as to tempt us to despair of finding the real thing. We see that no one desires anything except what seems to him to be a good, and so, when we see how many things people seek as goods, we doubt whether there is available any reasonable standard for deciding which goods are better and which goods are worse. When we hear Plato

5. Plato, *Symposium*, 205a.

tell us that happiness is to possess the good forever, we wonder if he might simply mean that, like the barn owl, we must continually refill our stomachs with mouse meat, or our ears with another three-minute pop song, or our eyes with a new image on television after the last one has faded.

Our familiar condition thus resembles that of the ancient Athenians for whom Plato was writing, who had an abundance of good things in their world to fulfill every desire the flesh could imagine, from food and drink to sex and warfare. But, at least according to Plato, they still were neither happy nor sure how to seek happiness. We are, even more so, in a position much like that in which the French mathematician, Blaise Pascal, found his contemporaries four hundred years ago in seventeenth-century France. Pascal wrote then,

All men seek happiness. This is without exception. Whatever different means they employ, they all tend to this end. The cause of some going to war, and of others avoiding it, is the same desire in both, attended with different views. The will never takes the least step but to this object. This is the motive of every action of every man, even those who hang themselves.[6]

It is incontrovertible, Pascal tells us, that everyone seeks happiness. But we are so constituted, or rather, corrupted, that both one thing and its opposite can be perceived as good and pursued by the same desire; some persons can even come to believe that their own extinction is their lasting good, their true happiness.

Pascal was a skeptical Christian, confident in the goodness of God, but even more confident that something had gone terribly wrong at the core of human beings. If we had once known what truly would make us happy, we had fallen away from perfect knowledge, and lost any reliable, reasonable means of rediscovering it on our own. All that remained in us of true desire, and true reason, was a "trace." Consequently, Pascal wrote, "there is nothing in nature which has not been serviceable" in appearing as man's true good. He then gives us a quirky list of examples: "the stars, the heavens, earth, the elements, plants, cabbages, leeks, animals, insects, calves, serpents, fever, pestilence, war, famine, vices, adultery, incest." He explains, "since man has lost the true good, everything can appear equally

---

6. Blaise Pascal, *Pensées*, trans. W. F. Trotter (Mineola, N.Y.: Dover Publications, Inc., 2003), §425.

good to him, even his own destruction," despite all the reasons we might give to the contrary.[7] His view of human beings, at first, might not seem to differ much from Kinsella's vision of the barn owl. Our search for the thing that will make us happy is so various, incorrigible, and contradictory that it also appears irrational, inexplicable, and futile. It seems to stretch on forever and to go in every direction without any defined path.

Thinking of Pascal's account of man's confused and corrupted appetites, T. S. Eliot once wrote of the

> Thousand small deliberations [that]
> Protract the profit of their chilled delirium,
> Excite the membrane, when the sense has cooled,
> With pungent sauces, [and] multiply variety
> In a wilderness of mirrors.[8]

We wander through that wilderness, seeking any shard of glass that may shine, any spice that may excite the tongue, and any sudden emotion, however morbid, that may keep our feelings heightened for another moment. Unable to possess the good forever, we seek out myriad broken mirrors that dimly reflect it, and we wander from mirror to mirror, as if hoping one will finally put an end to the wandering. But, as Eliot's lines tell us, though we never abandon the search, we have given up the hope: we come to take the mere sensation of desire as the only good that does not fail so long as we remain tireless in the experience of novelty and proceed from new to new, from the surprising to the still more strange.

Although I would dissent from the icy and stark light in which Pascal and Eliot put this account of mankind's dogged but wild search for the good, I do think they and Plato converge on a definitive explanation of what human life is all about. Desire, but not just desire. The hunger for real happiness. What causes so much confusion, heartache, and even despair in our world today is not the impossible worry as to whether we all really want to be happy. Rather, we find formidable obstacles set in our paths by the world that frustrates our discovering where that happiness may truly be found. We have no shortage of goods in this world, so how do we choose among them? Is there a good that lasts forever? Or do

7. Pascal, *Pensées*, §425.
8. T. S. Eliot, *Complete Poems and Plays 1909–1950*, 23.

all the short-lived pleasures of this world simply have to be clutched together, one after the other, stimulation after stimulation, as a hodge-podge tragic parody of lastingness?[9]

If conservatism can offer a just critique of the modern world, it is precisely on the grounds that the modern world provides us myriad false images of happiness and attempts to content us with them. Promising freedom of choice, including the choice of *how* to be happy, modern liberalism has served, by and large, only to add to the natural difficulty of determining what is that good which alone will make us truly happy. This is not primarily the case because it has been the coincidental regime under which a dazzling, cosmic marketplace of goods has come into existence with no purpose other than to await our consumption. Rather liberalism has been foundational to the categorical intellectual or spiritual negation that led to such a marketplace being built in the first place. Our age holds up many things for our desire, but it does so only by deliberately discounting the reality of other things that may compete for that desire and absorb it entirely.

In this chapter, I shall describe, first, what I see when I look out at the general culture of this age, what it is I observe being held up as good sure-fire-recipes for happiness in the streets, on television, and in that wide placeless world of the internet. But it will not do merely to describe the "wilderness of mirrors" constituted in our day by flat screens and touch screens. One might reasonably object, after all, that no one expects to find happiness in what the talking heads have to tell or to sell us. No one really confuses the often-fervent browsing we do on Facebook with the search for a good that lasts forever. Often though we turn to these things, it is not in seeking our salvation. For that we go elsewhere: we seek out education, for instance, precisely because it is supposed to make possible our discovery of what is truly good, to form our mind to desire the good, and to train us in the virtues necessary to obtain it.

How wonderful it would be if this were always the case. How much more wonderful it would be if the leading voices of modern thought

9. This tragic view is one the classical world took as probable and which we should acknowledge as a real possibility: see Aristotle, *On the Soul*, 415a. Unless otherwise noted, all quotations of Aristotle are from *The Complete Works of Aristotle*, ed. Jonathan Barnes, 2 vols. (Princeton, N.J.: Princeton University Press, 1984).

wished to cooperate with us in that discovery. In fact, however, many of those voices, during the last four hundred years, have sought to narrow the scope of education and to thin out or simply deny the traditional answers given to the question, "Where lies the true happiness of mankind?" I shall discuss several instances of this to indicate that education in modern times has not generally been the ally of human happiness, because many of its major authorities have sought to render meaningless the idea of a lasting good in order to clear away obstacles to a desire without end and rooted only in power. For, if Eliot is right that the modern mind mistakes the sensation of desire for the good desired, then it is only through power that we may keep our senses primed. Some of the most formidable minds during these last few centuries have, in practice, sought to make it *more* difficult for us to develop those skills of discernment that would save us from the condition Pascal woefully describes, in which leeks, cabbages, and disease can actually convince us they are the good we seek and the font of our happiness. They have offered us power in the place of goodness, the force of desire in place of knowledge of the desirable.

If this part of my argument is successful, it will demonstrate as far as possible that human reason and modern education as they are usually conceived in our day can be the very enemy of realizing our potential as human beings. The methods of apparent intelligence can be the enemies of truth; promises of advancement and upward mobility can distract us from the real pilgrimage we are called to undertake by our nature as persons.

I shall, second, try to offer a description of the realities that our age tends to look on askance or deny outright. In place of the impoverished goods on offer at large and in most of our places of education, I draw on the resources of the Christian Platonist tradition to propose that the possession of the good forever that constitutes human happiness is to be found in the contemplation of three realities that modern thought has tried to conceal, namely, those of truth, goodness, and beauty. I propose that this triad constitutes the fundamental terms of what is real, and yet their reality is routinely denied by many of the authoritative voices in our culture. However, if we can defend their reality, that will allow us to sketch a richer vision of human happiness, to explain the central role of education in providing us the means to its attainment, and to live out our humanity in a manner more in accord with its dignity.

Clues to Happiness in a Consumer Culture

I do not want to spend too much space rehearsing the goods that our society implicitly proposes as the makings of human happiness in our day. Complaints about them are nearly as common as the proposals themselves. We are all familiar with the popular conception that our lives are being thoroughly "commercialized," so that at any given moment someone is trying to invent a new need, that a new product might be manufactured to fill it, with the one constant being that the buying of the new itself remains a kind of perpetual desire, and the new is never in short supply. No wonder Kinsella wrote that unsettling sketch of the barn owl: to buy and to devour, and to rest that we may buy and devour some more, seems to be not simply the habit but the purpose of everyday life. It is not uncommon to hear of the "commercialization" even of those unconscious aspects of ourselves that we do not think available for exploitation by advertisers in actuality finding themselves increasingly to be targeted. Indeed, it has been decades since soft-drink bottlers began advertising their wares by making specific appeal to our desire not to be marketed to. The very fact that we are so wise to the ambitions of marketers to sell us happiness should put us on guard that our knowingness and cynicism may themselves be harnessed by some future advertisement campaign.[10]

What most impresses me about everyday life in our age is not so much the obsessive capitalization and consumption of the new, but the way in which so many of the commercial and non-commercial elements in our life are geared to giving us a sense of epistemic and communal connection—to the world of information and to other persons. While the sale of computers and smart phones is obviously big business, the desire for a perpetual contact with others—a desire to be recognized, seen and heard, and to hear and to see—seems to drive us even more than does the desire for the novelty of a new purchase. Our way of communicating generates a continuous stream of brief flickers, so that we are at every moment finding out something incidental about others and informing others of our incidental "status" through what is erroneously called "social networking" software.[11]

10. See Jonathan Crary, *24/7: Late Capitalism and the Ends of Sleep* (London: Verso, 2013).
11. Here lies one of the compelling truths behind Francis Fukuyama's *The End of History and*

A network is usually understood as a complicated and interdependent system that performs some function beyond itself. But the networks of our day serve chiefly to remind us of the incidentally active existence of others and to make them aware of ourselves, as if we felt a deep incompleteness that might be filled through acknowledgment by another person. Worse, our "networks" attempt only to fill it quantitatively, aggregating almost atomic instants of attention from others to keep our own attentions unevenly but perpetually occupied. In our appetites to be recognized and, as it were, to feel the new, we continuously search about us. Once, a friend told me of how such appetites can reveal themselves as both absolute and meaningless: he had heard of a study that claimed persons sometimes send emails to themselves just so they will have the satisfaction of clicking on a new message from someone.

Well, you say, it is certainly true that consumption and communication take up much of the mental space of modern life, but neither pretends to provide us happiness, nor do the myriad other claimants on our time in the present age. I would not deny that. But when we live in a condition where everything seems to melt into air, where the new becomes old with lightning speed, we become trained not to identify happiness with this or that thing—we are not so naïve—but to retreat from the fast and fading spectacles of the world into the feelings they stimulate. When we dwell always in a vast wilderness of mirrors, we discern, eventually, that the mirrors are just mirrors. What we conclude is that happiness must not attach to any one of them, but must be rather the fleeting-but-renewable feeling such things can give us. We come to define happiness as a feeling, usually a feeling of present pleasure, in which our appetites momentarily rest. And it is around this conviction that our lives tend to take form. We seek wealth, or public recognition, or power, in order to make it possible for us to enjoy, exhaust, and renew the pleasurable feeling we identify as happiness. This leaves us in an uncomfortable position: we doubt that anything specific in the world can of itself provide happiness to us, and yet we acknowledge that *only* things in the world can stimulate our deeply private, indeed entirely isolated, conception of happiness as a feeling in us.

the Last Man (New York: Avon Books, 1992). That the need to be recognized does not necessarily find its fulfillment in democratic capitalism merely testifies to our inability to predict—much less to channel—what is most fundamental to our natures as persons.

Such a conception of happiness may seem to adore the material world, but in fact it merely recognizes its dependence on the raw materials of that world so that we may harvest objects for exploitation. On the whole, it might better be called unworldly insofar as nothing in the world *in particular* can be considered essential to happiness, but only used as a stimulant.

In sum, the modern person concludes of happiness that it involves a novelty of appetites, a species of companionship and mutual recognition, and an interior feeling. I do not wish to reject these typical conclusions of the modern person out of hand. In fact, they seem to affirm three things worth holding onto. First, they suggest happiness is primarily an inward state; second, happiness is in some way tied to pleasure; and, third, our happiness is also, in some way, tied to the world, including the persons, outside us. More than two thousand years ago, the Greek philosopher Aristotle made three similar claims in his own account of happiness. And yet, happiness as typically understood in our day bears very little resemblance to how Aristotle or other great minds have usually described it.

A Hall of Modern Mirrors

Perhaps, we speculate, we have only to acquire a more rigorous understanding of what we need as human beings in order to reach a satisfactory consensus about what will make us happy. Surely an education will help with that, insofar as being educated is often thought to entail being familiar with what intellectual authorities have to say in their fields of study. If the surface life of our age does not give us a satisfactory account of happiness, that should be no surprise. Surfaces are superficial, after all. Surely, we tell ourselves, when we go in search of deeper answers, we will find real depths adequate to our curiosity. It is common for us to hear "ignorance" treated as a grave evil, and so perhaps we just need to be a bit better informed, a bit "enlightened."

When we turn to many of the intellectual authorities of the last three centuries and more, however, we are likely to be disappointed. They are often adept at methodical and "critical thinking," at seeing through the superficial conventions of their days, but they tend to do this in the process of hollowing out our lives rather than deepening them. They typically come offering a great insight, but that insight then serves to show us that reality is in fact even less rich or interesting than we thought it was. The new idea chiefly strips away, rather than adds to, the reserve of what had once been known. It prides itself on being a school of disenchantment. Let me offer a few examples.

I claimed above that some parts of the contemporary world promote buying and consumption as tools of our happiness. One of the most powerful critics of modern capitalism and consumption was the German philosopher Karl Marx, who believed that the perpetual exploitation of labor in the name of conspicuous consumption alienated human beings from the world and left them in a wretched, in some sense sub-human, state. What, we may ask, does Marx think a fully human person would be? He tells us in an early essay,

An animal produces only itself, while man reproduces the whole of nature. An animal's product belongs immediately to its physical body, while man freely confronts his product.... It is just in his work upon the objective world, therefore, that man really proves himself to be a *species-being*. This production is his active species-life.... By tearing from man the object of his production, estranged labor tears from him his species-life.[12]

We can certainly marvel with Marx at the human being's ability not only to reproduce himself, as do all living things, and not only to produce a specific sort of object, as bees produce their hives, but to make *anything* whose idea may be kindled in the imagination. But Marx goes further than marveling: it is this capacity for limitlessly varied production that defines mankind as a species. What is human nature? Production, says Marx. This does not seem so much opposed to the contemporary account of mankind as a consumer as it is the other side of the same coin. Market consumption was an evil, according to Marx, only because it alienated man from his productive labor. But he believed production was all there was to human life even in optimal conditions. We thus are rendered even more dependent on the world for happiness in his view of things than the contemporary popular story might suggest; for, he says, if our relation to making-things is compromised, we become estranged from our very natures and our selves are diminished.

12. Karl Marx, *Early Political Writings*, ed. Joseph O'Malley (Cambridge: Cambridge University Press, 1994), 76.

As I noted above, contemporary life does not just present buying and consumption as means to happiness. One can often consume the spectacles of modern life for free or very cheaply, but spectacle here means simply the experience of seeing something or someone novel, deriving a thrill from its witness, and then moving on to the next one. Novelty experienced rather than some substantial merit in a thing seen, heard, or learned is the essential characteristic of our spectacular society. One of the single most influential philosophers of the last three centuries would tell us roughly the same thing, if in more acute and sophisticated language.

The German Idealist philosopher Immanuel Kant wrote, late in the eighteenth century, that the ability to appreciate an object not because it is useful but because it provides delight in itself (in its "formal presentation" alone)—or, as we might say, it gives us pleasure in a spectacle through its novelty alone—is called taste.[13] When we express our taste affirmatively, we call something beautiful. But, Kant admonishes, while a person "will talk about the beautiful as if beauty were a characteristic of the object and the judgment were logical," it is in fact the case that "the judgment is only aesthetic and refers to the object's presentation merely to the subject."[14] When we look upon something and call it beautiful, we are not saying anything about the object so described, but only about our taste, about our feelings regarding the object. A thing cannot be beautiful, says Kant, but we may say it is in order to express our own inward emotion. Beauty is subjective, a *taste*. As such, what matters, so far as our tastes are concerned, is not the existence or quality of one thing rather than another, but merely that there be a multitude of objects in the world to which we might apply our taste-judgments. Novelty has a way of becoming everything for the old philosopher as it does for the modern urban denizens depicted in Eliot's poems. What we see does not in itself matter; only the sensation, the delight in our own tastes, matters. On this score, the roving search for novelty commonly exhibited by children and adults in our day would seem to throw us back on ourselves: we think we are going outward in search of something real and beautiful, but we in fact are burrowing ever deeper into our own inner feelings, so that they become the whole of our reality.

13. Immanuel Kant, *Critique of Judgment*, trans. Werner S. Pluhar (Indianapolis: Hackett Publishing, 1987), 1.5.

14. Kant, *Critique of Judgment*, 1.5–6.

Kant believes this to be a spiritual reality, and this contrasts markedly from Marx's emphasis on the material objectivity of human nature, but if Kant is right, beauty serves to save us from "estrangement" from ourselves primarily by proposing that we are locked up inside ourselves, where the feelings enjoy a spiritual freedom that transcends objective nature at the cost of being cut off from it.[15]

An intellectual descendent of Kant's, the literary critic and early psychologist I. A. Richards, would seek to borrow the materialism of Marx to lock us up even more securely. Explaining why people look at beautiful works of art and read beautiful poems, he denies as a matter of course that there is anything called beauty to be seen, or any spirit to be awakened to its freedom from material laws. On the contrary, it is one more physical law, for Richards explains that art's effects are due to

a greater number of [neurological] impulses which have been brought into co-ordination with one another.... [so that art leads to] the resolution, inter-animation, and balancing of impulses.... the conduct of life is throughout an attempt to organize impulses so that success is obtained for the greater number or mass of them ...[16]

If Richards is to be believed, artworks simply provide occasion for the multifarious "impulses" in our brains—electrons circulating through a maze of synapses, we suppose—to be brought into momentary order. "Taste" is in fact merely the capacity to experience this order in the brain. If, presumably, one could find a way to order impulses in the brain without any external stimuli at all, so much the better. Happiness would be achieved; a life would be well lived within the small compass of the brain. Richards suggests that the feeling of beauty is closely bound to human happi-

15. Kant's severance of beauty from being is decisive, and prepares the discussions of being to be taken up in subsequent chapters. His rendering beauty "subjective," as we shall see just below, prepares the way for the radical reduction of beauty to sensation or feeling. But, it is fair to note, this was on the whole far from his understanding of the beautiful. He understood beauty as subjective, yes, but universally so, such that every human nature could be expected to identify the same thing as beautiful (*Critique of Judgment*, 1.8). Furthermore, this universal subjective experience was the basis of culture, which broadens the mind, harmonizes the understanding and imagination, expands the sympathies, and makes possible a community of refinement and taste (*Critique of Judgment*, 1.9, 35, 41–42, 52, 60). His intentions are not to the point, however, since the opposite of them has been derived from his decisive first step of conscripting beauty into his system of transcendental idealism.

16. I. A. Richards, *Principles of Literary Criticism* (New York: Harcourt Brace, 1934), 61.

ness, but then he reduces both to what Kinsella calls our "staring" brains.

Kant and Richards may seem overly psychological, overly inward, to convince us they adequately grasp the conditions of human life and happiness. If the feeling of pleasure takes place within as an experience of beauty or "order," we usually find that it depends on things outside us, too. If pleasure is to be a sign of happiness, then, it would seem that goods outside us are necessary—and in great quantities. The most pleasure will be had by he who has the most goods, and he who has as many goods as he desires and the power to secure them with relative ease. So concluded Thomas Hobbes, the English philosopher, more than a century before Kant began writing. Hobbes was a far more terse and reductive thinker than Kant, more ready to dismiss as absurdity anything that did not seem empirically obvious. According to Hobbes, there is no inward psychology in the sense of a spirit or soul apart from matter. Rather, human beings are full of often irrational passions that are, in themselves, nothing more than microscopic movements of matter within us. Those small movements of intention break forth in the visible movement of action as human beings seek to attain material goods and to overcome the fear of those goods being taken away.[17]

In brief, Hobbes tells us that only matter is real, and human life consists of a wide range of irrational and unpredictable movements of passion, the foremost of which is fear. Because nearly all men fear death and other misfortunes, Hobbes, in his *Leviathan*, describes the "general inclination of all mankind" as "a perpetual and restless desire of power after power, that ceaseth only in death."[18] Desire for the power to secure more material goods is the universal condition of human life.[19] We would be back with our barn owl again, save that the barn owl at least experiences some blank cessation of hunger between feedings that might remind us of such words as peace and contentment. Such an association is mere folly, according to Hobbes.[20] We are far too fearful of losing what power and security we have attained to cease in the hunt for more. Life is itself motion—the motion of hunger for anything that is not death. Even sleep is a kind of restlessness.

17. Thomas Hobbes, *Leviathan* (Indianapolis: Hackett, 1994), 6.1–3.
18. Hobbes, *Leviathan*, 11.2.
19. Not necessarily more goods than others have, but "more" in the sense of always-yet-another.
20. Hobbes, *Leviathan*, 6.58.

We began with the claim that it was demonstrable that all actions seek some end. If Hobbes is right, that is not the case. If only matter is real, then we would expect all things to follow the laws of physics. According to the new physics of Hobbes, when "a body is once in motion, it moveth (unless something else hinder it) eternally."[21] What is true for any other material object must necessarily be true for the life of the human body; we cannot think of movement, including the movement of desires, in terms of ends-aimed-at, but only in terms of the motion itself. We are moved by passions that are by their nature separate from reason, and so move in unpredictable directions. Fear is the one nearly universal passion, which does not so much guide desire to a particular end—power—as chase us *away* from a condition of vulnerability that would expose us to death at the hands of another. In the world of Hobbes, nothing can truly be good. Actions happen, but they are not always aimed at some end, and when they *are* aimed at an end, that does not necessarily mean that the agent is seeking something identified as good. We may seek all kinds of things that we call "good," but no one of them constitutes the universal good for human life called happiness. For to reach an end would be to fall still, and to fall still would be, in Hobbes's view, not fulfillment but death.[22]

But Hobbes's account of things invites a question he goes to great lengths to make it impossible for his reader to ask: "For what positive end do we even bother fearing extinction?" Because extinction is death, answers Hobbes, and you are *probably* afraid of death. We do not have to regard life as a good in order to fear its loss, and his assertion is only conditional at any rate. If you do not fear death, well, then you do not need his counsel. But if we persist with the question, a ready answer comes to us from the nineteenth-century English naturalist, Charles Darwin. Darwin evidently agreed with Hobbes that only matter is real and that actions are driven by irrational processes.[23] In his *Autobiography* he observes that there "seems to be no more design in the variability of organic beings and in the action of natural selection, than in the course which the wind blows."[24] And yet, he tells us, everything "in nature is the result of fixed

---

21. Hobbes, *Leviathan*, 2.2.
22. Hobbes, *Leviathan*, Introduction.1.
23. Irrational in the sense that they are outside and independent of reason.
24. Charles Darwin, *Autobiography* (New York: W. W. Norton, 2005), 73.

laws."²⁵ Despite the lack of design, he nonetheless sees those fixed laws enforcing a definite aim in nature, writing that those who understand, like him, that

all the corporeal and mental organs ... of all beings have been developed through natural selection, or the survival of the fittest, together with use or habit, will admit that these organs have been formed so that their possessors may compete successfully with other beings, and thus increase in number.²⁶

Hobbes gave us the individual's fear herding us wildly from death to power after power; Darwin dilates this description of man to include the species of everything in nature, so that every species as a whole engages in competition to avoid extinction and to increase its number.

We need not do this consciously, according to Darwin, as how could the common garden snail know anything about the overall health of his species? If there is no design to it all, how did this competition for survival and the mechanism of natural selection become a "fixed law"? A world truly absent of design, one may expect, would be one characterized by an absence of universal qualities generalizable as laws, and it would be nonsense to speak of what generalizations there are as fixed.²⁷ It would seem probable, then, to conclude that whatever laws we hit upon with our reason are not the fixed and certain truths Darwin made them out to be.

One possible solution to this question-begging of Darwin's presents itself: the appearance of such laws is simply a useful creation; that is, we claim to believe something to be true not because it really *is* true, but simply because it would be convenient if it were so. One may protest, we really do believe some things to be true, not because we find them useful, but because we think them true. The last great German philosopher of the nineteenth century, Friedrich Nietzsche, had a ready response. *You* may believe something true because you think it is, but is it clear that there is really a "you" to take responsibility for that belief? If Hobbes is right that we are driven by all sorts of physical passions that may not form a coherent, much less a rational, whole, perhaps the very notion of an "I," of a self, is itself one more useful falsehood produced by some passions other than

25. Darwin, *Autobiography*, 73.
26. Darwin, *Autobiography*, 74.
27. That is certainly how Hobbes viewed the matter (*Leviathan*, 15.41).

ourselves. To see this, Nietzsche claims, is to *"recognize untruth as a condition of life."*[28] Every supposed truth is not the product of a natural desire to know, but the production of a "will to power" whose source is something other than ourselves and of which our sense of identity is just one more product. All supposedly rational talk of "cause, sequence, reciprocity, relativity, constraint, number, law, freedom, motive, and purpose" is just myth added to myth, untruth to untruth, devised by *us*.[29] But who are we? He does not mean that people are dishonest, for to speak of a lie would be to speak of a self that can take responsibility for falsehood. Untruth is not an occasional action, he tells us, but, again, the condition of our lives. To speak of "self-preservation" or other teleological interpretations of action is, as Hobbes already gives us grounds to suspect, misplaced. The will to power seeks simply to discharge itself.[30] The "I" (*ego*) may be simply the effect of this discharge, not its agent or cause.[31]

Let us take stock of this brief and dismal survey of some of the most formidable figures in modern thought. We began with the claim that everyday life offers us abundant but unsatisfactory suggestions as to what might be the good that a person must possess forever in order to be happy. Wanting to be wise, and finding the common answers of the present inadequate, we looked to several of the distinguished figures of the recent and not-so-recent past—to the sorts of formidable influences whose writings one might expect to read (or, more likely, whose ideas will be uncritically diffused) in a typical humanities course at a contemporary university. It is usually a good idea, finding one's friends' and contemporaries' talk about things inadequate, to turn for advice to our parents. But these intellectual parents, I propose, fail us. They do not contradict the common assumptions of our world by providing a vision of human life more rich and profound. Rather, they simply attempt to strip us of the capacity for belief in anything that might deter us from giving ourselves up to lives of consumption and spectacle: desire without end, pleasure without purpose, selves without integrity.

Far from telling us that contemporary life's apparent fullness conceals an even greater abundance if we can just get beyond its superficialities,

28. Friedrich Nietzsche, *The Works* (New York: The Tudor Publishing Company, 1931), 1:4.
29. Nietzsche, *The Works*, 1:23–24.   30. Nietzsche, *The Works*, 1:14.
31. Nietzsche, *The Works*, 1:18–21.

they tell us that, in the words of the philosopher Iredell Jenkins, reality is in fact "impoverished." Jenkins believed that modern philosophy had done a dreadfully persuasive job in establishing as a "settled conviction" in the minds of most modern persons "that nature is *in fact* much simpler and barer than it appears to us *in experience*."[32] In brief, modern thinkers generally tell us that, whatever our experience to the contrary, reality is in fact far less than it seems, and much of what we take for reality is just a projection of our minds onto the bare surfaces of matter, including that which constitutes our own bodies. Most modern philosophers, then, do not seek to divulge realities that exist beyond the experience of our everyday desires and which, once known, will transform them, but to show us that there may be *even less* to the world than our purchases, entertainments, longings, and curiosities would suggest, because there is no *beyond*. We journey not from a cave of appearances to a realm of boundless light, but into the heart of darkness of reality's dark continent. The realization that this was the trajectory of modern thought took centuries, and the philosophy of Nietzsche is the testament of a man who felt so poignantly the bankruptcy of modern beliefs that he wrote simply to trace down to the last its logical consequences. It is perhaps only a coincidence that he went mad.

If we tally up what these influential writers deny as real, however, we will generate a list worth contemplating. Marx defined only material production as real, denying the possibility of any *spiritual goods*. Kant, as an Idealist philosopher, gave to ideas the highest, spiritual reality at the expense of matter; but in making his case, he denied the reality of *beauty* except within the closed context of the mind, the house of ideas. Richards seems to have thought only matter was real, and to have believed *beauty* was simply a certain subjective coordination of impulses within the material organ of the brain. Hobbes, in a similar way, denied the existence of the *good*; we are moved to flee from the death we fear rather than to seek a happiness that would make life worth living. Motion is just motion; there is no "wherefore" to be found in nature. Darwin in slight contrast conceived of something like a *good* as the purpose of life in the "survival of the fittest" and the production of offspring, but such a good was a ceaseless

32. Iredell Jenkins, "The Postulate of an Impoverished Reality," *The Journal of Philosophy* 39, no. 20 (September 24, 1942): 535.

process that did not belong to any member of the species, accounting only for the total quantity of the species as a whole, which could never actually know such a good *as* good. Lastly, Nietzsche, seeing the work of these figures and seeing through the denials of beauty and goodness to a secreted assertion of power, concluded that there could be no such thing as *truth*.

One reason we are tempted to find reality "impoverished," it would seem, is that we have been told over and again that only matter is real; in consequence, we are expected to dismiss as subjective projections, mass delusions, or ideological conveniences those non-material things that make fruitful knowledge, desire, and joy—namely, *truth*, *goodness*, and *beauty*.

Our Experience—and Aristotle's—of Reality

Now, despite what I have said about the account of happiness offered by the popular culture to our age, our everyday lives do invite us to believe in truth, goodness, and beauty. We look about us and perceive that things are what they are; that is, we find the world to be true. We have already noted that the world seems to be overloaded with goods; our doubts arise only when we ask whether it is possible to discern an order intrinsic to the world of goods that survives and directs our appraisals, and by means of which they should be arranged so that we can know and seek after the highest good. As Kant suggests, most of us routinely use the word "beautiful" as if we were describing something present *in* the thing described and not merely something *in* us. What we lack is a vocabulary sufficiently developed to account for differences of beauty in terms independent of differences of taste, and that illiteracy leads us to doubt the value of our perceptions. As a rule, then, we all have not simply occasional but routine experience of truth, goodness, and beauty as realities that shape our lives. If our intellectual parents are correct to deny them, then they do so against rather than in confirmation of the evidence those lives provide. To disenchant the world they must first dismiss an awful lot of it—almost the whole of it.

I would suggest that, if our intellectual parents seem to be giving us poor nourishment—if their most powerful arguments tend to dismiss experience and diminish the possibilities of finding the happiness we already seek—we would do well to look back still further, and to learn what our intellectual grandparents, even our great-great-great grandparents have to tell us. Rather than attempt to mount a thorough-going response on behalf of ancient tradition against the reductive views we have touched on, in this chapter I shall meditate on just one text: a mere paragraph or so that, happily, contains all the resources we need to pose a serious challenge to the world-stripping modern philosophers and novelty-inebriated common sense of our age.

Recall my claim above that the common conceptions of happiness in our day tell us that it seems to be largely inward in nature, has something to do with pleasure, and yet is also bound up with the world around us. With these three attributes in mind, consider these words that open the *Metaphysics* of Aristotle:

All men by nature desire to know. An indication of this is the delight we take in our senses; for even apart from their usefulness they are loved for themselves; and above all others the sense of sight. For not only with a view to action, but even when we are not going to do anything, we prefer seeing (one might say) to everything else. The reason is that this, most of all the senses, makes us know and brings light to many differences between things.[33]

The ancient Greek philosopher gives us a whole history of hunger and happiness in these words. While we often use our eyes and ears to accomplish specific tasks, while we actively *look* and *listen* in order to find food or to avoid getting run over by a bus, by our nature, our minds go by way of our senses out into the world. And in response, the things of this world rush up to meet us. The world is *ob-jective*, it throws itself before us. It *discloses* itself every bit as much as our senses actively *uncover* it.

The philosopher D. C. Schindler has argued well that this comes as a consequence of the ecstatic natures of both the being of things and of reason itself. He writes that the neo-Thomist philosopher Jacques Maritain (whom we shall study in Part II) was correct to posit reason as having an intuition of being such that the mind is always extending itself so that it has a "primordial" and "true grasp" of what is real.[34] He goes on to note, however, that the phenomenologist Gabriel Marcel was correct to criticize

33. Aristotle, *Metaphysics*, 980a.
34. D. C. Schindler, *The Catholicity of Reason* (Grand Rapids, Mich.: William B. Eerdmans Publishing Company, 2013), 10, 5.

Maritain's claim as indicating reason somehow possesses being, whereas in truth our encounter of reality more closely resembles the reception of a gift. Intuitive grasp or generous reception, by themselves, inadequately describe the experience of perception and knowledge. Only when taken together does the whole truth appear; reason, Schindler writes, "is in being, and being is in reason."[35] If our encounter with the world were purely one of reason's taking possession of what is other than itself, then we would sense the act of knowing as a kind of conquest, wherein we master some phenomenon and impose a name upon it. And, in truth, we do give names to things. But what we name is always the fruit of discovery; the act of naming is possible only because the being of what is real has first disclosed itself, has first offered itself to us as an appearance to be wondered at and then a mystery to be contemplated. There is no time at which knowing as act is not also a knowing as reception; everything we know is first of all a gift given to us to be known.

The meeting of our desire to know and the reality of the things of this world giving themselves to knowledge begets delight, a pleasure in knowledge for its own sake. So much does the world around us offer, so much light does it throw upon the windows of our soul, and so many words does it seem to speak to us, that we often prefer simply seeing—simply taking the world's wisdom into us—to every sort of useful action. Our desire to know finds, simply through the act of the eyes, such ready nourishment that everything useful we might do seems of worth primarily because it allows the eye to see the light about it, and this light to bathe the mind in its rays. This indicates the first of three essential qualities that require us always to describe reason and knowledge in terms of vision—the claim that guides this entire study. For, sight is always an action performed by us, but one that cannot be performed if light is not simultaneously given to it: not light, then sight, but both at once so that they constitute a unity of activity and passivity, the seer going out of himself into the seen, and the seen going out of itself into the seer.

How can we name this condition, in which the mind stretches out through the senses for the reality after which it hungers, and in which reality answers back with a light that delights? Aristotle has an answer on

35. Schindler, *The Catholicity of Reason*, 8.

which we have already touched. It "is owing to their wonder that men both now begin and at first began to philosophize."[36] And he continues, "all men begin ... by wondering that things are as they are."[37] By nature, it seems, we dwell in the world in wonder. Contrary to Marx, who claimed man's nature was production, it seems more evident that our nature is defined by our orientation to wonder. We become estranged from reality not when the products of our labor are taken from us, but when this capacity to wonder about the world is deadened within us. Contrary to Nietzsche, the first instincts of our reason are not to harness truth for power, but to be overpowered by the delight of reality. Perhaps he was correct that a "will to truth" mischaracterizes this desire, at least insofar as such a phrase suggests a triumphant march, a sort of willful persistence that overcomes other possible avenues of action and takes *possession* of the world by storm.[38] Further, this desire *to know*, this delight in *seeing*, is deeper, more primordial, in us even than the will, even than the idea of truth, at least to the extent that *being*—my being, your being, the being that is *reality*—is an already complete and unified whole that stands rationally behind and beneath truth and makes it possible.

Let me unpack what this means. For Aristotle, wonder initially entails our seeing things as they are, witnessing them as effects, and wondering what their causes may be. In this respect, to be in wonder is to confess a state of ignorance, to confess that we see there is more in the world than is yet in our minds. The world presents itself for our inquiry and, inspired by what it gives us, we move from mere wonder *at* it, to a knowledge *of* it that is finally a presence *in* it.[39] We can see that things are as they are and can build upon that vision toward one that penetrates to causes. But knowledge of causes does not succeed in reducing the world to our domination; on the contrary, it allows us to see more fully, more widely and in greater detail, the infinity that first takes the initiative in allowing itself to be seen by our eyes. I would suggest that this taking of delight in our encounter with a world that gives itself to us to be known is our *fundamental* experience, and one which we retrospectively describe in speaking of the world as true. Truth is embedded in the world's existence; it stretches out to us from reality, and so, to see things is also to hear them *speaking* truth to us.

36. Aristotle, *Metaphysics*, 982b.   37. Aristotle, *Metaphysics*, 983a.
38. Nietzsche, *The Works*, 1:6.   39. Schindler, *The Catholicity of Reason*, 30.

This is what philosophers call "intelligibility." The world's truth speaks a language that we, by our intellectual nature, have the potential to understand.

We encounter this truth, Aristotle claims, through our own natural inclination. That is, we already experience what is true as good, as the object of our desire, before we enter into it (as truth).[40] And the way in which we desire to know the truth about things leads us not to find out what they are good for—to what use we may put them—but to find out their causes. That is, we want to know why the things about us were sufficiently good as to merit being put into being, and we sense them as good simply for being knowable.[41] We want to know the order of goods that leads everything to find its place in reality as something by something else desired and known. And we want to know the ultimate good for whose sake all other goods are pursued and in virtue of which all things wonderful simply are.[42] In sum, we have an interior sense of goodness that directs us to the goodness that, along with truth, is intrinsic to things.

Does wonder cease with our knowledge of truth and goodness? Some scholars have claimed that philosophy, for Aristotle, is precisely the reduction of wonder at the effects of the world to science, that is, to knowledge about their causes. Martin Heidegger even saw in the joy-in-seeing of Aristotle the seeds of the modern desire to reduce all things to their use-value, making them subject to our power (technology), through reasoning about causes.[43] But wonder cannot merely be the desire to move from an absence of knowledge to knowledge, a desire that diminishes in proportion to our arriving at knowledge. Nor, for that matter, is knowledge best understood as a kind of technical mastery. Aristotle *might* seem to suggest this so, insofar as wonder describes the condition of wanting to know the causes of things without actually knowing them. But he also tells us of the

40. Aristotle, *Metaphysics*, 1091b.

41. As Mark Shiffman argues in "Shaping the Language of Inquiry: Aristotle's Transformation of the Meanings of *Thaumaston*," *Epoché* 10, no. 1. (Fall 2005): 21–36, we may indeed initially wonder out of a desire to possess, but one of the wonders of inquiry is the transformation that takes place of the character of our wonder and the nature of the wonderful itself. We may initially find only the unusual wonderful, but, as Shiffman follows Heidegger in arguing, we eventually develop "a disposition of wondering at the unusualness of the usual" (23).

42. Aristotle, *Metaphysics*, 1072a–b. See also Rémi Brague, "Necessity of the Good," *First Things* 250 (February 2015), 47–52.

43. Schindler, *The Catholicity of Reason*, 181.

delight we take in seeing and knowing. Is it not also to be in wonder when we take delight in knowing the truth and goodness of a thing? To delight in, to experience *as good* by taking pleasure in, a thing that is known *as true* is to see its reality as having at once an orderliness to it as well as a certain excess, a mystery. This experience of truth as good, as something we may in some sense possess but also as something that exceeds our comprehension, that becomes more mysterious the more we understand it, is to encounter the beautiful.[44] Contrary to Kant, we have no reason to believe that beauty is something exclusively located in the subjective judgment as a *taste*; it rather is the name for that aspect of things that orders, unifies, and makes to shine from the depths of being (reality) their truth and their goodness. Kant quite helpfully defines beauty as a taste-judgment regarding the formal presentation of an object independent of its existence, and in the second half of that claim some of the words ring true but not as he intends them.[45] Beauty is the shining forth of the form that makes a being to be what it is such that it exists, is intelligible as true, and is desirable as good. "Form" does not prescind (in the sense of "stand apart") from being and existence; as we shall see, it is the name we give to the mystery that being shares with us in virtue of its fullness of actuality and in such excess that we can never cease to wonder.[46] As Maritain once observed, to define "beauty by the radiance of the form" is in reality to define it "by the radiance of a mystery."[47]

If Aristotle's terse initial commonplaces are to be believed, then, our everyday experience shows that we by nature desire not primarily to make or possess things but to know them as true, good, and beautiful. As is the case with the unsatisfactory account of happiness contemporary culture offers, the fulfillment of this desire would seem to be largely inward, but an inward experience intimately engaged with the world beyond us and receiving the blessings of truth, goodness, and beauty from it. When we

44. This is a *minimal* definition of the beauty of reality that attempts to capture what we shall call its convertability with truth and goodness. In later chapters, I will attribute to beauty a greater independence of identity analogous to that of truth and goodness.

45. Kant, *Critique of Judgment*, 1.1–2, 11.

46. The decisive argument for reason as convertible with wonder, because being is convertible with love and mystery, is to be found in the work of D. C. Schindler, most fully in *The Catholicity of Reason*, 163–228.

47. Jacques Maritain, *Creative Intuition in Art and Poetry* (New York: Pantheon Books Inc., 1953), 162.

receive these things, we take delight, we experience pleasure. And so, truth, goodness, and beauty are not only realities all around us that we routinely experience, they are the aspects of reality that seem to be primary ingredients in human happiness.

Once again, if Aristotle is correct, then the denial of the reality of these things, propagated by Kant, Hobbes, and Nietzsche, constituted not so much a set of realistic and disillusioned modern insights, as a perverse project often intended to strip the world of its contents, leaving only matter behind. If the world is reduced to matter, there is nothing to see, nothing to show, nothing to delight in, nothing to relish as good, as Aristotle understands these acts.[48] And yet, if it is reduced to matter, that matter becomes available as raw material for use by our desires. Reality no longer gives itself to us, but rather sits inert, passive before the domination, the use and the abuse, of such agents as can impose form upon it.[49] The modern thinkers I have referred to, therefore, are complicit in a project of unchaining and exacerbating human desire specifically by depriving it of the food it most requires. They encourage us to claim a greater freedom for our desires even as the material world seems less and less capable of affording them delight. We saw at the outset that Plato proposes happiness as the genuinely human good precisely because the word itself seems to bring all inquiry to completion. We do not have to ask the further question, "Why would you want to be happy?" But these modern minds, in supposedly freeing our desires, force us to ask, "Why do we go on desiring if there is nothing specific to be desired?" The only answer they can offer, as Hobbes well knew, is "power." But then we ask, "Power for what?", and are told in reply, "to attain whatever you desire." Only one of these responses actually answers the question, but to hear the answer is not only to discover what one already knew and was moving toward but to change one's life for good.

Here is the change. We come to see that wonder never ceases, and the mere experience of the truth, goodness, and beauty of the world around us cannot consummate that wonder in happiness, because it cannot give us those things forever.[50] Rather, as we engage the world in wonder, we

48. Schindler, *The Catholicity of Reason*, 127.

49. Karl Barth, *Protestant Theology in the Nineteenth Century*, trans. Brian Cozens and John Bowden (Grand Rapids, Mich.: Eerdmans, 2002), 23–24.

50. Thus, there is a difference between imperfect and perfect happiness. See Aquinas, *Summa Theologica*, I-II.2.8, I-II.3.2.

have to climb up ladders of truth, goodness, and beauty, until we encounter these things not *in things* but *in* and *as* themselves. Learning to climb those ladders is what Aristotle, Plato, and the western tradition in general have understood education to be. For, only our intellects can ascend a spiritual ladder, and the untrained intellect will almost inevitably slip and fall back upon the beauty in things rather than climb up to beauty itself. At the top, where those ladders converge, lies the life of contemplation, where we live in the presence of truth, goodness, and beauty in their permanent and perfect selves.[51] Only in that contemplation can we encounter these things in forms that will not fail, and so such highest and most perfected thought brings us into the life that Aristotle understood as the happiest one—indeed, he says that in this state we become as gods. All our other wants and desires exist to make that divine life possible.

We can conclude then with this thought. I have claimed that our common culture and its rarified modern influences give us either inadequate or outright vicious answers to our necessary inquiry into happiness. But ancient and not-so-ancient wisdom abounds to provide us more satisfying and compelling answers. It is the proper task of the conservative to resist the modern desire to strip-mine the world, and to seek instead to fulfill the principal urge of human nature, the hunger for reality, through the act of dwelling in the wonder that leads to happiness. What the conservative would conserve is that intellectual tradition, with its condign vocabulary and compelling conceptual architectonic, that help us so to dwell. And so, in the next chapter, we must go beyond a few references to an exemplary figure such as Aristotle in order to examine what constitutes the great tradition of the West that I called, in the last chapter, Christian Platonism.

---

51. Aristotle, *Metaphysics*, 1072b.

TWO

What Is the Western Tradition?

The Foundations of the West

We saw in the Introduction that conservatism seeks to defend a particular vision of human life that George Santayana defined as Christian Platonic in nature. In chapter 1, I considered one aspect of that vision: how it envisions human happiness in comparison with typical modern accounts of it. It now seems appropriate to ask a more foundational question. If conservatism seeks to conserve the western tradition, then what are that tradition's constitutive principles?

To answer this question, I should probably begin by stating an assumption that may no longer be obvious to some readers: there is a recognizable tradition of western civilization in which we all participate, even though, in many ways and over a long period, we have misidentified its fundamental characteristics. This misidentification has, in many instances, resulted in alienation, in an utter estrangement. Many westerners prize the wrong, or merely incidental, things in their native tradition, while others, perhaps in reaction, have come to despise the West as an idea. In a word, sometimes the western tradition is celebrated for certain reasons, and sometimes it is vilified for roughly those same reasons—but the problem is, in praise or blame, the reasons themselves inaccurately reflect the core features of the West.

We shall, then, have to take another look at those foundations that are always with us, and to wipe from them the obscurities that conceal their true strength—indeed their awe-inspiring genius. My hope is that these words will affect the reader not as an indifferent spectator but as an heir and potential perpetuator of the tradition I shall outline. I hope that they will make visible in a new way those foundations that are already *yours*: materials you may already handle with facility, but whose significance, whose vital brilliance, may not always be easy to pinpoint. Rather than beginning with abstract definitions, however, let us recall a particular, concrete moment. A moment that, I have already hinted and will contend now, is foundational for the West and yet one that may appear too fortuitous, circumstantial, and eccentric for so lofty a designation.

Rumors of Socrates

One day nearly two-and-a-half millennia ago, a fellow named Apollodorus passed on an anecdote he had heard of a drinking party held at the Greek playwright Agathon's house. The Athenian philosopher Socrates was there, and it is mostly because everyone finds him so curious and attractive that this story has been several times retold.[1] But all present at the dinner were noble citizens of Athens, and so worthy of gossip. Hung over from drinking the night before, those assembled have come only because Agathon has won the prize for best tragedy in the city's annual festival. None of them is in the mood for wine, but they must do their social duty; so one guest, Eryximachus, proposes they each give a speech in praise of love.[2]

Why not?, they reply, just before Socrates bumbles in, having gotten lost in thought down the street from the party. Phaedrus speaks of love as a god who possesses the lover, causing him to go out of his mind in the effort to earn praise and avoid shame. We praise this mania and those who die for love, however unreasonable they and we may be in doing so.

---

1. Indeed, Joseph Pieper rightly suggests that it is mere curiosity, as opposed to a love of wisdom, that leads others to ask Apollodorus to repeat his story. Pieper, *Leisure, the Basis of Culture*, trans. Gerald Malsbary (South Bend, Ind.: St. Augustine's Press, 1998), 73. As Shiffman argues in "Shaping the Language," "wonder" must be transformed if it is to fulfill us. St. Augustine will later emphasize the categorical distinction between unrefined and transformed wonder in coining with particular definitions the terms *curiositas* and *studiositas*. This is helpful insofar as it suggests even the studious, in this fallen world, may at times give in to idle curiosity. For a fine summary of texts on the subject, see Scott B. Dermer, "Augustine and the Virtue of *Studiositas*" (unpublished paper).

2. Plato, *Symposium*, 177a.

Indeed the supernatural quality of love seems to lie specifically in its capacity to make us do heroic things that are not in our own self-interest and that appear the more awesome to us the more they seem inexplicable.

Not quite, replies another guest, Pausanias. Love is a god indeed, or rather gods; those possessed of Pandemic love seek only vulgar and bodily satisfactions. But Uranian love is good, he says, as it is a love of what is noble and intelligent, drawing the older, who have virtue, to the younger, to whom they impart it. Those present probably recognize that Pausanias is defending his own erotic relationship with their host, the older Agathon, against social censure.

Eryximachus, who is a medical doctor, then speaks. Good love is ennobling indeed, for it is the pursuit of order or harmony. All things, at their optimum, are governed by good love and in harmony with themselves, but a more common sort of love leads to disorder. His medical advice is to harmonize the body through heavenly love, so that one may enjoy good health. The comic playwright Aristophanes, who has deferred his own speech on account of a case of the hiccups, at this point intervenes. Do you not know, he asks them all, the story of love? We were once whole creatures with four arms and four legs, but the gods, upset with our rowdiness yet jealous of our worship, have split us in half like a hardboiled egg.[3] Self-divided, we wander the earth seeking our other half, and spend our lives vainly trying to repair this physical bifurcation with frantic motions. Agathon speaks next, and his love is like a tragic hero: a forbidding and beautiful god, who gives birth to moderation in all he touches, shunning every disfigurement of excess.

Socrates did not choose this conversation, and claims to be no good at speeches. But, soon, he has dismantled Agathon's haughty poeticizing and, to amend for his rhetorical deficiencies, he recounts the story of a visit he once paid to Diotima, a Mantinean priestess. His tale echoes the other speakers, and yet silences them. Love is neither beautiful nor a god, but is the desire for the beautiful, and the beautiful is always good.[4] But this is not all: "Love *must* be a lover of wisdom" because wisdom is the most beautiful of things.[5] Socrates then reports that Diotima had asked him, why do people love beauty and wisdom? Because to possess it is to

3. Plato, *Symposium*, 190e.   4. Plato, *Symposium*, 201c.
5. Plato, *Symposium*, 204b.

possess the highest good, and to possess the highest good forever is the very definition of happiness.[6]

And she does not stop there. The possession of beauty is not itself happiness, but rather our desire drives us to the presence of beauty so that, as we draw near, we give birth to lasting things, we engender in beauty; in this fruitful diffusion of ourselves we become immortal, extending ourselves beyond ourselves through the having of children, the making of artworks, the codifying of laws, the performance of glorious deeds.[7] Though Socrates does not ask her to, Diotima then describes how one may rise above the life of the senses, from the beauty of mere bodies, to arrive in the presence of eternal beauty, which "always *is* and neither comes to be nor passes away."[8] Arriving at this pinnacle,

the lover is turned to the great sea of beauty, and, gazing upon this, he gives birth to many gloriously beautiful ideas and theories, in unstinting love of wisdom, until, having grown and been strengthened there, he catches sight of such knowledge, and it is the knowledge of such beauty…[9]

Diotima breaks off a moment, as if impatient with Socrates's slow wit, admonishing him to pay attention. She then defines that beauty, unmixed and immortal, after which every heart chases. One begins to suspect Socrates is no longer just relating an anecdote.[10]

In any case, this pug-nosed subject of gossip has made a coup, and Aristophanes's objections to some part of the speech are drowned out in applause. But, suddenly, the doors of the dining room fly open, and the drunken statesman and soldier Alcibiades barges in. Flushed and deaf with wine, he learns what the guests have been up to and sets out on an apparently unrelated speech that is three parts praise, one part diatribe, regarding the character of Socrates in love and war. He has fallen for Socrates, but never possessed him; he has fought alongside Socrates, and seen the philosopher stare down enemy armies and even save Alcibiades's life. "I shall never forgive you!" he shouts.[11]

More drunken Athenians straggle in, crowding the room, and Alcibiades's words break off. Some of the original guests excuse themselves, while

---

6. Plato, *Symposium*, 205a–206b.
7. Plato, *Symposium*, 206e–209e.
8. Plato, *Symposium*, 211a.
9. Plato, *Symposium*, 210e.
10. Plato, *Symposium*, 212a.
11. Plato, *Symposium*, 213e.

others stay up talking through the night. Agathon's house is full of drunks, despite the best of intentions. Aristodemus, the original source of this gossip about Socrates and company, remains to sleep among them, waking at the cock's crow to find Socrates still there, chatting about whether dramatists ought to be able to write both comedy and tragedy, or just one or the other.[12] This matter at last talked-out, the philosopher rises, and leaves to start his day.

What has happened here, in Plato's *Symposium*? We pass through the murmur of gossip to a drunken party, hear a series of vain or vapid speeches, followed by a brilliant one. But Socrates has scarcely finished before Alcibiades interrupts, hijacking the conversation with his self-possessed lament over the cruelties of the Socrates he admires and resents. And then, everyone putters on. One can read this dialogue for many reasons, and one can read it in different ways, for Plato has not given us a treatise but an event. He has not told us whom we must believe and, indeed, the most absurd speech on love, Aristophanes's, is the one that comes closest to the definition most modern persons take, and probably Socrates's contemporaries took, for granted. On what is this dialogue founded? How do its parts come together? Which are incidental, which important? Might we hear it as just so many rumors of salacious interest but no consequence?

This, in microcosm, is the problem we face in attempting to see the foundation, the defining tradition, of western civilization. So much has transpired in our history that is obtrusive and violent like Alcibiades, passionately irrational like Phaedrus, solipsistic like Aristophanes, pretentious and vapid like Agathon, self-serving like Pausanias, and reductive and therapeutic like Eryximaches. Clearly, Socrates constitutes the center of the dialogue, but what does it mean to identify him as such? Alcibiades's speech indicates that few of us, if any, know the real Socrates; there may always be the image of a different man hidden *within* the one we think we understand. As we shall see, with the West in general, as with the *Symposium*, we will find our true center, our clear foundation, in a word that Socrates speaks most forcefully only in quotation marks: Beauty. If we do not hold fast to that word, we have not simply missed something important, we have missed everything.

---

12. Plato, *Symposium* 223d. We shall return to this moment in Part III.

Inadequate Apologists for the West

If we were to retrace the accounts we members of western civilization have given of ourselves, of our essence or foundation, over the last few centuries, one might think indeed we have missed at least something. For, the apologies often made for the West tend to slip, in due course, into attacks on it, as if the apologies themselves were sufficiently obtuse as to bring about their own defeat. Defenders of the West as a single and singular civilization often get something right; at various times since the Renaissance, they have made reference to Socrates. However, it is seldom the Socrates of the *Symposium* of which they speak, but he of the *Apology*. That is, they hold up only the Socrates identified with a supposedly rigorous "critical reason" that leaves no stone idol upright, and whose dialectical method supposedly led to the methodical rationalism of modern politics and science.[13] On this account, the West is the civilization of reason, of a reason that examines received beliefs and generally argues them away, or of a reason that deploys its own laws primarily to gain mastery over the laws of nature. Socrates is thus reduced in our imaginations to the very thing from which he spends many of his dialogues trying to distinguish himself—a sophist.[14]

In another defense of our civilization, Socrates's Athens has often been cited as its cornerstone. As the birthplace of citizenship and democracy, it is sometimes rhetorically posed as the inspiration of our modern regime of political freedom and equality. We modern citizens fulfill the Athenian dream, this narrative, dating back to the Enlightenment, proposes. Others may refer to ancient Greece's slightly less ancient pupil, Rome. It was in Rome that law was first rigorously codified, and so to Rome we look for the principle of ordered liberty.[15] Most of us, conscious of Rome's legacy or not, reveal ourselves to share in this sense of foundation by our constant references to legality and rights as our particular distinction. What makes us westerners, by this account, is an obsession with the rule of law,

---

13. For an account of the "critical thinking" Socrates as a Victorian misrepresentation, see Mark C. Henrie, "Why Go to College?" *The Canon* (Spring 2008): 24–35.

14. See Plato, *Gorgias*, 482e, 483d–e.

15. For the hopeful, if ironic, birth of this conception, see, Virgil, *The Aeneid*, trans. Allen Mandelbaum (New York: Bantam Dell, 2004), 159.

not in the sense of wanting the police to have an iron fist but in wanting every aspect of our lives to be justified and protected by juridical appeal. Sometimes, of course, such an appeal is made to the Judaic law, particularly God's gift of the Decalogue.

Reason, freedom, equality, and the rule of law: these are venerable words and familiar ones, often voiced to defend the West against its ancestors, its earlier selves and inner contradictions, and above all against the civilizations beyond its pale. Their easy appeal slips all too readily into facile argumentation. We like the sound of celebrating the West as the home of critical and methodical reason, for who wants to be on the side of arbitrary irrationality? Freedom and equality are powerful words, especially when one envisions the alternative as a totalitarian regime, the foreboding clink of whose chain-mailed divisions can be heard marching out in the streets by the frightened plebes within. And, finally, the rule of law sounds brilliant so long as the only other possibility is an anarchic jungle. But this rationality so much vaunted may not be an obvious offspring from the reason of Socrates; modern democracy may not *actually* have preserved any of those aspects of freedom the Greeks prized; and, apart from young meritocrats studying public policy in the Ivy League, few can work up much enthusiasm for the prospect that one's civilization's greatest accomplishment has been the establishment of rigorous bureaucracies.

And so, alas, these keywords will not stay pinned. They slip from apologia to alienation, and they have provided convenient fodder for the West's most severe internal critics. Yes, indeed, the West is identified with the rule of law—too much so, say some. The Roman conception of ordered liberty begets two related species of western xenophilia or orientalism, in which we look to the East for an image of the more fluid self we are not but would like to be.[16] A post-War American version of this, which gave us the term "multiculturalism," treats the West as the inevitable law-giver to the nations, and seeks to understand other civilizations as complementary, so that we may

16. Romantic orientalism from Emerson to Nietzsche still exercises a surprising power on the western imagination. A more compelling instance of this has been the recent attraction to Eastern Orthodoxy as an alternative to a Roman Catholicism codified to the tastes of the late Empire; see, for example, Joseph Ratzinger, *Introduction to Christianity*, trans. J. R. Foster (San Francisco: Ignatius Press, 2004), 84–85, first published in 1968 by Kösel Verlag GmbH, Munich. The eastern and western are now understood—by the West, at least—as two lungs of the same ecclesial body (see John Paul II, *Ut Unum Sint*, Encyclical Letter, May 25, 1995, par. 54.2).

enjoy their art, their cookery, their imaginative, communal, or emotional life, as we seek to rule them justly. But this touristic imperialism has long since given way to the now familiar use of the word "multiculturalism" as a suspicion of the West's political ambitions that selectively venerates the non-western as an appealing image of otherness.[17] The non-western becomes good precisely because it is "transgressive" of all familiar forms of law and order.

But, some may reply, the West pioneered freedom and equality, and so these orientalist critiques are redundant. I shall argue, actually, that the West did arrive at a conception of freedom that is, if not unique, at least distinctive. But that distinctiveness lies not in anything specifically political. Those alienated critics of the West, however, do not reject this conception of political freedom so much as they seek to drive it to limits *ad absurdum*. They envision a total liberation of the person from every condition, including the conditions of his own nature, where the only image of goodness becomes one's own sense of an absence of pain.

Stephen Greenblatt's Pulitzer-prize-winning book, *The Swerve*, is only the most recent iteration of the rush to critique western ideas of freedom by encouraging its readers to envision human life as most fully achieved when an administrative state creates a wide field for the absence of pain, while one's own abstention from enduring love allows one to enjoy the finite pleasures of self-creation within its bounds.[18] According to Greenblatt, the Christian West derided and even loathed beauty, by which he evidently if indefensibly means the sensation of aesthetic pleasure. We shall refute that claim in due course, but here I would only note how such a critique takes advantage of the West's preening over freedom and equality to create an ideal vision of personhood as a life carried out in the absence of pain and punctuated by the pursuit of any pleasures that do not cause pain to others.[19] At war with the West, Greenblatt fashionably portrays his ethos as a resurrection of classical Epicureanism against the

---

17. Matthew Arnold's essays on Celtic literature, in *The Collected Works of Matthew Arnold*, vol. 11 (London: MacMillan and Co., 1903–1904), are prototypical of this early form of imperial "multiculturalism," while Chris Shannon has provided a brilliant study of the postwar American species with which we are more familiar in *A World Made Safe for Differences* (Lanham, Md.: Rowman and Littlefield Publishers, 2001).

18. See R. R. Reno, "A Philosophy for the Powerful," *First Things* 219 (January 2012): 3–6.

19. See Kalb, *The Tyranny of Liberalism*.

morbid asceticism of Christianity. His recovery of a lost, good West is in fact the celebration of ideas at some remove from what I shall portray as its real tradition.

So, also, does the western celebration of an undefined reason easily flip from apologia to alienation. The conception of Socratic reason as self-critical readily devolves into a sense of the rational as simply that which deconstructs all received ideas, and this gives way to a sleek nihilism, in whose book intelligence finds its fullest expression in a negation of all claims to goodness. If, in Greenblatt's world, tattooing the body might be a pleasure to be cultivated, for those alienated from a vague western narrative of the triumph of reason, tattooing becomes a deliberate disfigurement of the body—a way of showing that nothing interior, not even the self, survives critique, but dissolves in what has justly been called a culture of death.[20] One sometimes hears defenses of the West, from an older, liberal humanism that still reveres Socrates the "critical thinker." While they are often full of charming sentiments, they do not withstand what is probably the great positive contribution of Nietzsche to western thought: the reason of classical liberalism inevitably leads to irrationalism, the hermeneutics of suspicion, and, finally, nihilism.[21] To maintain the liberal humanist position is really just that—to maintain it, in the sense of refusing to trace to their logical ends the consequences of one's principles.

The more specific narrative of the West as the apotheosis of methodical reason in the full subordination of nature to technological uses leads to a similar alienation, whose end is, perhaps ironically, a fetish of technocracy. Such critics of the West experience horror at its technical accomplishments (they justly mock Richard Nixon's performance in the "kitchen debate"), and yet they look to still further advances to liberate us from their consequences. They stand appalled before the destruction of Hiroshima, but only on their way to dreaming up a post- or trans-human regime where the moral ambiguities of advanced technology dissolve in its therapeutic applications and more totalizing mastery.[22]

20. See Terry Eagleton, *After Theory* (New York: Basic Books, 2003); see also Lisa Ruddick, "When Nothing Is Cool," in *The Future of Scholarly Writing*, ed. Angelika Bammer and Joerres Boetcher (New York: Palgrave Macmillan, 2015), 71–85.

21. See, Alasdair MacIntyre, *After Virtue*, 3rd ed. (Notre Dame, Ind.: University of Notre Dame Press, 2007), 113–15.

22. See Peter Augustine Lawler, *Aliens in America* (Wilmington, Del.; ISI Books, 2002).

So, easy apologetic defenses of the West's accomplishments have be-
gotten critiques of the West that deride it as an oppressive regime standing in the way of our absolute self-creation as autonomous and denatured
individuals—whether conceived as "subaltern," epicure, punk, or cyber-
punk. My argument has not been that our civilization has inevitably
reached a state of unraveling, but that it has unraveled in consequence of
our failing to understand it. It is as if we have watched the drunk tableau
of Plato's *Symposium* and latched too much on to incidental detail—we
take Pausanias's pandering as indicative of the ideological dishonesty of
western thought, or Eryximachus as a sign that the western love of technology will ruin every good party—all the while ignoring that incomprehensible figure, Socrates, who dares to speak of an ineffable reality called
beauty.

The Six Great Insights of the West

I would, recalling that word, return us to the foundations of the West
and give my own account of its character: one governed by the concept of
beauty, a word which comprises in an eminent way the other keywords I
have just criticized as inadequate. I intend to do so by consciously echo-
ing Kirk's six canons, by discussing here six key insights about the nature
of the cosmos and of the human person that constitute the genius of the
West that we should all desire to share in, to conserve, and to cultivate.

We might think of these not so much as creedal propositions as we
should six coordinates bounding the map of reality itself, which make
possible in an unmatched way the fruitful exploration of that reality.
These insights are to be found already present in the culture of ancient
Greece at the time of Socrates, and they are also to be found in the Judaic tradition prior to its contact with Hellenic culture. But they find
fuller and more satisfactory articulation just before and during the first
Christian centuries, as the thought of Athens and Jerusalem engage one
another, exchanging the intellectual tools necessary to develop their own
potentials. And so, while we began with a scene from Socrates's Athens,
we should understand the philosopher himself as a representative figure
within a synthetic but readily unified tradition that no less profoundly depends on Jewish and Christian thought.

What I would offer, then, are the six definitive canons of what I shall describe in the broadest possible sense as the Christian Platonic tradition. Let me offer them in a list, and then turn to their explication. The West proposes:

1. that man is an intellectual animal;

2. that his nature is founded on a prior or foundational intelligibility in the world and that he is intellectually and erotically oriented toward a transcendent knowledge of it;

3. that this dual orientation proceeds by way of reason toward an intellectual vision perceptive of Beauty Itself, which is the splendor of truth;

4. that the world is itself ordered by and to Beauty;

5. that human dignity specifically consists in our capacity to perceive and contemplate that splendorous order, and, thus, the most excellent form of human life is that which is given over to such contemplation; and finally,

6. that this contemplation realizes itself in what we may call happiness or salvation, and it is characterized by an activity that resembles passivity, that is to say, not simply the absence of motion but a fullness of activity that is called peace and freedom.

In various forms, all characteristically western thought is structured by these six insights, and so, if we wish to understand and defend the integrity of the western tradition, it must be done on the strength of their value. If this is not sufficiently provocative, let us make it more so by noting some apparent contradictions in what I have said so far. I noted a moment ago that defining the West in terms of reason is inadequate, but now have claimed that man's distinction as an intellectual animal is in the event foundational. I dismissed freedom and equality as foundations for the West, but the fifth insight intimates a principle of equality, while the sixth mentions freedom outright. I cast doubt on the rule of law as the West's true foundation, and yet, in the second and fourth, I claim that there is an orderliness to reality that the West rightly affirms, and might not natural or positive law doctrines be precisely the result of that affirmation? Clearly, some explanation needs to be provided, and so let us turn to examine each insight in detail.

To claim that *man is an intellectual animal* is not strictly identical with claiming he is rational. First of all, "intellect," in the Christian Platonist tradition, means the faculty of thought itself, particular species of which we can distinguish and arrange in a hierarchy. "Mind" has sometimes been the preferred term, and "reason" will do so long as we distinguish it from what we shall define in a moment as the particular activity of discursive reasoning. Aristotle's understanding of God is of a thought that "thinks itself": its thought does not proceed outward but is always, immediately, and wholly present within itself.[23] Many centuries later, St. Thomas Aquinas would explain that this claim does not indicate that God thinks *only about* himself to the exclusion of all else, but that he *is* his thought, comprising the knowledge of all things in a single, simple essence.[24] From this highest mode of pure thought, all other thinking descends. God's thought is, in Aquinas's terms, a pure vision of himself, where he sees all in his essence and he *is* his essence.[25] Further, this thought is not receptive of what is, but constitutive of it; God thinks things and they come to be, not vice versa. His is the *creative* intellect.[26] But, as we descend the ladder of thought—passing through, in Aquinas's view, the angels—we arrive at a creature whose knowledge is neither immediate, nor primarily of himself, nor creative of things.[27] A human being comes to know other things first, prior to himself; he does so gradually and sequentially by means of discursive reasoning, and this act of knowing is achieved when his mind measures up to the already existent things known (it is not *their* measure).[28]

For all these distinctions, *ratio* or *logos*—in English, reason—is essentially a species of, a participation in, intellect—*intellectus* or *nous*.[29] This entails the following. On the one hand, relative to God, or to the angels—who are the intellectual creatures *par excellence*—man might best be de-

23. Aristotle, *Metaphysics*, 1072b20.   24. Aquinas, *Summa Theologica*, I.13.11.

25. Aquinas, *Summa Theologica*, I.14.7.

26. Aquinas, *Summa Theologica*, I.14.8. Cf. Jacques Maritain, *Art and Scholasticism*, 120–21.

27. Aquinas, *Summa Theologica*, I.14.2, I.87.1.

28. Aquinas, *Summa Theologica*, I.14.7, I.14.8, and I.16.1–2. Cf. Jacques Maritain, *The Degrees of Knowledge*, trans. Gerald B. Phelan (Notre Dame, Ind.: University of Notre Dame Press, 1995), 93–94, 116.

29. The italicized words are the Latin and Greek equivalents. See Pieper, *Leisure, the Basis of Culture*, 11–12; Aquinas, *Summa Theologica*, I-II.19.4. Efforts to distinguish Aristotelian or Thomist thinking on causality from the "participation metaphysics" of Plato or Augustine make a distinction in detail only (Maritain, *The Degrees of Knowledge*, 324–25). In every instance, we finally require a conception of participation, and of human intelligence as a participation in the divine (see below).

fined as a rational animal, because man knows primarily by discursive rational sequence rather than through a natural, immediate knowledge of himself.[30] But, considered absolutely, the human mind participates in intellect, and so cannot be understood merely in terms of its particular, discursive mode of thinking, but must also be considered in light of its participation in *intellectus*, in the form of immediate thought proper to the divine mind.[31] To identify human nature or the West with reason alone, therefore, would seem to speak only about the plodding, methodical procedure that adds thought to thought in order to formulate a conclusion.[32] It tells us little about the essence of reason apart from its peculiar gait. It does not inform us, for instance, of what becomes of reason as it arrives at a fuller understanding of truth.[33]

Nor does it consider what was, from the time of Plato onward, the distinctive attribute of thought and intellect—its immaterial freedom. "Thought," writes Aristotle, "is what it is by virtue of becoming all things."[34] A material thing is made what it is by its form or idea, but its matter constrains it to being *only* that. In contrast, the mind, as a spiritual or nonmaterial reality, is not so entrapped.[35] Aquinas explains,

intelligent beings are distinguished from non-intelligent beings in that the latter possess only their own form; whereas the intelligent being is naturally adapted to have also the form of some other thing; for the idea of the thing known is in the knower. Hence it is manifest that the nature of a non-intelligent being is more contracted and limited; whereas the nature of intelligent beings has a greater amplitude and extension.[36]

In the last century, it was common for existential philosophers to distinguish man as condemned to solitude by his thought. In virtue of his mind, he could know himself apart and alone in the universe. On the con-

---

30. Aquinas, *Summa Theologica*, I.58.3.

31. Aquinas, *Summa Theologica*, I.79.4, I.84.5.

32. Cf. Hobbes, *Leviathan*, V.1.

33. *Ratio* is assumed into, or restored to, the *intellectus* from which it began, Aquinas suggests, when he describes *intellectus* as the act of understanding in which the mind adheres "to the formed judgment with approval" (*Summa Theologica*, I.79.9).

34. Aristotle, *On the Soul*, 430a1.15.

35. Understanding is "an altogether immaterial operation" (Aquinas, *Summa Theologica*, I.50.2).

36. Aquinas, *Summa Theologica*, I.14.1.

trary, says Aquinas, it is only because of our reason as a species of intelligent and spiritual reality that we are not shut in upon ourselves. One of Aquinas's great modern interpreters, Pierre Rousselot, elaborates on this point in saying, to "know is primarily and principally to seize and embrace within yourself an *other* who is capable of seizing and embracing you: it is to live by the life of another living being."[37] Another important interpreter observes that it is only by means of this capacity of the mind to become another thing without losing its own substantial integrity that human beings may "escape from the individuality in which matter encloses them," to have contact and even communion with other beings.[38] Thus, what absolutely characterizes the human being as intellectual is not his distinct way of solving problems, but the essential openness to being, the capacity to drink in the whole of reality, becoming it virtually without ceasing to be himself, afforded by the spiritual operation of thought.[39]

Our intellect impresses not primarily in its orderly processing of data, but in the "limitless voracity" by which it "seizes being and draws it into itself."[40] If the mind can know all things, and everything that is is a being, and every being is true, the mind can potentially contain the universe, it can possess the fullness of being and of truth.[41] Indeed, Aquinas writes that the intellectual soul comprehends universals and, as such, "has a power extending to the infinite; therefore it cannot be limited by nature to certain fixed natural notions, or even to certain fixed means."[42] The only limit confronting it is that of what is or could be real.[43] And yet, within this freedom, the mind naturally seeks a law to guide it to its proper fulfillment.[44] The use of discursive reasoning reveals to us that thought has its laws, including those of logic. If this is so, then a mind that can know

37. Pierre Rousselot, *Intelligence: Sense of Being, Faculty of God*, trans. Andrew Tallon (Milwaukee, Wisc.: Marquette University Press, 1999), 7.

38. Maritain, *Art and Scholasticism*, 32.

39. Schumacher, *A Guide for the Perplexed*, 22.

40. Maritain, *Art and Scholasticism*, 5.   41. Aquinas, *Summa Theologica*, I.16.3.

42. Aquinas, *Summa Theologica*, I.76.5.

43. Aquinas, *Summa Theologica*, I.5.2. Schumacher speaks of the human mind as *capax universi*, having a capacity for all things (*A Guide for the Perplexed*, 35). Aristotle and Aquinas contrast the mind with the sense organs. The eye sees color, the nose smells odors, but the mind perceives realities so qualitatively different that they have only their reality—their being—in common, and therefore the proper object of the mind is all that is being, being *per se*, and finally Being Itself.

44. Aquinas, *Summa Theologica*, I.91.2.

everything nonetheless can become aware of something governing and conditioning its reason though not properly found *within* it.

It would, therefore, be an error—sometimes called rationalism—to presume that the process of discursive reason is the highest or only form of intellect, or that it outfits itself with its own criteria of, or means to, truth, as if anything that comes to it from outside its own workings must be dismissed as "irrational."[45] On the contrary, reason itself discovers its particular nature relative to the idea of intellect, which is absolutely prior to it and in which it participates. And reason finds in its very operation a truth beyond itself that is definitive of the human person. Namely, *that his nature is founded on a prior or foundational intelligibility in the world and that he is intellectually and erotically oriented toward a transcendent knowledge of it*. In brief, something precedes man's act of knowing, both in himself and in the world. Aristotle speaks of "comprehension" as that intellectual virtue whereby the mind "grasps the first principles" of thought that cannot themselves be demonstrated.[46] We can demonstrate truths by our reason's use of logic, but the principles that make reasoning possible cannot themselves be demonstrated. The presence of these first principles in the mind that make possible its life and activity indicates that human reason, *ratio*, has something necessary behind it, beyond its manipulation, but still inside thought, *intellectus*.[47] But this is not all.

If the Christian Platonist tradition places intellect at its center, it does so because it delights in burrowing down beneath the surface of reason to discover how much is always and already *given* to it. The most ancient authorities in the tradition emphasize that prior to our reasoning lies some kind of gift, visitation, or inspiration.[48] For Plato, every idea is a recollection (*anamnesis*) from the plane of eternal ideas, or pure intelligibles.[49] Centuries later, St. Augustine would stretch into the darkness of memory to find the presence of God—the one who makes the memory to be in the first place and who abides there as in all things.[50] Elsewhere, he tells us that

45. John Paul II, *Fides et Ratio*, Encyclical Letter, September 14, 1998, par. 45.

46. Aristotle, *Nicomachean Ethics*, 1141a1.9; *Metaphysics*, 982b1.4–5, 993b1.10–11.

47. Cf. Aquinas, *Summa Theologica*, I.62.8.

48. Pierre Hadot, *What Is Ancient Philosophy?*, trans. Michael Chase (Cambridge, Mass.: Harvard University Press, 2002), 19.

49. Plato, *Meno*, 81c, 86b, *Phaedrus*, 249c–d; *Phaedo*, 75e.

50. Augustine suggests that things known, as Plato claims, are learned by recollection (Au-

our knowledge of universals, which it should be said is the context of the knowledge of individuals, derives from a direct vision of "the inner light of truth which illumines the inner man and is inwardly enjoyed."[51] The mind reaches deeply into itself to recover what is infinitely prior to and beyond itself; what is prior fundamentally informs, gives shape to, reason and its action.[52] Taken together the *nous*, or *intellectus*, of first principles and the indwelling presence of things known, or the God who knows, serve to explain a remarkable fact. We do not know everything about the world around us, but, as we discussed in the last chapter, when we look out at the world we discover the intelligibility of reality itself; thought is possible only because idea, truth, was there first, already waiting to be cognized.[53] The same orderliness that provides the mind its first principles provides also to every being its potential to be understood.[54] Beings await, confront, and even speak to the reason as much as the reason seeks them out, grasps, and understands them.[55] That we can know things—that we can readily know *that* they are and *what* they are—tells us something about the objec-

---

gustine, *The Confessions*, trans. Maria Boulding, OSB (Hyde Park, N.Y.: New City Press, 1997), X.10.16; he makes the memory prior to the act of thinking *in* the self (X.16.25); and he passes farther into memory (deeper into himself) in search of God (X.17.26); there, he finds his mind enthroned (X.25.36), and farther *in* still, beyond the mind, because infinitely *above* it, God himself (X.26.37). Whereas the knowledge of a material object may come into the memory from without, God somehow has come into the memory from within: emerging from deeper within us than our minds are, to make his impression on the memory.

51. Augustine, *The Teacher*, in *Earlier Writings*, trans. John H. S. Burleigh (Philadelphia: The Westminster Press, 1953), 11.40; cf. 11.38. Cf. Augustine, *On Free Will* (in *Earlier Writings*), II.8.23 Augustine's account does not seem satisfactory, because it simply opposes the sense knowledge of individuals and the intellectual vision of universals. Most accounts are articulated thus, but for them to remain coherent, intellect, or *nous*, has to be foundational to all thinking and so the context in which everything is thought or known. Aristotle suggests this by speaking of intellect or "comprehension" as "concerned with ultimates in both directions" (*Nicomachean Ethics*, 1143a), by which he means with the knowledge of universals and particulars. The word "comprehension" describes the circle, the arena of thought on whose ground thinking begins and takes place.

52. That is, "reason has a wax nose," meaning, among other things, that its "shape is determined by theological convictions" (Tracey Rowland, *Ratzinger's Faith* [Oxford: Oxford University Press, 2008], 5). Reason has always to go beyond itself in order to be fully itself (Schindler, *The Catholicity of Reason*, 8–9, 20).

53. Cf. Hadot, *What Is Ancient Philosophy?*, 74, and Richard Viladesau, *Theological Aesthetics* (New York: Oxford University Press, 1999), 114.

54. Aquinas, *Summa Theologica*, I.79.3.

55. We considered this in the last chapter. Cf. Fergus Kerr, *After Aquinas: Versions of Thomism* (Oxford: Blackwell Publishing, 2002), 130.

tive intelligibility that precedes our knowing and greets us at every turn.[56]

The intelligibility of the world presents a road for the intellect that lies not just behind but ahead. If reason is perfectly human, it builds upon those first principles given to it in advance in order to reach an actuality that is decisively too great for it. So, Aristotle says that the life of contemplation is attainable for man only "in so far as something divine is present in him" that allows him to develop beyond the merely human.[57] Plotinus will suggest the arrival at truth comes like a "sudden" revelation beyond reason's ken.[58] St. Augustine will later define the mind—with its faculties of memory, understanding, and will—as an image of the Triune God. Only through having received God's image in his nature can the human being possess the capacity to know him. Indeed, what makes us human is not chiefly this prior impression of God's Trinitarian image; that impression constitutes a mere potency that comes most fully into act only in our turning to the contemplation of God himself.[59] Man can approach God by no material means, but only with the immaterial intellect, and yet "man is directed to God, as to an end that surpasses the grasp of his reason," writes Aquinas.[60] Reason does not rest in the first principles it knows more intimately than it knows itself, because it thinks *with* them rather than *about* them, and stretches beyond what can be comprehended to attain the most valuable knowledge.[61]

Aquinas contends we have a natural desire to know the cause of the effects we see.[62] So, as we saw, Aristotle begins his *Metaphysics* with the proposition that all "men by nature desire to know."[63] As Plato dramatizes in the *Symposium*, this is not just a potency of our intellect, but the ruling object of our love, our innermost desire.[64] Reflection on the intellect

56. Viladesau, *Theological Aesthetics*, 118–24.

57. Aristotle, *Nicomachean Ethics*, 1177b128.

58. Bernard McGinn, *The Foundations of Mysticism* (New York: Crossroad, 1991), 53.

59. Augustine, *The Trinity*, trans. Edmund Hill, OP (Hyde Park, N.Y.: New City Press, 1991), XIV.4.15–16.

60. Aquinas, *Summa Theologica*, I.1.1.

61. Aquinas, *Summa Theologica*, I.1.5 (on the "slenderest knowledge" of the highest things as "more desirable"); I.12.1 (on the natural desire to know God, who is "supremely knowable" in himself, but still "exceeds every kind of knowledge; which means that he is not comprehended").

62. Aquinas, *Summa Theologica*, I.12.1.

63. Aristotle, *Metaphysics*, 980a25.1.

64. Cf. Pseudo-Dionysius, *Divine Names*, in *The Complete Works*, trans. Colm Luibheid

we find in us, the intelligibility we see all around us, and the desire that by our very nature drives us—these all converge on the fundamentally *erotic* orientation of our mind to the apprehension of the highest reality.[65] By our natures—by our reason and will—we desire nothing less than the supernatural.[66] Because of first principles given to us, our mind has no trouble understanding beings: we naturally think in terms of *is*. But this ready comprehension *that* things are and of *what* they are provokes us to strain and exceed ourselves in trying to understand what it is To Be—or to glimpse something even beyond that.[67]

But what is this supernatural end?[68] The tradition proposes that *this dual orientation proceeds by way of reason toward an intellectual vision perceptive of Beauty Itself, which is the splendor of truth.*[69] The intellectual animal does not depart on an endless and infinite journey, but rather is directed toward a final destination. Aristotle demonstrates that there must be such a final cause at which all things aim. For "no one would" seek any good "if he were not going to come to a limit," and the world would not be reasonable if it did not act "for a purpose."[70] But we do find the world soaking in intelligible truths and desirable goods; we find purposive action everywhere. And so, the proper question is not whether there is a final cause, a highest good at which all things aim, but rather what is that good. Because of the mind's universal capacity, we know that whatever it may be, we may come to understand it.

We see in the *Symposium* that Socrates believes the name for this good at which our nature aims is Beauty. Plotinus will write, centuries later, that the soul's course lies in "the vision of the First Beauty itself."[71] But why

(New York: Paulist Press, 1987), 708B, and John Henry Newman, *Discourses Addressed to Mixed Congregations* (Notre Dame, Ind.: University of Notre Dame Press, 2002), 70.

65. See Joseph Pieper, *Faith, Hope, Love* (San Francisco: Ignatius Press, 1997), 222–24.

66. Jacques Maritain, *The Collected Works of Jacques Maritain*, vol 11, *Integral Humanism, Freedom in the Modern World, and A Letter on Independence*, ed. Otto Bird, trans. Otto Bird, Joseph Evans, and Richard O'Sullivan, KC (Notre Dame, Ind.: University of Notre Dame Press, 1996), 19.

67. "We lifted ourselves in longing yet more ardent toward *That Which Is*" (Augustine, *The Confessions*, IX.10.24).

68. See Henri de Lubac, *The Mystery of the Supernatural* (New York: Herder and Herder, 1998), 55, 100, 209.

69. Plato, *Phaedo*, 78d–79d.

70. Aristotle, *Metaphysics*, 994b1.13–15.

71. Plotinus, *The Enneads*, trans. Stephen MacKenna (London: Penguin Books, 1991), I.6.9.

should our minds and our wills find fulfillment in Beauty? Why should we not say, instead, truth or goodness or being? Such questions arise only if we lack the understanding of Beauty typical to the premodern West.[72]

We know that our discursive reason can add proposition to proposition and arrive at a truth. We know, also, that that which we rightly desire is good. We know still further that the good of the intellect—what the intellect by nature desires—is truth. When we arrive, by way of discursive reason, at the final knowledge, the highest good of the intellect, and come to possess it, the tradition tells us we do not know it any longer in terms of discourse but in the form of intellectual vision. According to Plato, our recollection of truths in our earthly, bodily life is simply an imperfect re-presentation of what was present to the eyes of the soul prior to its "fall" into the body. Augustine would treat the discursive thought of his *Soliloquies* as anticipations of a vision still to come. He has personified Reason say,

> Reason who speaks with you promises to let you see God with your mind as the sun is seen with the eye. The mind has, as it were, eyes of its own, analogous to the soul's senses. The certain truths of the sciences are analogous to the objects which the sun's rays make visible, such as the earth and earthly things.[73]

Here, Augustine speaks of the eyesight as the "soul's" sense, because he understands it not as a bodily function, but as a power of the soul whose act goes out into the world and immediately grasps its intelligible reali-

---

Plotinus finally affirms that the soul is ordered to the Good, which is "beyond-beautiful," while everything "until The Good is reached is beautiful" (I.8.2). Plotinus's development on Plato stems in large part from a desire to secure the absolute transcendence of the Good without risking anything that might compromise that transcendence. In consequence, the soul is indeed ordered by and to beauty, with beauty governing its whole "course." Though the Good is genuinely beyond beauty, it is still "the nature of Good" to be "radiating Beauty before it" (I.6.9). At the very least, then, we can affirm Plotinus as affirming our souls as ordered "subjectively" to beauty. But he has already affirmed that beauty is a "splendor as of light" (I.6.5), which is just what this radiance of the Good must be, and so it does not stretch the author's intention a great deal to say that the radiance of the Good that begets Beauty is itself a genuine radiance, "objective" Beauty Itself. What is finally at stake is how high into reality goes the participation of every beautiful being. Does the particular beauty of this being participate in the highest principle of reality, the Good? And, if so, is that being beautiful because it participates in the Beauty of the Good? Yes, Plotinus answers; he just refuses to identify the Beauty of the Good as the Good as such, thus securing the absolute transcendence of the Good.

72. See Viladesau, *Theological Aesthetics*, 6, 63.

73. Augustine, *Earlier Writings*, 30. Concerning the healing of that vision as failed mission of Plato that is efficaciously achieved in Christ, see Augustine, *Earlier Writings*, 226–27.

ties.[74] Just as the eye sets upon particular intelligible things in the material world, the mind's eye fixes on the highest spiritual truth. He, with most of the Christian Platonist tradition, considers the seeing of truth as the soul's vision of Beauty.

We speak truths as truths, but when truth presents itself to the mind's eye, it does so as Beauty.[75] In such vision, we encounter truth as more than a series of particular propositions; we see it whole, with all its multifarious aspects joined into a seamless unity, every part overflowing into every other like, again in Plato's words, a vast sea. Unlike a sea, however, this vision is not formless but perfectly formed, and the superabundance it presents to the eye of the mind readied for its vision does not necessarily blind or confuse, but reveals itself as splendor, as an overwhelming and reasonable goodness.[76] Louis Dupré has admirably expressed how central and formative this conception of truth-as-vision was for the ancient world, in writing,

If there is one belief the Greek thinkers shared, it must be the conviction that both the essence of the real and our knowledge of it consists ultimately of *form*. Basically this means that it belongs to the essence of the real to *appear*, rather than to hide, and to appear in an orderly way. By envisioning the real as such as harmonious appearance, the Greek view displays a uniquely aesthetic quality, expressed as much in architecture and sculpture as in philosophy.[77]

We are all familiar with the notion of true knowledge as the rising from material particulars to immaterial universals, which is normally understood as the process of, first, the senses encountering the form (essence)

74. Margaret Miles, "The Eye of the Body and the Eye of the Mind in Saint Augustine's *De trinitate* and *Confessions*," *The Journal of Religion* 63, no. 2 (April, 1983), 125–42. As we have noted, this active dimension must be coupled with the eyesight and the soul's receptivity if we are to have an adequate account of knowledge as the co-presence of reason in being *and* being in reason.

75. A difference inheres between truth as known discursively and as known perfectly and immediately by the intellect beyond discursive reason, to wit, intellectual vision. Not "every act of knowing is such that it mediates an experience of beauty," writes Richard Viladesau, discussing the work of Coreth: "A purely conceptual, logical, discursively rational knowledge does not grasp the beauty of what is known, but only a contemplative vision that is absorbed in the object and takes pleasure in it. What characterizes the experience of beauty is not the mediation of thought but the immediacy of 'vision' or intuition" (Viladesau, *Theological Aesthetics*, 128).

76. The convertibility of being, truth, goodness, and, or *in*, beauty, is central to Aquinas's understanding (*Summa Theologica*, I.5.4). Cf. Maritain, *Art and Scholasticism*, 173–74.

77. Louis Dupré, *Passage to Modernity: An Essay in the Hermeneutics of Nature and Culture* (New Haven, Conn.: Yale University Press, 1993), 18.

of a thing entirely "concealed" by, or compounded with, material individuality, and of, second, subsequently transcending that encounter in order to know the form in its purity, *sub specie aeternitatis*.[78] Following Aristotle, we may rightly think of this as a movement from the concrete to the abstract, and so knowledge would seem to be characterized by the condition of abstraction and to have nothing to do with "sight" as we normally understand that concept, which would seem to be nothing other than the sensation of the individual. This is true as far as it goes. But it would be more accurate to say that human reason, because of its discursive character, moves from an immediate intellectual vision of *some* things (first principles) and a sensible vision of *many* concrete particulars, by way of abstract reasoning, toward that condition where reality appears once more and is not just of *some* things but of *all*. The life of reason moves from its origins, which make possible sensation and reasoning, into sensible vision, onto abstract discursive reasoning, and, by way of such reasoning, it climbs higher, to another sort of vision that is intellectual rather than sensible. When we attain it fully, we rise to Eternal Beauty, that is, behold truth in its splendor.

This understanding was already normative in the ancient world. Plato's seventh letter, which may be the work of Plato but may also be evidence of how later readers assimilated the Greek philosopher's work into the tradition, describes just such a journey from the discursive to the vision of beauty. Plato writes, to the friends of his late disciple Dion, that the highest knowledge, that of philosophy

Is not something that can be put into words like other sciences; but after long-continued intercourse between teacher and pupil, in joint pursuit of the subject, suddenly, like light flashing forth when a fire is kindled, it is born in the soul and straightway nourishes itself.[79]

Other sciences may give us the (wrong) impression that they have been comprehended once we have sufficient discursive knowledge about them. But dialectic—the practice of mounting up by means of conversation within a community of lovers of wisdom—because of its absolute object, leads one eventually beyond words and conversation. Words give way and

---

78. Maritain, *Degrees of Knowledge*, 37–40.
79. Plato, *Letters*, 341c.

beauty flashes forth as a vision. For Plato, as for the tradition as a whole, we are rational *animals* insofar as we must speak and listen in order to acquire knowledge (because the body at once makes possible and hinders our journey to truth). But the whole aim of our speaking is a wisdom beyond words—an intellectual vision of beauty.

The most elegant hymn to this vision appears, unsurprisingly, in Augustine's *Confessions*. In Book IX, Augustine and his mother, Monica, are depicted following just the pathway of dialectic that Plato describes, and then all words and time fall away in a glimpse of the eternal God. In the following book, he moves beyond this narrative of ascent to enter into an interior dialectic, where the God nearer to him than he is to himself is the interlocutor. This inward, searching speech culminates in a moment of exultation mixed with remorse: "Late have I loved you, Beauty so ancient and so new, / late have I loved you!"[80] In the Patristic era of Christianity, beauty becomes more rather than less definitely the adequate name for the vision to which human beings are called by nature.

Nearly one thousand years later, Thomas Aquinas will accept it as a matter of course, speaking consistently of true knowledge as vision, of rational truth as spiritual light, of divine revelation as the "light of glory," and of the divine knowledge as akin to a single glance over all eternity.[81] The infused intellectual virtue of faith, of which Aquinas writes as a kind of hearing, is transcended only when we attain to perfect intellectual seeing: in the "manifest vision" of God.[82] Drawing together such testimonies as these, the theologian Hans Urs von Balthasar concludes that, "for the great thinkers of the West (from Homer and Plato via Augustine and Thomas down to Goethe and Hölderlin, Schelling and Heidegger), beauty is the last comprehensive attribute of all-embracing being as such, its last mysterious radiance."[83] Maritain, in a passage we have already cited, declares

---

80. Augustine, *The Confessions*, X.27.38.

81. For example, Aquinas, *Summa Theologica*, "the light of glory strengthening the intellect to see God," I.12.2; "the glorified eye can see God," I.12.3; "God is intelligible light," I.12.5, obj. 1; "God sees his effects in himself," I.14.7; God knows with "the knowledge of vision," I.14.9; his vision is a "glance … carried from eternity over all things," I.14.13; see also I.56.3, I.57.2. Cf. Pieper, *Leisure*, 12.

82. Aquinas, *Summa Contra Gentiles*, trans. Vernon J. Bourke et al. (Notre Dame, Ind.: University of Notre Dame Press, 2002), 3:40; and *Summa Theologica*, I-II.65.5.

83. Quoted in Viladesau, *Theological Aesthetics*, 33.

Beauty to be the "radiance of all the transcendentals united."[84] Far from being an incidental quality or perfection of material things, beauty in its purest sense designates a finality at which the human intellect arrives when it fulfills itself, when it is most fully saturated in reality. This is not to collapse truth into beauty, for truth loses nothing of its integrity when we know it so well that we see it. Rather, we see the truth, love it as good, and finally perceive it as a reality unto itself, a form, that stands in relation to all other things and speaks of their harmonious existence as created. Beauty is this total showing forth of *form and splendor*, distinct from truth because we may encounter it as an existence, as being, before we recognize it as true, but also distinct from truth and goodness, because in its vision these things are finally held together within the form, within the fullness of being. As we shall have occasion to discuss again in Part II, Beauty comes first and also last in our experience. As we shall see presently, this characteristic of beauty in our subjectivity finds confirmation in the realm of being as such.

Human beings are by their nature ordered to this vision of beauty, and the intelligibility of the world around us is not the least of evidences in favor of that proposition. This should suggest to us that beauty is not exclusively or even primarily a human "value," but *that the world is itself ordered by and to Beauty.* Though it has taken us some time to arrive at this insight, it is surely the keystone of them all, the definitive single claim. It is also one of the oldest. In the *Gorgias*, Plato proposes that "wise men claim that partnership and friendship, orderliness, self-control, and justice hold together heaven and earth, and gods and men, and that is why they call this universe a world order."[85] Nature must be understood in terms of well-ordered desires, that is to say, movement ordained to an intelligible end—which is, in turn, to say, form (being constituted in itself by a purpose beyond itself) ordered to splendor (intelligibility and fullness that holds all forms together in unity such that, in the perception of splendor, every form is seen always to transcend itself by innumerable relations including relation to the creative divine mind).[86] This, as we have already

84. Maritain, *Art and Scholasticism*, 173n66.

85. Plato, *Gorgias*, 508a.

86. We have already indicated Beauty's convertible relation to truth, goodness, and being, a crucial fact that von Balthasar discusses in *The Glory of the Lord*, 1:19. But it is essential also to see that what makes this convertibility possible, such that beauty may be first and also last in our ex-

noted and as we will return to, is beauty. In the *Timaeus*, Plato will elaborate this same cosmic architecture with a slightly different vocabulary. It is
a "work of craft" that is "most beautiful," he says, and then explains this in
terms of geometry.[87] We usually explain order by number, and so number,
here, is indicative of the beautiful. In just these two passages, Plato ad-
verts to the language of ethics, making, and mathematics, all of which cor-
respond in some fashion to both ancient and modern understandings of
the word "poetics." The cosmos is a poem, an artwork, a thing of beauty,
eternal and yet composed of movements or processions that give it a form
visible to the vision of the body and of the soul.

In a similar vein, the Wisdom of Solomon will praise the creative
knowledge of God for having "arranged all things by measure and number
and weight," that is, for endowing creation with the mathematical qualities of beauty.[88] This seemingly incidental passage will become a point of
reference for centuries, anchoring claims that God is Beauty and that all
he makes is beautiful.[89] Later, it will take on new life, finding more complete expression in the prologue to John's Gospel, where the eternal *Logos*,
the well-measured and ordered thought of God, creates everything from
nothing.[90] Aristotle effectively glosses all these passages in noting that
"the good and the beautiful are the origin both of the knowledge and of
the movement of many things."[91] He contends that all things are ordered
together and connected in an intelligible way;[92] and insists against his
opponents that geometry, and mathematics in general, are intimately involved in that intelligibility as beautiful.[93]

Medieval writers will embrace these concepts with alacrity, finding
the geometrical and numeric structures that saturate the material world,
the *cosmos*, as but signs of its origin in Beauty Itself and its orderly journey back to it.[94] It is hard to imagine a people more enamored, not just

---

perience and in the real as a whole, is its irreducibly polar nature as form and splendor (*The Glory of the Lord*, 1:19–20, 118). Cf. Schindler, *The Catholicity of Reason*, 69–71.

87. Plato, *Timaeus*, 29a.

88. Wisdom 11:20. All quotations of Scripture, unless otherwise noted, are taken from the Revised Standard Version, Second Catholic Edition.

89. Umberto Eco, *The Aesthetics of Thomas Aquinas*, trans. Hugh Bredin (Cambridge, Mass.: Harvard University Press, 1988), 23.

90. John 1:1–3.   91. Aristotle, *Metaphysics*, 1013a1.21–22.

92. Aristotle, *Metaphysics*, 1075a1.15–24.   93. Aristotle, *Metaphysics*, 1078b1.1–5.

94. See Umberto Eco, *Art and Beauty in the Middle Ages*, trans. Hugh Bredin (New Haven,

of the experience of seeing beautiful things, but of taking those mundane encounters as signs of God's goodness, presence, and intelligibility—and as anticipations of the vision of God himself. Augustine, early in *The Confessions*, would approach God by way of his own natural desires as a person and by the orderliness of things in general, proclaiming, "From you derives all manner of being, O God most beautiful, who endow all things with their beautiful form and by your governance direct them in their due order."[95] This rich perception would find its greatest single advocate and most sustained explication in Dionysius the Aeropagite, whose *Divine Names* holds that the universe is mapped as a great pageant begun in the divine Beauty of God, proceeding out into the precincts of creation, and returning once more to him. Dionysius writes,

And so it is that all things must desire, must yearn for, must love, the Beautiful and the Good. Because of it and for its sake, subordinate is returned to superior, equal keeps company with equal, superior turns providentially to subordinate, each bestirs itself and all are stirred to do and to will whatever it is they do and will because of the yearning for the Beautiful and the Good. And we may be so bold as to claim also that the Cause of all things loves all things in the superabundance of his goodness, that because of this goodness he makes all things, brings all things to perfection, holds all things together, returns all things.[96]

In discovering in ourselves intellect and desire, an intelligibility that precedes our thought and a light that fulfills it, Dionysius rhapsodizes, we have entered on the road to seeing the order and direction, source and meaning, of all things. One consequence of this insight regarding an existential truth would seem to be that there is a cosmic order comprehensive of justice that we have the capacity to understand and obey. This led eventually to the western conception of the rule of law as a good. The intelligible order of the macrocosm provides a model for the individual soul, the microcosm; the path to wisdom for the person consists in large part in the contemplation of and assimilation to that order.[97]

Conn.: Yale University Press, 2002), 17. (Evidently, Greenblatt has not read this book or the abundant materials on which it draws.)

95. Augustine, *The Confessions*, I,7,12.

96. Pseudo-Dionysius, *The Complete Works*, 79.

97. Rémi Brague, *The Wisdom of the World*, trans. Teresa Lavender Fagan (Chicago: University of Chicago Press, 2003), 31–34.

We suggested above, however, how impoverished this truth comes to appear when reduced to the merely juridical domain of positive law. The western genius for the law should not be understood in terms of its monumental success in suppressing and civilizing barbarians in the wilderness or in conquering the wilderness itself by means of technology and good government. The spirit of law does not culminate in the institution of a *Pax Romana* or a *Pax Americana*. More fundamental and universal than any ephemeral regime is the insight that there is a natural or cosmic law that gives meaning, relation, and order—form and splendor—to all things.

If all things participate in the orderly procession-from-and-return-to Beauty, they do not all do so in the same way. Things without intellects are ordered by a "natural desire" that moves them to their ends through the government of a higher intelligence.[98] Animals with a sensitive appetite, but without intellect, act under the power of their own wills, but that will is directed by instinct—by, as it were, the conclusions of reason implanted and fixed in their natures *from without*.[99] Intellectual creatures, on the other hand, are not merely directed to their end but direct themselves with a free will. That will is free, because they not only move themselves toward their end, but know it; indeed, it is specifically their capacity for knowledge, for the immaterial spiritual act of understanding all things, including their ends, by virtually becoming them, that allows human beings to fulfill themselves in freedom.[100] Because thought frees the creature from total imprisonment in matter, allowing the mind to become other than itself, to become another in knowledge, Aquinas writes that man's vision of the Divine Beauty leads, finally, to his assimilation to it. This, as Rousselot writes, is "indeed the most perfect form [of assimilation to God] of all."[101] As we saw above, the intellect allows for a unity among things, including between man and the divine, that is unique because it is intellectual rather than ma-

98. Aquinas, *Summa Theologica*, I.6.1.   99. Aquinas, *Summa Theologica*, I-II.40.3.
100. Aquinas, *Summa Theologica*, I-II.1.8.
101. Rousselot, *Intelligence*, 33. The poet and Jesuit priest Gerard Manley Hopkins writes that "God's utterance of himself in himself is God the Word" and that this word "outside himself is this world." The "world then is word, expression, news of God" (*The Major Works* [Oxford: Oxford University Press, 2009], 282). Created being in its act of existence is a word, an utterance or procession from God that constitutes his "grandeur" or glory. Every being, as God's word, is an expression of that glory in itself and, in its being, offers praise or glory to God (291). Man with all things is created, but man as a creation that knows himself and can speak, completes the return of all things to God, for his knowing and spoken word returns the glory of being to God: "This

terial; we do not dissolve in that vision, but realize ourselves in it.[102] Thus it is *that human dignity specifically consists in our capacity to perceive and contemplate that splendorous order, and, thus, the most excellent form of human life is that which is given over to such contemplation.*

One provocative and plausible opinion regarding Plato's dialogues is that they all seem to have been intended as a kind of "propaganda" to convince his readers that the distinguishing human function is this contemplative union.[103] So, also, in the Hebrew Scriptures, when Solomon proclaims "the desire of wisdom leads to a kingdom," and describes divine wisdom as a beautiful woman whom he loved "more than health and beauty," and declares that he "chose to have her rather than light, because her radiance never ceases," we justly hear a summons to contemplation as, morally speaking, the most desirable, because the best, life.[104] When a man capable of wisdom first learns of the life of philosophy, Plato's letters tell us, he "thinks he has heard of a marvelous quest that he must at once enter upon with all earnestness, or life is not worth living."[105] As Pierre Hadot has convincingly demonstrated, all ancient philosophies were conceived "above all [as] a way of life," rather than as a specific set of doctrines or conclusions.[106] In his discussion of the *Symposium*, he emphasizes that the dialogue tries to convince us that "philosophy is not wisdom but a way of life and discourse determined by the *idea* of wisdom."[107] We should wish to become lovers of wisdom, if we are not already, and this consists in a life shaped by certain practices and oriented toward a certain end, rather than in a specific knowledge. Aristotle more dryly observes that the life of happiness will "be in accordance with the highest excellence; and this will be that of the best thing in us."[108] That, he claims to have demonstrated, is the activity of the intellect, and the highest such act is that of contemplation. Indeed, insofar as man can, by something divine in him, attain it, contemplation will be itself a divine life. Aristotle elsewhere

---

then was why he was made, to give God glory and to mean to give it" (291). What may seem the special pleading of the devotional poet in fact expresses with singular clarity, in terms of being-as-word-as-glory, the perception of the orderly procession-and-return of Beauty.

102. Aquinas, *Summa Contra Gentiles*, 3:37. Cf. Ratzinger, *Introduction to Christianity*, 157–58.
103. Hadot, *What Is Ancient Philosophy?*, 72.   104. Wisdom 6:20, 7:10.
105. Plato, *Letters*, 340b–c.   106. Hadot, *What Is Ancient Philosophy?*, 4.
107. Hadot, *What Is Ancient Philosophy?*, 46.
108. Aristotle, *Nicomachean Ethics*, 1177a11–12.

demonstrates that this is not just a metaphor: eternal contemplation is the very life of God and the type of human life the gods most bless.[109]

When St. John writes his Gospel centuries later, however, such arguments have won out. He indicates in his narrative of Jesus's encounter with the Samaritan woman at the well that all human beings already are seeking this most excellent way of life; they just do not know where to find it. Gesturing to the well, the Lord cryptically tells her, "Everyone who drinks of this water will thirst again, but whoever drinks of the water that I shall give him will never thirst; the water that I shall give him will become in him a spring of water welling up to eternal life."[110] This image of water standing for the vision of beauty as the most excellent, because everlasting, life for the human being attempts to make us aware of something we already probably know. We thirst, and we wish our thirst to be quenched. So, the woman replies immediately, "Sir, give me this water, that I may not thirst, nor come here to draw."[111] Water and light are the recurrent images for the divine beauty, for the object of the contemplative life, because they indicate by analogy that this life is, first, natural to the human person and, second, stands in inexhaustible transcendence of him. In a dark room, we all immediately turn to a spark of light; we all thirst. We sense that light from above and water from below surrounds us as the inexhaustible reality we always need. When St. Paul speaks in the Areopagus, he approves the pursuit of the philosophical life already to be found there, and merely attempts to complete its assent to contemplation by revealing to them the name of the God who has made all things in beauty.[112]

This assumption that all men desire to know the truth, the pursuit of which constitutes a singularly dignified human vocation, would come to rest at the heart of the Christian West's self-understanding.[113] All human beings are called, in virtue of their intellectual natures, to what the pagan world had called the intellectual life—this much the Gospels dramatize and the early Christian apologists repeat. Christianity recognizes therefore the need for both philosophy and theology as complementary practices. Theology helps make it possible for the life of Christianity as a

109. Aristotle, *Metaphysics*, 1072b, and *Nicomachean Ethics*, 1179a24–30.
110. John 4:13–14.   111. John 4:15.
112. Acts 17:22–31.
113. For an authoritative argument to that effect, see John Paul II, *Fides et Ratio*, par. 1–6.

whole to become philosophy perfected, for it is "a way of life" that entails "living according to the *Logos*."[114] This sense of the philosophical life as a calling produced not by our individual circumstances but by our natures as such is the foundation, to be seen unmistakably in the Greeks, for a robust conception of human equality.

It must be said, however, that the principle of equality comes to appear impoverished and arbitrary when reduced merely to the political, as it has been in all those accounts of modernity and the West that speak of "equality" apart from this ontology of the human being. A strong defender of that ontological equality, Jacques Maritain, couched his political philosophy as a response to modern efforts to wrench the principle of equality from its foundation in human nature. He contended that "Metaphysics is a necessary prerequisite of ethics."[115] For,

> it is no more possible to rationalize the human elements without knowing what man is than to rationalize the production of a factory without knowing what a factory is. We must know then what man is: which is the office of metaphysics and even of theology. Ethics, which we may consider as the rationalization of the use of Freedom, presupposes metaphysics as its necessary prerequisite. Ethics cannot be constituted unless its author is first able to answer the questions: *What is man? Why is he made? What is the end of human life?*[116]

The equality of human persons is rooted not in a juridical fiat but in the vocation of all human beings to know and dwell in the divine names of truth, goodness, and beauty. "Man is a metaphysical being, an animal that nourishes its life on transcendentals," he writes.[117] A legal equality that frustrates this nourishment would be an offense against human dignity. And yet this is what we see in our day. Modern doctrines of equality tend to be asserted unapologetically without foundation and therefore seem to be rooted in mere political power rather than in any recognized truth about the human creature. In *The Person and the Common Good*, Maritain provides a political philosophy that defends modern democracy insofar as

---

114. Hadot, *What Is Ancient Philosophy?*, 247, 241.

115. Maritain, *Collected Works*, 11:10.

116. Maritain, *Collected Works*, 11:10–11. Simone Weil's understanding of equality and human rights is similarly rooted—see *The Need for Roots*, trans. Arthur Wills (London: Routledge Classics, 2007).

117. Maritain, *Collected Works*, 11:11.

it makes possible the fulfillment of the properly human vocation. The volume also condemns democracy and every other political regime insofar as these attempt to conceal or pervert the principles of human freedom and equality by denying the summons built into our natures as *intellectual* creatures destined for the truth.[118]

Implicit in such a rich conception of the equality of human nature and of the calling to know the truth, of course, lies also a potential for inequality: one cannot have dignity without the possibility of distinction. Though all are called, few may come.[119] And so, the two chief speculative concerns of medieval Christian writers would be, first, the theology of the attributes of God, and, second, the proper (metaphysical) definition of man as the *imago Dei*, whose earthly life is best spent in that "imperfect happiness" that seeks to know God.[120] Following from these, the main contribution the medieval writers would make to the western tradition was eminently practical and dedicated to cultivating the attributes of human dignity toward distinct fulfillment. That is, the particular strength of medieval Christian thought lay in its many attempts to perfect a discipline or habit for the living out of man's natural contemplative vocation in light of its super-elevation by God's grace.[121] Medieval Christians take the purposive orientation of human life for granted, and concern themselves with developing those spiritual techniques that may allow us most efficaciously to pursue it. Thus, from Evagrius Ponticus and John Cassian in the fourth century, to Richard of St. Victor in the twelfth, Sts. Thomas Aquinas and Bonaventure in the thirteenth, and Julian of Norwich and the anonymous author of *The Cloud of Unknowing* in the fourteenth, we find a remarkable flowering of philosophical and theological works whose primary focus is not to demonstrate truths, but to serve as aids or methods for their contemplation by the person living within the body of the Church.[122] Just as Plato's dialogues may not be primarily demonstrations

118. Jacques Maritain, *The Person and the Common Good*, trans. John J. Fitzgerald (Notre Dame, Ind.: University of Notre Dame Press, 2006).

119. Matthew 22:14. Cf. Weil, *The Need for Roots*, 19.

120. On imperfect and perfect happiness, see Aquinas, *Summa Theologica*, I-II.3.2, I-II.5.3. Cf. Alasdair MacIntyre, *God, Philosophy, Universities* (Lanham, Md.: Rowman and Littlefield Publishers, 2009), 75–76.

121. This is what Maritain defines as "practically practical science" (*Degrees of Knowledge*, 333–34).

122. See Evagrius Ponticus, *The Praktikos and Chapters on Prayer*, trans. John Eudes (Ka-

of philosophical truths but models of dialectic intended to seduce us into the practice of philosophy, of the life of dialectic in community, so these works are guides to the interior dialogue with God.

In Dante, we find an especially vivid poetic representation of the vital fact with which all these authorities grapple: human life can be spent as an aimless wandering, but it finds its true character in a long intellectual and erotic pilgrimage toward a vision of the Divine Beauty. Dante depicts the vision of God as three circles in "exalted Light," an image of form and splendor—to wit, Beauty.[123] In seeing it, his life finds fulfillment: "my mind was struck by light that flashed / and, with this light, received what it had asked."[124] Understandably, the medieval figures I have mentioned are more often discussed as belonging to the tradition of ancient and Christian mysticism. But such a grouping distorts their significance: in creating a phenomenon called "mysticism," one cuts off these writers from their intellectual foundations, as if they had personal experiences to share rather than accounts to render about the truth of the human person in his ordination to the divine. It would be more accurate to think of their accounts as especially practically minded expressions of Christian Platonist speculation, which work is essential to the actual living-out of the life of *theoria*, of true knowledge. Guides to devotion and contemplation do not stand outside the intellectual tradition incepted by the figure of Socrates; they are integral parts of it that bring to light the way in which the ordering of man to intellectual vision, and the ordering of all things by and to beauty, finds practical expression.[125] Such insights bequeath not primarily

---

lamazoo, Mich.: Cistercian Publications, 1981); John Cassian, *Conferences*, trans. Colm Luibheid (New York: Paulist Press, 1985); Richard of St. Victor, *The Twelve Patriarchs, The Mystical Ark, Book Three of the Trinity*, trans. Grover A. Zinn (New York: Paulist Press, 1979); Bonaventure, *The Soul's Journey to God, The Tree of Life, The Life of St. Francis*, trans. Ewert Cousins (New York: Paulist Press, 1978); Julian of Norwich, *Showings*, trans. Edmund Colledge, OSA (Mahwah, N.J.: Paulist Press, 1978); *The Cloud of Unknowing* (Mahwah, N.J.: Paulist Press, 1981). This is not an arbitrary list, but it does exclude many major figures; I have included only those whose work I know best. For a similar, but more methodical chronology more attentive to the Christian East, see Kevin Hart, "Contemplation: Beyond and Behind," *Sophia* 48 (2009), 435–59.

123. Balthasar, *The Glory of the Lord*, 1:21.

124. Dante Alighieri, *The Divine Comedy*, trans. Allen Mandelbaum (New York: Everyman's Library, 1995), 540–41.

125. Louis Dupré compellingly calls the modern uses of the word "mysticism" into question, seeking to restore the works so called to their true theological status, in *The Enlightenment and the Intellectual Foundations of Modern Culture* (New Haven, Conn.: Yale University Press,

specific bits of information so much as a whole way of life; they give us a terrain with a finite number of paths that we are called to inhabit. This is surely the best way to understand, for instance, the *Spiritual Exercises* of St. Ignatius of Loyola, just as it is the poetry and spiritual writings of his late disciple, Gerard Manley Hopkins.[126] The Jesuit practice of a life dedicated to *giving* God glory, these figures show us, comes in natural response to man's being as a creature spoken into being and so also to his species as a creature who can speak.[127] In giving God *glory* they indicate furthermore the freedom and gratuity of this action: it ends, on the side of the human subject, in free contemplation and, on the side of God, in the incomprehensible excess of his beauty.

The craving for a water that so quenches our thirst that we shall never thirst again, a light that answers our most gnawing question, anticipates our sixth and final insight: that *this contemplation realizes itself in what we may call happiness or salvation, and it is characterized by an activity that resembles passivity, that is to say, not simply the absence of motion but a fullness of activity that is called peace and freedom.* The whole of the Christian Platonist tradition converges on "happiness" and "beatitude" as the terms best suited to name the purpose of human life, and it tells us that all our activities are ordained to that end. Plato definitively characterized that end as the possession of the good forever.[128] Christianity would propose that such a state consisted specifically in the intellectual assimilation to God, in abiding in him.[129] Because one could achieve this only in a condition that transcends the present, fallen, earthly realm where all things pass away, Christians emphasize that happiness is just another name for beatitude as *salvation*.[130] But if every act and thought aims at some good, and all things together aim at the highest good—the final cause—we may well ask, what happens once we arrive there?[131] Our lives are largely conditioned by change, and so what kind of life could be lived "forever"? If an

---

2004), 318. Bernard McGinn, the authoritative historian of mysticism, similarly treats as dubious any hard line that would sever mysticism or "mystics" from philosophy and theology (McGinn, *The Foundations of Mysticism*, xiii, xvi).

126. Ignatius of Loyola, *Spiritual Exercises and Selected Works* (New York: Paulist Press, 1991).

127. Hopkins, *The Major Works*, 290–91.   128. Plato, *Symposium*, 206a.
129. John 6:68, 17:3.   130. Acts 16:30.
131. Aristotle, *Nicomachean Ethics*, 1094a1.1.

activity reaches its end, that activity normally ceases; if this is true of any familiar human action—including the journey to and through the contemplative life—then the cessation of motion would seem to be a death, and Christian holiness a bore.[132] If this end of movement were the cessation of activity, if it were a mere lapsing into passivity and potentiality, then this unhappy opinion would be correct.[133]

Perhaps paradoxically, the exponents of the Christian Platonist tradition characterize activity as we know it as a movement between the poles of potency and act; at every moment, we move between one and the other, we are a composite of potency and act, and indeed these words give us the measurement of movement *per se*.[134] The realm of change in which we dwell is one in which all things are only *actualized* in certain respects, while they are *in potency* in others. The achievement of an action should not be understood primarily as the cessation or finishing of movement, but as the realization or, as Julian of Norwich depicts it, the fullness, the filling-full, of an act.[135] Movement is the transition from a state of partial activity and potency to a state of being completely activated. As we approach the Eternal Beauty, as we become truly happy, we come nearer to the uniquely divine condition of existing as *pure act*.[136] We have seen that Plato describes the completion of the mind's assent to beauty as the height of fruitfulness: the perception of the beautiful and the good is itself diffusive of beautiful and good things. And we have seen that Aristotle, perhaps in contrast, characterizes perfect happiness as an inward self-completion, in which the subject

132. McGinn, *The Foundations of Mysticism*, 262. This equation of life with movement and stillness with death is the foundation of Hobbes's heresy within the Christian Platonist tradition. See Hobbes, *Leviathan*, 6.58 and 11.2. That this should be a heresy rather than an absolute break is demonstrated in the work of Yvor Winters, who largely accepts Hobbes's basic premise, and reconstructs the Christian Platonist contemplative ideal on its foundations. See Yvor Winters, *In Defense of Reason* (Athens: Ohio University Press / Swallow Press, 1987), 20–29, 200–202. But see also Yvor Winters, *The Collected Poetry of Yvor Winters*, ed. Donald Davie. (Chicago: The Swallow Press, 1978), 184. For commentary on Winters's efforts in this project, see James Matthew Wilson, "Representing the Limits of Judgment: Yvor Winters, Emily Dickinson and Religious Experience," *Christianity and Literature* 56, no. 3 (Spring 2007), 397–422.

133. Aquinas, *Summa Theologica*, I-II.9.3. obj. 1.

134. Aristotle, *Physics*, 201b1.25–201a1.14. Cf. Aquinas, *Summa Theologica*, I-II.9.1. To clarify: if we are *now*, then we are in potency to *later*, and if we are *here*, we are in potency to *there*. As soon as we pass from *here* to *there*, we attain "*there*" in act, but are thus rendered once again in potency to a new *there*, including the old *here*.

135. Julian of Norwich, *Showings*, 186.

136. Schumacher, *A Guide for the Perplexed*, 27; Aquinas, *Summa Theologica*, I.3.1.

thinking and object thought become identical, so that the act of thought can be completed without motion. To conceive the gods as acting-through rather than thinking themselves struck him as preposterous.[137]

The tradition will give up neither of these propositions, contending that happiness is at once an act of achieved stillness and an intrinsically self-diffusive and productive state.[138] Aquinas, for instance, affirms that only the contemplative life realized outside of time is perfect happiness,[139] and, crucially, this he describes as the dual-act of "knowing and loving God."[140] One knows God through the speculative—as opposed to the practical—intellect, and so in this respect happiness is act (knowing) without movement (*praxis*).[141] The love proper to the will reaches this perfect act, as well, but it also overflows in "delight" and "joy in truth."[142] For Aquinas, this actualization of the mind in knowing God is the very definition of fruitfulness.[143] The human person's participation in God as the eternal good is a fullness of act and stillness whose very nature is to diffuse or communicate itself to others.[144] There is a dynamism of the highest sort proper to stillness.

At the opening of the *Confessions*, Augustine famously writes, "our heart is unquiet [or restless] until it rests in you."[145] But he is at great pains to show that the happiness found in such rest is not a mere relapse into the absence-of-motion that is potency. It is the height of activity, in which the mind sees without comprehending, possesses without exhausting.[146] In this condition, rest and joy find their true identities. The tradition proposes that peace cannot be understood as merely the absence of war, and freedom cannot be defined as the simple absence of obstacle or determination. Rather, peace and freedom are the attributes of happiness, wherein the faculty of the intellect reposes in vision and the faculty of

137. Aristotle, *Nicomachean Ethics*, 1178b.

138. Maritain, *The Degrees of Knowledge*, 286.

139. Aquinas, *Summa Theologica*, I-II.3.2.

140. Aquinas, *Summa Theologica*, I-II.1.8.

141. Aquinas, *Summa Theologica*, I-II.3.5. Cf. Maritain, *The Person and the Common Good*, 24–25.

142. Aquinas, *Summa Theologica*, I-II.3.4.

143. Aquinas, *Summa Theologica*, I-II.11.1, I-II.11.3. Cf. I.19.2.

144. Aquinas, *Summa Theologica*, I.106.4.

145. Augustine, *Confessions*, 1,1,1.

146. McGinn, *The Foundations of Mysticism*, 253, 262. Cf. Aquinas, *Summa Theologica*, I.38.1–2.

the will overflows in the seeing of what it loves.[147] The attempt to express this condition has been the source of the most exhilarating writing in the western tradition, spanning from Plato to Augustine, and on to T. S. Eliot, in his Christian Platonic poem, *Burnt Norton*.[148] In such moments, the most familiar language finds itself transformed, validated, and violated, in the effort to take on absolute signification.[149] We are never so free and at peace as when we see into the heart of spiritual light that gives itself to our seeing.

A Classical Expression of the Six Insights: Plato's *Phaedrus*

Socrates's "Palinode to Love," given in the *Phaedrus*, offers one of the earliest and richest expressions of all six of these insights.[150] In his long "prose poem," Socrates reveals to us what, he says, no earthly poet ever could: a comprehensive account of what the human being is, of what his life consists, and its position within the order of the cosmos. He begins by noting that every soul is immortal. All souls travel in the trains of the gods, pursuing a circular motion at the limit of the universe. In this motion, the souls perform two distinct actions. First, they roam "among the stars" looking after all that does not have a soul (i.e., material beings), and governing "the cosmos at large."[151] In this dominion, souls may become ensnared and weighed down by matter, until they fall into an earthly body. But, second, those souls that remain free of matter revolve at the very "rim of heaven," where they "stand and gaze at things outside the heavens."[152] They see "the place of Being, the Being that truly is—colorless, shapeless, and untouchable, visible to the mind alone."[153] It is "the Plain of Truth,"

---

147. Aquinas, *Summa Theologica*, I-II.70.3.

148. Augustine, *Confessions*, IX.23–25; T. S. Eliot, *The Complete Poems and Plays, 1909–1950*, 122.

149. Maritain characterizes this in terms of language's meaning becoming "uncircumscriptive" and super-eminent, *The Degrees of Knowledge*, 240–41.

150. Plato, *Phaedrus*, 243b.

151. Plato, *Phaedrus*, 246b. In this discussion of the dialogue, I do not quote from the Cooper edition of Plato (cited elsewhere), but from Plato, *Phaedrus*, trans. Stephen Scully (Newburyport, Mass.: Focus Publishing, 2003).

152. Plato, *Phaedrus*, 247b.

153. Plato, *Phaedrus*, 247c.

where the forms of all things, including Justice and Beauty, appear to the soul.[154] As the soul "looks upon Being, she feels adoration, and when contemplating the truth, she is easily nourished and feels joyous."[155] In sum, souls order what is beneath them and contemplate what is above.

Thus far in the Palinode, Socrates has not assigned any privileged status to the form of Beauty akin to that he assigns it in the *Symposium*, where *To Kalon* appears as the form of forms, the desirable of all desirables, that orders human (erotic) life. Something similar happens when Socrates turns his attention from the preexistent souls of heaven to those that have fallen to earth and been imprisoned by the "oyster shell" of the body.[156] When the embodied soul looks "upon earthly beauty," such as that of a beautiful face, it is "reminded of the true" form of beauty itself.[157] It is "startled" into recollection of "beauty in its radiance," which the soul has witnessed prior to its embodiment.[158] For us embodied souls, beauty serves as a cause of such recollection (*anamnesis*) for a particular reason. The vision of the eyes is the sharpest of the physical senses and therefore its objects act on us more powerfully than others do, but this in turn reminds us that it is the property of the forms, as *form*, to appear to the intellect.[159] And so, the vision of the mind participates in the sharpness of the eye's vision, and the eye's vision in turn anticipates, or even participates in, the non-sensible vision of the mind. But that is not all. What the soul's vision sees is "pure light."[160] And "beauty shone brightly" amid all the forms.[161] This would suggest that beauty plays a distinctive role *for us* as embodied souls for whom sight is the most potent sense: visible beauty has a subjective power that allows us to experience the "cold shudder" of beauty as it draws the mind from the life of senses immersed in the flux of becoming, up to the eternal forms it knew before its birth, where Being alone abides.[162] But beauty, in the *Phaedrus*, seems to stand out from the other forms *absolutely* as well, not only because it is bright, but because all the forms would seem, as "pure light," to be beautiful in their turn.

Socrates's account of the soul contains many other details that account for the composition of superior and inferior souls and their concomitant

154. Plato, *Phaedrus*, 248c.
155. Plato, *Phaedrus*, 247d.
156. Plato, *Phaedrus*, 250c.
157. Plato, *Phaedrus*, 249d.
158. Plato, *Phaedrus*, 250a.
159. Plato, *Phaedrus*, 250d.
160. Plato, *Phaedrus*, 250c.
161. Plato, *Phaedrus*, 250d.
162. Plato, *Phaedrus*, 251b.

responses to the encounter with beauty, but from this brief summary we see drawn together the six insights we have been exploring. The immortal soul that has once seen the forms and so now has the capacity to know defines the essence of the human being (for Socrates, what bodily form the soul occupies is destined to change in any case, and so is incidental; only mind is essential). The embodied intellect depends for its knowledge on its prior experience as a soul traversing the heavens. Thus, *anamnesis* serves as Plato's way of accounting for why the world seems already intelligible to us and also for why our thought about this or that individual thing seems to lead us in the direction of a knowledge that transcends all individual things and that, indeed, transcends the mobile, temporal rim of the universe and has therefore the permanence of the eternal. Although other texts from the tradition more strongly assign to Beauty its status as the splendor of truth and, therefore, as the highest aim of the intellect, Socrates's oration both privileges the form of Beauty Itself, assigns beauty a unique "subjective" power in the life of the intellect, and interprets the appearance of the forms in terms of pure light and radiance, that is to say, in the conventional language of the beautiful.

Socrates does not confine beauty either to its subjective power or to its lofty preeminence, however. As the souls circle the limits of the universe, in contemplation of the forms, their movements cause the concentric circles of the cosmos to turn. That is to say, by way of the heavenly souls' simultaneous adoration of a beauty above them and governing motions of all that lies beneath them, Beauty Itself proceeds downward, through those that participate in it by way of contemplation, and gives life and motion to an orderly cosmos. Thus things proceed from beauty and, through the circular motion of bodies, and through the circular *anamnesis* of the soul (including its cycles of birth and rebirth), all things return to beauty, saturating the world in form and splendor in the process. In discussing the various possible responses of the human soul to the encounter with earthly beauty, Socrates makes clear that the dignity of the human being lies in a proper responsiveness to beauty. Some respond like animals and seek "to mount" the beautiful being, others may respond to it in jealous violence or tragic self-destruction.[163] The proper response, however, is one that recognizes the fittingness of the soul to rise up to the vision of

---

163. Plato, *Phaedrus*, 250e, 252c.

beauty. Indeed, the "Plain of Truth" is a pastureland that is "just right for the best part of the soul."[164] Thus, according to Socrates, the highest potentiality of the person lies in the contemplation of the splendor of truth, even though we often fail to achieve it. When we do achieve it, we enter the pasturelands of happiness, wherein a perfection of action (the circular motion of the soul) becomes identical with an unconditioned peace and freedom (the vision of the forms, beyond all motion). And so, a few pages of the *Phaedrus* would seem to contain all six of the insights that guide the Christian Platonist tradition. Alfred North Whitehead was in some sense correct to opine that all philosophy was a footnote to Plato, for Plato was at least one of the first to plant these six seeds in the soil of the West, making possible not mere annotation but enrichment, growth, and boundless fecundity.

Why the Soul Must See

Before we turn to some important implications of these six insights as a whole, we should draw together, from what I have just said about the *Phaedrus*, our thoughts about the nature of seeing and the vision of the soul that guides this study. As I mentioned in the last chapter, there are at least three reasons that Plato, and we with him, must privilege sight so as to understand the human person's intellectual nature as fulfilled in the soul's vision of truth-in-beauty. First, the sharpness of the bodily sense of sight seems to associate it most closely with the activity of the intellect. Plato's linking the two as distinct but mysteriously connected senses—one bodily, the other spiritual—only hints at what we should call their final unity in the person. It is the mind that sees *through* the bodily eye, so all sensation for us is at once a bodily and an intellectual act. However distinct the parts of this act may be in the reason, it is the person as a whole who sees and knows.[165] Jacques Maritain spoke of "intelligentiated-sense" to refer to this character of sensation in general, but especially as we experience it in those acts of the senses, such as the contemplation of works of fine art, where the life of the intellect seems most obviously to dominate the senses.[166]

164. Plato, *Phaedrus*, 248c.
165. Cf. Schindler, *The Catholicity of Reason*, 119.
166. John G. Trapani Jr., *Poetry, Beauty, and Contemplation: The Complete Aesthetics of Jacques Maritain* (Washington, D.C.: The Catholic University of America Press, 2011), 69.

Second, if the intellect always acts through the bodily sense of sight, so also the bodily sense of sight, as our "fullest" such sense, anticipates that still greater mode of sight, intellectual vision. The eye sees the sensible form (or shape) of things that derives from the invisible, because intellectual and ontological, form that constitutes the essence or nature of a thing. Only the eye of the mind can perceive intellectual form, which is the truth of being. Both acts are therefore rooted in one and the same form, with the bodily eye perceiving the visible expression of form and the intellectual soul perceiving the form that is truth itself. Our experience of the intensity or sharpness of our bodily sight anticipates and gives us a way to imagine (by analogy) the much more intense and sharp, because immediate, experience of seeing-the-form, of knowing the truth.

Third, and finally, as we have several times noted, this image of the mind as seeing captures the essential characteristics of knowing in its fullest state of perfection. It is an activity that is also a passivity, a movement of the soul out into the world it knows, and a movement of the forms of the world (things) entering into the soul as they come to be known. A fullness of knowledge is no longer a series of discursive steps, but an immediate reality beheld (some would say "intuitively," though "intellectually" is the only term unlikely to mislead us). The state of simultaneous passivity and activity that perceives immediately the form of truth is one where the mind rests in perception of a formal whole in itself and in all its harmonious relations with the whole of reality, and this, we have said, is beauty. A fullness of knowledge is indeed an intellectual vision, and the fullness of a form's presence to the mind, which is the presence of truth and so also the disclosure of being, will always give itself as beauty. To speak of the vision of the soul is, therefore, finally to perceive something about the nature of the person, the nature of beings as formally constituted, and the character of reality as a whole, which is being (*common being*, which means, in the terms of Scholasticism, all created, finite beings) perceived as an ordered whole of form and splendor brought into being by the divine Beauty, God himself.

The Christian Platonist Tradition as
the Tradition of the West

In introducing these six insights, I claimed that they were the central coordinates of the Christian Platonist tradition and that Christian Platonism was *the* tradition of the West. We have not seen to the heart of western civilization unless we know them and see how they provide that civilization its historical coherence, inestimable value, and the fruitfulness just noted. We can see easily enough why such ideas as reason, freedom, equality, and the rule of law, may describe some consequences of these six insights, while also feeling that they cannot adequately express them. For, none of those terms gets to the heart of the matter; the Christian Platonist tradition accepts Beauty as the first principle that gives order not only to the journey of human life but to reality as such, and so all things must be seen in relation to Beauty.

Having made such a broad generalization and bold claim, I need to point out what I do *not* intend. I do not say that Christian Platonism is the dominant tradition of the West in the sense that it might be contrasted with other competing traditions, such as Aristotelianism, Biblical Christianity, Stoicism, or some other designation. In the study on some particular author—Aquinas or Bonaventure, for instance—it is useful to make such specific distinctions. And if we were chiefly engaged in the study of intellectual history, we should have to register such minute distinctions as those between early, middle, and later Platonism, to say nothing of the variations proper to primitive and later Christianity. But my ambition has been to point out the six coordinates that give us the map of western thought in general; it holds in its bounds an immense variety of thought, much of it irreconcilable on the level of particular claims or details, and yet bound together by familial traits that lead us in a consistent, general direction. Such coordinates indicate how a vast and multifarious tradition may have held together and may still hold together; they leave unspecified a wide array of particular historical and philosophical questions to which a number of compelling answers may be given.

I would make another clarification. These six insights are hardly the exclusive property of the West. As modern writers such as Irving Babbitt, T. S. Eliot, Paul Elmer More, and E. F. Schumacher have shown, there are great continuities between the thought of eastern religious and contemplative traditions and Christian Platonism. They seem to have understood the six insights I mention as a perennial and fundamental legacy of the human race, rather than as a peculiarly western phenomenon. I would only slightly dissent from that understanding. I have no interest in praising the West for its exclusive differences, nor have I any hope that claims along the lines of "X has never been thought of outside of the western tradition" could be conclusively demonstrated. But I do hope I have been successful in highlighting the sustained, coherent, and dynamic tradition born in Athens and Jerusalem and developed in the West, which has given us not only a bountiful intellectual pluralism, but has also developed these six insights in profound and systematic ways. Whatever the variations in thought within the western tradition, what seems to drive its life is an adherence to these insights.

As we noted above, the philosopher George Santayana once diagnosed Babbitt, More, and Eliot as Christian Platonists; he failed to mention that it was also the case that he was a Christian Platonist, though he was also an atheist and a materialist.[167] What Santayana's testimony and example seem to reveal is that the six coordinates of the tradition are broadly spaced; they leave room for a wide range of beliefs; and yet they cohere so naturally as to form, upon examination, a visible whole, a unified tradition. For all its specificity, that tradition necessarily includes a great number of figures: not only Platonists who were not Christians and Christians who were not consciously Platonists, but also such figures as Maimonides and Averroes, who were neither Christians nor Platonists but, respectively, Jewish and Islamic commentators on Aristotle who helped the West develop its tradition. Let me encapsulate my understanding of this tradition's range in the following way. By defining Christian Platonism according to these six coordinates, we do not gloss over the multifarious and real differences between historical schools and figures; rather, we seek to establish the foundations that make those things intelligible to one another, and which, therefore, help account for the differences we do find as competing answers to a shared set of questions: How shall we understand reality? How shall we understand our role within it?

167. Santayana, *The Essential Santayana*, 567–69.

Are We Christian Platonists Still?

I began with the claim that many of us have missed the six intellectual foundations of the western tradition. It may seem reasonable to conclude that, if we are unaware of, or unfamiliar with, these ideas, then the tradition must itself be dead or in retreat, and something else must have taken its place. Such a conclusion has been characteristic of the modern West since the sixteenth century, at which time the major artistic and intellectual figures came to imagine themselves as glancing back to antiquity in order to begin something entirely new.

We have good reasons to question this thought, however. René Descartes believed himself to be doing something new, and many persons, including intellectual historians, took him at his word.[168] And yet, in addition to his direct dependence on specific medieval sources that have long since been illuminated by Etienne Gilson,[169] we may broadly observe that Descartes manifests, in however unsatisfactory a form, five of the six insights of the West. He defines man as minimally a "thinking thing," if not an intellectual animal.[170] His conception of innate ideas derives from the conception of *nous* or *intellectus*.[171] He views the intelligibility of things directly dependent on God as their cause and perceives that intelligibility in mathematical terms somewhat after the fashion of the ancients.[172] In addition, he makes gestures toward the contemplation of God as the chief human vocation and the cause of happiness and peace, and couches his major philosophical statements in a rhetoric that makes them appear as if they were the desultory consequence of a meditative way of life.[173] What constitutes his breach with—or heresy within—that tradition is his stripping away of the fourth insight—*that the world is itself ordered by and to beauty.* In each of the five insights he does share we hear the impov-

---

168. Etienne Gilson, *The Spirit of Mediaeval Philosophy*, trans. A. H. C. Downes (Notre Dame, Ind.: University of Notre Dame Press, 1991), 13–14.

169. See Etienne Gilson, *Études sur le rôle de la pensée médiévale dans la formation du système cartésien* (Paris: Vrin, 1930).

170. René Descartes, *Meditations on First Philosophy*, trans. Donald Cress (Indianapolis: Hackett, 1993), 19.

171. Descartes, *Meditations*, 22–23.

172. Descartes, *Meditations*, 29–31.

173. Granted, many of these gestures are extraneous ones. Descartes, *Meditations*, 35. Cf. Hadot, *What Is Ancient Philosophy?*, 264.

erishment that comes from not joining them all by means of that name.

We could perform a similar analysis with Descartes's contemporary and fellow mathematician, Blaise Pascal, who is no less a recognizably modern figure, but whose thought is imbued with Augustine, in terms of his understanding of reason as driven by desire and transcended by an intellectual vision that can be illuminated only by the light of faith.[174] What conceals this continuity is, once again, his modern rejection of nature as ordered by and to Beauty, and his conclusion that nature is so disproportioned and discontinuous as to be essentially unintelligible to us.[175] For Descartes and Pascal, as for most early modern figures, the meaning of the cosmos has been almost entirely neutralized.[176] Truth, goodness, and above all beauty can no longer be properties of being, simply because material being seems unworthy of such things, it has depth of quantity but not quality—except, perhaps, insofar as it becomes the receptacle of the human being's imposition of form upon it.

In German Idealism and the Romantic movement of the nineteenth century, we find constant reaffirmation of man as a creature distinguished by his spiritual nature and summoned to the contemplation of beauty. But these ideas are broadly reconceived in terms of spirit as emotion or intuition and in terms of contemplation as an act of the poetic imagination rather than of intellectual vision: feeling and interior making replace the seeing-that-is-knowing. As such, the human spirit comes to be understood as creative rather than as speculative or receptive of truth. Immanuel Kant, like Descartes, claimed to be doing something new; unlike Descartes, he really was.[177] His subjective account of truth, goodness, and beauty in the three *Critiques* marks a radical departure for philosophy. And yet, many of his disciples, including Wordsworth and Coleridge, were swift to draw his work back into the tradition, treating it as a modern, more adequate, foundation for ancient Platonism.[178] In a similar vein, P. B. Shelley translated Plato's *Symposium*, and a general interest in neo-Platonism visibly

174. Pascal, *Pensées*, §§425, 270–80.

175. Pascal, *Pensées*, §§72, 75, 792.

176. Brague, *The Wisdom of the World*, 194.

177. Immanuel Kant, *The Critique of Pure Reason*, trans. Paul Guyer and Allen W. Wood (Cambridge: Cambridge University Press, 2007), 113.

178. Claud Howard, *Coleridge's Idealism: A Study of Its Relationship to Kant and to the Cambridge Platonists* (Boston: R. G. Badger, 1924).

shaped the course of Romantic thought through his influence.[179] Its most striking break with the Christian Platonist tradition appears not in its sense of nature as ordered by beauty and of eternal beauty as transcendent of nature, but in its incapacity to believe this indicative of some final cause and ordering of human life to a particular transcendent end. This loss of finality exacerbates a dualism in the Romantics, in which the mind rises and falls between the realms of nature and spirit, showing itself free of, and superior to, the former, but not quite suited to remain in the latter.[180] The soul's distinction is its emotional and imaginative capacity for an experience of "natural supernaturalism" or merely immanent transcendence.[181] Such is the problem explored in Shelley's "Hymn to Intellectual Beauty" and John Keats's "Ode to a Nightingale," for instance.[182]

Later figures in the Romantic tradition, such as Friedrich Nietzsche and Martin Heidegger, would retain this conception of human life as a contemplative or artistic vocation that is both intellectual and erotic. For such projects, they would draw heavily on the resources of Greek culture. If we can discern a continuity with the Christian Platonist tradition even in these figures, then we must clearly understand that any modern break with it has been incomplete. Indeed, the best way to imagine the modern West would be as a sort of heresy—or variable series of heresies—within that tradition. Often, the key to understanding modern figures is to discern precisely how they are repeating, with a "heretical" difference, some earlier authority's footsteps.

We cited above Whitehead's old saw that all of philosophy is but a footnote to Plato, and it is accurate in two respects. First, the marked intellectual continuity in the western tradition makes it easy to discern the continuing presence of such founding figures as Plato and the authors of the Gospels. And, second, perhaps more provocatively, I would argue that a tendency to exegesis and commentary—to footnoting, as it were—comes

179. David K. O'Connor, ed., *The Symposium of Plato: The Shelley Translation*, trans. P. B. Shelley (South Bend, Ind.: St. Augustine's Press, 2002).

180. See James Matthew Wilson, *Timothy Steele: A Critical Introduction* (West Chester, Penn.: Story Line Press, 2012), 10–12. One may describe the same attributes of Romantic thought as monist or pantheistic with the same results: an immanent vacillation of the human mind between matter and spirit.

181. M. H. Abrams, *Natural Supernaturalism* (New York: W. W. Norton: 1973).

182. Percy Bysshe Shelley, *Selected Poetry and Prose* (New York: Rinehart, 1956), 228–31; John Keats, *Complete Poems and Selected Letters* (New York: The Modern Library, 2001), 236–38.

so naturally to that tradition that any claim to a serious or complete rupture ought to be greeted with skepticism.[183] Our modern heresies depart no further from the developed Christian Platonist tradition than did the Hellenistic schools—the stoics and epicureans, or the skeptics of the late Academy—from its early authorities. This is perhaps what gives to so much of modern thought, for the student of history, its quality of nauseating, impoverished, farcical repetition. It also gives us grounds for hope of a more genuine return. Just as the heresy of stoicism was eventually reintegrated to the tradition proper, by way of Plotinus, St. Augustine, and others, so have Kant and others been restored to the tradition, however insufficiently, by the work of such as Bernard Lonergan and Erich Voegelin. It is worth saying, in concluding this point, that I use the word heresy loosely. The six insights of the Christian Platonist tradition are not so much creedal propositions as first principles or predispositions that precede the development of fully demonstrable propositions.[184]

Picture Socrates in Fear

It is precisely because the West's six great insights see beyond mere propositions to the first principles of reality that they have proven so stable in their own right and fruitful for theological, philosophical, and artistic reflection during the last two millennia and more. Our experience indicates that the misunderstanding of them, or the loss of consciousness of them, does not mean they somehow cease to be relevant to our lives, but rather would suggest that they endure, and that human life simply goes on, impoverished by its forgetting.

In the *Symposium*, Socrates looks at his intoxicated, amorous, and rhetorical companions and intimates that however content they appear, however brilliant they may think themselves, their deepest longing is for the eternal beauty that alone makes for happiness. In our age of relative political freedom, of comfort and pleasure readily facilitated by the tech-

183. There is an "exegetical" character to western thought, in which every new thought emerges consciously as a commentary on one already established (McGinn, 3). This is not merely a trait of, say, Scholasticism with its highly developed discipline of the commentary, but of the West as a whole. See Rémi Brague, *Eccentric Culture: A Theory of Western Civilization*, trans. Samuel Lester (South Bend, Ind.: St. Augustine's Press, 2002).

184. Dupré speaks of this in terms of a "primitive intuition" in *Passage to Modernity*, 18.

nology that methodical reason has made possible, of a modern state that tests our water for pollutants, our banks for credit-worthiness, and our children for scoliosis, we may well wonder what the use is of some reborn Socrates introducing old gods. The new gods of the city suit us just fine, we think. Leave well enough alone.

Rather than taking this account of the Christian Platonist tradition as a vain attempt to rehash the part of a Socratic disturber of this sort of peace, it may be worthwhile to turn for a moment to an often overlooked portrait of Socrates. In the *Euthyphro*, Plato depicts the philosopher in the central marketplace of Athens. He is on his way to answer charges of impiety before the magistrates; and we readers of the *Apology* know that he will be convicted of these charges and condemned to death. On the way to this fateful rendezvous, he meets Euthyphro, who is just now returning from leveling roughly the same charge against his father.

Socrates has been accused of impiety. He sees that Euthyphro has just accused his own father of that crime (to wit, murder), and, not wishing to be similarly condemned, he says he desires to become as pious as Euthyphro. Therefore, Socrates asks the young man, "what is the pious"?[185] Surely he must know, or he would not have accused his own kin of failing in it, and Euthyphro claims to know indeed. "What is dear to the gods is pious" he says, "and what is not is impious."[186] Socrates pursues the question. Do the gods hold all the same things as dear? No. Then how do we determine what we should do to please them?[187] Euthyphro is not forthcoming, and so Socrates proceeds with the usual examination, inquiring from every angle; and yet he gets nowhere, and grows more and more anxious as each of his questions fails to coax Euthyphro to offer a satisfactory definition of piety. The "pious is what all the gods love," he offers, but then does not reveal what they love.[188] If we could just learn, Socrates thinks, whether something is pious because it is loved by the gods or loved by the gods because it is pious, we might find a beachhead. But, he complains, "you did not wish to make [piety's] nature clear to me."[189]

Socrates's life is on the line; he cannot let the subject drop. And so, he pursues it by still other angles, until he believes he has found one that

---

185. Plato, *Euthyphro*, 5d.   186. Plato, *Euthyphro*, 7a.
187. Plato, *Euthyphro*, 7e.   188. Plato, *Euthyphro*, 9e.
189. Plato, *Euthyphro*, 11b.

will allow Euthyphro to give him a final answer. "Tell me then, by Zeus," he begs, what is the final cause of our piety, of our service to the gods? If we just knew what purpose piety served, we would have at last a grip on its nature. Euthyphro replies—with a glib smile, I imagine—"Many fine things, Socrates."[190]

Many fine things, indeed. Plato's dialogues are known for their irony and humor. But when I read this dialogue, knowing Socrates's fate; when I hear these opaque words of young Euthyphro; when I read of Socrates again taking up the mantle and trying, once more, to get a straight answer from a self-righteous parricide; and when, finally, I hear Euthyphro excuse himself because he has somewhere else to go, and the dialogue abruptly ends, I do not picture Plato laughing, or Socrates satisfied that he has shown that the chief difference between himself and the young traitor is between one who knows nothing and is unaware of that fact, and one who knows he knows nothing and so seeks the truth.[191]

Rather, I picture Socrates in fear, scared, eyes searching the back of Euthyphro as he fades down the dusty road—a bit like the Samaritan woman at the well, or a middle-aged Dante lost in a dark wood, the howl of animals in the shadows behind him. I picture him not as a philosopher, but as a person like all of us, as one who is not always certain what lies beneath one's feet. We look at the world around ourselves, and we know that we need to know the truth. We sense that our lives depend upon it. But the world rushes in so readily to tell us "many fine things," that we begin to think, before we hear a true word, *we may just die.*

To return to the great insights of the Christian Platonist tradition is not an act of backward piety. I do not know that there is anything pious about it except insofar as it was pious of Socrates to summon his fellow citizens to pursue the love of wisdom. I think of it, rather, as an act of survival. Those six insights help us to pin down the map of reality against the raging winds, so that we may begin to examine it, and to make our way across it. They have proven, as much as anything may be proven, the means by which we may not lose our lives but save them, so that our minds and our hearts may make a course and home in on happiness.

190. Plato, *Euthyphro*, 13e.
191. Plato, *Symposium*, 173d.

PART II

ART,
BEING,
AND
BEAUTY

THREE

We Must Retranslate *Kalon*

Even before the elections in November 2008, particularly astute conservatives had lamented that many of the supposed victories for their cause were in truth nothing to celebrate. In the years since, the volume of this lament has grown to the point of becoming audible within the main corridors of contemporary political debate. Most of these persons were "paleo" or traditional conservatives, who saw in the George W. Bush administration little that was genuinely conservative and much that testified to the further usurpation of the word "conservative," and of the Republican Party, by a neo-conservative agenda.[1] That agenda was largely repugnant to those who believed in local and limited government founded on enduring cultural traditions, stable and self-sustaining communities, and, above all, the Christian intellectual legacy that informs all things by means of faith and reason. They, naturally, saw even less to admire in the candidacy of John McCain. But the traditional and neo-conservative animus was not then and is not now reducible to competing definitions of "conservative" or even to competing public policy platforms.

When, at the 1992 Republican National Convention, Patrick Buchanan, that arch-paleo-conservative, railed that America was locked in a culture war, his observation was perspicuous but generally understood in unhelpful ways. The media and even most admirers of Buchanan drew the

---

1. While examples of this are legion in the periodicals, a good post-election example is Tom Pauken, *Bringing America Home* (Rockford, Ill.: Chronicles Press, 2010).

113

lines in that war between an abstract conservative theory of culture on the one hand and those who actually "manufacture" culture in our society, the culture industry located mostly in Hollywood and New York City. As such, the culture war appeared to be little more than disgruntlement of the heartland against the coasts, of consumers against retailers, of passive recipients against makers, or, at best, arm chair theorists against commercially successful practitioners, the categories of whose success went undisputed.

The conservatives generally did not attack the conceptions of art that modern artists and the culture industry maintained, but couched their anger in terms of what, to the artists and industry, appeared extrinsic matters—for example, they protested against certain features of content from nudity and vulgarity to blasphemy, without accounting either for why, first, so much of this offensive material enjoyed commercial and critical success or for how, second, that content related, or failed to relate, to a thorough-going vision of the nature of the fine arts. Sometimes, conservatives opposed Andres Serranos and Robert Mapplethorpe's photography with Allen Bloom's *The Closing of the American Mind* and William Bennett's *The Book of Virtues*.[2] But they seldom read the books they championed and it seems not to have occurred to them they might just take better pictures on their own. Instead, conservatives let the walls hang bare—or covered them with banal abstract oil painting, the radical art of a past age that never so much shocked as flattered.

Needless to say, not all critics of contemporary art and mass culture were so visceral and limited in their jeremiads. From the beginning of the "New Conservative" movement in the 1950s, a substantial number of thinkers have orbited about the conservative discontent with contemporary artistic practices and standards in variously tight and wide circles. They *did* write novels; they *did* start little magazines of art and culture. But they also have always been kept at a distance from those who form opinion and policy in mainstream conservative circles. Just since 2008, conservative philosophers and journalists Patrick Deneen, Rod Dreher, and Jeremy Beer have been prominent among those who observed that the supposed conservative revolution of the last thirty years foundered

---

2. See Claes G. Ryn, "Allan Bloom and Straussian Alienation," *Humanitas* 25, no. 1–2 (2012): 5–19.

largely because it focused exclusively on party politics and institutional power at the expense of a broader intellectual program.[3] Whatever Reagan Republicans were doing in Washington, they largely left the culture industry to form and reform American consciousness.

So wide was this chasm between institutional success and cultural formation, that most of the children raised in the age of Republican ascendency have arrived at adulthood with, perhaps, their explicit political principles informed by a vague belief in free markets and low taxes, but with their imaginations and sensibilities entirely formed on the mass cultural excretions of music, film, and television—and their cultural politics in turn molded by that sensibility. To offer just one consequence of this, most persons in their early twenties cannot conceive of why one would oppose the legal codification of homosexual unions, because, in their moral imaginations, a free and expressive sexuality is a continuous presence taken for granted and an "individual right." Their music palpitates sex and their narratives have promiscuous misadventures as the chief element of plot—and none of this strikes them as having anything at all to do with the removed realm of the political. Rather, it belongs to the private realm of personal freedom and self-creation. To make matters worse, our civilization as a whole has chosen to pretend that politics is not merely the extension of ethics to the broader social structure. We ignore, in consequence, the formative role law plays on moral character. And so, the young come to identify legal with moral permissiveness without quite recognizing it, and their moral antinomianism leads, in turn, to a legal one.

Deneen's keenest arguments have testified to the organic nature of culture and insist, therefore, that Republican obsessions with electoral and legislative victories not only blinded conservatives to their intellectual and emotional foundations but mutilated their arguments.[4] And Beer has noted that matters might have been different had conservatives worried less about success in Washington and entered more into the practice of transforming the culture from within.[5] Had there been fewer bureaucrats at the FCC and lobbyists decrying blasphemous art, and more talented

3. See Rod Dreher, *Crunchy Cons* (New York: Crown Forum, 2006).

4. See, for example, Patrick J. Deneen, "Counterfeiting Conservatism," *The American Conservative* 9, no. 4 (April 2010): 16–18.

5. Jeremy Beer, "By the Book," *The American Conservative* 8, no. 9 (May 4, 2009): 19–20.

conservatives starting production companies or writing good books and poems, had there been more organizations like the Wedgwood Circle (and had it been founded much sooner), our present climate might look considerably different, more decorous and more flourishing. Politics, as they say, lies downstream from culture. Instead, an aging cohort of Reaganites chant and re-chant their political principles while even their children find such slogans—and even such sound ideas—unintelligible, because increasingly disconnected from a complete way of life. We now bear witness to what some have diagnosed as the William F. Buckley Jr. problem: sharp, sardonic, and refined argument cannot long stand athwart the Jacobin transformations of history, when such bearers of conservative wit leave to their enemies the writing of a culture's stories and the shaping of its tastes.

This belated awakening to the need to cultivate and inform a culture rather than merely rail against its malformations does not tell the whole story, of course. Some few persons have found a foothold in the higher precincts of culture, where they have at least provided a critical voice for compelling conservative judgment of the arts and a forum for new work of true value. One thinks above all of Hilton Kramer and Roger Kimball's *The New Criterion*; their magazine has done as much to promote new, good art and to excoriate the bad as one can by means of a confident hauteur and astringent sensibility. Nevertheless, the greater achievement of that periodical has been critical rather than cultivating; the new writer one discovers in its pages is more likely to be a forgotten great than an inchoate unknown, and the journal's standards remain overly (not to say exclusively) beholden to the canons of high British modernism. Of even greater creative import, Gregory Wolf's *Image* magazine has, in an appropriately meek way, sought to rekindle in contemporary art and letters a sense of the transcendental nature of Beauty and the particular vocation of the Christian artist in an ostensibly post-Christian world. I might mention also the high achievement of promoting good work in the plastic arts done by the *American Arts Quarterly*, and the new poems that appear in *First Things*, and in such poetry journals as *The Hudson Review*, *Measure*, and *The Formalist* (now defunct). These have all provided substantial forums for good work for that smallest of contemporary audiences—those who still believe that the fine arts are fine because they are the arts of the beautiful.

The mention of poetry perhaps suffices to indicate how restricted these nonetheless important successes have been in the reconstitution of a conservative sensibility and the generation of "conservative" fine arts; it also suggests how impossible it would be simply to re-channel conservatives' previously intense focus on institutional politics to the diffuse and broad cultural landscape. None of these few good efforts has penetrated the major centers of the cinematic arts. And, while it is the case that the art of the spectacle that necessarily governs television and film needs to be displaced as the *primary* living art form of our culture, it is also true that these forms are bound to remain *central* for the generations to come. Thus, while it may not be impossibly hard to achieve a reformation of literature on conservative principles, it will be infinitely more difficult to effect a cultural sea change in an age driven by a capital-intensive, highly profitable film and television industry.

The controversy a few years ago over Mel Gibson's *The Passion of Christ* was outrageous for a number of reasons, among them that the film was ambiguous on several theological questions and as a work of art; but none of those more vital, critical questions could be raised for sustained discussion because of the shrill voices of secular identity politics which are even more deaf to questions of art and beauty than are the most dogged conservative party hacks. I mention that film and the ridiculous frolic of denunciations it received only to suggest that the real practical task for conservatives concerned with the arts would be the extension of good art outside of certain small intellectual circles in New York and the only slightly larger circles that have formed on provincial college campuses such as Sewanee, West Chester University, and the University of Evansville, where at least some good new fiction and poetry sees the light of day.

Everywhere conservatives have access to the public realm, they ought to be working for the creation of a new, or rather, regenerated practice of the fine arts as they do for the more typical partisan causes; this includes, of course, the conventional political action in education policy and school boards, but especially means cultivating more serious attention to resurrecting high and popular arts in our daily lives. The difficulties posed to any such project are forbidding—quite apart from the present lack of resources, venues, or audiences for good art and literature and the almost astronomical timeframe required by a cultural politics that seeks conversions of heart rather than changes in officeholders.

I have long since noted that the conservative sensibility that found a voice in the culture war and continues to speak against the decline of humanities education in the college classroom is beholden to a particular aesthetic, one that I would call a "politicized aesthetic." Because a similar term, "political aesthetics," is already in common usage among social theorists, I shall have to outline carefully how I differentiate it from the phrase just introduced. Political aesthetics *per se* indicates the fluid relation between, on the one hand, the forms of political arguments, of politicians and political programs, ideas, events, and characters, and, on the other, the formal principles of art and beauty. When one speaks of political aesthetics, one primarily intends that politics is not merely a matter of dialectical argument, nor even a matter of the beauty consonant with rhetorical persuasion or other superficies; rather, the whole enterprise, like the whole of reality, has a *form* and therefore is somehow bound up with and perhaps even comprehensible in terms of beauty. In the next chapter, I shall return to the claim I made above that proposes conservatism as just that body of thought that sees in politics an inextricable relation between aesthetic form and ideas, wherein the measure of sound ideas is to be found in their conformity to Beauty. But when I say that conservatives have tended to sympathize with a politicized aesthetic I mean something that is, to my mind, entirely admirable but of less philosophical scope and which, finally, poses a problem.

Let me approach the concept anecdotally. Years ago, I matriculated into a Masters of Fine Arts program in poetry writing. My ambitions were fourfold: to find time to write, relieved of the demands of a fulltime career; nonetheless to be able to subsist by teaching courses on a rural university campus; to take graduate courses in literature, anticipating my eventual departure for a doctoral program in literature; and, finally, to commune with other young aspirant poets.

The last goal was the one least satisfactorily met. Aside from having no particular interest in or potential for the intellectual life, my classmates were generally engaged in the composing of what I thought to be trash—not merely in execution, but in *theoria*, in formal principles. Their work consisted chiefly of brief effusions of juxtaposed images plastered on the page with no attention either to meaning or rhythm. Their chief impact on my own work was to inspire me to write satires on theirs. As years passed, the prominence of disjointed, fragmentary, deliberately ugly and unintelligible poetry in literary magazines convinced me that my classmates had pursued the dominant conventions of our day and that there was very little positive I could learn for my art from the vast majority of other writers then publishing.[6] Nonetheless, I appreciated that such a creative writing program had its uses, for it exposed me to what I instinctively loathed, giving me opportunity to formulate counter principles. When I left after two years with a degree that seemed more *memento mori* than honor earned, I nonetheless felt that I had apprenticed myself in writing by engaging my contemporaries in a meaningful manner.

While on vacation after my first year in the program, I met a bright young conservative undergraduate. When he learned that I was a Master's student in the writing of poetry, he remarked on the spot, "Oh, so you all read Hesiod and Horace!" He said this with such envy and relish that I only reluctantly disabused him. Very little of the reading required in the program involved things written more than a few years previous, and, strangely, that meant very few of the students in the program knew how to write anything but tattered words trickling in unpredictable streaks down the page—a practice that, could they only have known it, they inherited from the surrealists with none of the interesting if naïve theories by which the surrealists had justified their practice. David Yezzi of the *New Criterion* was correct to diagnose these ignorant heirs of surrealism as mere "unrealists."[7] Having noted the dogged presentism and indifference to craft in the program, I reported to this undergraduate that I *had* actually been spending my days reading and rereading the Elizabethan and Jacobean drama and lyric poems, and so benefitted in my own writing from the extended contemplation of a properly English classical period, rather than the Greco-Roman one the very thought of which sent my friend careening toward the vastness of the sublime. What troubled me in his expression, however, was the evident confusion regarding what it might mean to study writing as a craft, to write great literature rather than to caress its gold-stamped leather spine.

6. Diagnosing and moving us beyond such species of contemporary poetry is the central purpose of my book, *The Fortunes of Poetry in an Age of Unmaking* (Bismarck, N.D.: Wiseblood Books, 2015).

7. David Yezzi, "The Unrealists' Return," *The New Criterion* 24, no. 8 (April 2006): 24–27.

It is, again, the fit of joy this friend experienced that I want to scrutinize, for I think it representative of something typical of conservative arguments about culture in general—something good in itself, but also restricted and inadequate. Conservatives in our age, if they have any intellectual calling, have tended toward law and the social sciences, particularly—as might seem appropriate—political theory and history. As such, while they often have a profound enthusiasm for certain works of literature and great art, their tastes tend to be informed not only by their *a priori* political commitments, which can be a good thing, but by their commitment to the explicitly political as well. This can prove stifling. The catalog of favorites tends to begin with the political allegories of George Orwell, swiftly skips back to the historical romances of Sir Walter Scott, and then plummets into the sublime and ennobling depths of Shakespeare so long as he is telling us about a Caesar or a General, before plunging, at last, into the classical world. *Homer! Hesiod! Virgilio mio!* More generally, one hears the rich-toned deference and reverence at the mere issuance of the phrase, "Great Books." One sometimes suspects that in praising the *Aeneid* they are really just dreaming of its vision of how a good empire might look.

I do not mock this sensibility; I am its willing vassal as much as anyone. But we need to understand its source and its shape if we are to see not only that it remains incomplete but that it can provide only narrow foundations for the revival of the arts in a fashion amenable to the other great principles conservatives share.

In brief, this is a politicized aesthetic: the reverence and deference conservatives naturally and rightly feel for inherited institutions and the legacies and traditions of their forefathers applied—not thoughtlessly but secondarily—to works that have accrued a triad of characteristics. First, their content is immediately comprehensible in terms of ethics; while Homer's is not a bald didacticism, one must truly be numb not to experience a kind of moral fear and awe when confronted with a full vision of the noble virtues of Achilles. Such is also the case with the piety of Aeneas, which may have been a subject of scrutiny for Virgil but takes on a glorious simplicity in the minds of many of his readers. I would not argue that conservatives tend to admire only artworks with patent ethical content, as if they could skip over questions of beauty or artistic achievement entirely in the rush to celebrate the stirring moral. Rather, they admire a real beauty in the moral, but, as I shall elaborate, conservatives tend to venerate only *one form* of moral beauty.

Second, much literature before the age of the novel gave absolute primacy to both public life and public virtues. As such, the classical authors remain keenly attractive to those already by nature inclined to attend to the explicit prescriptions of public and social life to the neglect of the obscure subtleties of the "private sphere." Conservatives often appreciate the poetry of action and grow impatient with the interior dynamics of the psyche (which, Roy Campbell's poetry suggests, they attend to chiefly as an object of satire). If a work is Christian, conservatives seem to appreciate it more if it is "religious" rather than theological; if I may risk obscurity, they consistently prefer the allegorical to the ontological.

Sir Walter Scott's romances are but scarcely novels in the modern sense, but are prose narratives that anticipate the techniques of the novel while retaining many conventions of classical epic and history. And, of course, Orwell's two best fictions were intended neither to be conservative nor to be novels at all. That his sensibility tended to exploit the genres of the fable and dystopian fantasy suggests that it was in a key way alienated from an age that loved the interiority of the novel—and his alienation is something in which his conservative readers share. They appreciate such works not merely because they are ethical in content, but because they are concerned with public action, with external or social forms, in much the same way that political theory or the other social sciences generally are.

Third, in their own right and by dint of venerability, the kinds of works conservatives tend to cherish are, in several senses, Great Books. That is, they have in themselves and in their dusty gold-edged pages the attributes of the noble and the great. Here lies, I think, the decisive feature of the conservative politicized aesthetic: a somewhat narrow sensitivity to only that kind of beauty that merges with what the classical tradition called the sublime, and whose style was called the noble or the grand.

This identification of nobility with beauty—or rather, the making of nobility into the particular kind of beauty conservatives can appreciate—has itself a noble history. Aristotle, in the *Rhetoric*, says, "The noble is that which is both desirable for its own sake and also worthy of praise; or that which is both good and also pleasant because good. If this is the noble, it follows that excellence [virtue] must be noble, since it is both a good thing and also praiseworthy."[8] In his usual fashion, Aristotle insists that what is good in itself is at once useful and pleasant, and holds forth virtue as a leading example. One attempts to be virtuous because the practice of virtue is itself good, but it will also lead to a good end beyond itself (fruitfulness) and the actor will take pleasure in the activity. But the "for its own sake" is comprised under the idea of "the noble." We can understand this, of course. Even in our day, one might be called noble for doing something one need not do (for use or one's pleasure), but which we can see one nonetheless ought to do. We associate the word with the bow of grace to duty and service and with the submission of strength and greatness to a law above themselves. Nobility is a peculiarly attractive sort of goodness.

"Noble," however, is not the best available translation of Aristotle's word, and it has the effect of concealing something central to Aristotle's argument. This makes it hard, in turn, for us to see why it should be the case that there is a form of goodness that is distinguished for its attractiveness. "Noble" serves here to translate the Greek *To Kalon*, the typical rendering of which, in other contexts, is given as "beauty." We might say that in rhetoric, the only art form that is intrinsically more public even than architecture, nobility bleeds into beauty. We might still better say that nobility characterizes the kind of beauty that is especially suited to rhetoric. If we remain unaware of this translation, we are left to think that the noble pertains only to the context of persuasive speech and the practice of virtue (ethics). But what Aristotle reveals to us with that crucial Platonic word *To Kalon* is the substantial identity between these things and beauty. Nobility clearly pertains to ethics insofar as the exercise of virtue is inherently noble; but nobility and virtue alike are caught up in the beautiful; beauty gives goodness its final justification.[9] So we see that Umberto Eco's *The Aesthetics of Thomas Aquinas* translates this passage as "The Beautiful is that which is both desirable for its own sake and also worthy of praise."[10] The Noble is at once an ethical and aesthetic category for reasons we discussed above: beauty is the ordering principle of reality, and so also orders the natural process of things toward their good. As Joe

8. Aristotle, *Rhetoric*, 1366a33–35.
9. See Balthasar, *The Glory of the Lord*, 1:19, and Aristotle, *Nicomachean Ethics*, 1168a.
10. Eco, *The Aesthetics of Thomas Aquinas*, 42.

Sachs has written of Aristotle's vision in general, the "true and the good stem from one source, and converge in the Beautiful."[11] The noble is good for its own sake, but this quality of being an end-in-itself becomes fully intelligible to us only when we see that goodness is convertible with, or, in Sachs's language, converges in the beautiful. "Why should I be good?," a child asks, and the parent stutters. But no one asks, "Why should I want to look at this beautiful thing?," because no one has to order one to do so. That which is good in itself, it must be understood, is finally good *for beauty's sake*. If you see a thing's beauty, you already desire to gaze upon it. And so, fundamentally the noble *is* the beautiful, but they are distinct in our experience. In consequence, some of us are more predisposed to the perception of the beauty of nobility than we are to beauty in general.

Conservatives verifiably have a particular appreciation for noble words, and the kinds of artworks they appreciate best tend, naturally, to be "Great Books"; that is to say, those kinds of literature that most obviously possess a nobility of spirit in virtue of the moral excellence, sublime scale, or venerable reverence with which they are associated. Such works remain valuable for that spirit even should they lack nearly all the other species of the beautiful or attributes proper to the fine arts. This limitation in taste became, in our age, a limitation in argumentation. Those to whom the suave prose of the *National Review* in its glory days delivered a certain tremor felt their aesthetic sensibilities satisfied and may not even have realized that there is more to art and beauty than noble rhetoric.

Complacent with rhetoric, they ignored *poiesis*, the making of plots. By this, I do not mean conservatives were indifferent to narrative and story. On the contrary, they have shown themselves admirably enamored of the essential stories of our civilization at a time when the Left is signified chiefly by its hatred, terror, manipulation, and silencing of the past. As I shall argue in Part III, narrative is foundational to the fine arts and above all to the practice of reason, and so a thorough "indifference" to stories would be impossible in any case. But admiring noble stories told and presupposing them in the practice of rhetoric are both distinct from the actual telling of stories. Conservatives sometimes seem to rely on the broad strokes of a plot grown so familiar to them as no longer to require the telling.

11. Joe Sachs, Introduction to *Nicomachean Ethics*, by Aristotle, trans. Joe Sachs (Newburyport, Mass.: Focus Editions, 2002), xxv.

More to the point, someone who venerates the great and noble comes to do so in virtue of his having taken some path, having lived some story of his own; while habit, instinct, or intuition certainly play a role in one's coming to admire greatness, that is not the whole story, and such admiration is neither irrational nor incommunicable. But it has been treated as such, and so conservatives have frequently proved negligent in telling the stories that show the fusion of reason and habituation. They appeal to tradition without keeping in currency the story that constituted the tradition in the first place. Nobility may be self-evident in itself, but it is not self-evident to most persons, whose senses and sensibilities must be refined by long experience and discipline. And so, if you want others to venerate what you venerate, you must, at the least, equip them to do so by means of narrative. If you would do this, you must enter into the arts.

As we shall consider below, because Mnemosyne is the mother of the muses, the recollecting of memories, the making of plots, is *the* activity in which all art forms engage (even music, despite superficial appearances to the contrary). Conservatives have proven themselves connoisseurs and conservators of the great stories on which a flourishing human culture depends, but in their veneration of the Great they have often been better at admiring the verdigris than penetrating to the substance. They have admired the beauty of only those artworks that seem most readily translatable into the language of politics and morality, and have left neglected both the more difficult beauties of the fine arts and the more accessible beauties attainable in popular arts and mass culture. They have thus been derelict in their duty to sow in our culture new stories, new works, new images that could inspire the young, deepen the mature, and challenge the perverse as Rilke tells us the Belvedere Torso should challenge us all.

Policy prescriptions can help a society to some extent, but what we always and ever need are instances of made beauty to fortify our culture with the resources it needs to render every facet of it more human and more humane. Our age in particular needs to recover *not only* what Burke called the moral imagination, but indeed *all* the precincts of memory, understanding, and will, which depend upon not only nobility but Beauty writ large. We must retranslate *Kalon*.

FOUR

Style and Truth

CONSERVATISM AS LITERARY

MOVEMENT

In the Anglo-American tradition, conservative thought was born of beauty, particularly literary beauty. If conservatism is a movement, it is first a literary one. By this, I do not refer to Dr. Johnson and Dean Swift, who, along with many other great men of letters of the eighteenth century, were Tories—a detail that may help explain the essentially backward look of satire in that or any period, but does not in itself forge a necessary link between the Tory cause and literature. Rather, I refer to that moment when Tory thought was transformed and diluted into a new compound called conservatism: that moment, in the furnace of the French Revolution, when Edmund Burke set down his *Reflections*. While I was able to indicate the importance of this fact in the Introduction, I should like now to return to its context to provide a richer sense of conservatism's aesthetic pedigree. I hope it will suggest how surprising it should be that contemporary conservatism seems so merely political while also offering some direction as to how all persons, whatever their political sympathies, might recover the rich conception of beauty discussed in Part I.

The ideologues of the age attacked Burke's arguments directly and indirectly, countering his claims, but above all deprecating the very style by which he set them forth. What he said was beautiful, they granted, but such beauty concealed a thousand vices, as Burke himself confessed. Mary Wollstonecraft above all would reply that Burke's argument against the Revolution and the demolition of French state, custom, tradition, religion, and society was founded on sensibility: on appeals to sensations of the sublime and the beautiful, rather than to reason. In her acerbic first volley, Wollstonecraft condescends, or rather con-ascends to the ether of which she believes Burke's arguments to be compounded. She informs Burke that

> it is natural to conclude, that all your pretty flights arise from your pampered sensibility; and that, vain of this fancied preeminence of organs, you foster every emotion till the fumes, mounting to your brain, dispel the sober suggestions of reason. It is not in this view surprising, that when you should argue you become impassioned, and that reflection inflames your imagination, instead of enlightening your understanding.[1]

With this call for sobriety, she invites them both to quit "now the flowers of rhetoric[;] let us, Sir, reason together."[2] If reasoning entails the presentation of arguments, Wollstonecraft has already carried the day, not because Burke's *Reflections* lacks for clear, specific—indeed, up to that time, unsurpassed factual—argument, but because Wollstonecraft has presumptuously denied their identity as such. Whatever their content, Burke's remarks may be swept aside as pretty flowers and stage theatrics, so that only her voice remains. It does not matter that she proceeds to declaim a theory of liberty that Burke had already dismissed as impractical abstraction and "political metaphysics," as unreal and irrelevant in their thin ugliness as she claims his words are in vaporous beauty. Burke had called the revolutionaries rationalistic barbarians; Wollstonecraft accuses Burke of being a sentimental poet puffed with sensibility. His appeals to beauty, and the exaggerated beauty of his prose Wollstonecraft takes as damning proof that what he says cannot be true.

We could say much in support of Wollstonecraft's more specific arguments, though it seems her pretending her arguments were rational while Burke's were not (hers founded on reason while his are founded on the preening unrealities of the aesthetic) is at once the central and weakest

---

1. Mary Wollstonecraft, *A Vindication of the Rights of Men and A Vindication of the Rights of Woman*, ed. Sylvana Tomaselli (Cambridge: Cambridge University Press, 1995), 6–7.

2. Wollstonecraft, *A Vindication*, 7.

claim in her *Vindication of the Rights of Men*. She accuses Burke of beautifully defending forms of gratuitous beauty—the vanities of estate, throne, and court—while ignoring the plight of the expropriated peasantry; Burke, who gives us the prototypical defense of an organic culture and society flourishing under the same conditions as would an oak tree, may seem in fact to be defending pleasure gardens rather than hamlets plotted with the rolling, irregular lines of peasant free holds, those small productive farms producing the necessities of country and the materials of familial and communal happiness.[3]

Wollstonecraft may have been right.[4] If we could truly identify Burke's defense of polity—as founded on an organic culture finding its way through historical challenges by means of a deep fidelity to tradition—with the interests of a narrow Whig oligarchy whose ascent was secured in 1688, then he has passed off as the common good a mere class interest. I am not sure such an identity is as obvious as she suggests; more probably, Burke's theory of state and constitution provides us a familial theory of the premodern society even more reflective of actual western practice than was Aristotle's *Politics* reflective of the Greek polis. Burke tells us how societies work and must work, while Wollstonecraft and her liberal contemporaries fumed rationalizing theories whose imposition by force inaugurated a new politics of alienation and destruction. But, if the argument I hope to provide fully in the next several chapters is correct, we might more justly say that Burke did not ignore reason in favor of beauty, but that he attended to only one form, or part of the form, of the wounded macrocosmic beauty of European society. That, in ignoring the deformations of a society produced by enclosures, urbanization, and the ensuing expropriation of the great agricultural masses—deformations to which Wollstonecraft nobly draws our attention—Burke was *inadequately* attentive to the beauty of social and political forms, rather than overly so and to the exclusion of reason.

I begin with this observation regarding the partial justice of Wollstonecraft's criticisms of Burke in hopes of hinting that a worthy defense of art and beauty will be one that succeeds in articulating the importance of those things in their own right, but that also demonstrates the organic relation, indeed the *metaphysical identity*, between the beauty that the

3. Wollstonecraft, *A Vindication*, 60.
4. Kirk, *The Conservative Mind*, 21–22.

fine arts make visible to us and the questions of the Good to which ethics, politics, and theology always refer. Burke was in principle aware of
this—but Wollstonecraft suggests he may have ignored matters that his
own theory of government should have condemned. But my particular
interest here is to show that the appreciation of this identity quite specifically characterizes the aboriginal expression of conservative thought
and has been its constant refrain during the last two centuries: so much so
that conservatism, insofar as it may be deemed a movement, has been primarily an artistic and critical rather than institutional-political one. The
perceptions of discursive reason and the perceptions of beauty may be distinct in means, but they are one in faculty and one in end: they both are
seated in the intellect and converge in being. This is the primordial insight
that bucked conservatism into existence and the perennial blindness that
has defined liberalism from the eighteenth century to the present. It is the
insight that led to the word "culture" becoming a ubiquitous category of
modern social and political debate—even as the prevalence of this word
has, historically, also been the chief means by which conservative thought
has persisted doggedly only *at the margins* during the long rise of the liberal state and administered society to the domination it enjoys today.

Let us, then, take the lachrymose and florid exchange between Burke
and Wollstonecraft of two centuries past as the moment in which the
idea of "conservatism" was born. We see that, by nature of the occasion
and the subject, it was a political birth. But, in view of the defense Burke
made of an organic and yet "artificial" social order founded on the forms
of natural beauty and, further, the arguments he made for ethical truth
as a reality discovered by means of dramatic action (theater) rather than
dispassionate, "metaphysical" logic, we may justly say that Burke's position presupposed an identity between all true thought, good politics, and
real beauty—this, as we shall see, despite the overall inadequacy of the
aesthetic theory of Burke's youth. In contrast, Wollstonecraft's response
was founded primarily on the competing assumption, one which has been
central to the liberal spirit, that a politics founded on beauty is not natural
but artificial—in the sense of "false"—and so, like the fine arts, is of limited function and value. Very well, she suggests, that the beauty of art appeal to the sensibility; but when it seeks to impose itself beyond that circumscribed field some kind of mystification occurs. Reason's sovereignty

is violated by sensibility's dreams. The tradition Burke initiated therefore affirms the claims of the beautiful on our quotidian lives, while the liberal tradition whose provocations precede it, stirred it to life, and which nonetheless was still coming into being years after Burke's death, would try to dismiss conservatism as a "mere aestheticism," a literary affectation utterly anodyne were it not for its all-too-aesthetic appeals for the legitimacy of past or threatened social and political forms.

Misguided though the dismissal Wollstonecraft attempted may have been, it confirmed the association between the political and beauty Burke himself had articulated, and it inadvertently prophesied the form the conservative tradition would take in the hands of its major exponents in the coming two centuries. Conservatism has been, from its beginnings, something of a literary movement. That has been the basis on which it has been alternately ignored, absorbed, or attacked. The conservatism of the later Wordsworth and Coleridge would be attacked by the younger literati of their day. But its deep structures would become foundational for Romantic thought, as would many of their ideas be absorbed into the liberal intellectual culture of subsequent generations. Taken straight, the critique of modern society by Wordsworth and Coleridge elaborates on the genius of Burke to offer a damning indictment of industrialization, urbanization, rationalism, and the soul-killing leveling of mass society. It was not taken straight however; it was cut with saccharin, and their wisdom about the "secret ministry of frost" preaching to the spiritually vital dwellers in the countryside would be melted to wistful sentiment and flow smoothly with the liberal and industrial drift of English society in particular and western society more generally.[5] Conservatism almost from the beginning, that is, from Burke to Coleridge, could be attacked directly, but such was its appeal that its critics would tend to absorb its aesthetic dimensions, patronizing them, and thus at once preserving and marginalizing them within the society it tried to stand athwart.

Shelley's sonnet "To Wordsworth" offers an admiring valediction, praising the older poet's past achievement, which includes its elegies for things lost, while denying the political implications of that achievement. Wordsworth's art undoes itself—or its age and admirers—at just that mo-

5. Coleridge, *Major Works*, 89.

ment when it suggests that the destructiveness of modernity might be addressed not only with beautiful lamentation but also with political argument. For some, this might seem like integrity, but Shelley preserves in amber the Wordsworth he likes by deeming it a betrayal. He cries,

> Poet of Nature, thou hast wept to know
> That things depart which never may return:
> Childhood and youth, friendship, and love's first glow,
> Have fled like sweet dreams, leaving thee to mourn.
> These common woes I feel. One loss is mine
> Which thou too feel'st, yet I alone deplore.
> Thou wert as a lone star whose light did shine
> On some frail bark in winter's midnight roar:
> Thou hast like to a rock-built refuge stood
> Above the blind and battling multitude:
> In honoured poverty thy voice did weave
> Songs consecrate to truth and liberty.
> Deserting these, thou leavest me to grieve,
> Thus having been, that thou shouldst cease to be.[6]

Wordsworth has wept for good things lost, and this, for Shelley, is admirable. Further, he had worked in "honored poverty" to praise "truth and liberty," but for seeing the poor life of the rural peasantry as a reality best honored, preserved, and even restored by a return to tradition, Wordsworth is accused of negating his own essential self. Shelley writes off Wordsworth's development as just the opposite, as a desertion and a death-in-life. Liberalism was prepared to venerate the beautiful traditions it had undermined so long as these things were safely exiting stage-right. Should they turn back around, they lost their charm and came to appear as irrational manias.

William Hazlitt, that exemplary English liberal and hagiographer of Napoleon, would perform a similar valediction of "absorb and dismiss" on Coleridge and Sir Walter Scott, admiring and appropriating their "cultural beauty," vertiginous ambition, and eloquence while deprecating the political visions that inspired them. His essay on Coleridge, for instance,

---

6. Percy Bysshe Shelley, *The Selected Prose and Poetry* (Ware, U.K.: Wordsworth Editions Limited, 2002), 120.

paints a picture of an imaginative mind and wholly admirable man, but one grown infirm by some spiritual malediction, so that he is left hobbling down a spiral staircase that disappears into the oubliette of the past:

> Mr. Coleridge has a "mind reflecting ages past;" his voice is like the echo of the congregated roar of the "dark rearward and abyss" of thought. He who has seen a mouldering tower by the side of a chrystal lake, hid by the mist, but glittering in the wave below, may conceive the dim, gleaming, uncertain intelligence of his eye: he who has marked the evening clouds uprolled (a world of vapours), has seen the picture of his mind, unearthly, unsubstantial, with gorgeous tints and ever-varying forms.... Our author's mind is (as he himself might express it) *tangential*.[7]

He can paint the beauty of such a mind safely only once it has been relegated to the museum. Hazlitt's essay proceeds to etherize Coleridge's ideas so that they remain at once imaginatively intoxicating and politically vaporous. Incapable of finding rest and concentration in any one idea, the claims of Coleridge's polymath genius are not to be taken seriously in themselves, and the man himself is to be explained away. His counter-revolutionary principles are to be indulged as the unhappy consequence of what an unjust and revolutionary age does to its most brilliant minds:

> It is not to be supposed that Mr. Coleridge could keep on at the rate he set off; he could not realize all he knew or thought, and less could not fix his desultory ambition; other stimulants supplied the place, and kept up the intoxicating dream, of his early impressions. Liberty (the philosopher's and the poet's bride) had fallen a victim, meanwhile, to the murderous practices of the hag, Legitimacy. Proscribed by court-hirelings, too romantic for the herd of vulgar politicians, our enthusiast stood at bay, and at last turned on the pivot of a subtle casuistry to the *unclean side*.[8]

Having too much integrity to become a servant of Legitimacy, as had Wordsworth and Robert Southey, Coleridge was confused but not corrupted by its claims—forced into the sort of mystical retreat already to be found in "France: An Ode" (1798). There was no good argument for Coleridge's position, Hazlitt indicates—only a Jesuitical "casuistry" that legitimates by subtlety what is patently immoral, and the poet testifies to this objective error within his subjective authenticity and genius by not

---

7. William Hazlitt, *The Spirit of the Age or Contemporary Portraits* (London: Henry Colburn, 1825), 58.

8. Hazlitt, *Spirit of the Age*, 68.

becoming a servant of the regime. Instead, he lapses into "vain imaginings, his lips idly moving, but his heart for ever still."[9] Coleridge's mute heart was still on the side of liberalism and liberty, suggests Hazlitt; his lips still form the words of poetry, but we cannot hear their content. Thus, the form of Coleridge's literary achievement remains, but with its political implications now silenced. But Hazlitt goes further in his apology. Coleridge's turn to the right is just one of many inevitable sorrows and sufferings of an age as corrupt as theirs:

Such is the fate of genius in our age, when in the unequal contest with sovereign wrong, every man is ground to powder who is not either a born slave, or who does not willingly and at once offer up the yearnings of humanity and the dictates of reason as a welcome sacrifice to besotted prejudices.[10]

One may be tempted to explain away Hazlitt's frequent recourse to pharmacological tropes in the essay as unsubtle suggestions regarding Coleridge's dissipations by the use of opium. But it is no less the case that Hazlitt deploys such language for therapeutic ends in a particularly modern sense. Coleridge's conservatism is a thing to be diagnosed as a social pathology: the symptom of an age, or rather of an age's disposal of a wayward and drifting genius. His thought, once become a malady to be treated, ceases to be an argument to be refuted. Just as Burke's words were deemed effete vapors of sentiment, so Coleridge's are dismissed as the suppressed moans of a fevered intelligence. The beauty of those words, so strongly attractive, is thus cut off from goodness and reason. They are rendered a kind of sublime pap to nourish the tastes of a liberal regime without otherwise affecting it.

Wollstonecraft's husband, the utilitarian William Godwin, would level a similar, but more anguished and erotic attack on Edmund Burke in his novel *Caleb Williams*.[11] There, a Burke-like nobleman is the paradigm of sensibility, of moral and aristocratic beauty—but persecutes and hunts the title character to the point of death with an irrational monomania. As many critics have observed, Godwin's attraction to Burke's genius seeps through the cracks of this otherwise unblemished and monotonous at-

9. Hazlitt, *Spirit of the Age*, 68.
10. Hazlitt, *Spirit of the Age*, 68–69.
11. William Godwin, *Caleb Williams* (London: Penguin, 2005).

tack on the abuses endemic to aristocratic society. Indeed, the writings of Hazlitt and Godwin collectively express a fear within the Anglophone liberal Protestant tradition that Diderot had also contemplated from within French Enlightenment liberalism: the world to which liberals were committed politically would be one true to Wollstonecraft's words, building a metaled wall between sensibility and reason, between goodness and beauty. That is, the world they fought to bring into being would prove one no longer worth imagining, no longer capable of giving aesthetic pleasure, of holding together by its own form rather than through the impositions of political force and continuous administration. The world of freedom they sought to bring into being was a great vacancy incapable in itself of eliciting our love however much it may unchain our lusts. To invoke another familiar image, liberalism was a *hortus siccus*, incapable of bearing fruit from its own seed; its fiercest advocates selectively rooted for and sought to transmute the fructifying waters of conservation and reaction that Burke, Wordsworth, and others came to represent. In this respect, conservatism in the post-Revolutionary world might better be described not as *a* literary movement but as the continued source of literary and aesthetic achievement in an age whose commitment to a defecated rationality left it dry. If liberalism could not have indulged in this emotional siphoning, these conservative figures would have been entirely vilified, marginalized, and forgotten. Such has been the fate of most conservative and reactionary thinkers whose work remains intractable for absorption into the pathological sentimentalities of liberalism.

We might reasonably attribute the multiple instantiations of authentic conservatism during the last two centuries to the occasional citizen who comes across and studies this absorbed, appropriated body of conservative thought and somehow sees—most likely, by a combination of good fortune, alienation from meritocratic tastes, and a predisposition to the noble and venerable—its complete form, its radical (as in, to the roots) meaning. So it was with the Oxford movement, rediscovering the ancient Church by way of the curious provocation of Wordsworth's poems. So it would be a century later, as agrarians, traditionalists, and orthodox Christians—from John Crowe Ransom, Caroline Gordon, William Faulkner, Allen Tate, and Robert Frost, to W. B. Yeats, T. S. Eliot, Wallace Stevens, Edith Sitwell, Christopher Dawson, and Graham Greene; from Cleanth

Brooks, Richard Weaver, and M. E. Bradford to Russell Kirk, Peter Stan-lis, and William F. Buckley—discovered the dry powder of conservatism tucked away in the base of the heaving, plodding windmill of modern liberal society. Such discovery comes as an explosion. But, because con-servative thought survived primarily as literary rather than political gun-powder, its blast only occasionally echoed beyond the ivory tower, literary salon, or front porch.

In the twentieth century, conservatism was generally dismissed as sum-marily as were Burke's appeals by Wollstonecraft. The southern agrarians, men of letters all, were lampooned as literary dreamers with only the silken threads of nostalgia tying them to the land. This doubt about the conserva-tive's seriousness seems inevitable. Liberalism's impoverished imagination leads it to take its vision of things as self-evident; departure from its or-thodoxies takes not only courage but a willingness to compromise when those orthodoxies have something good about them. John Crowe Ransom stood out as the ostensible leader of the Southern Agrarians when they published their symposium, *I'll Take My Stand*, in 1930. By 1945, he was singing the praises of Criticism, Inc. and the efficiency of the modern divi-sion of labor from his editorial office at Kenyon College. He went from uncompromising to capitulation in the space of a few years. Conservatism does not require any such dualistic absolutism, but when it seems to, it be-comes the easier to ignore. And, for every case like Ransom's, we may name others that testify to the sincerity and supra-literary or lived justification of conservative principles (Andrew Lytle, Ransom's friend, for instance, or Wendell Berry, his apotheosis). Even so, Buckley, Kirk, and, curiously, the conservative radio announcer, Alan Keyes, have all seen their arguments defanged nevertheless with the faint petting of being called "eloquent." There seems to be no occasion on which being praised as "well spoken" does not serve merely to excuse one's auditor from listening.

Only with the rise of Ronald Reagan did conservatism seem to stand up entirely from the writing desk to stretch its legs on the soap box or in the halls of state. This would prove an ironic victory as Reagan effected two transformations. He translated conservative sentiment to practical politics—primarily by unfolding the rhetoric of conservatism as a veil over what in fact was a pursuit of many of the same old liberal statist goals first essayed in the age of the French Revolution. So truly was this form of "literary" or rhetorical conservatism a veil lightly worn that few seemed to notice when Reagan changed the face beneath: without a pause for breath, the expansive optimism and destructive Jacobinism of Thomas Paine, and for that matter Mary Wollstonecraft, was issuing from the mouths of the leaders of the "conservative" revolution. How could the age of chivalry be dead if it was always Morning in America? Decades later, we could ask, How did a fidelity to "little platoons" comport with a regime of far flung bases and routine U.S. adventures abroad? Indeed, we may productively debate whether Reagan's policies were meaningfully conservative; some of them clearly were and some of them were only compatible with liberalism through prudence or the ambiguity that necessarily accompanies such much-used, little-understood, terms as conservative and liberal. But there can be no question that *rhetorically* he changed the substance of conservatism—and we can hardly take that as a mere semantic curiosity given the primarily literary character of the conservative tradition. So long without power, if we do not at least have words, we have only tears. And true conservatives weep today for the invasions wrought in their name.

Despite this perversion of conservative rhetoric as its apparent expositors seized real political power, Reagan and the success of politicians like him give us at least some grounds for hope. For, though many conservatives, Whittaker Chambers for instance, were pessimistic regarding the future of the West, Reagan confirmed what conservatives from Burke to Tate to Kirk always believed: there is a salutary populism, a potentially wide practical political appeal, to conservative thought that belies what, for the better part of two centuries, was taken as its merely literary, merely intellectual, vaguely aristocratic, pretensions. As G. K. Chesterton so often suggested, the "common sense" of the average person does not amount to the reductive materialist rationalism of Thomas Paine, but rather bespeaks a natural and general desire to live in a society whose ends transcend either individual material comfort or the uprooting and restructuring of society to conform to the bureaucratic logic of power, efficiency, and predictability. As Burke's *Reflections* propounded, political forms are prudent, limited, but ordered to the perfection of man, and man is ordered to an "eternal society," the divinization of eternal life in God. However much greed the decade of Reagan's leadership exhibited, it also suggested that two centuries of liberal statism and utilitarian rationalism had failed to kill the love or desire for the Good Itself native to the human person. For Reagan's appeal as a "Cold Warrior" stemmed from his willingness to speak in terms of good and evil, of our duties to God, and of the empty hungers of atheism. His words were appeals to beauty, specifically the beauty of the noble that, I have argued, tend to define the modern conservative, for good and for ill. If we are to reconnect his noble rhetoric with the profound insights of Burke and Eliot, we shall have to leave behind the terrain of party politics and head for the heights of the beautiful.

We must begin again to contemplate the foundations *not* of the conservative tradition but of culture as the social mediation—the works and forms—of our perception of the beautiful. The following chapters will do just that, taking three avenues. We begin with a reflection on the reading of Dante in an age of unreflective philosophical materialism to consider the way in which the arts of the beautiful can lead us beyond crass rationalism and therapeutic idealism through the power of the imagination, the openness and freedom of the *what if?* Imaginative beauty may be a pathway to a richer conception of truth and being, as many conservatives since Coleridge have proposed. However, even the radical left, for all its debts to the historical materialism of Karl Marx, can take beauty seriously. Indeed, it sometimes grasps the reality of beauty with bracing insight. And so, we shall consider the aesthetic theory of Theodor W. Adorno, whose reflections on mass culture have several affinities with conservative cultural criticism and whose theory of beauty helps reveal its spiritual and political importance. Dante can lead the imagination to contemplate truth and beauty in terms of being. Adorno's aesthetics instances an anguished but ontologically rich critique of the reality and truth of beauty that stands apart from, and in fact resists, what he would consider "totalizing" metaphysical claims.

These two reflections on the beautiful are completed and, as I think, surpassed by a third. In the philosophies of art and beauty articulated by Jacques Maritain, but rooted in the theology of St. Thomas Aquinas, we find at last the full dimensions of the beautiful. As I argued in Part I, the western tradition is specifically characterized by the insight that reality as a whole is ordered by and to Beauty. In Maritain, and in the line of inquiry he fostered, this insight finds a rich expression that makes it possible for us at once to see why the fostering of the fine arts and a broad culture is essential to the flourishing of any society and why, furthermore, the beauty we may discover in the work of art provides a criterion and guide for our moral and political judgments. Beauty, Maritain gives us reason to believe, is a property of being. It is specifically that property of being where being's form appears in itself, in its depths, and in the fullness of its relations. The encounter with it cannot finally be understood as an experience of possibility (imaginative openness) but as a direct entrance into the mystery of being by an avenue distinct from but analogous to that of the abstracting intellect. A robust metaphysical realism does not undermine or stand in the way of this encounter, as Adorno would propose, but deepens it and makes it more fruitful. For the power or shock of beauty, which we shall discuss in our consideration of Adorno, is ultimately attributable to beauty's reality, the way it at once stands as one of the transcendental properties of being, alongside truth and goodness, as something that *is*. It is itself the mystery of existence as really given. And so, we shall consider the way in which beauty seems to enfold being, truth, and goodness—giving itself to us *first* and immediately in our everyday experience, sometimes in ways that strike and shock, while also returning as the *final* and highest reality that holds truth and goodness together and that accounts for the whole ontological structure of reality. The beauty that first strikes and arrests us comes to appear through reflection as the stable fullness of being in its form and splendor. It is, as it were, the quality that reveals things in their individual integrity and the one that reveals the relation of all things and that holds all things together as one reality, good in order, and intelligible in truth.

FIVE

What Dante Means to Us

In our day, we tend to shrug off discussion of metaphysics, as if no knowledge were to be gained from learning what it means *to be*. The distinction between the practical and the speculative has come to appear as the divide between proof and make believe. We are concerned with facts; facts are real; but, as to what makes a fact a fact, we think the matter beyond discussion and perhaps even beneath contempt.

When we enter a book emporium at the mall, we may find an entire row under the heading "Metaphysics," but this intends something other than the philosophy of Being. It means the new-age trash that sates the unaccounted-for superstitions and desires of the recently de-Christianized. This curious nomenclature of inventory came to pass, not because the long-established meaning of the word was deemed secondary to this novel one, but because some ingenious store manager heard the word and thought, "Yes, that conveys a sense of importance and 'spirituality' without actually disclosing any content or imposing moral prescription." Such an anonymous manager resembles the classmate of mine years ago who, when asked to explain a poem of W. B. Yeats, wrote, "He's, uh, being philosophical." Indeed. These and myriad other persons who compose the contemporary West have become expert in short-circuiting all thought by dispatching all things of no immediate concupiscent use to a reverent and vacuous place on the shelf. Purchase it there, those who will.

Brave words with no meaning, transcendent sounds with no definite concepts are an abuse of rhetoric that became endemic in the Victorian age, as its more refined consciences tried to extricate themselves from the dreck of an increasingly gruesome and greasy commercial culture.[1] Its echoes could still be heard as late as 1916, calling the lads of Princeton off to their rendezvous with death.[2] In the early, spirited rhetoric of the Great War, one heard of truth, goodness, beauty, and God as things about which there was no doubting the humane goodness, the noble usefulness, but about whose truth one—tacitly—had serious doubt. The shelf-headings of our day have lost none of the pretension, some of the deception, and all the grandeur. By "metaphysics," they intend transcendent feelings without actual claims about knowledge. But to speak of being would make the modern "metaphysician" uncomfortable; it would require a dangerous flirtation with reality. It threatens to ensnare our desire to feel free with a truth that binds. Above all, it seems to ask of us a kind of belief that our blithe, materialist culture cannot muster.

This contemporary incredulity—which would seem to inoculate us against metaphysical claims—in fact results in persons' occupying alternately and erratically what in fact are two extreme metaphysical positions. Most elements of our culture tend to some species of materialism, that is, the belief (inconsistent though it must be) that nothing is real that cannot predictably be made manifest to the senses. This is, of course, a metaphysical claim: it says that what is real, what has being, is that which *is* material and only insofar as it is material. Much of the time, this is a very easy position to occupy. Only when confronted with our own thoughts does materialism directly and compellingly come under challenge in most persons' experience. For, to be a strict materialist, one has to say that thoughts *per se* do not exist. They are just the effects of certain chemical processes in the brain. Our knowledge of reality, for all its dynamism and power, is less real than the things it pretends to know and even than those things it causes to be.

This absolutizing of matter as the source and sum of reality has had a long, indeed a tenacious, legacy, and one hesitates, for that reason alone, to dismiss it out of hand.[3] But it is one that requires a great deal of faith, in the

1. See Denis Donoghue, *Speaking of Beauty* (New Haven, Conn.: Yale University Press, 2003), 169.
2. See David Brooks, "The Organization Kid" in *The Atlantic Monthly* 287 (April 2001): 40–54. Cf. Malcolm Cowley, *A Second Flowering* (New York: Viking Press, 1976), 6–7.
3. See, for example, Lucretius, *On the Nature of Things*, trans. Anthony Esolen (Baltimore: Johns Hopkins University Press, 1995).

peculiar modern sense of "unverifiable trust."[4] Through certain technologies, we can all perceive and measure that the brain undergoes certain physical changes when the mind thinks. But to identify those physical processes as thought itself can be done only on trust. One will always have the experience of ideas as ideas, of thought as thought; to persevere as a materialist, then, one must deny the reality of that experience, presume it misleading, and rationalize, "What appears to me as thought is in fact a series of separate physicochemical actions that produce only a sensation that other, similar physical processes cause me to call 'thought.' In fact, those actions are reducible to themselves, and thought is reducible to them." The mind equals the brain; thought, the "firing of synapses," even though we can have no experience of this identity; we cannot even explain what it would mean to experience this identity, since the experience *of* the explanation would be a mere appearance produced by processes of the brain that *possess* no true unity or consciousness but only *produce* it as a delusion, an unreal after-effect.

This has not stopped everyone from supposing. Steven Pinker and other "new atheists" have asserted that our inability to experience thought *as* a merely physicochemical process is probably just a limitation of our unevenly evolved brain.[5] But I can suffer a muscle spasm in my tricep, and I can choose to flex my tricep, and these two experiences are radically distinct; I could not reduce one to the other. If this analogy holds, then we have no basis for reducing thought to brain activities of which we have no first-person experience. If the analogy does not hold, it would be because thought seems more, rather than less, an activity of the mind transcendent of the body however much it may work in concert with it. But, enough. Materialism may never go away, despite the impossibility of making a compelling argument for its assertions, simply because it is a position most of us only *sometimes* hold—and that only when it is convenient. That is, when materialism frees us to equate knowledge with power, with what *can be done*, it also relieves us of the burden of knowledge as truth, that is to say, as the binding order of things—to wit, one that might impose itself on *our* wills.

The alternative position common in our age seldom exists by itself, but rather intervenes amid the everyday materialism of most persons: an

4. Schumacher, *A Guide for the Perplexed*, 45.
5. See Steven Pinker, "Evolutionary Psychology and the Blank Slate," in *What Scientists Think*, by Jeremy Stangroom (London; New York: Routledge, 2005), 23–36.

extreme form of dualistic idealism. Repelled by the idea of reality as reducible to material things and processes, the idealist insists, with an optimist's smile and an insecure heart, that the only true reality lies in thought. Matter may be real, after its fashion, but in the heaven of free ideas lies our proper concern. More often than not, the idealist is one seeking a refuge in a world where knowledge-as-power works most of the time, because it is *our* knowledge we are talking about, but where, sometimes, the knowledge of another undermines our sense of freedom, dignity, or worth.

Some idealists will locate reality in objective thought, suggesting that all persons share in one intellectual life among themselves. This is the therapeutic application of idealism: I may be alone in body, but we are all blissfully united on some imprecise level that we need not hash out, because it makes us feel so much the better the more vaguely it is proposed. Others prioritize the idea in its absolute subjectivity, and thus become voluntarists and relativists, who believe that reality consists primarily in their own perceptions and desires. This is the liberating application of idealism: it frees us to become our own criterion of truth, value, and desire. Our deepest desires are ours alone—our private property—and are dear—so valuable that no one could ever share in them or dare to trespass upon them. Incommunicability and even irrationality become a sign of one's ideas' truth.

Again, no one maintains these positions consistently or for very long. Many persons, who are subjective idealists about their own sexual activities, become strident and conventional moralists upon the theft of their pocketbook. Some people blissed out in the vibe of transcendental unity at their local Unitarian church or in the midst of a grinding bass line at Lollapalooza return to their banker's desk or cash register, on Monday morning, to view every human face a threat and the whole world a villain.

These idealistic effluvia tend to emerge as knee-jerk responses to either the ugliness or the rational inadequacy of materialism. Confronted with the impossibility of living as if we were just a sack of cells randomly conjoined, the everyday materialist momentarily turns idealist and tries to reimagine the self as a living soul whose reality transcends the material world as a little deity: as an agent of freedom and sole maker of meaning. This plays itself out in familiar scenarios. The person who tries to live as an occasional or circumstantial idealist clings to some eccentric superstition—astrology, the occult, or the existence of ghosts—in order to humanize the material world. "To humanize" means, here, to reserve some small, safe place for the existence of ideas, emotions—an order of meaning that is supra-material. For the rest, so long as the material world does not obviously violate a person's sense of selfhood, coherence, and worth, such a person lets the implications of materialism govern how he sees the world. Only should he suffer an occasional fit of existential angst does he need to play his little trump card of idealism: dialing the number of a psychic hotline or thumbing through the latest syncretistic, big-print treatise on Buddhism and psychotherapy, by "Dr. Beverly Tuffle, PhD."

As I have already indicated, it would be impossible to maintain pure materialism or pure idealism for any length of time, because both account for reality in ways we do not experience. The materialist says thought is unreal. "All right," one concedes, "but I can never know what that means without also knowing that I don't really know anything, because even the thought of thought-reduced-to-physical-process would give me the 'delusion' of thought-as-transcendent-of-matter. And, while I can understand that some thoughts may be delusions, I make that judgment in comparing one thought with another, not thought *per se* with matter." The idealist says all reality resides in the idea or the mind. "Fine," says Dr. Johnson, and then he kicks a real stone with his real foot and feels real pain.

We cannot escape metaphysics, then. But we can lose the vocabulary necessary if we are to make rationally compelling claims about reality; and once we lose this power of the reason, the world in which we live so confidently when unconscious of it becomes haunted by a nagging sense of insecurity and doubt, the moment we make a conscious effort to think about it. Such is the peculiar curse of the modern age. We radically divide truth from goodness, knowledge from desire, and idea from reality, in hopes of saving ourselves. But, in fact, we leave ourselves ill-equipped for rational reflection on anything that is not reducible to matter. That anything besides matter could have a serious weight that binds the reason after the fashion of the law of gravity seems almost an impossible dream. This, not incidentally, explains that curious phenomenon in modern intellectual life—to wit, the celebration of the naïve and primitive.[6] Accounts of earlier ages,

6. This is the pathology of romanticism, which we already discussed insofar as it has preserved conservatism as a species of "naïve and sentimental" culture. See Friedrich Schiller, *Essays*, ed. Walter Hinderer and Daniel O. Dahlstrom (New York: Continuum, 2005), 179–234.

when things—when the world itself—seemed charged with a degree of meaning in which all persons could believe with the same natural intuition that directs us to eat or sleep, have pullulated for more than three centuries now as a kind of forlorn fantasy. The modern person, we are told, because he is so self-conscious, so knowledgeable, and therefore so skeptical, makes the impossible wish, from time to time, that he were a bronze-age tribesmen or a medieval villager, so that he could instinctively believe that the sense of and need for meaning in this world *do* find confirmation in everyday reality.[7]

Our everyday materialism and idealism are themselves symptoms of this sense of loss. And this sense of loss tends to haunt non-student readers of the great literature of the western tradition, including the works of Plato and Aristotle, the Scriptures, and St. Augustine's *Confessions*. That is, a contemporary college student encountering these texts in a class will find them mere obstacles to be climbed over. He will be inoculated against taking their content seriously, trained to think meritocracy the sole reality. All that student chases down in such texts is a paraphrase of their internally coherent ideas, regarding which, belief would seem a foreign and irrelevant super-addition. In contrast, when the modern Christian, whose daily life is informed more by materialist assumptions than anything else, turns to Scripture or Augustine, he must steel himself for a fierce act of will, that he might find there something more than curious, strange, and arcane systems. We can see, for instance, that Augustine believed in form and matter, in the creative love of God as the cause of all existent things, and in the teleology that all persons desire happiness and will find it finally only in the simple, eternal unity of God. The Christian says, we no longer can believe these things the way Augustine did, or even see the reasons for their belief, but we have to assent to them in some vague fashion ... or we will no longer be Christian. Because one wants to be Christian, one wills the belief.

But, for the casual reader neither driven by the requirement to write a college essay nor the instinct to shore up a crumbling identity, even saying these ideas aloud can make them sound a bit unreal. One wonders how such ideas even came to be proposed, save as the evolution of some irrational or nebulous intuitions. "Can we really *believe* in *that*?" one asks.

7. An unsatisfactory effort to work through this modern problem is to be found in Hubert Dreyfuss and Sean Dorrance Kelly, *All Things Shining* (New York: Free Press, 2011).

I take so much time to describe modernity's erratic materialist-idealist complex, because one *useful* answer to the question asked just above has been that, when we leave aside our extrinsic purposes and agendas, and turn to the great literature of our tradition, we can find a middle passage between a power-hungry but empty materialism and a therapeutic and liberating, but ultimately vacuous, idealism. A passage, that is, that may lead to substantive knowledge about being that is solid and coherent enough to stand firm in an age such as ours, where appeals to experience rather than metaphysics often seem the last possible ground to defend a rich vision of the self and the world. When we allow ourselves to entertain the fictions of literature with a careful passivity and openness, the imagined becomes not simply the unreal but the possible. Make-believe becomes a kind of experience to set alongside all the others in which we discern truth, and so finally it becomes a mode of wisdom. Or, it may.

The reader will recognize here the deeper purpose behind Coleridge's famous "willing suspension of disbelief." One suspends disbelief not to pretend, but rather one pretends in order to discover the essential form of what one does not yet, but may come to, believe. Irving Babbitt and the New Humanists emphasized this as the essential exercise of liberal education: the dogmatic beliefs of others are taken non-dogmatically; doctrine becomes a world to be temporarily inhabited by the imagination. Truth is explored only insofar as it finds expression in beauty, but with the proviso that truth as theory could, perhaps, someday come to being in us in practice.[8] This is the basic answer Mark Edmundson gives us to the question "Why Read?" in his book of that name.[9] Literature holds open *possibility* in order that we might be nourished and cultivated in turn.

Let us consider this theme of experience and imagination, openness and possibility, as a path to the definite, of beauty as a path to truth, in terms of one of the perennial touchstones of its various advocates: the case of Dante's *Divine Comedy*. Dante, in part thanks to his self-critical account of his poem, has always been taken as that figure who straddles the litoral between imagined beauty and believed truth. His dedicatory letter to Can Grande proposes a mode of exegesis for his imaginative poem that

---

8. See Irving Babbitt, *Literature and the American College* (Washington, D.C.: National Humanities Institute, 1986).

9. Mark Edmundson, *Why Read?* (New York: Bloomsbury, 2005).

was normally reserved for books of Sacred Scripture.[10] Literature and theology are identical, he implies, in that they are both approaches to truth,
but one is mediated imaginatively while the other is immediately revealed
in Scripture. Boccaccio would write in his *Life of Dante* that, one day, as
Dante was

passing before a door where many women were sitting, one of them said softly to
the others (but not so softly that she was not clearly heard by him and by his companions), "Do you see the man who goes to hell, and returns when he pleases, and
brings back news of those who are below?" To this one of the others responded
naively, "Indeed, you must be speaking the truth. Don't you see how his beard is
crisped and his complexion browned by the heat and smoke that is below?"[11]

Dante, we are told, smiles silently, content that his poem had already won
so much fame as to become not simply a great story but a kind of history.
He dared to say for himself that, at its highest level of meaning, his poem
could be interpreted in the same ways as Holy Writ, but his tacit assent
here speaks to the possibility of, the openness to, reading the literal fictions of literature as if they were the facts of reality.

These early moments of the poetic seeming to trespass on the truth-
claims of history and theology may be more vivid, but they are far more
subtle than the claims that would be made for Dante in the nineteenth
century and after. Dante begins to feature much more largely in western
culture. Matthew Arnold took Picarda's line in the third canto of *Paradiso*,
"*E 'n la sua volontade e nostra pace*," as a touchstone of "culture."[12] Arnold
never defines what culture is, and he does not intend for us to take Picarda
at her literal word. And yet, for Arnold, culture is "the best that has been
thought and known in the world."[13] Dante's poem should serve as an example of the highest achievement, shape one's sensibility, and guide one's
pursuit of perfection; one just need not actually believe it. In a slightly
later and more comprehensive thinker like George Santayana, Dante joins

10. See Dante, *The Literary Criticism of Dante Alighieri*, ed. Robert S. Haller. (Lincoln: University of Nebraska Press, 1973).

11. Giovanni Boccaccio, *Life of Dante*, trans. Philip Wicksteed (Richmond, U.K.: Oneworld
Classics, 2009).

12. "And in His will there is our peace." Dante, *Paradiso*, trans. Allen Mandelbaum (New
York: Bantam Dell, 2004), 3.85.

13. Matthew Arnold, *Culture and Anarchy and Other Writings* (Cambridge: Cambridge
University Press, 1993), 79.

Lucretius and Goethe as paragons of the "philosophical poet."[14] He is the one poet who fully renders in sensuous and imaginatively compelling images a complete and thorough vision of reality (the "cosmic landscape," as Santayana calls it). While Lucretius and Goethe are also "philosophical" in Santayana's sense, they lack the cosmic scope of Dante.[15]

One may read Augustine or Thomas Aquinas and think one understands them, that one sees the internal logic of their claims, but still be unable to bring oneself to believe that what they say is a true description of reality, rather than a nice ideal superimposed on it by force of will. Their formulation of arguments as meant to be considered and accepted may itself be forbidding for the modern reader who finds the climate of late neo-Platonism or high Scholasticism alien. Between understanding and belief may loom an impassible chasm. However, amid the unsatisfactory dualistic tensions of materialism and idealism that alternately constrict our visions in modern times, a certain privilege has consistently been maintained for the imagination. For the imagination seems to be the place where the naïve and the primitive person truly surpassed the modern, Schiller and other Romantic philosophers once told us. A story, a poem, any work of the imagination, contains thought and ideas. But it puts flesh on them, it gives them a sensuous reality that is of course not identical with the reality of our everyday life but stands in some uncertain but undeniable relation to it. "I know this didn't *really* happen," I murmur over Homer, "but I know that if it were to happen, it would happen just as the poet said." The literary imagination is a kind of experience, the experience of being open to the possible.

Thus, the vividly imagined world of Dante has for generations been a way in which readers in our fragmented or distended world of materialists and idealists have been able to entertain the possibility of all reality cohering, of the world as created, as intelligible, as loved, lovable, and ordered to love and meaning, beauty, truth, and goodness. He proposes these things as facts of being in a way that rivals our age's presentation of knowledge as facts-under-power. And, in consequence, those things mod-

14. George Santayana, *Three Philosophical Poets* (Cambridge, Mass.: Harvard University Press, 1922).

15. Irving Singer, *George Santayana, Literary Philosopher* (New Haven, Conn.: Yale University Press, 2000), 140.

ern persons relegate to the ghetto of "value" seem to take on weight, as if they too were material truth. And yet the weight does bear heavily upon our feeble capacities for belief. Moreover, Dante also presents his reality as poetic details in a poem whose turning upon itself as a self-conscious work of art is so vertiginous that Dante the wayfarer several times faints for dizziness. The modern idealist finds such a realm congenial, as it draws him in without tying him down.

Dante's poem is very "thorough." But it is not so thorough as Augustine's writings or as the *Summae* of Thomas Aquinas, which Dante seems to have known well and to have incorporated partially into the structure of his *Comedy*. But the thoroughness of Dante is a freely *imagined* one. Because the poem is a fiction, we can encounter all that it says initially in a spirit of play; I can believe such-and-such for the moment without having to commit my will to it in real, everyday life. It seems almost a masterful version of those books on the "Metaphysics" shelf at the contemporary chain bookstore.

But, and here we reach the point of this inquiry, the capaciousness of Dante tends to have an effect that transcends such joy in pretending. Because it is so comprehensive, it tends to lead us from the world of imagination as fiction to the world of imagination as vision. Rather than remaining a world apart, Dante's world, because so vivid, may gradually come to have implications for our world. And when that happens, we may turn again from poetry to metaphysics and theology, from Dante to Augustine and Aristotle, and be able to encounter their ideas as reality for the first time. This slow "conversion" has happened before. Only a few months ago I met two graduate students, who were married and who had converted to Catholicism before their marriage. "Why did you convert?" I asked. "Because of Dante," the husband said. "There was too much that we accepted as reality that we could not accept unless we also accepted Catholicism."

Early in the last century, T. S. Eliot read medieval philosophy and theology as if it were poetry. A student of Babbitt and Santayana, he could suspend his mind in that condition of openness that leaves the whole western intellectual tradition an imaginative one. In a letter to Herbert Read, he notes that this exercise may prove only a "stimulant to the mind and imagination," wherein one accepts the beautiful architectonic of Scholasticism, but not its truth content, and seeks to emulate it in one's mental life.[16] His other writings indicate, however, that it was Dante who first drew him into the reading of the Scholastics. Further, when Eliot finally accepted the truths of Thomas Aquinas *as the highest of truths*, it led him to nothing less than a long essay on Dante wherein his mind consistently returns to the relation of poetry and belief.[17] The express concern is to demonstrate that one can appreciate Dante as a poet without assenting to the beliefs of Dante as a Catholic, but the current that seems to guide Eliot's meditations is his amazement that he has been brought, by way of the free, imaginative contemplation of poetic beauty, to the binding conviction of religious truth.

But why does this sort of thing happen? The concepts and words of Augustine are not those of our culture. We can understand them, but to assent to them we would need to be capable first of envisioning them within the framework of a whole way of life, a culture. It is one thing to say, I accept this or that point of a philosopher; but really to believe or accept as true—and bindingly so—what he says, one must become capable of thinking within the framework, the culture and tradition, that generated that point and holds it together.

To enter into a culture is not only to become conscious of a series of abstract propositions, but to enter into the context, the lives' worth of experience, that gives birth to them and in which they are embodied. The only way one experiences any life is as a story, and the way to enter into the experience of another is to enter into the story of another. Once we can do that, we can hear every proposition or truth that another may make and have some foundation to stand on in order to judge if he be right or wrong. We shall return to this relation of story and reason by another avenue in Part III, but here I wish only to consider the particular role literature may play in leading us to take beauty as something more than an epiphenomenon of matter. Beauty understood in this familiar sense might be thought of as truth at play.

Dante's narrative poem, we might say, provides a gateway, a point of access where the reasoned truths of moderate realist metaphysics and Christian theology take on full form, flesh, and blood, and can be seen

16. T. S. Eliot, *The Letters of T. S. Eliot*, volume 2, *1923–1925*, ed. Valerie Eliot and Hugh Haughton (London: Faber and Faber, 2009), 797.

17. T. S. Eliot, *Selected Essays 1917–1932* (New York: Harcourt, Brace and Company, 1932), 229–31.

in full rather than as atemporal abstractions. I would hold up Augustine's *Confessions* as another possible instance of this, but there is something particular to Dante's poem, with its subordination of all things to a coherent *and concrete* poetic and universal form, that gives one the sense of having seen a world first, and only then—only subsequently—reading into that world to discover the propositions that give it form. That such a journey is possible has everything to do with beauty, or rather, with beauty's identity as a transcendental property of being alongside the Good and the True. When we encounter being in beauty, we sense a kind of ordered liberty that can be described only in terms of form, proportion, of "what is fitting." The beautiful speaks to the same reality as the modes of goodness and truth, but without appearing to lead inexorably to imperatives of the will or convictions of the reason.[18] Kant held that the appreciation of beauty was a concern for form that is indifferent to its actual existence.[19] I reject this as an accurate account of beauty in itself, but I wholly embrace it as helping explain one possible experience we may have of beauty. We see Dante's world as beautiful, though it does not exist. But then, we gradually, perhaps imperceptibly, leave that conception of beauty behind, and discover that the order that seemed to exist only in the imagination is in fact the order of reality. What the imagined world lacks in compulsion may cause it to appear trivial to the casual eye, but may also make it that much the more attractive to the uninitiated but watchful, so that they can see what they otherwise would deliberately ignore.

As I just noted, in Eliot's long essay on Dante, his theme was that one need not actually believe in the Scholastic system and Christian cosmos that informs Dante's poem in order to appreciate it. Rather, one need only to understand those things and accept them within the confines of the poem. But the fact of Eliot's recent conversion to Anglo-Catholicism looms over his words. Dante's poetry was a continuous presence in his imagination, and we have reason to go beyond this empirical observation and to suspect that the poetic "system" of Dante contributed to Eliot's conversion to a religion that accepted much of that system as true.

What I have been trying to account for is the state of mind that might have been Eliot's as Eliot-the-poet cherished and defended Dante's literary

18. An insight Aristotle suggests in *Metaphysics*, 1078a.
19. Kant, *Critique of Judgment*, I.2.

achievement independent of its religious implications, while Eliot-the-convert seems to have been led gradually from the gates of Dante's fictive hell to the real portals of the Church. The point at which these two characters cross in the same person is that where one accepts, however reluctantly, that the imagination, with its habit of freedom, play, and of entertaining propositions as an experience rather than submitting to them as real, may be the only road, at present, to sincere belief in the metaphysical realism our intellects, however modern, require.

A few years after writing his essay on Dante, Eliot would observe that there "are two and only two finally tenable hypotheses about life: the Catholic and the materialistic."[20] As I have suggested, the modern idealist and his superstitions are really just pathologies of materialism. The alternative, as Eliot describes it, is between an anxiousness that can be evaded and numbed but never settled, or the assent to an understanding of a meaningful order as real, whose reality requires a realist metaphysics in turn grounded on the Divine. Eliot saw that if the choice was stark, and the allure of one over the other equally so, it was the rational foundation for justifying that choice that seemed so evidently wanting in the modern age. But to reason well, one must be capable of entering into a particular tradition of reasoning; to do that, one must first be able to envision what it would mean to live within that tradition—and it is to this that Dante offers a gateway if nothing else.

In an instructive misreading, E. F. Schumacher once interpreted the meaning of Virgil and Beatrice in Dante's *Divine Comedy* not as allegorical figures of reason and faith, but of poetry and faith.[21] The life of the imagination may serve as a kind of initiation into the life of supernatural faith in an age such as ours, where a distrust and misunderstanding of reason seem to dam it off as a path to the divine. What Dante means to us is that we have not surrendered the medieval identity of truth, goodness, and beauty as properties of being. We have not even given up real metaphysics. We simply lack confidence that discursive reason can deliver to us a compelling account of these things, and, no less, we fear the possibility that it might. Though Virgil, the poet, led Dante on a fearful path, Dante, the poet, holds open the possibility that the imaginative contemplation of beauty may lead us however gently beyond itself to an encounter with what is real.

20. T. S. Eliot, *Essays Ancient and Modern* (New York: Harcourt, Brace and Company, 1936), 181.
21. Schumacher, *A Guide for the Perplexed*, 130.

SIX

"Only What Does Not Fit into This World Is True"

To speak, in contemporary society, of art and beauty in the same sentence, much less as realities integrally involved with one another, is to risk becoming the object of smiling condescension. The great philosophers of beauty in the eighteenth century, including Burke, Hume, and Kant, treated beauty as a matter of sensation or taste, as either a physiological experience or a spiritual one, but always a subjective one. The arts of the beautiful were thought "to gentrify" the soul, softening it, making it more sympathetic in itself and sociable as part of a culture.[1] They succeeded in providing to the nineteenth century its canons of taste, but during that same period the rhetoric of the beautiful came to stand in stark contrast to the language of knowledge, science, and truth. The ideal beauty of Plato could be invoked, but as a subjective ideal alone, set apart from the smudges and smells of human trade and toil. Such appeals came to appear as a noble pose, as a willing suspension of disbelief that required an ever-greater strength of will in the face of the metaphysical materialism of the advocates of Charles Darwin and the moral materialism of the advocates of capital and free trade. In the poetry of John Keats, most obviously in the "Ode to Psyche" and "The Eve of St. Agnes," we find all

---

1. Edmund Burke, *A Philosophical Enquiry into the Sublime and the Beautiful and Other Pre-Revolutionary Writings*, ed. David Womersley (London: Penguin Books, 1998), 90–91, 177. Kant, *The Critique of Judgment*, 1.60.

things beautiful as belonging to a lost world, at which the poet looks with the vision of a sentimental conservative and a rational liberal. The poetic imagination becomes the one place where what of the past is beautiful (and good) may still abide, stripped of its status as real fact, as truth believed, and so is to be preserved as an idyll worshipped by the taste alone.

The high rhetoric of Keats will endure through the century, but in ever more attenuated expression, in the works of Walter Pater and Matthew Arnold. All this the modernists of the twentieth century will see through as mere ornament or affectation posing over the abyss. The language of beauty concealed the facts of reality with increasingly banal idealizations, while art took on new life and freedom as the expressive reification of the depths of subjectivity.[2] The romantic Platonism and liberal humanism of Arnold and Pater, modernists such as T. S. Eliot and T. E. Hulme would reject in favor of Aristotle. The language of beauty they would leave behind altogether for the language of form.[3] Those who spoke of beauty now expressed merely vain, vague, and nostalgic longings for Gainsborough landscapes or Tennyson's King Arthur, while talk of the aesthetic, in the restricted sense of the work of art as a form, could become increasingly serious—indeed, glum and humorless—even as it grew impermeable to rational explanation and debate.

We could almost sketch a historical graph of the last couple centuries showing that the falling fortunes of the idea of beauty bear an inverse relation to the ever more lofty or "professionalized" reputation of art and aesthetics: a yawning separation so great that the advent of cultural studies has made possible serious formal discussion, confined of course to academic conferences, of some very unserious "art," during which any reference to the standards or reality of beauty would be, at best, a cause of embarrassment and, at worst, occasion for an intricately formulated debunking of one more "bourgeois ideology." The discipline of literary studies has recently enjoyed the revival of formalism, that is, of an approach

2. See the whole of Abrams, *The Mirror and the Lamp*, for the most lively and thorough discussion of this transformation.

3. For a fuller account of this moment in the history of art and criticism, see James Matthew Wilson, "Ancient Beauty, Modern Verse: Romanticism and Classicism from Plato to T. S. Eliot and the New Formalism," *Renascence* 67, no. 1 (Winter 2015): 3–40, and "An 'Organ for a Frenchified Doctrine': Jacques Maritain and *The Criterion*'s Neo-Thomism," in *T.S. Eliot and Christian Tradition*, ed. Benjamin J. Lockerd (Lanham, Md.: Rowman and Littlefield / Fairleigh Dickinson University Press, 2014), 99–117.

to works of art that appreciates their formal properties as irreducible, complex realities, even as they are ultimately thought only to reveal the cultural and political conditions of the work's historical context.[4] Art can be serious; it can reveal truth; but beauty is an imposture.

The consequences of this division of art and beauty proliferate. We observe, for instance, the strange congruity of our culture's suspicion of any substantive claims about the beautiful with its increasing, everyday ugliness in architecture, urban planning, worship, speech, and manners. And we note, as well, the still further division of art into such purely modern groupings as "mass culture," "popular art," and high or "elite" art. One cannot help but think that we abet the exacerbation of the former in denying ourselves a condign language to describe that with which we cannot possibly be content; in a fashion typical of modern rationality, we resolve our discontent by rendering it mute, and we "mute" it by pretending it is unreal and by denying it a vocabulary with any moral force. Similarly, one can hardly avoid the conclusion that the radical division of the arts into the "entertainment industry," or "mass culture," and the stuff still taught in schools—supported by philanthropic foundations and the welfare state—and collecting dust in museums, and displayed at art shows in the Hamptons, amounts to something other than the natural hierarchical division of art works into lesser and greater, or even simple and difficult. Rather, artworks, in the view of our society, have lost their ontological integrity in being denied a foundation or reality in beauty, and so have been entirely subordinated to diverse instrumental uses. If you will not decide between the beautiful and the ugly, you will end up substituting some class, political, or commercial marker in their place.

Naturally, the works themselves are transformed in this subordination. The great mass of western persons now live in a poppy dream of consumption and repose; the "entertainment" they imbibe comes brilliantly adapted for digestion, distraction, and a speedy market oiled by evanescence and fueled by novelty. Meanwhile, the bohemian and "high" art-consuming elites make use of obscurities to flatter their sense of political enlightenment and to express a feckless form of cultural power. Supposedly politically "conscious" art serves to confirm the latest feminist or "ethnic"

4. See, for instance, Verena Theile and Linda Tredennick, eds., *New Formalisms and Literary Theory* (Basingstoke, U.K.: Palgrave Macmillan, 2013).

cause—not because anyone looks at it and is changed, but rather, because its presence in mostly empty public space gives testimony to the virtue of those corporations or universities who sponsor it and to the expert qualifications of those who administer it to manage "diversity" in our enlightened institutions. Elsewhere, austere rehashes of an earlier age's love of abstraction, or pornographic titillations, more truly attract elite audiences, who like to be reminded of their winnowing, ascetic sensibilities while also having their generally unmastered sensuality pandered to and "affirmed." The rise of homosexual-themed art is to be explained simply by the fact that it accomplishes all of the above.

If artworks in every age have served instrumental ends—and they have—the ends in ours are attenuated and debased compared even to the vain adornments that artists provided sovereigns in the early days of the modern absolute state. In those days, artists assumed a Virgilian role to proclaim (and so, perhaps, subtly admonish) their patrons to be better men than they actually were. Our age flatters its elites by telling them they are just fine indulging whatever desires they might feel so long as they pepper it with knowing gestures, contempt for bourgeois morality, and a smarmy appeal for donations to third-world or women's causes.

As might be expected from this shrill survey, I wish to argue for a restored sense of the philosophy and practice of the fine arts as bound up inexorably with the reality of beauty, but not merely, as the last chapter suggested, as a kind of imaginative openness. Rather, the beauty of the fine arts—the arts of the beautiful, as they are rightly called—needs to be understood as an intentional and perfected expression of the beauty to be found in every being insofar as it has being. The fine arts in their beauty reawaken the soul to the perception of beauty as a property of being in general, and so they initiate or train us in the seeing of reality in its fullness.[5] We shall return to this point at the end of our inquiry.

We have already considered an approach to art that understands its beauty as primarily imaginative and as an avenue of openness and possibility by which one may tenuously approach truth. We shall now turn to a thinker who brooked no metaphysical debate about the being of beau-

5. See Friedrich Schiller, *On the Aesthetic Education of Man*, trans. Reginald Snell (Mineola, N.Y.: Dover Publications, 2004), and especially Kevin E. O'Reilly, *Aesthetic Perception: A Thomistic Perspective* (Dublin: Four Courts Press, 2007), 47–50.

ty, but who provides a compelling account of its reality and its effects in non-ontological terms. This will prepare us for a more complete consideration of beauty in terms of being, and, in turn, the relation of beauty to the whole of reality.

The most ingenious mind of the Frankfurt school, Theodor W. Adorno (1903–1969) spent much of his life in study of art's truth in the age of ideology and enlightenment. His account of the function of art is intensely historical and sociological; it owes its starting premises to the Enlightenment idealism of Kant, and yet it stands in decisive opposition to the historicism and "bourgeois relativism" that obscure or soften the difficult vision of truth art can sometimes open. The vertiginous turning of his dialectical theory of art is interesting in its own right as a byzantine refinement of Marxist historical materialism, but it also merits attention because of its explanatory power regarding the difficulties of modern art and its implications for why postmodern art at once owes a debt to the modern and yet is an incoherent falling off from it as well. He offers us an account of art that likely reflects the terms in which many modern artists have conceived it in their practice, and yet, crucially, his aesthetic theory refuses to loosen art's clasp on either truth or, perhaps surprisingly, beauty. Moreover, he locates art as a reality bound to but distinct from any society's particular "ideology," and rehabilitates for social theory the medieval notion of art as derived from the intelligibility of the cosmos, as a reflection and imitation of the "Book of Nature."[6]

In subsequent chapters, we shall turn from Adorno to an early treatise by the French neo-Thomist philosopher Jacques Maritain. While prolific as a philosopher of art and beauty for much of his life, Maritain's *Art and Scholasticism* (1920) and *The Frontiers of Poetry* (1926)—two essays eventually gathered and published as one volume—offer a concise, suggestive, and convincing account of these matters, one that remains an indispensable touchstone for all subsequent discussion of art and beauty in the Christian Platonist tradition. If much of Adorno's writing is retrospective, trying to understand the currents of modern art after most of them had

---

6. Much of my thinking on Adorno and the "Book of Nature" was stimulated by a seminar given by J. M. Bernstein at the University of Notre Dame in 2004. Bernstein's discussion of these points may be found in "'The dead speaking of stones and stars': Adorno's *Aesthetic Theory*" in *The Cambridge Companion to Critical Theory*, ed. Fred Rush (Cambridge: Cambridge University Press, 2004), 139–64.

run their course, Maritain's writings are contemporary with the developments they seek to explain. Indeed, the power of this early book is partly lodged in Maritain's almost polemical campaign for his contemporaries to understand their work differently than they actually did. He would reveal the plenitude and finality of what, in most modern art, remained but an inchoate tendency. It is a work of philosophy that would reinterpret apparent historical contingencies into a more permanent language—without, for all that, losing sight of the historical transformations of art from culture to culture or age to age.

Adorno and Maritain alike saw art in the modern age as having achieved an unprecedented degree of "spiritualization," a consciousness of its autonomy and its function to pierce the flesh of everyday life and discover truth in that mortal wound. Their claims merit our attention *not* primarily as theoretical expressions of the modernist sensibility, but as accounts of art and beauty that cannot be laid by, and which, in fact, help us to arrive at a perception of art and beauty that not only explains the oddities of modernism in decades past, but that genuinely accounts for these things in themselves. For Maritain at least, the experiments and aberrations of modern art served primarily to make visible what had always been the case for the fine arts; even if one ultimately rejects modernist works, they make possible a fuller understanding of the arts of the beautiful in their essence.

As a late western intellectual heir of Karl Marx, Adorno developed his thought on the structure of dialectical historicism. For Marx, the dialectic served to explain how real evils (above all, the alienation of the subject from his labor) ultimately serve the interest of an apotheosis or end of history, so that one could understand agricultural and feudal social formations preparing for the rise of bourgeois capitalism and industry, and these social forms would eventually be superannuated by the emergence of a stateless dictatorship of the proletariat. Following Hegel, Marx's dialectic suggests that apparent evils in fact serve a historically *necessary*, or good, function, and even evident falsehoods—ideology—at once reveal and conceal historical truths.

Adorno accepted the dialectical movement of historical reality, but stripped it of its teleology; history is not moving toward a total synthesis that will resolve and end its shiftings.[7] Belief in any such necessary jour-

7. See Theodor W. Adorno and Max Horkheimer, *Dialectic of Enlightenment* (London: Verso, 1979).

ney was the prototype of the ideology of Enlightenment, of modernity; Adorno believed that the truth of history could be expressed only in the fragment, the essay, the shudder or glimpse, where ideology momentarily ruptures.[8] Indeed, it should *only* be so expressed; philosophies of totality conceal the truth to which they lay claim. The only adequate philosophy is that which confesses its perspectival partiality. In "Why Philosophy?" he explains,

Philosophy guided by a sense of responsibility for everything should no longer lay claim to a mastery of the absolute, should in fact renounce all such notions, in order not to betray them in the event, without, however, sacrificing the concept of truth itself. The province of philosophy lies in such contradictions as these. They confer on it a negative character.[9]

Truth appears in critique, in the moment of negation, where what has previously been accepted as truth is made visible in its falsehood and is momentarily transparent. One has no steady gaze on truth, but one may stand in shifting relation to it by means of critical agility. Robbed of the teleology that the realization in history of a final and complete system would provide, the dialectical movement itself becomes problematic, for it has no end against which to measure itself, but only the immanent perception of untruth, which is like the glazed sunlit side of a leaf that conceals the reality on the dull obverse, until, for a brief moment, we turn the leaf over. As such, Adorno's dialectical analysis of reality tends to spiral in a fashion more sophisticated and more elusive than that of other post-Marxist social theorists. Everything worthy of analysis expresses a historical situation compounded of truth and falsehood; every social change may offer us a glimpse of truth on its obverse, but some new falsehood dwells on top.

The charter document of this historical theory is *Dialectic of Enlightenment*, which Adorno co-authored with Max Horkheimer, another prominent thinker of the Frankfurt School. According to Adorno and Horkheimer, the conception of rationality heralded by the figures of the Enlightenment (which they view as an event reaching back before the seventeenth century and as the condition under which we now exist) worked

---

8. Thus, the form of philosophy becomes the essay rather than the Hegelian totalizing volume: Adorno, "The Essay as Form," in *The Adorno Reader*, ed. Brian O'Connor (Oxford: Blackwell Publishers, 2000), 91–111.

9. Adorno, *The Adorno Reader*, 43.

to dispel earlier conceptions of reason, myth, magic, and religion. The promise of Enlightenment was the promise of liberation from superstition and the dissolving of falsehood in the light of rational truth. But the method of Enlightenment, instrumental reason, was soon transformed from its finite function of dissolving primitive social forms into a social form itself; the method of instrumental reason did not last as a tool of Enlightenment, but became the standard, the substantive belief, of Enlightenment as a regime. Anything that does not conform to the method gets dismissed as false or irrational. What was supposed to have begun as a project of intellectual liberation, in which thought frees itself of calcified ideology by means of critical reflection, becomes itself the calcified ideology that stultifies reflection.

However, Enlightenment is distinct from other social forms in its totalitarian ambitions. It seeks the "reification," rationalization, and administration of all things; it would reduce and reify all things to the order demanded by its method. Begun in the name of luminous truth, Enlightenment may entirely conceal truth by the absolute ambitions that all things be made to fit, be subjected to instruments of administrative reason. This account grows darker in light of the general dialectical framework Adorno elsewhere provides. All apparent goods conceal within themselves evils; real progress carries within itself real barbarisms; appearances of freedom and rational "disenchantment," whatever truth they may show forth, hide new enslavements and enchantments in their shadows. The totalizing claims of Enlightenment thus hint not only at the size of its promise but the severity of its threat. He writes, "All enlightenment is accompanied by the anxiety that what set enlightenment in motion in the first place and what enlightenment ever threatens to consume may disappear: truth."[10]

In his magnum opus, *Aesthetic Theory* (first published in 1970), Adorno critiques several of the German idealists for at once misunderstanding the nature of art and yet modeling their philosophies on artworks. The idealists, Hegel above all, viewed artworks as justified insofar as they were the pre-conceptual or non-conceptualized other of thought, of Idea Itself. The concrete and sensuous was thus dialectically integrated as an inarticu-

10. Theodor W. Adorno, *Aesthetic Theory*, trans. Robert Hullot-Kentor (Minneapolis: University of Minnesota Press, 1997), 80.

late promise of Absolute Idea. However much this seems to depreciate the importance of art, reducing its matter and formal specificity to an incidental, present expression of the as-yet-absent Absolute, it actually takes the dialectic of the concrete artwork and the ineffable truth it contains as exemplary of how all things operate. The particular always mediates the revelation of the universal.[11]

A similar criticism could be directed at Adorno, though he is entirely aware of what he is doing and makes a method out of the contradiction. He views the flattened, banal surface of modernity as a patina of pure ideology concealing, and so inadvertently revealing, truth by its very operation. We are at every moment reminded of our freedom and set at greater remove from it. We are informed of our happiness even as we become less and less capable of reflecting meaningfully on what it might be. The tail-finned world of Enlightenment is all shiny steel surface welded to iron cuff. Insofar as an artwork makes an inassimilable appearance, insofar as it momentarily stands forth as unintelligible within the scheme of modernity, it causes a "break or rupture." These fugitive moments of rupture manifested in an artwork are the shattered moments where truth shines like a shard in the otherwise seamless enamel of ideological order. As such, the lyric poem may be the emblem of art in general and, indeed, the exemplum of the difficult and ephemeral means by which truth appears in an order arrayed against it:

The idiosyncrasy of poetic thought, opposing the overpowering force of material things, is a form of reaction against the reification of the world, against the rule of the wares of commerce over people which has been spreading since the beginning of the modern era—which, since the Industrial Revolution, has established itself as the ruling force of life.[12]

Adorno's essayistic philosophy is modeled on art's idiosyncrasy. *Aesthetic Theory* comprises, effectively, one long undivided paragraph whose stylistic density makes one think that each sentence is a new thesis advanced rather than a supporting plank within a sustained argument. Sustained argument would be itself a weakness, a concession to totalizing systemization that would lose its critical perceptions in the process of vindicat-

11. Adorno, *Aesthetic Theory*, 84.
12. Adorno, "Lyric Poetry and Society," *Adorno Reader*, 215.

ing them in the eyes of modern standards of rationality. In this respect,
Adorno follows the aphoristic philosophy of Nietzsche as a methodical
improvement on the "scientific" form of Marx's thought; and yet, he emphasizes again and again that in sacrificing argument he is not sacrificing truth, but making the vision of truth briefly possible in the stillness
between two waves of ideology.[13] Only "what does not fit into this world
is true," he writes, and this, not because the truth transcends the world as
Plato's forms transcend appearance, but because the particular work of art
appears only because it does not seem congruent with the "disenchanted
world" of enlightened society, and because it bears the conflict of ideology and truth within itself.[14]

If art is the form of his philosophy, what is art itself, and whence
comes the truth it bears and reveals? The shattered dialectical mirror that
Adorno gives us offers myriad answers, of which I shall provide just four
in the next chapter: religious enchantment, *fait social*, suffering, and natural beauty.

13. Adorno, "Lyric Poetry and Society," *Adorno Reader*, 214.
14. Adorno, *Aesthetic Theory*, 59.

SEVEN

Re-Reading the Book of Nature

In the last chapter, I concluded with the observation that the form of Theodor W. Adorno's philosophy is patterned on his vision of the artwork. We must ask, then, what is art itself and whence comes the truth it reveals? I shall discuss four ways of thinking about art that seem to command the attention of the skeptic who doubts its value as anything more than an empty gesture of liberal humanism. These four ways are also, in a qualified way, consonant with the account, which is a central claim of this book, of the reality of beauty as a property of being, and they offer a provocative if not finally satisfactory way of approaching that claim. They are: religious enchantment, *fait social*, suffering, and natural beauty.

Adorno always theorizes art historically rather than ontologically, presuming it to be internally situated within a historical society and to take its definition only from that situation; even so, he insists that artworks do not merely express the ideologies of their age as epiphenomena. Indeed, as he notes, in "Lyric Poetry and Society,"

Ideology, as a concept, must not be taken as meaning that all of art and philosophy amount to some particular persons' passing off some particular interests as general ones. The concept of ideology seeks rather to unmask false thought and at the same time to grasp its historical necessity. The greatness of works of art lies solely in their power to let those things be heard which ideology conceals. Whether intended or not, their success transcends false consciousness.[1]

1. Adorno, *Adorno Reader*, 214.

While Adorno rightly leaves open the probability that ideology cleaves to the work of art, the work's meaning is not reducible to a mere expressive relation, where society or its ideology gives the artwork its content and the artwork gives that content a particular form or voice. The greatness of, say, Virgil's *Aeneid* lies not in flattering Augustus Caesar, even if that were the intention of the epic, but in the way its formal autonomy makes visible a truth beside, within, but other than the ideologies of empire.[2] In modernity, art is autonomous because it is at once useless and, in its greatness, beyond use, but it seems also, historically, to draw on other social forms that transcend the useful.

In exploring this aspect of art, Adorno routinely returns to the putative connection between it and the "pre-modern" social forms of religion, myth, and magic. The stark, primitive forms of much modernist art and the critical theory that accompanied it frequently indicated that the modern artist sought to restore the ancient identity of art and religion as if by sheer force of will. Rilke was Adorno's national *bête noir* in this regard, but in the Anglo-American tradition nearly all the major literary modernists engaged in some such "religio-poetic" voluntarism.[3] The drive to craft a new religion of and for art in W. B. Yeats, George Santayana, or Wallace Stevens; to recuperate the "old time" religion, whether evangelical or Catholic, in Allen Tate and John Crowe Ransom; the ritualism in the dramatic ambitions of Yeats, T. S. Eliot, and W. H. Auden; the esoteric theophanies of Ezra Pound, H. D., and, more tenuously, William Carlos Williams: all these instances speak to a curious modernist belief. Art depended on religious forms, myth, and ritual; and so, for art to be possible in the modern world, those things must be restored at least as ancillaries of art.[4]

Adorno refuses such thinking out of hand. He acknowledges the historical origin of artworks in cultic and magical use; as such, artworks have internal to themselves an unmistakable trace of enchantment. But the essence of art cannot be deduced from its origin. Further, the historical En-

2. On autonomy as potency and weakness in art, see Adorno, *Aesthetic Theory*, 1.

3. Theodor W. Adorno, "Theses upon Art and Religion Today," *The Kenyon Review* 7, no. 4 (Autumn 1945), 678.

4. The single most pained and ambitious effort to give these practices a sociological basis may be found in John Crowe Ransom, *God without Thunder* (London: Gerald Howe Ltd., 1931). For figures such as Yeats and Stevens, the association of art and religion seems scarcely to require proof, just passing assertion as a given for anyone who knows what art is.

lightenment disenchanted the world, removing us from the conditions of
religious or magical belief. If artworks in some sense carry into modernity
a trace of those archaic conditions, their truth content must nonetheless
stand not in dialectical relation to a society that is gone, but to the society that is the present. As such, the enchantment of artworks derives not
primarily from their past instrumental function in religion, or as memoirs
of an extinct, unified religious culture, but by means of their inassimilable
difference from the modern order of instrumental reason.[5] Indeed, insofar as an artwork is art rather than a cultic instrument, it has always found
its meaning in this difference. In a short essay, "Theses upon Art and Religion Today," Adorno contends,

> art, and so-called classical art no less than its more anarchical expressions, always
> was, and is, a force of protest of the humane against the pressure of domineering
> institutions, religious and others, no less than it reflects their objective substance.
> Hence there is reason for the suspicion that wherever the battle cry is raised that
> art should go back to its religious sources there also prevails the wish that art
> should exercise a disciplinary, repressive function.[6]

Art's truth lies in its protest against, not in its comportment with, this or
that social order—much less a *sacred* order of society's "Sunday institutions."[7] This is not to say that art is merely a protest; only that, insofar as art
reveals truth, it does so unsystematically and in a condition of dialectical
opposition to whatever ideology is normally taken for the smooth surface
of "everyday" reality. Truth appears as what does not fit in with the world,
and so, Adorno writes off as barbaric or infantile romanticism the effort to
recover a social order in which the truth of art conforms with the systematic order of religion, myth, or magic, as if a renewal of the bonds of art and
religion would lead also to a re-enchantment of the entire social order, a
dispelling of the Enlightenment's dehumanizing rationalism.[8]

Adorno's theses on art and religion result in a constellation rather than
a unified theory. The connection between art and religion is genealogical
(art emerges from religious practices and meanings), rather than intrinsic.
The effort to make art religious so that it may have a higher truth value

5. Adorno, *Aesthetic Theory*, 2.
6. Adorno, "Theses upon Art and Religion Today," 678.
7. Adorno, *Aesthetic Theory*, 2.
8. Adorno, "Theses upon Art and Religion Today," 677.

and social authority would in fact neutralize that truth value, absorbing art within the domain of ideology.

And yet, the autonomy of art and the way in which it reveals, really does bear an analogical resemblance to religion properly conceived. In his *Leisure, the Basis of Culture*, Pieper underscores that divine worship is an activity cut off from all use, standing in opposition to all use, and this only because it is above all use. The "temple" is the locus of freedom, festival the time set outside the clock of work.[9] In this place, the reality that appears is given to us, rather than made by us. It is what is given from above, from the gods, and which cannot be touched by the social order we generate from below.[10]

The connection between the transcendent revelation given in religious rite and what Adorno characterizes as the socially transcendent truth afforded by art is more than historical. Or, rather, it is more than the remnant of prehistorical and primitive "enchantment." For, it was Kant who first systematically theorized the autonomy of the arts of the beautiful, and he did so in a peculiar way.[11] First, Kant eliminated the contemplative dimension of philosophy and theology, so that philosophy becomes a kind of work and religion the highest guide to our moral duty.[12] Both are thereby restricted to the roles of explaining or directing our practical lives.[13] Only in our encounter with the beautiful does Kant carve out a place for contemplation, for a human activity of the spirit that transcends our other activities in the world.[14] What the Christian Platonist tradition held, and holds, up as the greatest dignity of religious life—the contemplation, the loving knowledge of God—becomes a specialized preserve for our encounters with beauty in nature or in art. Religion and art are not only connected by art's primitive history as an instrument of cult; the autonomy and transcendence of use won for art in modernity comes about only through its being directly modeled on a conception of religion that Kant rejects as true religion, but reconfigures and reserves for art.

---

9. Pieper, *Leisure, the Basis of Culture*, 67.   10. Pieper, *Leisure, the Basis of Culture*, 71.

11. Kant, *Critique of Judgment*, 1.32   12. Pieper, *Leisure, the Basis of Culture*, 27.

13. Kant writes, "Whatever, over and above good life-conduct, man fancies that he can do to become well-pleasing to God is mere religious illusion and pseudo-service of God." *Religion within the Limits of Reason Alone*, trans. Theodore M. Greene and Hoyt H. Hudson (New York: Harper Torchbooks, 1960), 158.

14. Kant, *Critique of Judgment*, 1.12, 42

Pieper and Adorno both resist as "blasphemy" this Kantian effort to harness religion, to put it to work, for some secular (including any secular aesthetic) purpose.[15] And, as much as Adorno is convinced of the necessary separation of art and religion, he also understands it to "bear the imprint of its magical origin," and this may be seen, at the least, in the autonomy and "uselessness," as well as in the anti-because-supra–social truth-revealing of the work of art.[16] If this imprint were itself to be challenged, we would face the possibility that art is no longer possible, that Enlightenment had come to total dominion—a prospect that Adorno repeatedly holds up as a real one.

We have seen that, in this denial of an ontological connection between religion and art, Adorno deemed it possible for art merely to express a society's ideology, but also, simultaneously, to stand outside and against it in a manner at least analogous to the revelations of the sacred. In his dialectical imagination, these are not mutually exclusive alternatives. To what extent, then, does art's origin lie in its being a *fait social*, a production or epiphenomenon of its society?[17] And to what extent may art really be understood to stand outside social history, whether as a rupture or as something autonomous, above history, as post-Kantian aesthetic theory tends to affirm?

Answering such questions is rendered onerous by the fact that the very conception of art as autonomous is itself a *fait social*. If one source of art's autonomy is its historical distance from cultic use coupled with the persistence of religion's "magical" imprint, another is its uselessness in an Enlightenment society committed to the triumph of instrumental reasoning. Did Kant, for instance, elevate beauty to the last site of contemplative joy, only because he did not know what else to make of it? I would say, yes. And so, still another source is the meeting of that uselessness with the modern conception of the division and specialization of labor. Art thus becomes the particular division of labor responsible for a certain kind of uselessness—purposive purposelessness, or creation without a concept, as Kant had put it.[18] An age of utility thus renders art its useless other;

15. Adorno, "Theses upon Art and Religion Today," 679.
16. Adorno, "Theses upon Art and Religion Today," 680.
17. Adorno, *Aesthetic Theory*, 5.
18. Kant, *Critique of Judgment*, 1.11, 16.

an age of specialization makes a fetish of this uselessness as possessing a certain elevation, a technical autonomy. Such autonomy also appeared as a mirror of the emerging "bourgeois consciousness of freedom that was itself bound up with the social structure."[19] Thus, the artwork is not only the other to modern, administered society, but may also mirror the self-image of the modern individual who feels autonomous, choosing his purpose and ends independent of all norms and nature much as does a work of art.[20]

Even so, Adorno does not reduce the modern conception of the art-work as autonomous to a reflection of a regime that dominates everything in the name of liberation and individual freedom, as if the self-consciousness of modern art were a mere further working-out of the logic of liberalism. However many ways art may be social—and he lists many others besides those I have noted here—it registers resistance to society, it seeks to critique and render itself autonomous in the face of ideology. On the one hand, it must be made—reified—and so enters into the concrete relations of the so-ciety in which it is situated; on the other, as an object made, it stands forth as something independent that, at least briefly, resists integration into the logic of its age. As such, art "criticizes society by merely existing."[21]

Adorno speaks of the resistance or protest of artworks' being "neutral-ized" with time; his classical example of this is the opera, which shows forth for a period as true art, but eventually becomes an eviscerated form that is perpetuated as social fashion retaining and reforming the vestiges of serious art as a simulacrum produced by the "culture industry."[22] We must remember that the value of the opposition art manifests is not re-ducible to the opposition itself. Art absorbs and expresses the conditions of its age; it reveals them for the untruth—the ideology—they are, but it also may show forth a truth that primarily stands apart from, rather than in opposition to, ideology. The negativity of art is coupled with its "utopic" element, one constituted not by dialectical opposition to society but by an immanent process that "immerses [artworks] in twilight."[23] In

19. Adorno, *Aesthetic Theory*, 225.

20. "*Genius* is the talent (natural endowment) that gives the rule to art" (Kant, *Critique of Judgment*, 1.46).

21. Adorno, *Aesthetic Theory*, 226.

22. Adorno, *Aesthetic Theory*, 18, 314.

23. Adorno, *Aesthetic Theory*, 233.

acknowledging this, we emphasize that art is a matter of truth just as everyday life is a matter of unreality. Neither can be understood in terms of mere subjective feeling or experience, and art, above all, is not resolvable into that cliché American feeling of authenticity as derived from a causeless rebellion, a standing in opposition as "nonconformist."

Thus, in the essay "A Social Critique of Radio Music," Adorno dismisses those accounts that would paint artistic pleasure as relative, as mere sensation and personal opinion. We may find this artistic relativism easy to believe only because it conforms so neatly with the broader forms of relativism essential to an advanced capitalist society in which human freedom is controlled and extinguished by being reconstituted as "consumer choice." One believes art is subjective, a matter of *personal* taste, only to the extent that one has accepted its conformity to an instrumental and dominating logic of standardization and commoditization. Music in modernity changes not because "tastes change" and "the people" demand what they want, but because music must be reconfigured to fit this totalizing social logic.[24] Adorno demurs and does so decisively:

> Music is not a realm of subjective tastes and relative values, except to those who do not want to undergo the discipline of the subject matter. As soon as one enters the field of musical technology and structure, the arbitrariness of evaluation vanishes, and we are faced with decisions about right and wrong and true and false.[25]

I can think of no more cutting and concise defense of the integrity of artworks as manifesting truth in their inherent form. Adorno's historicism leads not to relativism or to a philosophy of history that will culminate in liberation (including liberation from the authority of the aesthetic); it takes the form rather of a desperate defense of the true made present in works of art against the temptation to conceal everything within a lying logic of Enlightenment.

The historical-dialectical nature of Adorno's philosophy would seem an unpromising one for a defense of truth. He cannot intend truth as the

---

24. "The less listener has to choose, the more is he made to believe that he has a choice.... The consumer is unwilling to recognize that he is totally dependent, and he likes to preserve the illusion of private initiative and free choice. Thus standardization in radio produces its veil of pseudo-individualism." Theodor W. Adorno, "A Social Critique of Radio Music," *The Kenyon Review 7*, no. 2 (Spring 1945), 216.

25. Adorno, "A Social Critique of Radio Music," 216.

ultimately coherent, intelligible system of reality—the *Logos*—for that would suggest that truth might have its apotheosis and the instrumental cunning of ideology might at last be overcome. For Adorno the historical destiny promised by Marx was part of, rather than a transcendence of, the Enlightenment mania for totality.[26] There is no way out of the darkness in which we live, but only the fragmentary encounter with truth, broken off from every whole, every apparent oneness. As Conor McCarthy has observed,

History is, for Adorno, a catastrophic process, a Spenglerian narrative of decline and failure. The potential and hope embodied in Enlightenment has resulted in domination and fascism. Only in the realm of art can resistance any more be located.[27]

Adorno describes this encounter in ways that will be familiar to the reader of Plato. Artworks deliver a "primordial shudder"; they are "neutralized [i.e., no longer religious] and thus qualitatively transformed epiphanies"; they are "resembled by the *apparition*, the heavenly vision"; and so, they "become eloquent by the force of the kindling of thing and appearance. They are things whose power it is to appear."[28] In their appearing or speaking, they produce images or promises of what is not, a sort of "unstillable longing in the face of beauty."[29] This tremor, this shudder, this vision is of truth-in-beauty, even though it is a truth in several senses produced by falsehood; not merely does art show us, by means of artifice, what is not, but it depends upon the ideological assumptions of its society for much of its form and content.

But what kind of truth thus appears? I shall advance only two answers—those that seem most distinctive to Adorno's theory and central to our effort to renew our understanding of the fine arts as the arts of the beautiful and of beauty as a property of being. Art may be produced by a society's ideology, but the demand for it derives from what remains foreign to that ideology, which means also what is suppressed by it. In a sense, art speaks a nondiscursive language of real suffering. This seems

---

26. Martin Jay, *Marxism and Totality* (Berkley: University of California Press, 1984), 259, 261.

27. Conor McCarthy, "Seamus Deane: Between Burke and Adorno," *The Yearbook of English Studies* 35 (2005), 243. One wonders, however, whether Spengler is not one more totalizing narrative of Enlightenment in Adorno's eyes—see Theodor W. Adorno, "Spengler after the Decline," in *Prisms* (Cambridge, Mass.: The MIT Press, 1982), 63.

28. Adorno, *Aesthetic Theory*, 79–80.

29. Adorno, *Aesthetic Theory*, 82.

primarily, but not exclusively, a specifically modern formulation of art's claim to truth. In the ages of Enlightenment, suffering is the experience that cannot be assimilated into bureaucratic order and it is also the product of the rational rage for such order. Adorno writes, early in *Aesthetic Theory*,

> If thought is in any way to gain a relation to art it must be on the basis that something in reality, something back of the veil spun by the interplay of institutions and false needs, objectively demands art, and that it demands an art that speaks for what the veil hides. Though discursive knowledge is adequate to reality, and even to its irrationalities, which originate in its laws of motion, something in reality rebuffs rational knowledge. Suffering remains foreign to knowledge; though knowledge can subordinate it conceptually and provide means for its amelioration, knowledge can scarcely express it through its own means of experience without itself becoming irrational. Suffering conceptualized remains mute and inconsequential, as is obvious in post-Hitler Germany.... [art] takes into itself the disaster ...[30]

Art speaks a suffering that cannot be spoken in the discursive language of society without losing the truth of its content. One is often disgusted with the modern propensity to provide technocratic or juridical solutions to moral or intellectual problems; in the age of such continuous "ameliorations" that address suffering as a project for technocrats, art provides the useless and inassimilable language that does not betray the experiential truth of its meaning. The limitation of this answer to the content of the truth of art is precisely its historicism; suffering is the underbelly of an age of rationally distributed delights. As Adorno instructs, art's teleology is immanent and particular, and so its identity is distinct in the age of Enlightenment from what it might be at other times. His insights in this regard are confirmed by the most distinctive works of modern art, from Picasso's *Guernica* to the spiritual writings of Simone Weil, the poems of Paul Celan and Anthony Hecht, and, perhaps most striking of all, the fictions of Flannery O'Connor.[31]

Can art make eloquent something more profound than the suffering produced by, but excluded from, rational history? Perhaps surprisingly,

---

30. Adorno, *Aesthetic Theory*, 18–19.
31. See James Matthew Wilson, "Socrates in Hell: Hecht, Humanism, and the Holocaust," *Renascence* 63, no. 2 (Winter 2011): 147–68.

Adorno gestures toward such a fundament, located precisely in that which modern aesthetic theory is thought to have transcended: natural beauty.

Recall Adorno's phrase "primordial shudder." Great art can deliver a kind of shudder that is the image of the fear and awe man encountered in the premodern "enchanted" world. While, as we have seen, Adorno resists the "infantile" effort to tie the essence of art to religion, he understands well that the premodern encounter with the natural world as enchanted or, better, intelligible and creative (ordering us, rather than we it), was a real one. Kant tried to define it in subjective terms, when discussing the sublime in the *Critique of Judgment*, but succeeded only in suggesting man's spiritual domination of a physically intimidating natural world.[32] Adorno seeks to recover the real, trembling existential character of man's encounter with the "Book of Nature."[33]

The natural world once appeared authored and thus intelligible to us, filled with meanings that were necessarily mute or pre-conceptual for our yearning, uncertain intellects. Nature's beauty is specifically its appearance of saying "more than it is."[34] Its objects promise a reality, a significance, beyond their ontological presence as things. Or rather, the things of nature strike us as things insofar as they refuse merely to be themselves, to disappear into the shape of instruments for our use, but maintain an aura of speech that is withheld, that refuses to be heard, defined, and possessed. It may in fact seem to promise a word that will possess us, enchant us. This experience of enchantment is at once unifying—we feel ourselves fitted into a kind of reciprocity with nature—and alienating—we sense its power and inscrutable intention and so rightly fear it.[35] We encounter an intimation of identity with nature that only leads us further toward what Adorno emphasizes as its "non-identity," its existence as other or apart from us and our concepts.[36]

Adorno thus resents and dismisses the banal elations declaimed by na-

32. Kant, *Critique of Judgment*, 2.25.   33. Adorno, *Aesthetic Theory*, 67.
34. Adorno, *Aesthetic Theory*, 78.

35. Adorno remains very close to Kant here, but whereas Kant (and Burke before him) finds a sociality and harmony in natural beauty, Adorno finds a reminder of our alienation from true society. A poem Adorno would have despised, as he despised the work of Rilke, T. S. Eliot's *Four Quartets* in its several parts explores this elusive, mute intelligibility of nature as identity and non-identity, as cause of significance and shudder, of purposive harmony and threat to every harmony of a merely human, technological order.

36. Adorno, *Aesthetic Theory*, 68.

ture enthusiasts or romantic landscape painters. Such persons, as it were, patronize nature, making it simpler than it is: a place of pure, unmediated pleasures, a consolation where one can be at one with oneself and all things. On the contrary, "What is beautiful in nature is what appears to be more than what is literally there…. Natural beauty is perceived both as authoritatively binding and as something incomprehensible that questioningly awaits its solution."[37] Nature does not restore us to tranquility and oneness of identity, it rather bespeaks mystery after the fashion of the Christian mysteries of faith, above all the Paschal Mystery. The exploration or contemplation of nature, its enumeration, does not exhaust its meaning. Natural beauty makes sense to us and yet resists comprehension; it invites further attention and threatens us with the unpredictable, unspoken, and unconquerable at once.[38]

Artworks are produced and signify as if according to the method of nature; they are an artificial image of natural beauty not according to content (Adorno regarded landscape painting as a sign of bad conscience) but according to operation.[39] As such, they reproduce in us the shudder of man before primordial nature in a secondary, neutralized, or autonomous way. As art becomes more "spiritualized," moving away from representation and imitation, it approaches the being-in-itself with which nature confronts us; art grows more "natural" the less it imitates the content of nature.[40] Because the enchantment of nature has been overcome and subjected to instrumentalization in the modern age, the artwork becomes the only place where the Book of Nature still appears; the metaphor becomes literal. Adorno concludes,

The total subjective elaboration of art as a nonconceptual language is the only figure, at the contemporary stage of rationality, in which something like the language of divine creation is reflected, qualified by the paradox that what is reflected is blocked [for we know artworks are human creations]. Art attempts to imitate an expression that would not be interpolated human intention…. If the language of nature is mute, art seeks to make this muteness eloquent.[41]

Art thus strives to make present to us a primordial truth that—while never simple, pure, or "immediate," as the romantics or modern art-religion

---

37. Adorno, *Aesthetic Theory*, 70–71.
38. Adorno, *Aesthetic Theory*, 73.
39. Adorno, *Aesthetic Theory*, 71.
40. Adorno, *Aesthetic Theory*, 77.
41. Adorno, *Aesthetic Theory*, 78.

advocates claim—touches the reality of the human condition buried beneath ideology. Art's autonomy from modern use reminds us of, or reveals to us, the autonomy of the natural world in whose bosom all human beings uneasily live.

The importance of art as resistance is thus quite other than the familiar kinds of "resistance" or "protest" we expect to find besmirching college art museums and right-thinking galleries in our day. The "happenings" of the '60s, with their hope of restoring ritual and participation to art in a supposedly post-Christian, democratic age, Adorno eyed with disgust; they were perfectly intelligible to the sense of "false needs" in modern society, reducing art to one more means of integrating persons with social controls. As his students at the University of Frankfurt organized mass protests and demonstrations late in that decade, Adorno did not recognize himself in their idea of revolution and retreated further into works like those of Samuel Beckett and Paul Celan that truly resisted the logic of Enlightenment.[42] Any art or thought immediately susceptible to praxis—even the praxis of destroying public property—he saw as already reconciled to ideology. Freedom was not a condition in which one could live, and no political action or "engaged" art would bring it about; freedom rather was an experience one might have when encountering the mute language of true art in its broken isolation. The only response to such experience was a shudder.

One can readily imagine what Adorno would make of art in the decades since his death in 1969. He celebrated art's "mute eloquence," and yet most art now is subsidized to speak loudly and clumsily, oblivious to, even contemptuous of, its essential dependence on form. He clearly found the instrumental categories of modernity dehumanizing and destructive; yet the postmodern practice of treating distinction and aesthetic judgment alike as just one more ideology obscuring the essential indifference and equality of all things would strike him as exactly the *wrong* lesson to learn.

Most postmodern thought reduces everything to expressions of ideology, so that there is neither the possibility of a fragmentary shudder of truth's appearance nor any truth to appear—only joy in the simulacra that

42. Brian O'Connor, Introduction to *The Adorno Reader*, 10.

constitute human experience. For many years, Adorno reserved particular scorn for jazz music. Jazz presented itself as an act of rebellion, resistance, and freedom even as it was almost unprecedented in its degree of standardization and commoditization: "The range of the permissible in jazz is as narrowly circumscribed as in any particular cut of clothes."[43] Little interested in the aesthetic, "jazz fans" nonetheless wore their devotion as a badge of "non-conformist" individuality. He saw there the first instance of art *not* slowly being "neutralized" and absorbed by society, but rather, an art form conceived from the beginning to be marketed as a commodity whose specific (purchasable) content was a rejection of commodity society.[44] The myriad identical teen malcontents gazing at their shoes from within a veil of black-dyed hair as they sway to repetitions in a minor key, or those causing neighborhoods to quake with car stereos technologically altered merely to maximize the subcretinous thud of bass, are just a late manifestation of this commoditized rebellion against commodity, of standardized de-standardization.

Adorno thus stands as one of the great advocates and interpreters of "spiritualized" modern art. So penetrating was his critical intellect that he understood how the truth of artworks had found poignant expression in and against modernity, while also anticipating that its protest qualities would be reified and absorbed. His account of art's truth is too austere by half; in modernity, only art that was hermetic and difficult could be beautiful and make truth appear. Beckett's writings become the plausible angel of modern art, for they almost alone resist art's absorption without despairing of art itself, of form in its incongruous integrity, as a locus of truth.[45] Furthermore, the effective stasis and impotence in which Adorno's dialectical theory seems to leave us is predicated on an assumption that what is necessary cannot be objectively good, but good only in the eyes of ideology. He interpreted the reductive and, it would seem, power-dependent account of conceptual reason found in Kant in a way calculated to depict it as sinister and exploitative, but he never seems to have considered that Kant's might simply be a poor account of human reason. So, finally, his account of Enlightenment may rightly perceive its

---

43. Adorno, "The Perennial Fashion—Jazz," *Adorno Reader*, 270.
44. Adorno, "The Perennial Fashion—Jazz," *Adorno Reader*, 271.
45. Adorno, *Aesthetic Theory*, 81–82.

subtle and pernicious stratagems, but it refuses the possibility that even falsehood might be founded on the good-seeking essence of all actions.

This, I propose, stems from a typical modern error. Adorno understood well the Platonic vision of the beautiful as a visceral encounter with an order of reality that transcends and critiques the present, as changeless being inevitably "critiques" becoming insofar as it shows *how* it can be at all and *why* it is not fully what it could be.[46] But he makes a telling mistake, no doubt attributable to the Marxist atmosphere of his thought, in viewing the "promise" of beauty as a gesture toward the non-existing and utopic, which becomes visible only through its opposition to the present. In contrast, Plato, in the *Phaedrus*, tells us that the beauty we encounter in the flux of sensual, worldly experience participates in the form of beauty that is already present, achieved, and stable. We could not perceive realities in the flux if the forms that are truth and being were not already present; what changes is knowable only because it already participates in the truth of the forms beyond all change. In displacing the form of beauty from its proper realm, on the plain of truth, of pure intelligibility, and inserting it into that of Plato's utopia, Adorno confuses ideas with the ideal, and imprisons thought and reality alike. He circumscribes everything within the horizon of history, where ideology will always dominate, where necessity cleaves to untruth, and where truth can do no more than briefly appear. Truth does not reveal to us what is—and is eternally—but what could be. It is never present, for Adorno, the way it always and already is in knowledge, for Plato. And this has the unfortunate effect of perverting the longing (*eros*) provoked by art's appearance of beauty for a pure vision (*theoria*) into a search for *praxis*, for the Marxist harnessing of the intellect to bring about utopia.

And yet, for Adorno, there can be no *praxis*; that is precisely what he rejected in Marx's view of history. We are left then with an account of art's truth as one of stasis and presence, but with no place in Adorno's world for these things simply to *be*. It evidently exasperates him that for beauty and being to be present to us, we have only to know them, to see. And we may know them fully regardless of what historical or social effect that knowledge might ultimately have. Indeed, if Plato is correct, one's joy in

---

46. Adorno, *Aesthetic Theory*, 82.

the vision of the Good will generally be repaid, on the plane of history, with execution.[47] He may say this only to underscore that truth, goodness, and beauty are more real than what participates in them on the plane of history, such that they are always waiting to give themselves to us, are always already here wherever the mind is awakened to their light, even if the flux of the temporal remains dark. We err to confuse the presence of truth with the arrival of utopia. In teaching this, Plato was simply recapitulating the common experience of mankind.

Despite this serious weakness, Adorno's writings on art shine forth as singularly important. In an age anxious to reduce everything to ideology, "opinion," and "subjective" feeling, Adorno practically defined ideology for our century and showed that its opposite was not an anti-intellectual "bourgeois relativism" but a savage and pained adherence to truth. In an age when critics were (and are) largely enthralled to species of western Marxism, he refused the reduction of art either to *fait social* or to an instrument of *praxis*, even while attempting to make the nature of art intelligible in terms of those things. Finally, in an age of rationalists, sensationalists, and psychoanalysts, he argued for the real truth and formal significance of art. In the process, he demonstrated that it was possible for an aesthetic theory to be thoroughly historical without giving in to mere historicism. Art is a matter of truth and falsehood, right and wrong, of beauty and ugliness; to view it otherwise is not a sign of progressive, knowing enlightenment but of infantile commodity fetishism. The pretension of our elites, who hold so much of bourgeois life in contempt (from the family, to religious belief, to conformity with natural law), is belied by the fact that they are themselves the consummate bourgeoisie. In appearing to transcend the nickel-and-dime concerns of the average person, they expose, not a sensibility for true art, but simply a taste for more expensive modes of consumption. At this, Adorno's writings do more than weep.

Art, its beauty, and natural beauty are realities on which our lives depend, Adorno tells us, however muted or washed over they may appear in our time. But, as my brief discussion of his work in contrast with Plato's should suggest, his historical account of these realities is at best provi-

47. Plato, *Republic*, 361e–362a.

sional. It is instructive, insofar as it shows we can take art and beauty seriously even if we share neither a particular reverence for the imagination
nor have a developed metaphysics of being. But we do, at the last, need
such a metaphysics. What matters to us will always be that which we understand *to be*, and *to be* not just for us but in itself. And so, in the following chapters, we turn to Maritain, who offers one of the most compelling
accounts of the metaphysics of art and beauty voiced in the modern age.
Only in the Christian Platonist tradition out of which Maritain writes do
we see beauty take on its full existential dimension, as a reality given to
the senses, as drawing the mind to the perception of being and truth, and
finally to a vision of beauty as the ordering principle of reality as a whole.
Only in the light of such an account can we see why it is that beauty not
only unmasks untruth or makes truth's shards momentarily appear. It saturates all things; it cleaves to being and, with being, is chief among the
terms by which the soul sees reality. Fine art takes on a new importance,
not because of its isolation from society or politics, but because it attunes
us, awakens and habituates us, to the perception of the ordered whole of
reality.

EIGHT

Art as Intellectual Virtue

Jacques Maritain's *Art and Scholasticism* (1920) constitutes one of the French neo-Thomist philosopher's briefest and most austere works; and yet, belying the more or less serviceable prose and apparent modesty of scope, it is a wide ranging series of interventions on nearly every significant philosophical question of Maritain's—or any—day. In speaking of beauty, Maritain sought to guide the intellectual life of an entire age. This can make the short treatise and the essays and notes later appended to it difficult reading: one cannot fully appreciate the significance of Maritain's claims if one does not also sense the positions to which he responds. Added to this, Maritain sent his little book off into the intellectual circles of Paris, in 1920, knowing quite well that its identity, or rather, its literary genre would seem more than a little ambiguous. Was it, as its extensive footnotes suggested, an academic treatise somehow escaped from the under-siege and well-policed corridors of post-*Pascendi dominici gregis* (1907) official seminary philosophy?[1] Was it, conversely, in that age of avant-garde movements, yet one more manifesto detonating on the Left Bank in the years after Symbolism, Futurism, and Cubism, and contemporaneous with the emergence of the Surrealists? Historical philosophy or explosive manifesto?

1. For a superb summary of the ways the Catholic Church's often admonitory response to theological liberalism and modernism provided an occasion for the revival of Catholic intellectual life in general, see Kevin Starr, *The Lost World: American Catholic Non-Fiction at Midcentury* (Bismarck, N.D.: Wiseblood Books, 2016).

Naturally, what it was would shape how its words must be read, but Maritain's genius left this, too, ambiguous. *Art and Scholasticism* has therefore lived multiple lives, speaking to discontinuous audiences. Or rather, it speaks to us individually as distinct audiences, initiating us in a deliberate manner so that, if we read it as secular skeptics, pious faithful, or seasoned Christian philosophers, we will, at each turn to the text, discover something new. The book told its first audiences, and tells us now, that if we would know what is real, what is true, what is good, we must first and finally discover *all* within the radiance of the beautiful.

In method of argument, Maritain's small book reads much like the sundry theses and manuals on the thought of Thomas Aquinas and medieval Scholasticism that issued from the Catholic academy and press in the first half the twentieth century. The questions of the Schoolmen were not quite those we ask in modern times, works in this genre always began by confessing; and so, the careful scholar must sift through the *Summae* and Commentaries in search of the rare, often isolated, passages out of which some clear theory might be constructed. Maritain's small book assembles roughly forty references to the *Summa Theologica*, and nearly as many more to the minor works of Aquinas, Albert the Great, or John of Saint Thomas. What he reports to us calls into question some of what the modern world has presumed about art and beauty, while putting much of what it gets right upon entirely new foundations: Maritain affirms and modifies what artists from Baudelaire to Maurice Denis and Jean Cocteau had suggested, by equipping them with Thomist moderate-realist arguments.[2] This act of affirmation did not simply provide a Scholastic scaf-

---

2. All Christian Platonist thought is realist in nature (i.e., it holds that ideas, universals, are in some sense real and constitutive of beings). For Maritain and much of his generation, however, Aquinas's "moderate realism" was not only found to be convincing in itself as the true account of metaphysics, but also thought to counteract the insincere or rhetorical Platonism found in the liberal humanism of the nineteenth century. Moderate realism affirms the reality of ideas as formal causes and of forms as constitutive of beings, and present *in* beings; it denies, however, that the forms exist in themselves and as independent substances in which material things participate as mere imitations. Aristotle and Aquinas, in their realism, were thought to give a proper ontological and epistemic dignity to individual beings, whereas Plato was taken for an "exaggerated intellectualist" (*Art and Scholasticism and the Frontiers of Poetry*, 53), as an unworldly dualist, who denigrated the worth and denied the existential reality of individuals in favor of the ideal forms. On the significance of moderate realism, with its affirmation of the concrete "whole substance" rather than exclusively the "substantial form," for the theory of beauty, see Eco, *Art and Beauty in the Middle Ages*, 74–83. For more on modernism and Aristotle, see James Matthew

fold in support of modern notions—it drew them in new directions, as if to show us in the most gradual and unassuming manner possible that modern aesthetic theory, when it works itself out, will converge with that left implicit in Aquinas. The modern artist, in turn, when he thinks through what he already believes, will discover that his pursuit of beauty in the work of art has led him down such unexpected avenues as to leave him standing on the threshold of the Church.[3]

The suavity of this argument led to multiple conversions in France in the 1920s, and in the English-speaking world in subsequent decades. To the modern artist, *Art and Scholasticism* read like an avant-garde manifesto that only gradually disclosed its power as an apologetic. To the neo-Thomist philosophers and theologians of Maritain's and subsequent generations, it would appear as an enduring contribution to the revival of Scholasticism—inciting more extensive and historically sensitive work on medieval aesthetics, even as it retained the kind of academic authority for which few works could hope. The book sat on converts' shelves, but also appears in the footnotes of medieval scholarship to this day. If, as with much of Maritain's work, it was more a point of departure than the final word (including for Maritain), it has remained one of immense value. Again, the treatise told us, at once, what the modern world had forgotten about beauty, and yet also what its deepest instincts and intellectual appetites inarticulately craved.

Maritain's method follows the rudiments of Scholastic practice, distinguishing the smallest possible parts of any given argument with the intention of uniting them as an understood whole. His first such distinction in the treatise is between the virtue of art and the transcendental of beauty. Since Kant, we have tended to think of "art" as intending the fine arts exclusively, and to interpret beauty primarily in terms of its role in the fine arts; consequently, we have misunderstood both.[4]

The virtue of art is a practical rather than a speculative one, ordered to action rather than knowledge, to outward reification rather than the

---

Wilson, "Louis MacNeice's Struggle with Aristotelian Ethics," *New Hibernia Review* 10, no. 4 (Winter 2006): 53–70. For a rebuttal to the persistent but finally inadequate reading of Plato as denigrating rather than showing the true value of material reality, see Schindler, *The Catholicity of Reason*, 119–29.

3. Maritain, *Art and Scholasticism and the Frontiers of Poetry*, 174n73.

4. Maritain, *Art and Scholasticism and the Frontiers of Poetry*, 4.

interior complacency of the intellect. Art takes on further specification when contrasted with prudence. The practical, moral virtue of prudence is that by which a person acts suitably in a given situation, applying a general moral principle to a particular event. The prudent man knows how to do what is right here and now. Art is a practical virtue, but an intellectual rather than a moral one, ordered intrinsically to making, the "undeviating determination of works to be made."[5] If prudence proceeds from certain abstract laws to contingent actions whose consequences may vary radically, art is ordered to the realization of a definite idea in matter; prudence adapts to circumstance, art adheres strictly to the idea of the thing to be made. Prudence concerns the whole good of man *qua* man, art the activity of the man *qua* artist as one directed to a particular artifact.

Here, Maritain follows high Scholasticism to suggest to us the limited truth of modern notions of aesthetic autonomy.[6] In itself, the virtue of art has no end but the thing made; everything else is extrinsic to it. Indeed, the artist in possession of this virtue "will need a certain heroism in order to keep himself always on the straight path of Doing [prudence], and in order not to sacrifice his immortal substance to the devouring idol [the form to be reified as a work of art] that he has in his soul."[7] The artist *qua* artist has no end but the good of the thing to be made, but there is no such thing as the artist who is not first and always a man, just as there is no being that exists in isolation from all things else. Maritain clearly wants us to think of those great painters and poets who wasted away their being, so obsessed were they with realizing their spiritual vision. Hence his frequent references to Oscar Wilde and his longer-lived French counterpart, Andre Gide.[8] But we should think no less of the carpenter or watch maker in his workshop, holing himself up in the single-minded practice of his craft.

Maritain clearly admired the ascetical and heroic vision of such an immanent but nevertheless unworldly dedication. It leads him in many of his writings to slip by way of a pure romance of ideas from a Scholastic

5. Maritain, *Art and Scholasticism and the Frontiers of Poetry*, 9.

6. For Aquinas, the virtue of art, as an intellectual rather than a moral virtue, "does not presuppose the rectitude of the appetite" that is the work of prudence and the foundation of the other moral virtues (Aquinas, *Summa Theologica*, I-II.57.4–5).

7. Maritain, *Art and Scholasticism and the Frontiers of Poetry*, 16.

8. Maritain, *Art and Scholasticism and the Frontiers of Poetry*, 92.

style to something more lyric, not to say purple, which must have seduced his first audience, the modern poets and painters. "This work is everything for Art," he writes,

Hence the tyrannical and absorbing power of Art, and also its astonishing power of soothing; it delivers one from the human; it establishes the *artifex*—artist or artisan—in a world apart, closed, limited, absolute, in which he puts the energy and intelligence of his manhood at the service of a thing which he makes. This is true of all art; the ennui of living and willing ceases at the door of every workshop.[9]

Maritain flatters the artist *qua* artist with an autonomy that is also an ecstasy. The virtue of art leads the artist to make a sacrifice of himself for the realization of its end. This is all calculated to draw in his audience, since modern artists already operated with a sense of their work's "autonomy" and the heroism of the pursuit of its unworldly difficulty. The French philosopher makes it sound as if we would speak falsely to suggest that artistic work has any intrinsic moral or instrumental purpose. But this is not, finally, what he says. For, we would also speak falsely to suppose a man can live strictly as an artist without losing his humanity—and even his soul. The identity of someone as an artist is an accidental essence within the substantial reality of his being as a person. Thus, the artist, or artisan, has an intrinsic obligation to the thing he would make, but that thing may ultimately be subject to other considerations proper to orders of reality external and superior to the criteria of art.

To what use would a new invention be put?, we ask of the useful arts. Such a question is far more complicated with the "fine arts," whose thing made is not something useful but something ordered to the manifestation of Beauty Itself. According to Maritain, the Greeks subordinated the fine arts to reason, humanizing it by refusing to surrender it entirely to its own interior impulse, not to mention the many human and cultic uses that occasioned it and gave works of art their central place in ancient society. The medievals similarly subordinated art and beauty to the virtue of faith—a matter to which we shall return.[10] In those civilizations, beauty really did have its uses and so the arts were circumscribed alternately by faith and reason, sacrifice to the gods or the evangelization of the faithful. But, as

9. Maritain, *Art and Scholasticism and the Frontiers of Poetry*, 9.
10. Maritain, *Art and Scholasticism and the Frontiers of Poetry*, 161nn46, 22.

we shall see in the next two chapters, by the very fact that a work of art is ordered to beauty as its end, it stands in a necessary and intrinsic relation to multitudes: to other beings, to the ordered whole of reality, to God. In his opening salvo, however, Maritain elects to speak only of the limits set on beauty by things apparently external to it, to further reinforce the sketch he has given us of the artist as ascetic, as the one who heroically gives of himself for the sake of his work.

Only in the Renaissance do we see the artist cease to give himself up for his art precisely by denying to the beauty of his work its ordination to anything beyond itself. At that time, the artist became conscious of the "wild beast Beauty" as the sole and autonomous end of his work. But this new knowledge caused the artist to emancipate his genius from his humanity, at once exalting himself but also rendering himself *less* capable of producing the truly beautiful thing. For, if the work of fine art is ordered to Beauty Itself, beauty bears within it a more profound and mysterious order and identity than the fine artist's genius may discover working independently of faith and reason. In consequence, the artist may see and represent the beautiful, but be driven mad by it as well, climbing into those airy towers proper to the megalomania of one who thinks himself the divine origin of beauty, or lapsing into the void, the misery of one who can find no answer for the beauty of his work in the cosmos outside of it.

If Maritain initially affirms, for the virtue of art itself, the modern notion of it as autonomous and as having a self-absorbing and undeviating telos for the work made, he steers a more critical course between two other modern misconceptions. Above all, romantic and post-romantic aesthetics often reduce—or "elevate"—art to a kind of emotional excretion, whether as akin to the leaves on the trees or something more visceral. Conversely, in Maritain's day, self-styled neo-classicists held up the French playwright Jean Racine as the model of art as an ornamental exercise of the reason, or wit (*l'esprit*), of perfect method devoid of subjective, emotional, or spiritual interest. Maritain, here and in all his aesthetic writings, argues that art has more or less rightly come to be perceived as autonomous because it has become self-conscious and spiritualized as an *intellectual* virtue. The discovery of this truth belongs to the Romantics.[11] While

11. Walter Raubicheck, "Jacques Maritain, T. S. Eliot, and the Romantics," *Renascence* 46, no. 1 (Fall 1993): 71–79.

his later reflections on the telos of the fine arts as beauty will speak to this most powerfully, in the early pages of his treatise, he concerns himself with the more modest task of establishing art as intellectual rather than merely emotional, and as an intellectual rather than a moral virtue. If it is eminently practical in having its end as a *material* thing made, artistic work is nonetheless no mere decoration or ornament but a power of man as an essentially intellectual animal. It is

the properly human work, in contradistinction to the work of a beast or the work of a machine.... When work becomes *inhuman* or *sub-human*, because its artistic character is effaced and matter gains the upper hand over man, it is natural that civilization tends to communism and to a productivism forgetful of the true ends of the human being.[12]

The work that most befits man, as a rational animal, is the intellectual one of art, in which the idea impresses itself upon matter, subordinating, not to say dominating, it. It is worth our pausing to note that one hears an anthropology of human dignity in work here that Maritain's friend, Yves Simon; the English artist, Eric Gill; the Welsh poet, David Jones; and the great phenomenologist, Pope John Paul II—among many others—would subsequently elaborate.[13]

While the virtue of art is seated in the intellect and not in the powers of the body, art, even fine art, remains a kind of work. The practice of the virtue essentially entails reification, the ordering of an intellectual form to actualization in matter.[14] It cannot be, as the romantics might have had it, and as certain modernists dreamed of it, an effervescence of individual, oracular intuition that might someday free itself of matter altogether (more on this below). Rather than legitimizing art in an age given over to utilitarian and pragmatic—not to mention communistic materialist—concerns, however, Maritain seeks to demonstrate the dignity of artistic work as intellectual; in the art of logic, it even crosses over from the practical to the speculative and gets taken up into the contemplative life of the

12. Maritain, *Art and Scholasticism and the Frontiers of Poetry*, 154n4.

13. John Paul II's encyclical *Laborem Exercens* (September 14, 1981) is probably the fullest expression of this tradition of Catholic theology of work inaugurated by a Maritain footnote. For reasons that George Weigel has catalogued, however, this encyclical may be the *end* of that tradition as well, because of the radicalization and volatility of the conditions of work in our age—see Weigel, *Witness to Hope* (New York: Cliff Street Books, 1999), 421.

14. Maritain, *Art and Scholasticism and the Frontiers of Poetry*, 13.

philosophers and theologians.[15] He will elsewhere suggest that the fine arts similarly approximate this super-elevation—that they, indeed, form an analogue to the super-elevation of prayer made possible by the Holy Spirit.[16] As if expanding Joseph Pieper's great defense of leisure and contemplation from the degradation of a world of "total work," Maritain thus aligns art properly understood with a society ordered to dignified work, but also seeks to vindicate "true making" as a form of leisure and contemplation.

Maritain primarily wishes, however, to defend the intellectual nature of art from those modern artists and aestheticians who identify it with a mere emotional intuition. Man does not reduce himself to a beast of animal impulses to engage in "creative" work, shedding his reason like so many mind-forged manacles. Nor can he rightly reduce the exercise of his intellect to a series of categorical methods and mechanical practices, as Descartes and modern rationalists attempted to do with every previously distinct human activity.[17] At best, this reduces the intellect to the discursive operations of human reason, and at worst it reduces even that reason to the positivist and utilitarian ideal of the machine (Maritain here resists the Cartesian dream of comprehensive method, which has for ambition the hope that, "if we can just discover the correct *method* for art, even an idiot can become an artist").

Maritain turns to Aristotle and Aquinas alike for the vocabulary to save his intellectual vision of art from emotivist (romantic) and mechanical (neo-classical) reductions. He notes that art, like any virtue involving action, is a *habitus* of the practical intellect, and a *habitus* is the disposition of a person's appetites or inclinations. In this respect, art lies outside the reason or, rather, participates in aspects of the human being that are outside the *discursive* operations of the reason. But every virtue is a *habitus* specifically ordered by reason and, along with the will, is seated within the intellect.[18] All virtues are perfective of that person's intellectual nature rather than aberrant from it. We acquire a practical virtue "through

---

15. Maritain, *Art and Scholasticism and the Frontiers of Poetry*, 12. Maritain here follows but does not cite Aquinas, *Summa Theologica*, I-II.57.3.

16. See, for instance, Maritain, *Art and Scholasticism and the Frontiers of Poetry*, 130, and *The Situation of Poetry* (New York: Philosophical Library, 1955), 69–70.

17. Maritain, *Art and Scholasticism and the Frontiers of Poetry*, 39–40.

18. On the virtues' ordering of will to accord with reason, and the will's situation within the intellect, see Aristotle, *Nicomachean Ethics*, 1144b25–30, and Aquinas, *Summa Theologica*, I-II.9.5.

exercise and use," but it always "attests the activity of the spirit" and resides in the "intelligence or the will."[19] One can be taught to obey a slavish
method, but the *habitus* of art can only be imparted by apprenticeship, by
the kind of personal practice that gradually elevates the soul so that it may
accomplish, by its own inner direction, the making in matter of an idea
already in the mind. Through practice, the intellect becomes *connatural*
to the determining of a work. Thus, the virtue of art is truly intellectual,
gained only through the perfection of some aspect of the mind, even as
we may come to possess it as a second nature that seems to draw from resources outside the reason and that may even be experienced as a flashing
intuition whose swiftness seems almost a defiance of reason's sequential
ploddings.[20]

The *habitus* of the typical artisan, such as a carpenter, might mislead
us, however, into believing art far less intuitive and far more rationalistic
than it is. We see that he has a particular end in mind—a good house—
and that the principles of a better or worse house may be adjusted by an
explicit and predictable method to accord with what use we expect the
house to serve. But if this is, in truth, inadequate to the genius of the carpenter, how much more it is to that of the fine artist, in whose operation
the object to be made cannot be judged immediately in terms of its instrumental value in serving an end outside itself. The end of the fine arts, after
all, is the making of a thing whose primary end is not an extrinsic function
but an immanent beauty.[21] As such, the *habitus* of the fine artist obeys
rules connatural to himself, but these rules are neither as evident nor read-

---

19. Maritain, *Art and Scholasticism and the Frontiers of Poetry*, 10–11.

20. Maritain will later risk situating the act of the fine artist as the exemplar of "creative intuition" that really does stand outside the reason, but always within the intellect. As we saw above,
the second great insight of the western tradition is that the *ratio* of reason is grounded on the
intellectus that precedes, informs, and ultimately fulfills it. Maritain would choose to explore this
facet of the poetic (in the poet and the poem) in terms of a "spiritual unconscious" (*Creative Intuition in Art and Poetry*, 91). This gives his later writings on aesthetics a distinctly modern, rather
less "Scholastic," timbre, but is substantially coherent with Aquinas and the rest of the Christian
Platonist tradition. My focus in the following two chapters will fall on Maritain's philosophy of
beauty, which I take to be his aesthetics' greatest and most illuminating insight. Maritain, however, would become fascinated by his theory of the artist's creativity—by the operations of creative intuition and poetic knowledge. This is where the burden of his aesthetic works falls over
the course of more than three decades. For a systematic treatment of Maritain's philosophy of
"poetry" (meaning of artistic creativity), see Trapani, *Poetry, Beauty, and Contemplation*.

21. Maritain, in response to an uncharitable review by Montgomery Belgion, underscores

ily evaluable as are those of the arts in general. Because beauty "like being, has an infinite amplitude," there "is always an infinity of ways of being a *beautiful* work."[22] I shall elaborate on and qualify this claim in the chapters ahead. But for the present, it will suffice to note that Maritain has herein found a way to account for the infinite variety of beautiful forms in the fine arts that is superior to the theory of genius found in Kant, and which draws fruitfully on an insight found in a stray note by Pascal.

Maritain's neo-Thomist philosophy in general follows in Pascal's track as an apologetics of the *reasonableness* of Christian faith: one that is founded on a conviction that the intuition and sense of beauty can lead us into the waiting room of grace. Here, though, we find a specific debt: Maritain's discussion of art as *habitus* echoes Pascal's own meditations on method and poetic beauty:

> As we speak of poetical beauty, so ought we to speak of mathematical beauty and medical beauty. But we do not do so; and the reason is that we know well what is the object of mathematics, and that it consists in proofs, and what is the object of medicine, and that it consists in healing. But we do not know in what grace consists, which is the object of poetry. We do not know the natural model which we ought to imitate …[23]

Pascal's observation invites contradiction at several points, not least of which is the ancient and enduring perception that mathematics makes visible the convertibility of truth and beauty. As we saw in Part I, numbers can disclose truth to us (a "proof") but also reveal the formal structure of that truth as beautiful. We shall return to this near identity of number and form, truth and beauty, presently. But what I want to emphasize here is the note on which Pascal concludes. Derived from a model, but from one not even the artist may truly know in advance, *habitus* may appear esoteric and exclusive in its direction: the modern world wants efficiency and uniformity, it wants everything that counts as knowledge to be "re-

---

that he has never asserted "that the fine arts were ordered *exclusively* to beauty and that the other arts produced nothing beautiful", but only that "what distinguishes the fine arts from the other arts is not solely the social situation of the artist who practices them, it is above all the fact that in the fine arts the spiritual element introduced by the contact with beauty becomes preponderant" (Maritain, *Art and Scholasticism and the Frontiers of Poetry*, 114).

22. Maritain, *Art and Scholasticism and the Frontiers of Poetry*, 44.

23. Pascal, *Pensées*, §33.

vealable" to every half-intelligent mind, and so has trouble accepting that, while "method is for all ... *habitus* is only for some."[24]

We cannot hope to memorize the rules of art and then make good art, but neither can we rest on the assumption that some inspiration, some will not our own, is the source of that virtue. The romantic doctrines of natural ability, emotional intuition, and spontaneity are wrong, because they ignore the essentially intellectual source of art. However mysterious its resources, the intellect of the artist, rather than his kidney, conforms to a higher rule that is internal to the particular work and its particular beauty and that participates, as we shall see, in Beauty Itself. In Kant's theory of the artist as genius, we hear that the genius is the one who "gives the rule to art."[25] Kant's purpose is to show that, because the beautiful is not a concept or a perfection, it can draw on past models but should never imitate them. Past works of art serve as what Matthew Arnold would later call "touchstones" to train the taste and ready that of the genius to create works of genuine originality.[26] The variety of beauty in works of fine art is to be explained in subjective terms: those works are the products of individual geniuses who, in their art-work, are law-giving, not law-following. In contrast, Pascal intimates that the artist really is imitating. His work is an imitation of what has not yet been seen. The artist does not give rules and produce what is original, but discovers rules, dimensions of reality, hitherto unknown, for the sake of showing forth what transcends even the mind of the most formidable genius—the splendorous form of grace. It is the work itself that reveals to us its own rule, a rule by which it was already governed before it came into being. The good, the beauty, the being, of the work made remains the end and so also the expression of the law governing its realization. It is being that is infinitely various, not the intuitive mind of the artist. It is being that rules art.

Maritain's theory of art insists upon the humility of even the fine arts as work; the artist, in bringing a new beauty into the world, does so by way of selfless imitation of the hitherto unseen. But, in this submission to the being of the work, Maritain shows us the artist's and the work's spiritual and intellectual nature and glory. He grants to art a kind of self-directed

24. Maritain, *Art and Scholasticism and the Frontiers of Poetry*, 40.
25. Kant, *Critique of Judgment*, 1.46.
26. Kant, *Critique of Judgment*, 1.47.

autonomy, but he elsewhere shows that this autonomy is always informed by the complete way of life of an individual man and a human community, and is finally subject to the rule of divine love.[27] Perhaps surprisingly, given Maritain's status as a disciple of the medieval schoolman Thomas Aquinas, it is only because of the right ordering of all these attributes that he reserves a special place for the sacred artisans of the Middle Ages:

In the powerfully social structure of medieval civilization, the artist had only the rank of artisan, and every kind of anarchical development was forbidden his individualism, because a natural social discipline imposed on him from the outside certain limiting conditions. He did not work for the rich and fashionable and for the merchants, but for the faithful; it was his mission to house their prayers, to instruct their intelligences, to delight their souls and their eyes. Matchless epoch, in which an ingenious people was formed in beauty without even realizing it, just as the perfect religious ought to pray without knowing that he is praying; in which Doctors and image-makers lovingly taught the poor, and the poor delighted in their teaching, because they were all of the same royal race, born of water and the Spirit!

Man created more beautiful things in those days, and he adored himself less. The blessed humility in which the artist was placed exalted his strength and his freedom.[28]

But then came the Renaissance, and with it the relocation of the end of art in the exaltation of the individual genius, the pretensions of human making to divine creativity. While one hears in Maritain's work the notes of a certain romantic medievalism welling up, one hears also the craving for humility, for spiritual discipline and metaphysical realism that defined intellectual life in post–World War I France.[29] The soldiers dead in the trenches had suffered a similar "natural social discipline" not for the sake of merchant or banker—to wit, that bourgeois monstrosity, the *laïc* Third Republic—but for the *patria*, the French nation; all they lacked was a civilization worthy of their bodily and spiritual sacrifice. As Stephen Schloesser has shown in his book on Maritain, passages like this one speak not only of an age lost, but of an age that must yet come to be if only for the sake of the recently buried.[30]

27. Maritain, *Art and Scholasticism and the Frontiers of Poetry*, 71–75.

28. Maritain, *Art and Scholasticism and the Frontiers of Poetry*, 21–22.

29. Jacques and Raïssa Maritain, *Oeuvres Complètes* (Fribourg: Éditions Universitaires, 1984), 3:363.

30. Stephen Schloesser, *Jazz Age Catholicism: Mystic Modernism in Postwar Paris, 1919–1933* (Toronto: University of Toronto Press, 2005).

A revaluation of the nature of art as intellectual virtue and of human work as a *habitus*, at once rational yet above bourgeois mechanical formulae, addressed the needs of the age even as it set down permanent philosophical truths. It justified the proliferating, esoteric methods of modern art even as it recalled artists to an intellectual discipline they had explicitly eschewed. Once again, *Art and Scholasticism* shuffled with agility and ambiguity between manifesto of the moment and perennial philosophy. It explained with clarity the ascetical devotion of the artist to his work; it challenged the modern world to take such artistic discipline as a model for its moral and religious discipline; and, in these early pages, it summoned both to a renewed understanding of human life as a whole as something ordered by the intellect to the divine. Maritain's book had much to teach. It has much to teach us still, the most important being that art, as intellectual activity, finds its finality in a beauty that is one ("convertible") with truth. The rules of art, therefore, illuminate the laws of reality, and do so not merely by opening imaginative possibilities or revealing a utopian "other" to the superficial rationalism or ideological untruths of society. The fine arts touch on beauty and so do they on being and truth. It is to this electric point of contact that we now turn.

NINE

Beauty as a Transcendental

One can readily see how Maritain's Thomistic reflections on art at once flattered and admonished the artists of Paris's Left Bank and beyond. He corrected the romantic intuitionism of those who had learned from Kant that artistic beauty was that which pleases universally *without a concept*, but who had blended that philosopher's theory of genius with the sensationalism of Hume and Burke so that art had come to be thought of as not only beyond all intelligible rules save those the genius himself imposes, but also derived from something other than the intelligence. Maritain did this by rearticulating whatever truth there might be in those claims in terms central to Thomist philosophy: Being and Intellect.[1] Further, he argued that the romantics had been right on at least one count; they had made art conscious of itself and, in so doing, they had awakened it to its spiritual telos.[2] This new consciousness specifically perceived that the fine arts operate according to what he later would call "poetic knowledge" and "creative intuition": non-abstractive (concrete), non-discursive (intuitive) intelligence proceeding in accord with the ineffable logic of the artwork's internal laws.[3]

1. In this, Maritain helped give a properly philosophical foundation to the "classicism" T. S. Eliot had already begun to popularize in England. Eliot's classicism would eventually make explicit its connection to Thomism in the pages of *The Criterion*. See James Matthew Wilson, "Style and Substance: T. S. Eliot, Jacques Maritain, and Neo-Thomism," *Religion and Literature* 42, no. 3 (Autumn 2010): 49–81, and "Ancient Beauty, Modern Verse: Romanticism and Classicism from Plato to T. S. Eliot and the New Formalism."

2. Cf. Maritain, *Art and Scholasticism and the Frontiers of Poetry*, 115.

3. Maritain, *Art and Scholasticism and the Frontiers of Poetry*, 52, 192n123.

What was the proper end of this knowledge, this intuition, of fine art as a whole? Was it an autonomous encounter with existence that could become a little god in a rarified religion of its own? Was art the idol to the divine creativity of the artists?[4] Certainly, that seemed to be the assertion of advocates of "pure poetry," to whose aesthetics Maritain cautiously demurred.[5] Art drives toward *being* by way of *beauty*, Maritain would answer. Only in grasping that movement do we discover the way in which art is produced by natural reason but ordered to the absolute. It is oriented to God in a purely analogous and asymptotic fashion that may be usefully contrasted with theology in telos and from metaphysics in method.[6]

In philosophy, he would say, one reasons discursively by means of abstraction toward a knowledge of the truth; in poetry, the artist's knowledge subsists in the idea of the thing to be made and is communicated purely in the concrete work he brings into being. Art conveys knowledge without abstraction and so, in some sense, without a concept; even so, it is an intellectual act, more intuitive and elusive than the demonstrations of the metaphysician, but also more concrete and existential in character.[7] This particular contrast and complementarity between metaphysics and poetry proved an abiding interest to Maritain and underlies everything he has to say on the nature of art.

In *The Frontiers of Poetry* he would speak of metaphysics as a science that "gives chase to essences and definitions," while poetry accepts intuitively and passively any "flash of existence glittering by the way."[8] Because all created being is constituted by the union of essence and existence, metaphysics and poetry converge upon the same reality, but by the distinct paths of essence and existence.[9] So, also, in his larger philosophy of knowledge, Maritain would establish metaphysics and poetic knowledge as two natural (and perforce, asymptotic) analogies to the infused and elevated knowledge of faith and mysticism: each of them served as a way by which the human being could encounter the depths of being, which is

---

4. Maritain, *Art and Scholasticism and the Frontiers of Poetry*, 120–22.

5. Maritain, *Art and Scholasticism and the Frontiers of Poetry*, 122–23.

6. Maritain, *Art and Scholasticism and the Frontiers of Poetry*, 122.

7. Maritain, *Art and Scholasticism and the Frontiers of Poetry*, 162n56.

8. Maritain, *Art and Scholasticism and the Frontiers of Poetry*, 128.

9. See Thomas Aquinas, "On Being and Essence," chapters 2 and 4 in *Selected Writings*, ed. Ralph McInerny (London: Penguin Books, 1998), 32–37, 41–43.

Being Itself, though these natural ways suffered intrinsic limitations that divine grace alone could remove.[10] In "The Majesty and Poverty of Metaphysics," he would dilate:

There is a sort of grace in the natural order presiding over the birth of a metaphysician just as there is over the birth of a poet. The latter thrusts his heart into things like a dart or rocket and, by divination, sees, within the very sensible itself and inseparable from it, the flash of a spiritual light in which a glimpse of God is revealed to him. The former turns away from the sensible, and through knowledge sees within the intelligible, detached from perishable things, this very spiritual light itself, captured in some conception. The metaphysician breathes an atmosphere of abstraction which is death for the artist. Imagination, the discontinuous, the unverifiable, in which the metaphysician perishes, is life itself to the artist.[11]

If Maritain seemed to reject yet refashion the romantics' finally anti-intellectual theories regarding the origin of art, his theory of the fine arts' *final cause* performed a similar task in regard to the modernist ideas gaining currency in post-War Europe. The thirst for a realism that cut through the sentiments and fantasies of romantic spirituality—one that affirmed the poet is just a man, and man is just a creature subject to misery and bodily death more often than he is privy to elevating emotions—had led to a proliferation of doctrines of "classicism" and "impersonality" among post-War literati. These doctrines sometimes took for model the blueprints of the mechanical engineer, wherein the austerity of design seemed to sober up a mind grown bloated on the indulgence of sentimental watercolors. If this cold, dispassionate vision of art as design appeared, at first, realistic in the sense of reducing the artist to engineer and the world to what the positivist and rationalist mind could quantify with certainty, it was finally realistic in another, transcendent, sense.

The absolute exigencies of mathematics and mechanics bespoke, to modernists as they once had to Pythagoras, a changeless order beyond the vicissitudes of quotidian life, at once inaccessible to the human spirit and chastising of it. Biological life is slush; the absolute is hard, numeric. A realism that aspires to the photograph can only document appearances; a realism that abstracts and penetrates beyond the surface of things, in con-

10. Maritain, *The Degrees of Knowledge*, 5.
11. Maritain, *The Degrees of Knowledge*, 2.

trast, may capture the eternal presences in a world of flux.[12] Maritain's account of art as work-in-humility and as intellectual rather than emotional flattered these notions, even as he directed them to unexpected ends. Once again, he would say, art is a virtue of the intellect, and the work of the fine artist is ordered to beauty. Before his audience could sneer at how "Victorian" and Paterian all this was, he would add: he did not mean the beauty of the early Burke, of the aesthetes, or the beauty of decadent sensualism, the beauty of the soft line or the tender melody, much less the beauty of bourgeois Europe, with its moralistic and preening sensibility. The nerve centers and heart strings were too imprecise an instrument for what he had in mind. Beauty for the Schoolmen was a metaphysical principle, a transcendental property of being. If one would grasp what *is*, what exists, what is real—then one had better understand beauty with exactitude. For beauty reveals being in its fullness, and beauty is most difficult.

The historical success of Maritain's account of beauty, which would launch a thousand theses and make the philosophy of beauty the site of neo-Thomism's widest dissemination in lay and non-Catholic culture in the twentieth century, only confirms its success as philosophy. Although he took as his starting point the fashions and prejudices of his age, the greatest contribution of *Art and Scholasticism* would be to provide us the foundations for an enduring and satisfactory account of beauty as a property of being—one sufficiently clear that through it we can better understand the fine arts and any beautiful thing, and by means of which we can judge the artistic tendencies of any age. In his later writings on art and beauty, Maritain would always insist that he approached his work as a philosopher, not a practicing artist; if this appeared the qualification of the inexpert, it was really intended to suggest the lasting, if abstract, character of his observations.[13] His little book may have played the manifesto to its early Parisian readers, but its ultimate audience was man, whose eyes by their nature seek out the beautiful form that provides a gleam of the beatific vision—man, no matter his historical condition, in search of the real.

Following Aquinas, Maritain sets before us three related definitions of beauty, which we might sum up as beauty as first perceived, beauty in its

---

12. These sentences paraphrase the modernist aesthetic theory of T. E. Hulme. See T. E. Hulme, *Speculations* (London: Routledge and Kegan Paul, 1987), 8–11 and 82–85. Cf. Schloesser, *Jazz Age Catholicism*, 164.

13. Maritain, *Art and Scholasticism and the Frontiers of Poetry*, 119.

interior essence, and beauty in its relational fullness of being. The first is beauty as it initially strikes us in experience: the beautiful is "that which, being seen, pleases: *id quod visum placet*."[14] The second defines the essence; Saint Thomas assigned three conditions to beauty, which Maritain preserves:

> *Integrity*, because the intellect is pleased in fullness of Being; *proportion*, because the intellect is pleased in order and unity; finally, and above all, *radiance* or *clarity*, because the intellect is pleased in light and intelligibility.... *splendor formae*, said Saint Thomas in his precise metaphysician's language: for the form, that is to say, the principle which constitutes the proper perfection of all that is, which constitutes and achieves things in their essences and qualities, which is, finally, if one may so put it, the ontological secret that they bear within them, their spiritual being, their operating mystery—the form, indeed, is above all the proper principle of intelligibility, the proper *clarity* of every thing.[15]

Third, and finally, Maritain would syllogistically draw this definition of the essence toward the final cause, beauty as that property of being that manifests the form in itself and in all its intelligible relations, including its relation to God as Beauty Itself. If form is the principle of being of any and every thing, and if it is form that constitutes beauty, then beauty must be convertible with being: every thing, insofar as it has being, must have to that extent beauty. Along with unity, goodness, and truth, beauty must be one of the transcendental properties of being—and, as God is Being Itself, so these properties must name God.[16]

Each of these three definitions merits inspection. Maritain cannot entirely avoid condescension regarding Aquinas's first definition. The beautiful pleases, it delights *us* who see it. In the climate of post-War Europe, this appeared to locate beauty in the subjective experience of the person, perhaps idealizing the capacities of the human subject but only at the expense of "objective" reality. By no coincidence, the wider phenomenon of this sort of idealization—in epistemology, metaphysics, and theology—would be the target of Maritain's sustained criticism. We cannot understand the *visio*, as it has come to be called, subjectively, says Maritain. Rather, Aquinas intends us to understand this statement as an affirmation of the onto-

14. Maritain, *Art and Scholasticism and the Frontiers of Poetry*, 23.
15. Maritain, *Art and Scholasticism and the Frontiers of Poetry*, 24–25.
16. Maritain, *Art and Scholasticism and the Frontiers of Poetry*, 30.

logical reality of beauty: the human mind is fundamentally intellectual or rational; it is therefore fundamentally oriented to that which is *intelligible*, and what is intelligible par excellence is being. The beautiful pleases us because we are encountering a kind of reality that, as intelligible, is proportioned to our intellects. Or, better: by our very natures, we move toward the reality outside ourselves, to which we are ordered. If we are pleased, it is because beauty is a reality known rather than a sensation had.

Because our delight in beauty is ontological—because it is an encounter of the intellect with being—it tells us something about the particular way human beings know. Because of our reason, we can come to a knowledge of anything that is intelligible, no matter how abstract, but we tend to call beautiful primarily that which is sensible. Human reason, because embodied, apprehends most naturally sensible or material things.[17] The beautiful, insofar as it is concrete, is thus so perfectly oriented to our comprehension that it is *given* to us without effort: the intelligence, here, "does not have to disengage an intelligible from the matter in which it is buried, in order to go over its different attributes step by step; like a stag at the gushing spring, intelligence has nothing to do but drink."[18]

Far from entertaining those post-Cartesian problems of idea and reality, of mind and body, which he would elsewhere show to be false dilemmas, Maritain suggests that the experience of beauty acts as a proof that the human intellect is an embodied one and effortlessly *sees* being and beauty in the real.[19] So immediate—indeed, intuitive—is this perception that Maritain views any conceptual delineation of the beautiful as either retrospective or preparatory; we fashion concepts in order to understand the distinct parts of what we already know in seeing, and while the discourses of "education and instruction" can prepare us for receptivity and perception, they are not to be confused with it.[20] Of the two hundred fourteen endnotes in the book, one of the longest, the fifty-sixth, provides the critical background to Maritain's conclusions: there, he demolishes and reconstructs Kant's *Critique of Judgment* in order to show the superiority of the Schoolmen. If Kant spoke correctly in saying the beautiful is *without a concept*, his followers misread in believing that beauty stands

17. Maritain, *Art and Scholasticism and the Frontiers of Poetry*, 24.
18. Maritain, *Art and Scholasticism and the Frontiers of Poetry*, 26.
19. Maritain, *The Degrees of Knowledge*, 78.
20. Maritain, *Art and Scholasticism and the Frontiers of Poetry*, 26, 165.

apart from the intelligence. Rather, beauty is, in a sense, the intellect concretized, form shining on matter, in the case of sensible beauty, and form as a reality in itself, shining forth in all its intelligibility, in the case of intellectual beauty. In either case, beauty owes its initially non-conceptual nature to its supra-rational intelligibility, its richness rather than poverty of being, to its being the very visibility of the form that actualizes things as real.

To the essential account of the extra-mental reality, the interior essence, of beauty Maritain turns next: Integrity, Proportion, and Clarity. Wherever these three qualities are found, according to Aquinas, there is beauty—and, when seen, it pleases. How one defines and orders these three qualities will determine how one understands beauty more generally. We shall consider in detail Maritain's discussion of them, in this chapter, and then consider some criticisms that deepen and fill out his discussion, in the next.

Maritain rightly understands integrity as wholeness, the completion of a thing according to its nature.[21] When something is mutilated, lacking what it should possess, we find integrity wanting and the thing itself ugly. This is easy enough to concede in terms of natural beauty, as anyone who has seen a severed limb can attest. But in the fine arts, Maritain quickly affirms, the integrity of the artwork is distinct from what it represents: "if it pleases a futurist to give the lady he is painting only one eye, or a quarter of an eye, no one denies him the right to do this: one asks only—here is the whole problem—that this quarter of an eye be precisely all the eye this lady needs *in the given case*."[22] The *virtue* of art alone can determine a given work's integrity—the standards or laws of a work are internal rather than external to its nature.

Maritain spends little time discussing proportion, as if the intrinsic instability of measuring one thing relative to another discomforted him. It discomforted Plotinus and Edmund Burke, too. Plotinus found an aesthetics rooted in proportion absurd, because in such a case, beauty would be a mere relation, not a reality in itself. But, as we saw above, the One has no relation, because of its transcendence, and yet its light is beauty. Intellectual beauty must therefore be a brilliance that transcends all fig-

---

21. Maritain, *Art and Scholasticism and the Frontiers of Poetry*, 27. Cf. John W. Hanke, *Maritain's Ontology of the Work of Art* (The Hague: Martinus Nijhoff, 1973), 21.

22. Maritain, *Art and Scholasticism and the Frontiers of Poetry*, 27.

ure, even if the beauty perceptible by the senses have proportions specifically because it is delimited by matter and so is subject to measurement. For Burke, writing in the mid-eighteenth century, the notion of beauty as rooted in proportion posed a different challenge. It suggested that beauty was convertible with number and that there could be, in consequence, a mathematical equation for beauty that would simply be "struck" over and over again in every beautiful thing.[23] "Mathematical ideas," he argues, "are not the true measure of beauty."[24] He sees neo-classical aesthetics, with its veneration of symmetry and geometrical forms, as the consequence of an aesthetics of mere proportion. But these features are more a cause of boredom than pleasure.[25] The beautiful, if it is to induce pleasure and love as Burke says it must, should "shun the right line, yet deviate from it insensibly."[26]

Maritain's account, which owes a great deal to neo-Platonism as does it to Burke's romanticism, is sensitive to both these objections. And yet, if he is to be faithful to his reading of Aristotle and Aquinas, he can no more ignore proportion than integrity because both powerfully speak to the ontological nature of beauty. Aristotle writes in the *Metaphysics* that "definition is a sort of number."[27] By this he means that the formal principle of a thing, the nature, that makes it to be *what* (the kind of thing) it is may be in some sense understood as a ratio, as a relative addition and subtraction of qualities. A plant has life, but a dog has life and the capacity for movement, and so on. This suggests not, Aristotle argues, that all things are reducible to number. That was the error of Pythagoras.[28] Rather, it teaches us that natures are perceptible as forms, as measures or proportions, and everywhere there is being there is form. When we speak of proportion, of what is ordered and fitting, we are always speaking of form, and the union of form and matter constitutes complex beings in reality. Integrity is the term for a proportion that describes the internal relations of the form to itself; in a material thing, its shape, in an intellectual one, the arrangement of its conceptual or intelligible elements. In every case, integrity is the proportion of the existent individual to its nature or essence—it measures how fully a thing has become what it is, how fully it has realized

23. Burke, *A Philosophical Enquiry*, 130.   24. Burke, *A Philosophical Enquiry*, 137.
25. Burke, *A Philosophical Enquiry*, 140.   26. Burke, *A Philosophical Enquiry*, 157.
27. Aristotle, *Metaphysics*, 1043b34.   28. Aristotle, *Metaphysics*, 1002a–b.

its own essence. To be fitting to oneself, to be whole, to be truly oneself, is to *have* integrity. Let us note, then, that the singularity of a thing as being itself—as having integrity—is in itself relational. It places a being in relation to something beyond itself—in this case, its essence. Being would seem to be relational, and the encounter with *integritas* discloses one particularly fundamental relationship that may be thought of in terms of the proportion of individual to universal, of thing to form, and of existence to essence. Maritain scarcely touches on all this in his philosophy of beauty. In his later metaphysical writings, however, stimulated by the existential Thomism of Etienne Gilson, Maritain will brilliantly explore the paradoxical proportionality or relationality—what he calls "a species of polarity"—of essence and existence.[29]

While proportion certainly refers to this integral relation of a thing to itself, Aquinas most obviously intends by it what the young Saint Augustine comprehended under the term of harmony: the relation of distinct beings and their formal elements relative to one another.[30] Maritain seems to take this aspect of proportion primarily in terms of *composition*, the spatial arrangement of things relative to one another, rather than in the more expansive sense that Aquinas intended: proportion must be understood in terms of the total number of relations between a thing and everything else, and the degree to which those relations are fitting, or well proportioned. To this we shall return, not only because I believe Maritain errs here, but because, for reasons neither Plotinus nor Maritain grasped, it is the primary condition of beauty without which one cannot understand the rest. The evident reason Maritain pays it little mind is that he views the term proportion as bearing less weight than it in fact does, and he does so because he has inadvertently followed Plotinus in silently transposing much of this important aspect of proportion into the third quality of the beautiful: *claritas*.

Clarity, the splendor of the form, Maritain refers to above all as "radiance," and treats it as by far the central and most capacious element of the beautiful. It may begin with the material radiance of color, which is our familiar analogue for it, but it primarily describes the attribute we

29. Jacques Maritain, *A Preface to Metaphysics: Seven Lectures on Being* (New York: Sheed and Ward, 1940), 63–65.

30. Augustine, *Confessions*, IV.13.20.

encounter when we discover the inherent intelligibility and signification of things. We perceive this radiance in terms of the relative power of
the human intellect to receive the form of a being into itself, but we also
perceive it in terms of what can be known but never comprehended: the
manifestation in the form of the mystery of being, of the absolute *Logos*,
the creative intelligence of God, who causes all things to exist and to be
knowable. When we detect the radiance of a thing, we are encountering
it as a mystery that makes sense: something obscure, because its essence is
concealed from us, but also something self-revealing, because ordered to
being and intellect at once. If integrity and proportion sound to some sen-
sualist, subjective, and relative in nature, clarity denotes the stark confrontation of the mind with the ontic reality of things as formed for existence
by the absolute intellect of God. We delight in understanding and uncertainty at once, in seeing things existing, in seeing their *be-ing*, and we
sense their radiation of Being Itself whose effect they are: "the deep-seated
splendor one glimpses of the soul, of the soul principle of life and animal
energy, or principle of spiritual life, of pain and passion ... [and] there is
a still more exalted splendor, the splendor of Grace."[31] This ontological
splendor of beauty stands out as our encounter in concrete terms with being and with Being Itself; in beauty we *see* in existence what metaphysics
can only describe and define in terms of essence and by means of the discursive reason.

   At the risk of repeating these observations, it is worth quoting Maritain's lengthy footnote on radiance:

By "radiance of the form" must be understood an *ontological* splendor which is in
one way or another revealed to our mind, not a *conceptual* clarity. We must avoid
all misunderstanding here: the words *clarity, intelligibility, light,* which we use to
characterize the role of "form" at the heart of things, do not necessarily designate
something clear and intelligible *for us*, but rather something clear and luminous
in itself, intelligible *in itself*, and which often remains obscure to our eyes, either
because of the matter in which the form in question is buried, or because of the
transcendence of the form itself in the things of the spirit. The more substantial
and the more profound this secret sense is, the more hidden it is for us; so that, in
truth, to say with the Schoolmen that the form is in things the proper principle
of *intelligibility*, is to say at the same time that it is the proper principle of mys-

31. Maritain, *Art and Scholasticism and the Frontiers of Poetry*, 29.

tery. (There is in fact no mystery where there is *nothing to know:* mystery exists where there is *more to be known* than is given to our comprehension.) To define the beautiful by the radiance of the form is in reality to define it by the radiance of a mystery.[32]

In rushing past integrity and proportion to clarity, Maritain reveals his powerful attraction to, even fixation on, the single most potent insight of the Christian Platonist tradition, though one which is comparatively obscure in Aquinas: the status of beauty as a transcendental property of being.[33] Defined immanently, something is a transcendental if it is present in any and every thing regardless of the kind of thing it happens to be.[34] One may not find it very illuminating to be told that "thing" is a transcendental, because every thing (being) is by definition a thing. Nor is it immediately startling to learn that unity is a transcendental: everything that is *something* is by definition *a* or *one* thing and not multiple, even if it is composed of multiple elements or qualities. I know that a book is made of a cover, pages, some thread, and some glue—but taken together these things become a unity (an "accidental nature") to which I refer when I say, "book."[35]

But, even on the side of immanence, the transcendentals do begin to instruct us more profoundly than this. That all things that exist are true tells us a great deal: that beings, in their very being, are real, and that the substance the intellect drinks when it knows, truth, is one with the stuff of reality. That things are true tells us at least two things about them: that the existent thing, to the degree that it is true, conforms to the creative idea that puts it in being; and that the one who perceives and knows the thing possesses its truth to the extent that the idea adequately conforms to the thing.[36]

---

32. Maritain, *Art and Scholasticism and the Frontiers of Poetry*, 28.

33. Sufficiently obscure that many interpreters of Aquinas prefer to render Beauty not a transcendental property, but to follow quite strictly *one* of Aquinas's statements that beauty is a *tertium quid* standing behind truth and goodness as a union of them, rather than standing alongside them as a property of being. See Jan A. Aertsen, "Beauty in the Middle Ages: A Forgotten Transcendental?," *Medieval Philosophy and Theology* 1 (1991), 68–97. I reject this "demotion" of beauty for several reasons discussed in previous chapters and below.

34. See Jorge J. E. Gracia, "The Transcendentals in the Middle Ages: An Introduction," *Topoi* 11, no. 2 (September 1992): 113–20.

35. It may not be startling, but it should be! That beings are one gives us in fact the whole mystery of form in little. See William Carroll, "Illusions of Unity? Mind, Value, and Nature," *Public Discourse* (www.the publicdiscourse.com), September 23, 2013.

36. Maritain, *The Degrees of Knowledge*, 93.

Good as a transcendental tells us even more: everything, insofar as it exists, is good. It may be a greater or lesser good according to the degree of its nature, and so we sense an intelligibility to the order of things expressed as hierarchy. Moreover, we detect an internal ordering to things, their nature; a thing is a good thing when it *is* as its nature orders it to be (as it should be when fulfilling itself, its telos). Thus, we note a further intelligibility in things when recognizing that something is "evil" or "bad" insofar as it is not what, by its own nature, it should be; we understand all things in terms of a basic positive affirmation of being of which evil is a *no-thing*, a negation. These hierarchical and internal perceptions of the goodness of things are rooted in what Aquinas describes as a threefold goodness of things:

first, according to the constitution of its own being; secondly, in respect of any accidents being added as necessary for its perfect operation; thirdly, perfection consists in the attaining to something else as the end.[37]

When we call something good, we may mean any and all of these things. The existence of a thing is the outcome, the final cause, of its maker's intention; insofar as a thing is intended, it is the good of some prior operation. But that thing, now having existence, becomes better insofar as it increases in being: the plant grows, the student learns, the man acquires moral virtues, the electric clock receives a fresh battery. In every case, something accidental to the being allows it to become more fully itself. But, finally, something must guide the being in this act of fuller existence. An end, beyond the existence of a thing, draws that thing toward it—that is, there is some good beyond itself at which the thing aims. Clearly, goodness adds to truth, but it does not stand really apart from truth as something *other*, because inquiry into the goodness of something is inquiry into the causes that make a thing to be, and to be true, in the first place. To deny the presence of goodness in things would be to deny the intelligibility, and therefore the *truth*, of beings.[38]

Extending this observation to the beautiful comes naturally, although doing so may lead us to conclude, as does Maritain at one point, that it is just a *kind* of good: we know most goods as goods because our will, our

37. Aquinas, *Summa Theologica*, I.6.3.
38. Aristotle, *Metaphysics*, 994b10–14. Cf. Maritain, *The Degrees of Knowledge*, 25.

appetite, knows rest when they come into our possession, while the beautiful is that quality in a thing which allays our appetite on sight—as soon as it is possessed by the intellect through the senses.[39] On this account, to affirm the reality of beauty would do no more than to say that what is known as true can, simply through that knowledge, be enjoyed as good. We shall see that Maritain's whole account invites us to step beyond this conclusion.

As much as Maritain emphasizes the real being of the transcendentals in all their immanence, he hedges his account of them quite closely in his endnotes, conceding that in "the things of this world … truth, beauty, goodness, etc., are aspects of being *distinct according to their formal reason*, and what is *true simpliciter* (absolutely speaking) may be *good* or *beautiful* only *secundum quid* (in a certain relation)."[40] Thus, each of these attributes "command distinct spheres of human activity, of which it would be foolish to deny *a priori* the possible conflicts, on the pretext that the transcendentals are indissolubly bound to one another."[41] This prismatic, immanent disunity of the transcendentals may, in a sense, make the world sad, bespeaking its fallen and fragmented state. And this sadness may explain why Maritain's treatise must throw down the gauntlet on the reality of beauty: the positivism and utilitarianism of the age has a firm, if perverse, conception of what is true and what is good respectively. True things are the evident end of the reason, and good things of appetite or will, but "empirically speaking" there did not seem to be much basis for talk of beauty except as a loose, cloudy adjective for certain unverifiable sentiments a peculiarly sensitive form of clever animal might sometimes feel.

Maritain wishes to drive us beyond the affirmations we can make based merely upon the apparent surfaces of things. If truth, goodness, and beauty in things are relative and imperfectly perceived, his realist metaphysics nonetheless drives us to the certitude of beings. Further, the perception of beings leads the intellect to the principle of Being, and the transcendental reality of Being Itself who is God. We relative beings are only analogous to God as Being Itself, and so, if the transcendentals are immanently convertible, so also, the unity, goodness, truth, and beauty of things are also ana-

---

39. Maritain, *Art and Scholasticism and the Frontiers of Poetry*, 26.
40. Maritain, *Art and Scholasticism and the Frontiers of Poetry*, 174n68.
41. Maritain, *Art and Scholasticism and the Frontiers of Poetry*, 174n68.

logues to God as the super-substantial eminent realization of these properties.[42] He is the transcendent or absolute transcendental. In brief, "God is beautiful.... He is beautiful through Himself and in Himself, beautiful absolutely." "Thus Beauty is one of the divine names."[43]

Maritain's thought, as a whole, can be understood as concerned primarily with metaphysics and epistemology; the philosophies of art and beauty, along with his theories of mysticism, are simply exemplary and unusual cases within that concern. That is, he tried to reorient his age to recognize that it perceived being, and that, in perceiving being, it perceived truth. In analogous fashion, he tried to show that we perceive beauty and, in perceiving it, once again, our mind flashes upon being and truth. Taken together, all that we see, with the senses and with the light of the intellect, is an analogue of God and leads us to him. Because beauty "belongs to the transcendental and metaphysical order," Maritain writes, "it tends of itself to draw the soul beyond the created."[44] The quintessential poet of modernity, Baudelaire, had seen as much, apprehending the "theological quality and tyrannical spirituality of beauty."[45] Beauty is the end of the fine arts; it is an absolute in itself. But all things are intrinsically self-transcending, with lesser things touching upon higher by way of anticipation. And so, it is the *claritas* of beauty, the way this form here before me discloses a splendor that seems to radiate from behind and above itself, that in fact stirs us toward a vision of God as Beauty Itself.

The analogy we make between relative beings and Being Itself, beautiful things and Beauty Itself, affirms the fundamental Platonic insight to which the Schoolmen, for all their supposedly hardheaded fidelity to the moderate realism of Aristotle, clung: the beautiful reveals not simply our creaturely yearning for God, but our existential *participation* in him. The clarity of the beautiful does not show forth a likeness in the sense of a comparison (a strict formulation of analogy), but rather confronts our senses and intellectual vision with the presence of God in things and the participation of things in God. The discursive process of abstraction, which may gradually lead us by deduction to some knowledge of God,

42. Maritain, *The Degrees of Knowledge*, 14, 241.
43. Maritain, *Art and Scholasticism and the Frontiers of Poetry*, 30.
44. Maritain, *Art and Scholasticism and the Frontiers of Poetry*, 32.
45. Maritain, *Art and Scholasticism and the Frontiers of Poetry*, 32.

though particularly proportioned to the human reason, is far more mediated and far less adequate than this encounter with God in Beauty. We
see him under the mode of Beauty. Our sensible perception of beauty in a
beautiful object is not so much a mediation as a manifestation of a divine
reality; this accounts for its intensity, which the most lucid demonstration cannot rival.[46]

When Maritain speaks of fine art as ordered to beauty, therefore, we
cannot object to the supposed quaintness of this claim and marshal forth
the myriad "ugly" artworks of the last century, much less the ugliness of
historical atrocity. For Maritain does not mean that artists make pretty
things. Beauty is not a perfection of some beings, but a property of all. His
claims are, in this respect, entirely in concert with Adorno's description of
the "shudder" produced by great art. Maritain means that the virtue of
art is, in the case of the fine arts, ordered to the making of what is real as a
revelation of form: in the artwork's participation in being, it participates
in an order of absolute truth—one which is given to us not by the mediation of reasoning but by the direct, concrete participation of the thing in
Beauty Itself, the capacity of form to manifest itself to the intelligence in
itself and in all its relations. This is, again, "tyrannical." Should we stop
anywhere short of beauty, we have stopped short of what is real: we have
foiled the natural orientation of our intellects, settling for half-truths only
because beauty is so difficult.

Maritain's realist philosophy of art and beauty gives us an invaluable
account by which to interpret our own historical situation. It also makes
a definite advance upon its classical sources. We know from experience
that even an aesthetically ugly work of art can manifest being in such a
way that it announces itself to the intellect in terms of "clarity," of "radiance," of "splendor," and that this disclosure of the work of art's being is at
once hard to account for and yet universal enough to challenge even our
most careful attempts at explanation. Aristotle, of course, long ago sought
to define the power and unique quality of works of art by investigating
their sources in human nature and behavior. In the *Poetics*, he explains the
origin of poetry in terms of man's natural desire to imitate, and his equally
natural delight in "works of imitation." This delight is so catholic that

46. Cf. Aquinas, *Summa Contra Gentiles*, 3.39.

though the objects themselves may be painful to see, we delight to view the most realistic representations of them in art, the forms for example of the lowest animals and of dead bodies. The explanation is to be found in a further fact: to be learning something is the greatest of pleasures not only to the philosopher but also to the rest of mankind.[47]

The ugly work would seem to be a cause of delight, according to Aristotle, because, despite the absence of pleasing beauty in what is represented, the work itself is an imitation (*mimesis*) of reality that causes us to "learn," that is, it causes our intellect to acquire and hold an additional truth from a reality before us, swathed in the veil of wonder. This, famously, leads Aristotle to speculate as to the nature of this learning, and so he compares poetic writing to historical writing, whose name means *inquiry*. He concludes,

poetry is something more philosophic and of graver import than history, since its statements are of the nature rather of universals, whereas those of history are singulars. By a universal statement I mean one as to what such or such a kind of man will probably or necessarily say or do—which is the aim of poetry, though it affixes proper names to the characters.[48]

Man delights in works of imitation, which themselves reveal by reproducing the discrete truths of individual beings. Since, for Aristotle, true knowledge is always of universals, those individual imitations must tell us something universal as well, or they would not delight as they do. Aristotle's treatise is primarily concerned with establishing the typology of poetry, its parts, and how they work, and so he leaves this line of inquiry aside as soon as he has established that the natural delight in imitation includes the imitation of things that would, in themselves, be ugly, and that this delight passes through concrete imitation by way of the intellect to the universal. Although he will later consider poetic form in terms of beauty, and although the role of beauty in being is frequently explicit and always implicit throughout the Aristotelian corpus, Aristotle's primary concern in these passages is to establish poetry as a natural human practice, in accord with our rational natures, and a legitimate mode of inquiry into truth.[49]

Maritain, we have seen, assumes roughly the same foundations for art

---

47. Aristotle, *Poetics*, 1448b9–15.
48. Aristotle, *Poetics*, 1051b5–10.
49. On beauty, see Aristotle, *Poetics*, 1450b–1451a, and *Metaphysics*, 1013a20.

as does Aristotle, but with his emphasis on *claritas*, he, for the moment, passes by the question of imitation and dares to specify how the "noetic" power of art is rooted in the reality of beauty as a transcendental property of being. In foregrounding the participation of all beautiful things in God, Maritain explains why our encounters with beauty seem cultic: oriented to a spiritualization of the self and an arrival at a state of awe, if not worship, seldom explicable merely in terms of the empirical details of the thing.[50] What is most manifest in the delight of an artwork is not that it is an imitation we recognize as true, but that its beauty *is itself* in part the splendor produced by a particular form's participation in a reality that transcends the thing itself.

Maritain's repeated underscoring of the *analogous* nature of beauty helps him account for why the modern tendency to remake art's already spiritual nature into an autonomous religion of its own goes awry (a phenomenon that Adorno also attacked, as we saw, from an opposite perspective). Such a tendency isolates beauty as an idol, as if it were absolute precisely because it is discontinuous with and independent of the total order of reality. It thus fails to see that things are beautiful because they *are*, because they have being, and so, when seen, flash like beacons so as to make visible also their standing in a relation to the whole cosmic order of beings—and within, above, and beneath all that, the divine splendor of God as Being Itself in which they participate.

Maritain relished the paradox, or rather, the asymptote here. Beauty is an absolute and, as we saw above, can therefore wield a tyrannical power. But when beauty is seen in itself, as the splendor of form, it also points beyond itself. Our delight in beauty will not be complete until we pass beyond—or, better, *within*—Beauty as a divine name, beyond—or *within*—even Being as a divine name, to God named in and as himself. To do this the radiance of beauty must be situated in the whole to which it bears immediate witness. Writing of modern art, with its consciousness of beauty as absolute and revelatory of being, Maritain concludes,

it is only in the light of theology that art today can achieve self-knowledge and cure itself of the false systems of metaphysics which plague it. By showing us where moral truth and the genuine supernatural are situated, religion saves poetry

50. Maritain, *Art and Scholasticism and the Frontiers of Poetry*, 75.

from the absurdity of believing itself destined to transform ethics and life, saves it from overweening arrogance. But in teaching man the discernment of immaterial realities and the savor of the spirit, in linking poetry and art itself to God, it protects them against cowardice and self-abandonment, enables them to attain a higher and more rigorous idea of their essential spirituality, and to concentrate their inventive activity at the fine point thereof.[51]

As was the case even in Maritain's first forays into the definition of the fine arts, he here seeks to establish its proper autonomy *as it is in itself* and then to insist that, just as the artist is simply a man viewed under a certain light, so all discrete realities, even the autonomy of beauty, are only distinct under a certain rational light and must ultimately be reconciled to a larger, unified whole in being.

Most artworks witness to the truth of these observations, their beauty opening to reveal a radiance that transcends them, and that radiance opening onto the whole plane of being. Many others seem not to do so— as if it was just this experiential chain that they were trying to deny or sever. Much of the art of the last century, especially of the last half-century, has set itself up as a minor cult of ugliness that ultimately bespeaks a despair of being, of existence itself. The modernists excelled at turning this kind of ugliness to positive account: the startling and disturbing could wake us to an encounter with being, and so the superficially ugly opened onto an ontological splendor. Think, for instance, of Mina Loy's troubling poem about a *mutilé du guerre*, "Der Blinde Junge," which has no obvious ambition beyond capturing the grotesque pathos of a blinded and disfigured street urchin:

> this slow blind face
> pushing
> its virginal nonentity
> against the light[52]

Loy's poem strives to be shocking in both subject matter and technique. The child has been made grotesque by the war and the word choices emphasize this so as to "defamiliarize" us, to force us to into a confrontation

---

51. Maritain, *Art and Scholasticism and the Frontiers of Poetry*, 139.

52. Mina Loy, *Lost Lunar Baedeker*, ed. Roger L. Conover (New York: Farrar, Straus and Giroux, 1996), 83.

with being by making it strike us as unaccountable, piercing, and new. The comic eros in some of William Carlos Williams's poems, the humorless mystified anatomy of Rilke's Apollo, or the initially frightening angles of the sculpture of Jacob Epstein, Karl Harmann Haupt, and the cubists, similarly present bare, inhuman, or *overly* human and visceral, images that will not stay put in signifying only their literal surface ugliness. Shape laid bare, however grotesque—indeed because it was grotesque—opened up a passage both in and out of time. This use of the ugly to reveal the transcendental source of every being in Being Itself is what Gerard Manley Hopkins intended when we spoke of the "odd" in his letters to Robert Bridges, and when he celebrated the strangeness of "Pied Beauty" in his poetry.[53]

Much contemporary art, on this scheme, reveals its own incoherence. It debunks, debases, and mocks every sensible dignity in human persons and in the order of things, as if to tell us that there is no goodness, truth, or beauty—that these things are oppressive and must be overcome. And so, by implication, this work tries to bring goodness, truth, and beauty back under the cover of freedom or liberation. Such art's critical turn seems to allow some kind of vision of the good to persist, but it is coded as mere negation. Superficial ugliness is a sign that the depths of being are empty and so should not summon us in ecstasy beyond ourselves.

The title of Tony Kushner's play, *Angels in America* (1993), provides a laughable instantiation of this. The homosexual figures it represents would be as angels, beings of pure freedom, and so would become angels, beings of pure goodness, if only the old America—a stodgy place of moral customs and restraints, all of which serve merely to drive sincere desires into closets and restrooms—were replaced by a new America, a birthright of freedom *from* all limitations and *for* delectation of the senses without responsibility to the body. In such an America, condoms serve as the last concession to the flesh before our souls fly off to a consumer's heaven to preen their plumage. AIDS serves to give this beauty its tragic element, an epidemiological analogue to Dorian Gray's picture—a parody of the wound in Jacob's thigh after his wrestling with the angel. One could mock nearly every facet of contemporary culture in similar terms, for from high art to soft drink commercials, the flourishing human life is always understood as that which maximizes pleasure without acknowledging the limits of mortal-

53. Hopkins, *Major Works*, 132, 234.

ity and eternity except insofar as these become a source of morbid delectation—the pleasure taken in discovering pleasure to be dangerous. This hedonism that is also a kind of death wish seems, in the same breath, to propose that there is an absolute that transcends us and that art reveals, but to refuse the existence of such a thing insofar as it would seem to impose a binding meaning and order on human life. The absolute must, therefore, be simply the experience of pleasure we have when we are shocked.

In *The Frontiers of Poetry*, Maritain addresses these attributes of modern art, for they had already appeared as the tendencies of modernist works to what he calls angelic suicide and materialist sin. The undeviating and autonomous nature of art wants to forget that it subsists as a virtue in a human person and that the work itself will enter a finite world as one more finite work within it.[54] It wants to become, itself, an absolute that transcends the matter of human life and the embodied human intellect, and so to aspire to an absolute world-scorning spirit. While Maritain is more critical of the tendency to materialism, in which art gets reduced to an ornamental display of human reason to flatter certain social classes, his sympathy for the tendency to angelism—to a suicide of the person and of human arts, committed in hopes of becoming pure, immaterial spiritual intelligence—leads him to warn artists against it all the more emphatically.[55] His warning comes in the form of an antinomy that follows logically from the "asymptote" of beauty we discussed above. The fine arts tend of their nature to absolute beauty, but, because the artist is a man, he cannot afford to give this tendency free reign. He must subordinate the *habitus* of art to the stewardship of reason and faith, and must further make some concessions to the weakness of the flesh: if art ignores the embodied condition of persons, it will become opaque, rather than intriguingly obscure, to them.

These warnings are sound. Indeed, they provide some of Maritain's most instructive reflections on the human condition—insights that will later guide his panoptic account of human knowledge and his influential "Thomist Personalist" political philosophy.[56] And yet, they also reveal the one severe weakness of his analysis of the conditions of beauty. In a word, he slights proportion in favor of clarity. Let us now give it due attention.

54. Cf. Maritain, *Art and Scholasticism and the Frontiers of Poetry*, 71.
55. Maritain, *Art and Scholasticism and the Frontiers of Poetry*, 123–24.
56. See Maritain, *The Degrees of Knowledge* and *The Person and the Common Good*.

TEN

The Need for Proportion

As I noted in the last chapter, how one defines and orders the three qualities of beauty will determine how one understands beauty as a whole. One can accept integrity, proportion, and clarity as the three conditions or elements of beauty and still, by emphasizing one over another, arrive at strikingly incompatible accounts of the beautiful. It will be the purpose of this chapter to consider the three different possible emphases and to examine their various implications. This will include a partly negative critique of Maritain's emphasis on *claritas*, which will lead us, finally, to a judicious appreciation of proportion as the singular and central term necessary for any discussion of beauty. As I shall repeat, beauty must finally be understood in terms of proportion, and proportion is the genus of which *integritas* and *claritas* are species. The constitution of beauty at last settled, I shall close with four brief reflections: first, on beauty as a property of being rather than as a "perfection"; second, on the relative position of beauty among the transcendentals; third, which follows logically from the second, on the position beauty should hold in our acts of knowledge, including moral and political reflection; and, fourth, on some qualifications about the role of the fine arts, in light of beauty's status as a property of being.

James Joyce's *alter ego*, Stephen Dedalus, provides a good first example of the bizarre consequences that follow from one plausible interpretation of the condition of beauty. Joyce has Dedalus define the conditions not in terms of the being of beauty, but rather in terms of the stages of aesthetic perception. This has the advantage of drawing a clear connection between, as it were, the objective elements of beauty and the experiential or subjective account of beauty first forwarded by Aquinas, "*id quod visum placet*." It has the disadvantage, however, of collapsing the former into the latter and therefore stripping Aquinas's aesthetics of what makes it most compelling and most firmly in continuity with the Christian Platonist tradition, namely, its understanding of beauty as a property of being and so the study of beauty as a branch of metaphysics and epistemology rather than of sensation. Dedalus himself might have sympathized with this criticism. For, as we shall see, even on his account, what is most striking about beauty is how it discloses form, how it reveals being; how we respond to our experience of that disclosure is important but still secondary.

In Dedalus's excursus on the elements of beauty, in *A Portrait of the Artist as a Young Man*, he places primary emphasis on integrity as the key to the beautiful. The distinct thing-ness or closed-off unity of a thing—its being *this here* rather than something else—is the foundation of Joycean aesthetics.[1] Although Dedalus's expatiations on Thomistic terms are generally acknowledged as a bit of self-parody, with Stephen using the language of Aquinas like second-hand equipment that exposes him (to his own shame) as a poor beggar at the margins of European civilization, Joyce's writings as a whole *do* testify to integrity as their fundamental aesthetic principle. For Joyce, the individual word or phrase, the individual image, regardless of its particular content, is beautiful so long as it is distinct. Dung, advertisements, pornography, an ignorant mispronunciation or malapropism—these things are beauties in Joyce's world because they stand out from the flat backdrop of the quotidian. Stephen's subsequent definition of clarity as *quidditas*, the "whatness" or particular essence of a thing, would seem to subordinate it to integrity: the farthest depth of our understanding of a thing is to specify its individuality. He more or less ignores proportion; how else could dung and poetry be equal—sliding into one another—than if beauty's measure is oriented purely to each

---

1. James Joyce, *The Portable Joyce* (New York: Penguin Books, 1975), 479–80. For an elaboration of this discussion of integrity, proportion, and clarity, see James Matthew Wilson, "John Paul II's 'Letter to Artists' and the Force of Beauty," *Logos: A Journal of Catholic Thought and Culture* 18, no. 1 (Winter 2015): 46–70.

thing having its own integrity, each thing being an equally distinct entity, while it ignores their suitability or fittingness in respect to other things?

In the last chapter, I proposed that *claritas* is an encounter with the proportion of a particular being to the minds that know it: above all, to the mind of God that constitutes a thing in existence at all, and secondarily, to those minds perceptive of its existence. To speak of *claritas* as *quidditas* would seem to get something right and something wrong about this. On the one hand, to ask *what* something is, to enquire after its essence, is indeed to proceed from the individual being to the universal of form, type, or kind. As such, it would be to speak of the proportion of an individual in relation to its own essence. This, however, we identified in the last chapter as belonging to the element of integrity (to which we shall return in a moment). *Claritas* reflects something else. It refers not to an individual being as expressive of a universal essence, but to its being as expressive of a creative intelligence. When we perceive the clarity or splendor of a thing, we remark above all that its existence is intended, that the fact of its existence testifies not to the reality of a universal essence on which it is based, but on the mediated revelation of a divine mind whose knowledge is causative of being. *What* that being is, its relation to form, is one way of getting purchase on the mystery *that it is* in the first place. Joyce's subjective account of beauty robs it of its existential dimension and flattens out the dimensions of beauty in the process.

He does not mean to, however. As Dedalus explains himself, *quidditas* sounds more like what Gerard Manley Hopkins would celebrate as *haecceitas*. What we recognize in perceiving a particular form as separate (integrity) and as having an order proper to itself (proportion) is not its identity with a universal at once greater in intelligibility, but lesser in particularity, than itself (*quidditas*), but the full force of the individual thing's particularity of being. Not *whatness* but *thisness*, not the intelligibility of essence but the experiential slap of existence perceived. Despite his subjective couching of aesthetics, Dedalus finds in Aquinas a resource for understanding the way things exist and the way they can be perceived as beautiful precisely because, in themselves, they manifest the mystery of being.

Maritain's account of integrity as wholeness is more adequate than Joyce's, and yet, it is much too brief because, conversely, he gives *dispropor-*

tionate weight to clarity. As he describes the beauty of being, every form seems about ready to catch fire and direct us straight to God, if we only let the senses rest on it for a moment. Maritain found in poetry and metaphysics, in the poetic knowledge of the poet and the intuition of being of the philosopher, a kind of natural grace, a special epistemological case, that sometimes seems to absorb his imagination more completely than beauty and being themselves.[2] While there is a great deal of truth to his account of being as casting a radiance that sweeps us up, if only we perceive it for what it is, his persistent return in his later work to the epistemology of art and beauty—his interest in poetic knowledge and creative intuition as analogues for natural and infused mystical experiences—diverted him from giving a full reckoning to the conditions of beauty in general. It even kept him from providing a sober account of the nature of the idea of *claritas* that rightly absorbed him.

Maritain's concern in his philosophy of beauty was to describe how the movement from the particular to the absolute could be rendered more certain and compelling, how it could avoid dissolving the works of art it wishes to explain in a murky sea of beauty. The love of beauty has been described as ecstatic since the time of Plato, but Maritain wanted to explain, as it were, what was so ecstatic about it. This concern of his regarding the intellectual "intuition" of beauty has attracted much critical attention in subsequent decades, but it is his account of beauty as a transcendental that was most fundamentally important to his age and, perhaps even more so, to ours. His over-emphasis on clarity, in consequence, makes for that account's greatest vulnerability, not because clarity is less important than the other conditions of beauty, but because Maritain is so enthralled to its primacy that he fails to see how all the conditions of beauty are coherent and logically bound together.

It may surprise us to find that, here, Maritain more closely follows the reasoning of Pseudo-Dionysius and Plotinus than he does the particular understanding of these great figures developed in the works of Aquinas.

---

2. As we noted above, Trapani's study of Maritain focuses on his account of poetic knowledge, and for the reason just stated. See also Jacques Maritain, *A Preface to Metaphysics*, where he discusses the "intuition of being" as kind of special insight, not necessarily a "species of mystical grace," but at least a "gift bestowed," a natural grace, proper to the metaphysician but not necessarily available to all persons (48).

For Plotinus, *clarity* may truly be said to be Beauty Itself: the light of the *Logos*, of the Rational-Principle, and the Ideal-Form that is divine, immaterial, and transcendent is where real beauty is situate.[3] Human beings, because embodied and reliant on the senses, tend to identify beauty with the symmetrical, the proportioned, and the fitting in material things. If such measures gave us the whole truth about beauty, then it would not be a quality of some one unity, some one thing, much less a substantial reality in itself; it would be a mere relation. But, asks Plotinus, is not the formless beauty of sunlight more beautiful than the finest proportion? Further, are not such realities as moral virtues in the soul, and ideas in themselves more beautiful still?[4] Proportion is the outcome when the intellectual light of beauty shines upon unformed matter, which is itself dark, unintelligible, and ugly, and brings it to form.[5] Proportion is matter's formal participation in beauty, but is not Beauty Itself. Beauty is intellectual form-beyond-form, and certainly beyond the measurable proportions of matter.

Umberto Eco, in *Art and Beauty in the Middle Ages*, has shown that what Plotinus gives us in his discussion of beauty are two potentially, but not necessarily, compatible accounts of beauty: an aesthetics of light that views beauty primarily as an intellectual form-giving principle itself transcendent of form, and an aesthetics of proportion that understands the beautiful primarily in terms of fitting relations and formal properties.[6] In Plotinus, the beauty of proportion is no more than a stimulus to the pursuit of true beauty—a pursuit whose finality leads to the laying by of the body as the solitary soul at last passes into the solitary One beyond being.[7] Maritain enacts an analogous distinction in his work, where he at one point seems to understand beauty specifically as the result of form's proportioning of matter, and at others to understand proportioned matter as merely a lower mode of, but a genuine participant in, Beauty Itself.[8]

---

3. Plotinus, *Enneads*, I.6.3.   4. Plotinus, *Enneads*, I.6.1.
5. Plotinus, *Enneads*, I.6.3, 5.
6. Umberto Eco, *Art and Beauty in the Middle Ages*, 28–30, 49–50.
7. Plotinus, *Enneads*, VI.9.11.
8. See Maritain, *Art and Scholasticism and the Frontiers of Poetry*, where, citing Albert the Great and Plotinus, he seems to tie beauty to form's ordering of "proportioned parts of matter" (25), but see also his account of God as "beautiful absolutely" (30–31). Maritain is right to distinguish types of beauty, for as a property of being, beauty always and only manifests itself analo-

Maritain's efforts to restrain the tyranny of absolute beauty sometimes appear as nervous efforts to resist the Plotinian implications of his account of the *claritas* of beauty, but they are unsuccessful. With Plotinus, Maritain consistently sees the beautiful in proportioned matter always radiating the light of transcendent and indivisible life of the divine. This explains his consistent preference for works of visual art that are not abstract, but are slightly abstracted in character: by refusing to pretend to be simulacra of sensible reality, they serve the better to reveal a transcendental principle beyond themselves. A strict realism, such as that found in the academic painting of William-Adophe Bouguereau, on the other hand, seems to have struck Maritain as an almost atheist and positivist trust in appearances.[9] But, as we shall see, not only is there no reason for proportion to be a subservient effect, a mere participant, in the splendor of true beauty, but proportion may be the key to a proper understanding of *claritas* and of beauty as a whole. I do not mean heuristically, as it is for Plotinus, but absolutely.[10] And I say this not to deny the transcendent unity of beauty for which Plotinus argues, but rather to affirm it as compatible with a theory that holds proportion as an element of not just sensible but all beauty.

Eco's previous study, *The Aesthetics of Thomas Aquinas*, with its careful attempt to establish a historical understanding of Aquinas's definition of beauty, offers a needed corrective to Maritain on proportion. The book as a whole can be quite troubling, if unconvincing; Eco refuses Maritain's speculations on the "lightning" intuitions of aesthetic perception altogether, and ultimately accuses Aquinas's thought on beauty of incoherence, because of its grounding in individual forms of which we can have no direct knowledge.[11] For Aquinas, he rightly argues, we have direct sense perception of individuals, but our knowledge of their forms or essences comes indirectly by way of abstraction. If beauty (for Aquinas) is a matter of the intellect's seeing the splendor of the form, and yet, if the

---

gously (30), and so he is also correct to note that, though sensible beauty is the mode connatural to us, it is not the highest kind absolutely speaking (25).

9. Maritain, *Art and Scholasticism and the Frontiers of Poetry*, 27.

10. I explore this possibility for multiple angles elsewhere. See Wilson, "Ancient Beauty, Modern Verse," and "The Splendor of Form," *Dappled Things* 8, no. 1 (Candlemas 2013): 43–55.

11. Umberto Eco, *The Aesthetics of Thomas Aquinas*, 62–63.

experience of beauty as we have it is one of an immediate sense perception, Eco asks, what could Aquinas's account of beauty have to do with
our experience of it? We can know forms by intellectual abstraction, and
we can perceive concrete sense objects directly, but we have no immediate
intellectual apprehension of the concrete.

In fact, there are multiple legitimate Thomistic ripostes to Eco's criticism. One could argue with Kevin O'Reilly, in his recent *Aesthetic Perception: A Thomistic Perspective*, that Aquinas does in fact give us an intellection by intuition as Maritain claims; how else could we know first
principles, since they do not admit of demonstration?[12] As I argued in
Part I, all our reasoning (*ratio*) is founded on a prior intelligible principle
in us (*intellectus*), one of much greater scope than the particular movements of discursive thought, such that all our abstractive thinking occurs
within the act of immediate intellectual vision, not as a thing set apart
from it.[13] Also, as I shall elaborate, the abstraction of the form may occur,
in principle, *after* sense perception, but this does not entail it must occur
temporally afterward. When was the last time anyone had sense experience
of a bowl of pretzels and only secondarily recognized it *as* a bowl of pretzels? The bodily senses are ordered by their nature to the intellect and, indeed, the *experience* of beauty Eco mentions would not be an experience
of beauty were they not so ordered.[14]

Beauty is not, for Aquinas or for Maritain, a type of sensation, but
a reality perceived (an existence, or relation of existents), a form beheld
(an essence, or relation of essences), by the intelligence.[15] They are faithful to Plato's *Phaedrus* and the Christian Platonist tradition as a whole
in considering beauty as a reality perceived by the whole of the human
person. The bodily eye may directly perceive sensuous beauty, but it does

12. Kevin E. O'Reilly, *Aesthetic Perception: A Thomistic Perspective*, 45. This refers, of course,
to the *nous* or *intellectus* that is the condition of possibility for the vision of the soul that underlies this entire study.

13. One of the weaknesses of St. Augustine's otherwise compelling *The Teacher* is his articulation of the distinction between the knowledge of sensible and of intelligible things. He *does*
make them to seem not only different objects, but different modes of knowing altogether (12.39).
The proper account would be to show that what is known by way of the senses always comes into
act within the faculty of "the inner light of truth which illumines the inner man and is inwardly
enjoyed" (12.40).

14. Aquinas, *Summa Theologica*, I.76.5.

15. Maritain, *Art and Scholasticism and the Frontiers of Poetry*, 23.

so in unity with the intellectual senses, the vision of the soul. It will not do to say, as Eco does, there is no place for this in the epistemology of Aquinas, because it is just this experience of the unity of vision with vision that Aquinas takes for granted and then seeks to explain. It will, however, prove fruitful to distinguish within the reason the distinct "moments" of sensation and coming to knowledge in the reason that occur within the act of perception of a being as beautiful, and so we shall return to that question below.

But let us turn from this question for now by considering one important respect in which Eco's historical judgment seems largely sure, the implications of which are immense for our whole discussion. If one wishes to understand integrity, proportion, and clarity properly, one must acknowledge a certain redundancy to them as a definition, Eco tells us. To wit, proportion (as a kind of measurement and numeric *ratio*) is *per se* central to the idea of being as having an intelligible form, and so it must be the central term in our understanding of beauty as a whole, since form is the *sine qua non* of beings.[16] We recognize something as beautiful, because it seems justly proportioned and fitting, both in itself and in relation to those things that meaningfully surround and interact with it. By this last clause, I mean whatever can possibly come into relation with it, including the mind that may come to know it and the divine mind that in knowing causes all things to exist.

Eco's account of the three conditions defines them just in terms of this grasp of form as itself a proportion, and so rejects the Plotinian notions that light and proportion are somehow opposed as substance and relation are, or that proportion is a mere material effect of the formless light of beauty. Substance is in itself already a kind of relation; ideas have a *ratio* proper to themselves (though it should not of course be confused with the divisible *ratio* or measurement of material things). Integrity, according to Eco, signals merely an affirmation that the *first proportion* is that of a thing to its nature, its existence to its essence, its fulfillment of its end as a particular kind of thing and its internal self-coherence.[17] *Claritas*, he says, may well mean what Maritain says it does, but not just that. It indicates a participation of the individual thing in the absolute; but *more*

16. Aristotle, *Metaphysics*, 1043b33–1044a2.
17. Eco, *The Aesthetics of Thomas Aquinas*, 99.

than this, it bespeaks the proportionality of the thing to a series of acts of seeing and knowing (being illuminated), of making-to-be known and showing-forth (illuminating).[18] Most importantly for Eco, when something is proportioned to our senses and our intellect, we perceive it as showing forth a certain radiance, a certain splendor. Here, he reconnects the essential qualities of beauty with the definition Aquinas gives "for us," that beauty is that which pleases when seen. Clarity, by Eco's account, is above all the kinesis of that pleasure, the experience of the *visio*, the spark of an intelligence encountering what is suited to it: intelligibility is clarity, it is the form of something recognized as proportioned to itself *and* to us. He summarizes his account thus,

Clarity is the fundamental communicability of form, which is made actual in relation to someone's looking at or seeing of the object. The rationality that belongs to every form is the "light" which manifests itself to aesthetic seeing.[19]

Whereas Maritain absorbed proportion into clarity as its mere hand-maid, Eco insists that clarity is a secondary or phenomenal attribute of proportion. Integrity and proportion constitute the "objective" criteria of beauty, whereas clarity comes into being only through the proportionate encounter of a thing with a knower. The listing of three conditions of beauty by Aquinas may mislead: integrity and clarity are species within the genus proportion, rather than conditions *other* than proportion. Eco confesses that clarity may comprehend much more than this, or rather, that its definition accumulated a plurality of reconcilable meanings, as it passed from the hands of Dionysius the Aeropagite to Albert the Great and on to Aquinas, with Maritain reproducing Albert's thought and ignoring Aquinas's.[20] Understandably, scholars have been drawn to these provocations regarding which interpretations of "clarity" most accurately reflect its use in medieval documents, but their arguments seem less important and less convincing than what Eco illuminates by reorienting beauty to proportion.

In sum, the proportion of a thing that is a condition of its beauty is not reducible to any one relation, not even to the particularly important relation of a thing's existence to its essential nature, which integrity de-

18. Eco, *The Aesthetics of Thomas Aquinas*, 104.
19. Eco, *The Aesthetics of Thomas Aquinas*, 119.
20. Eco, *The Aesthetics of Thomas Aquinas*, 111, 250n130.

scribes. The proportion of a thing to its knower, and of a thing's essence to its existence, are just two of the most important relations that must be "fitting" if a thing is to be beautiful. Moreover, so numerous are the possible relations of a real thing to itself and to another (to other things), that the proportion of a material thing to the senses—something Maritain celebrated—is not essential to beauty. And, again, *pace* Plotinus, something need not be material to bear proportion, because proportion is proper to the form or essence of a thing regardless of whether that thing is material (the human body) or spiritual (a mathematical equation).[21] A thought can be as or more beautiful than a face: the "fact is rather that proportion, because it is constitutive of beauty and thus coextensive with it, has its own transcendental character. Proportion therefore has an infinity of analogues."[22] The fingers of a hand may be "proportioned" relative to each other, individually to themselves, and also relative to the whole human body and—long though the study may be in determining this—they may also be proportioned to their use (their instrumental good) and to the creation of which they are one small part (their final good).[23] With mesmerizing insight, Eco concludes the proportion that constitutes beauty is

not a single type of relation between two things, but rather a dense network of relations. It can pertain to a relation between one item and another item, or between two items and a third. In fact we are free to consider the relation of three, four, or an infinity of things, proportionate among themselves and proportioned also in respect to some unifying whole. This unifying whole may then be taken as one item in a new set of items unified in their turn among themselves; and so on to infinity.[24]

The totality of these proportions, which, again, comprises integrity and clarity, constitutes beauty. Something may be somewhat beautiful, if it is "fitting" in a certain number of relations, but not in others. And, naturally, these proportions form an order, and potentially lead us intellectually

21. Eco, *The Aesthetics of Thomas Aquinas*, 87.
22. Eco, *The Aesthetics of Thomas Aquinas*, 97.
23. Aquinas mentions the proportions of the fingers as a way of discussing the proportions of the moral virtues within the individual man: "thus the fingers are unequal in size, but equal in proportion, since they grow in proportion to one another" (*Summa Theologica*, I-II.66.2). Whenever proportion or fit is mentioned in Aquinas, it becomes clear, we are in the realm of beauty as that property enveloping goodness and truth and making them measurable by the intellect.
24. Eco, *The Aesthetics of Thomas Aquinas*, 89–90.

to ever greater and higher levels of order until we arrive at a vision of God and all things in relation to him. Thus, Eco continues,

All creatures have an order of congruity in respect to one another, and beyond that there is a superior order in virtue of the fact that all creation is oriented toward God. This idea of a universal order is the source of a number of central features of Aquinas's thought: his teleological conception of the created world, his conception of divine providence as an ordering force, his conception of a Supreme Good realizing itself in things.[25]

The path from a being's individuality and interior wholeness (integrity) to its fullest realization as an intelligible radiance reflecting and participating in the light of the divine intellect (clarity) is one that proceeds on a proportioned path from proportion to proportion. As we saw in our discussion of the *Phaedrus*, Plato perceives the ideal beauty that transcends all things as also the source of the world-order, the *cosmos*. Beauty may well strike the vision of the eye and of the soul with its initial, isolated singularity in this or that particular form, but that initial seeing is but the opening of the soul to a comprehensive vision of all things, the whole of reality in its formal intelligibility. We do not thereby pass beyond beauty on to truth, but from that first shock of beauty productive of ecstasy, outward, beyond ourselves, to truth, and finally upward to beauty in its fullness, where all forms, all truths, are seen in themselves and as constituting the single, unified order of reality.

Maritain's idea of *claritas* seeks a shortcut from the immanent interior order of a work of art's integral beauty to the beauty of God. His brief advertences to integrity and proportion would seem to indicate that he actually believed a certain shock brought on by what seemed *disproportionate* or grotesque to the eyes of this world might actually serve beauty by sending us in search of the inner mystery, the luminous form of being hidden beyond appearances and waiting to share with us its intelligible splendor.[26] Recall, for instance, the futurist painting with the quarter eye. Right Maritain was to insist with such grace that all beautiful things do participate in God as Beauty. But, in ignoring the role proportion plays in

---

25. Eco, *The Aesthetics of Thomas Aquinas*, 90–91.

26. I mentioned above his (to my mind) perverse contempt for Bouguereau (Maritain, *Art and Scholasticism and the Frontiers of Poetry*, 27).

beauty, he ignores the perceptible means of this participation; he presses too hard for an intuitive vision; and he gives inadequate attention to the intimate link between the vision that sees and knows beauty and the more gradual means of reasoning that guide us from one perception upward to another until we have attained a vision of the whole. Truth and beauty, art and metaphysics, abstract intellection and intellectual vision, are even more closely joined than Maritain acknowledged—an odd oversight for a metaphysician, but understandable for someone convinced that there must be not only *degrees* of knowledge but also distinct *ways* of knowing.

The value of Eco's correction is not limited to the regrounding of beauty in proportion. Beauty remains for us, in one sense, always indeterminate insofar as we can always theoretically add another relation to which a thing might suitably be proportioned. "Such-and-such is fitting in *this* respect, but does it belong to a particular thing's beauty also to be fitting in *that* one?" we may ask. Thus, Maritain would seem to have erred somewhat in suggesting that a work of art could theoretically be autonomous and in-human—that it could be beautiful objectively, proportioned only to the divine beauty, without necessarily conceding any proportion to us as sensuous embodied beings or to the whole realm of the good, including the morally good. If art might justly be proportioned to the absolute spiritual beauty of the divine, and if we are to judge it to be thus beautiful, it must *also* be oriented to our human reason and perhaps to our senses—however much inferior these things may be to the eternal and divine intellect. Lacking this, the object would be short at least one sort of proportion—and not the least important one, for the purposes of the fine arts.

Maritain actually has not erred, but his exposition creates an interpretive problem that leaves most readers thinking he has. In "The Purity of Art," he addresses those passages from Aristotle we cited above in order to broaden Aristotle's account of art as imitation. Far from meaning that works of art primarily imitate by creating likenesses of things found in nature (though they generally do this), art imitates nature in the sense of, like nature, bringing material things into being under the proportioned law of the intellect. The pleasure or delight caused by something beautiful remains, first and always, its *claritas*, its intelligibility overflowing into the appetite.[27]

---

27. Maritain, *Art and Scholasticism and the Frontiers of Poetry*, 54.

How does this imitation proceed? A work of art, says Maritain, first makes a thing known as a thing; second, it makes itself known as a sign, "as making known something other than" itself.[28] And this thing signified may be a sign in turn, so that "the more the object of art is laden with signification ... the greater and richer and higher will be the possibility of delight and beauty."[29] The finality of this potentially infinite train of signification is the radiant manifestation of "a form, and therefore of a *truth*."[30]

In Maritain's account of art, richness of signification takes the place that proportion holds in Eco's version of Aquinas. In some ways it is a satisfactory alternative. By speaking in terms of signs, he underscores the ordering of beauty to the intellect. Furthermore, as Eco himself emphasizes, medieval aesthetics issued, in practice, in arts that were intensely symbolic and allegorical. Proportion, put into practice in art, will generally appear to us as a sign or symbol, that is, as the fitting of one concept to another by way of analogy, figure, and trope.[31] So, also, because creation is itself a book of nature authored by God, reality itself must be understood in these terms.[32] And yet, there are liabilities to Maritain's account, not least of which is the strain it takes to integrate his discussion of signification in art into Aquinas's conditions of beauty without conceding the obvious: to speak of "signification" is to speak of fitting analogies, where one thing can stand for, and so direct the mind to, the knowledge of another, and this is necessarily a kind of *ratio* or proportion, or it is nothing at all. A related liability is that *signification* is only one species of proportion, and so cannot help us understand the perception of beauty in those instances where some formal and intelligible *ratio* may be very clear to us but where little seems to be signified besides the ratio itself.

The greatest weakness, however, will become obvious when we consider how open-ended "signification" may be and how clearly specified "proportion" is, as a term, with its immediate implication not just of meaning, but of measured meaning and meaningful measure. However extensive the proportions of beauty may be, they bear within them a sense of intelligible

28. Maritain, *Art and Scholasticism and the Frontiers of Poetry*, 55.
29. Maritain, *Art and Scholasticism and the Frontiers of Poetry*, 55.
30. Maritain, *Art and Scholasticism and the Frontiers of Poetry*, 57.
31. Eco, *The Aesthetics of Thomas Aquinas*, 139–40.
32. Aquinas, *Summa Theologica*, I.1.10.

circumscription, and this helps us to account for why it should be the case that a "representation that exactly conform[s] to a given reality" generally does strike us as beautiful more readily than would a work whose *mimesis* is buried in the depths of signification.[33] Maritain's aesthetics wants to delegitimize academic classicism, with its precise realism of appearances, in favor of one of ontological mystery. To the extent it does that, it is less rather than more comprehensive and adequate as a philosophy of art—however much it gained as a Parisian manifesto. In contains within it, however, all the conceptual seeds we require to account for works of fine art that are at once proportioned to sensible reality and to the mystery of being.

If these are the most obvious immanent problems in Maritain's account of signification, there is a transcendent one as well. The best art is clearly not simply the most complex, or the draftsmanship of M. C. Escher would qualify as the most significant art in virtue of the sheer quantity of graphite strokes on the page. The language of proportion helps us always to keep in view the whole of the work (its integrity) and the whole of its relations, even if that should include the infinite reality of God. It helps us to do this specifically in terms of the work's wholeness and fittingness, wherein we can discern that some acts of signification would be out of place in a given work. Proportion, as Aquinas well knew, gives us a vocabulary of measure, order, weight, and number that we need to make these sorts of judgments. In contrast, "signification" would seem to suggest, with uncritical restraint, "the more the merrier."[34]

I would now turn to a series of four considerations that concerned Maritain chiefly in view of the fine arts and his theory of "poetic knowledge," but which concern the whole Christian Platonist tradition for they support two of its six chief insights: the status of beauty as a property of being—a reality present wherever there is being—and its implications for how we perceive and know it.

In everyday speech, we generally refer to the beautiful as a perfection

---

33. Maritain, *Art and Scholasticism and the Frontiers of Poetry*, 56.

34. Maritain does propose a limit, actually, but one in which proportion does not enter, but only the judgment of relative "obscurity" (Maritain, *Art and Scholasticism and the Frontiers of Poetry*, 59).

rather than as a property of being. Since the eighteenth century, and particularly since the treatises of Burke and Kant, aesthetics has attended the beautiful as a perfection, as well, hence its particular attention to the fine arts and scenic nature, two instances where a "perfect uselessness" seems to come to the fore and leave behind all other concerns. But I would note that our everyday language refers to truth and goodness as perfections, as well, but in all three instances this can be misleading. To say "this cheese is good" does not mean that all other cheese is not, but rather to note that the goodness of the cheese has come to the fore. So also, when we affirm something as true, as in these lines from a poem by Yvor Winters, wherein he describes fish swimming in a "small dark pool" on his father's property:

> From cloudy caves, heavy with summer dews,
> The shyest and most tremulous beings stir,
> The pulsing of their fins a lucent blur,
> That, like illusion, glances off the view.
> The pulsing mouths, like metronomes, are true.[35]

The mechanical pulse of their mouths, so measured and precise, reminds the poet that within what he senses lies the intelligibility of being, the potential to judge was is real as true. The rest of reality is no less true, but some things have the ring of truth; they make us conscious of the convertibility of being and truth. So it is with beautiful things. What we are moved to proclaim as beautiful will simply be an instance where a fullness of being makes beauty especially present to the mind. But everything, insofar as it is, is beautiful. I have at several points referred to Burke's early aesthetic treatise, *Philosophical Enquiry into the Sublime and Beautiful*. It is probably adequate to account for the suggestions of an aesthetic theory in those passages I quoted in Part I, but if so, only just. Burke wants us to model our morality and our politics on an aesthetic vision, on a vision of loveliness, of perfect beauty.[36] But for the analogies between these things

35. Yvor Winters, *Collected Poems of Yvor Winters* (Chicago: Swallow Press, 1978), 128.

36. He provides a basis for doing so in his early account of beauty; see Burke, *A Philosophical Enquiry into the Sublime and the Beautiful and Other Pre-Revolutionary Writings*, where he argues that beauty is a kind of perfection (138) to be understood as "that quality or qualities in bodies by which they cause love" (128). Our capacity to be moved by the beautiful is rooted in our natures, including our bodies, as constituted by God, their creator (90, 141). And so, while Burke understands us as designed by God to respond to beauty, which is "calculated" to cause

to hold, beauty would have to be a property of each of them. *Reflections on the Revolution in France* therefore seems to ask for a richer theory of beauty than the young Burke had provided.

This leads to my second note. Despite our most conscious experience of beauty as a perfection, the capacity of beauty to reveal being, to be the disclosure of individual forms and the form of things as a whole, testifies to its status as a distinct property of being, standing alongside the other "relational transcendentals" of goodness and truth. Since Aertsen, the argument for truth and goodness alone to be admitted to the table of such transcendentals has gained strength for both historical and philosophical reasons. For those who accept Aquinas's "faculty psychology" of the soul (that is, his theory that the soul is composed of the two faculties reason and will), rather than Augustine's triune account of the soul as containing memory, understanding, and will, it would seem as if "truth" accounts for being's relation to the reason as knowable, and "goodness" for being's relation to the will as desirable—and that leaves no room for anything else to be added. Beauty then is given a second-order status as the truth perceived as good. It is taken for a relation of truth and goodness at one remove from being. I have argued, and wish only to emphasize here, that beauty is that property of being that relates, and so reveals, form as the active principle of being. To perceive beauty is to perceive form anterior to recognizing its truth and goodness, and to perceive form once again after being, truth, and goodness have been affirmed as united by it. It is to perceive the form as having an intelligibility and desirability in itself, and as standing in relation to other beings, to all beings, and to God as Being Itself. This seems irreducible to either goodness or truth. If we are to understand beauty in terms of faculty psychology, then let beauty be that property of being that becomes perceptible when we grasp being *as a whole* and so *in its fullness as real*.

This account of beauty has considerable implications for how we know and live in the world. And so, a third note. A work of art made by a person must surely be proportioned either to that person or to the human condition in general. Its beauty is just that property that bespeaks

---

love in us, his early treatise does not have a theory of beauty as a property of being. Far from it; beauty is more like a rare trick that works on our bodies like liquor.

its potentially infinite relations to other beings. It takes its place among the world of things, but also among the world of actions and events. As such, and once again, the fittingness of a thing to the human world is not the least of its attributes and is one that we can address best in terms of "moral beauty." A woman with beautiful features who spits into the cup of a beggar cannot be wholly beautiful. Goose-stepping Nazis impressed the world with the beauty of their discipline and organization, but their image often makes us shudder now, for we know the great evils to which they are bound and which deform their potential beauty with violence. Such things are not without proportions that make them beautiful—they just evidently lack others of greater metaphysical weight.

One cannot say that a woman's actions are extrinsic to her facial features, or an army's discipline a separable matter from its cause. For the order of beauty is a metaphysical order; it judges all things in terms of totality and being. If all things participate in the absolute beauty of God, they do so imperfectly—in one way, but not another, or in some ways better than others. Our judgments of beauty therefore may often be as partial as are those about what is true or what is good. And yet, proportion describes and measures form, form constitutes beings, and beings *do* lead us to conceive the principle of all things, Being Itself. And so, Maritain was surely right to tell us that in beauty we discover intelligibility and mystery at once: we drink in the orderliness, the fittingness, of things and sense that they conceal within themselves no relative and private mystery, but clues to the eternal reality of God. Works of art, in virtue of their proportioned internal order of beauty, can provide us an education in sensibility so that we may perceive that *the world is itself ordered by and to Beauty*.

I have called into doubt Maritain's focus on creative intuition and poetic knowledge in one respect and affirmed it in another. Such ideas lead him to think of the perception of beauty as intellectual but pre-conceptual: beauty is the splendor of form radiating on matter. While he was right to try to account for the immediacy of the perception of at least some forms of beauty, and to suggest that this perception leads us from the particular encounter with the beautiful existent thing to an encounter with Beauty Itself Who is God, I noted it leads him to give short shrift to proportion. This oversight has consequences. As Harold L. Weatherby notes in a brilliant but neglected study, *The Keen Delight: The Christian Poet in the Mod-*

ern World, Maritain's non-conceptual conception of beauty neglects an aspect of our experience that a solid understanding of beauty as proportion clearly explains. The better we *know* something, the more beautiful it becomes.[37] The more conscious we are of the fitting proportions of a work, the more brightly the work glows. True, in trying to account for the interior rules of art, Maritain observes that

the artist's friends, who know what the artist sought to accomplish—as the Angels know the Ideas of the Creator—derive far greater enjoyment from his works than the public; so it is that the beauty of certain works is a hidden beauty, accessible only to a small number.[38]

Maritain intended this experience only as an instance of non-discursive connaturality: friends share in the nature of the artist, and so grasp intuitively his particular virtue of art. But, as Weatherby argues, such knowledge can be conveyed by discourse—it can even be written down in a scholarly monograph!—and is frequently so communicated in fact. If I look at a Vermeer painting—say, "Woman Holding a Balance"—I may find it beautiful immediately; the more closely I examine its absolutely focused and minute details, the more beautiful I may find it. If I can follow the invisible threads of its proportions *beyond* the canvas, to the narrative of which it represents an eternal moment, to the narrative of its creation in the work of the artist, to the great body of cultural symbolism its elements manifest—if I discover each of these things, the painting becomes more vividly beautiful to me. Most persons in Shakespeare's day and in ours can *hear* the beauty of the playwright's verses if they are well spoken, but a trained audience tends to hear, understand, and connect them in myriad ways that deepen the impression of their beauty.[39]

This deepening of knowledge seldom dulls but rather concomitantly deepens the experience of beauty—even though, since the time of Kant, the prejudice in favor of the immediate and intuitive nature of beauty has filled the popular imagination with clichés to the contrary and reaches a dead-end in such monomaniacal workings-out of the theory as Martin

---

37. Harold L. Weatherby, *The Keen Delight: The Christian Poet in the Modern World* (Athens: University of Georgia Press, 1975), 125–40.

38. Maritain, *Art and Scholasticism and the Frontiers of Poetry*, 165n56.

39. Weatherby, *The Keen Delight*, 143–44.

Heidegger's pursuit of unselfconscious presence. The unlimited number of possible proportions we may perceive helps explain not only why we often find most beautiful that which we most richly understand, but also why objects of very minor beauty may, to an informed sensibility, seem particularly exquisite. We need not dismiss such instances of rapt appreciation as either eccentric or subjective; to one who sees into the depths of the form of something, who sees into the network of its proportions, a superficially minute object may take on grandeur. The bricklayer especially appreciates well-pointed bricks not because of a merely subjective proclivity, but because he knows more than the average Joe. We may rightly call this "eccentric" only in those instances when such a person, swept up in the depths of some one object, fails to discover the even greater and more various beauty in other things; he deforms his own beauty in such disproportionate fixations. If, then, beauty sometimes strikes us like instant combustion, it just as often stretches itself out in time like the slow, deliberate burrowing of a hedgehog.

Because beauty is a transcendental property of being, it subsists in all things. If beauty is a property of being rather than a perfection, why should this discussion of beauty take place in the context of a discussion of the fine arts? This is the concern of my fourth and final note. Maritain distinguishes between the beauty of the fine arts and ontological beauty in general simply by noting that the fine arts are specifically *ordered to* beauty as their end. David Foster Wallace's *Infinite Jest* fulfills itself in the proportions proper to its intricate and ironic story, and not the useful but inessential proportion that also allows it to serve well as a doorstop. So Maritain's account rests. But we should emphasize the way, already noted, in which the beauty of fine art tends to train the intellect, honing its capacities of attention to see the form of all things with greater penetration. As O'Reilly argues, here lies the great value of aesthetic education. While objects and proportions may vary infinitely, beauty is one, and so learning to perceive form in the comparative "experimental" isolation of a work of art prepares one to see the forms that constitute creation and to perceive the ordered network of which they are a part.[40] We saw this first in the *Phaedrus*. Beauty seemed at first a mere propaedeutic to the discovery of

40. O'Reilly, *Aesthetic Perception*, 49–50.

the soul's intellectual nature: the beautiful face shocks us into a recollection of the Being we have known. But, finally, what we discover in our
recollection is the ordered beauty of the cosmos and the eternal beauty of
the form itself. This is the prototypical account of the experience of the
fine arts, those works especially calculated to disclose their own form, to
be beautiful, so that the form becomes the object of our contemplation.
We enter thereby into the contemplation of reality in its formal fullness.

This has two great consequences, which draw together all the observations we have made in Part II as they help explain the central insight of
the western tradition regarding the distinct status of beauty discussed in
Part I. With these we shall close.

First, when the Schoolmen listed the transcendental properties of being—if they did so at all—they ordered them as follows: unity, truth, goodness, and beauty. One first perceives the singular "it-ness" of a thing; then,
that it can be known as a form; then, its purposive worth and function (its
good or end), and finally one discovers its goodness, order, and depth as a
form, its beauty. Without calling into question this ordering, I would suggest that in experience there is no significant temporal differentiation between the perception of these ontologically identical but conceptually different properties. Beauty therefore stands out as the most "inclusive" of the
transcendentals, containing all the rest, enveloping them even, and drawing
them into conceptual relation (or proportion). Taking some liberty with
his Scholastic sources, Maritain advances a formulation that other scholars,
including myself, have rightly found irresistible: "Strictly speaking, Beauty
is the radiance of all the transcendentals united."[41] If this is true, then the
more we approach to perfect knowledge of the reality of a being, the closer
we come to its beauty. Perfection of knowledge is to perceive the splendor
of truth. But also, because beauty is a property of the form of every being,
it seems that it is contemporary with the truth and goodness of a thing. Because it is so directly tied to the seeing rather than the discussable knowledge (in the sense of the naming) of a form, it may even, in our experience,
seem to come first. Our first perception of a reality's form, as well as the fullness of knowledge of that thing as real, as true, and as good in distinct ways,
both constitute an encounter with beauty.

41. Maritain, *Art and Scholasticism and the Frontiers of Poetry*, 173n66.

Because Maritain was anxious to preserve beauty from the conceptual, he could not fully appreciate the consequences of this: our encounter with reality comes to us as fully and with as much validity in terms of beauty as it does in terms of truth and goodness. As such, arguments from beauty ought to have greater binding force on us than our culture likes to acknowledge. I will say something even bolder: they, in fact, do have such force on us, but because we, as a culture, suspect beauty almost as much as we suspect truth, we tend to have no way to explain this power except in terms of misleading clichés about rhetorical "artifice," "superficiality," "feeling," and "image." The modern age routinely denies the existence of things simply by denying itself a vocabulary to express them, but if we would be true to reality, above all the reality of our experience, we would acknowledge that much of our lives, meaning our intellectual lives above all, are formed and moved by the perceptions of the beautiful.

Proportion is to beauty what reasoning is to truth. Beauty and truth are both perceptible in terms of different types of *ratio*. When perfected, such measures converge in intellectual vision, the vision of the soul, perceptive of form and splendor, of truth and being illuminated as beautiful. This may seem to suggest that beauty has little logical weight, but it also entails that it has a claim on us as real, and so teaches us about reality by means distinct from but equally binding as those of logic. Aristotle argues just this in the *Ethics*, when he observes that "one ought not to demand a reason in all things alike ... but it is sufficient in some cases for it to be shown beautifully that something is so, in particular such things as concern first principles.[42] Showing the patterns of the beautiful to another, or teaching him the truth by reasoning, serve the same end. As many Arabic interpreters of Aristotle insisted, the *Poetics* should stand alongside the books of the *Analytics* in Aristotle's Organon, the "poetic syllogism" rooted in proportion being an exact equivalent to the logical syllogism rooted in discursive reason.[43] The discerning mind will find there is a clear logic to the poetic, as will it find that logic is one manifestation of the beautiful order of the intelligible and the real.

Whether, as it were, one ought to show beauty or argue truth depends

42. Aristotle, *Nicomachean Ethics*, 1098b.

43. See Alberto Rigolio, "Aristotle's 'Poetics' in Syriac and Arabic Translations: Readings of Tragedy," *Khristianskii Vostok* 6 (2013), 141–43.

largely on the circumstances and the particular matter under consideration. Moreover, demonstration from beauty informs us of first principles, which are themselves the foundation of reasoning toward the truth. John Keats was correct to declare, "Beauty is truth, truth beauty", but for reasons the mature Burke could explain, not Keats.[44] At minimum, beauty and truth are "equal" approaches to reality; but, as Aristotle suggests, if we must choose between them, beauty is actually *prior* to truth because nearer to the form that constitutes a being. It reveals the foundations of reality that reasoning cannot establish but only work within. And, to repeat, the experience of the beautiful is that of a complete vision obtained *posterior* to reasoning as well—because it gives us the formal attributes of truth seen as good, and of both as rooted in form, where alone is revealed the depths of reality.

A keen sense of the various proportions that contribute to the beautiful is thus necessary if one is to understand what is real. A mere aestheticism that prizes only the sensuously beautiful truth, or a "politicized aesthetic" that registers only the beautiful as noble, serve as just two instances of a myopia before the real. Our culture thus lies to itself in denying the reality of beauty, and barbarizes and narrows its intellect in treating aesthetic education as unimportant to the formation of a complete human being. Within that culture, conservatives willfully fragment its sensibility and everyday life by treating only certain modes of beauty as relevant, while liberals perform an even more radical disservice to the society they purport to help "progress," by seeking to scour the public realm of the claims of the beautiful in an effort to reconstruct society along isolated, desiccated, and often perverse forms of rationality.

The burden of my argument has been to call for a renewal of the role of art and an appreciation for the reality of beauty in an age and culture that minimizes, deprecates, or denies the worth of these things. But we arrive now at a second consequence of the reality of beauty—one that extends well beyond works of fine art. Rather, we arrive back at the concept I mentioned near the beginning of Part II, that of the political aesthetic. If the political aesthetic is something for conservatives to transcend, it also reveals something about the nature of beauty. Because the beautiful is the

44. Keats, *Complete Poems and Selected Letters*, 240.

mode under which reality appears to our first perceptions and our most perfect knowledge, it must be one way of knowing that would inform our conceptions of ethical and political life. When we think ethically, we are asking ourselves questions about what a good life *looks like*—what is its form.

This is no novel insight, but lies at the heart of the western tradition. As Michael Davis argues, for instance, in his superb commentary on the *Poetics*, that treatise is at once an account of narrative poetry and of human action, precisely because it is the thinking-through of human actions as poetry, as a story, that allows us to understand them. Poetry reveals three things that in human action itself otherwise remain hidden: the meaning of an action in terms of its interior motive, its completed form, and its broader narrative context. Consequently, "poetry would be the necessary condition for moral virtue generally," because it "is what allows us to experience our lives as wholes."[45] In seeing our actions as part of a poetic story, we see them as others *will* see them. Moreover, all our performed actions are already imitations ("performances") of the poetic or beautiful form in which they participate, insofar as the action is preceded by the intention of the agent: to intend is to create an ideal image that is subsequently realized or imitated—however imperfectly—in the action.[46] If the vision of poetic form is the precondition of ethics, so also is it the condition of the still greater scale of politics: political speculation tries to imagine the desirable form of communal life. No society can understand itself without understanding and seeking its proper form, and so no society can exist without being graspable in terms of beauty. Such was the insight of Edmund Burke; such was the insight of the Christian Platonist tradition on which he drew; and such remains the insight of those conservatives who dwell in the shadow of his legacy.

To preserve and reform political forms according to a vision of beauty is the distinctly conservative claim on our age's attention. If that summons has too frequently sounded narrow, even monotone, and so failed to resonate with as wide a range of sensibilities as it might have, that has been a problem of aesthetic or metaphysical vision first, and only secondarily one

45. Michael Davis, *The Poetry of Philosophy* (South Bend, Ind.: St. Augustine's Press, 1999), xviii.
46. Davis, *The Poetry of Philosophy*, xvii, 9.

of particular policies or practical politics. Thus, in drawing the attention of conservatives specifically back to a knowledge of the beautiful, I hope to point out shortcomings present in individual persons, in a portion of our society, and in our culture in general. If we would do what is right, what conforms to reality at its depths, we must grasp with clarity and conviction the being revealed to us in the enveloping hands of beauty.

The arguments I have made, both for the centrality of beauty among the transcendentals and for beauty as the ordering principle of reality should, naturally, unsettle what have become conventional beliefs. It forces, among other things, our understanding of goodness and, above all, truth to shift. And so, we turn now from an investigation of the relation of art, being, and beauty to see what consequences it might have for our grasp of reason, narrative, and truth.

PART III

REASON, NARRATIVE, AND TRUTH

ELEVEN

Reasoning about Stories

Years ago, it was not uncommon to hear literary theorists proclaim ours a postmodern age, by which they meant an age so suspicious of stories about our cultures and civilization as to have lost the means of reciting its own story to itself.[1] Eventually, someone got around to noticing that to say that we have passed through an age beholden to comprehensive ("master") narratives into one that refuses all such narratives is, well, itself a staggeringly comprehensive narrative.[2] And so it is. All historical discussion, all arguments about one age or another, including that of conservatives about the modern condition or traditional civilizations, are fundamentally arguments about stories. Though the means of disputation remain perpetually unsettled, it is still the case that to argue about who we are, who we should be, as individuals, as a people, or as human beings *per se*, has as its stake the story we shall take as true and tell over to ourselves as the truth. The conservative intellectual tradition has always recognized as much and distinguishes itself from other traditions not merely in offering a narrative of its own, but in defending story itself as the essential, unmatched means to knowledge about truth and goodness.[3]

1. The once authoritative account of this claim was to be found in Jean-François Lyotard, *The Postmodern Condition: A Report on Knowledge* (Minneapolis: University of Minnesota Press, 2002).

2. Fredric Jameson, *Postmodernism, or, The Cultural Logic of Late Capitalism* (Durham, N.C.: Duke University Press, 2001), xi.

3. Cf. Gerald Russello, *The Postmodern Imagination of Russell Kirk* (Columbia: University of Missouri Press, 2007).

The disciplinary disputes among historians illustrate this fact most obviously, since the major trends in that field during the last century have been away from particular or more-or-less grand story telling toward a positivistic mapping of the surface of things. Some aspirant postmodernist or modernist, frenetic and at the edge of his seat, chirps, "Yes, the triumph of space over time!" And some conservative observes, while retreating to the back of his club, "How sad. Where shall the young discover their heroes?" And the conservative has a point, for it is unclear how one could engage in fruitful inquiry about what is good without granting to story-telling at least a moral authority.

The argument about and defense of stories extends well beyond the sheltered halls of academic historical research, however, even though popular books of history tend to retain, in our day, the form and sense of elegant narrative and to eschew, thereby, the standards of academic history. It is not only in the purveyors of high theory or serious scholarship, but in the forgetfulness of everyday life that story-telling comes under suspicion or the threat of "positivist" superannuation or "postmodern" forgetfulness. Wendell Berry has with good reason observed in his essays that the rise of isolated small societies centered on taste preferences and consumption (the modern nuclear family in its suburban home) has resulted nearly in the extinction of story-telling and so the further isolations of those societies.[4] Far from sitting semi-circle about the hearth to while away the hours of darkness with good talk and laughter, the members of modern families retreat from one another to their individual screens and watch in total passivity as narrative spectacles unfold before their eyes. Berry contends that the loss of story-sharing amounts to the loss of community. A family that does not tell tales together and that does not work together, can scarcely be said to live together, and certainly lacks the bonds that seal physical propinquity as communal solidarity. Not only, then, does a loss of story-telling hamper moral inquiry, it undermines our realization of a static good to which absolutely no one objects: the goodness of being together.[5]

Berry's observations—which so many of us feel in the blood—offer a humbler and more domestic account of what the German romantics

4. Wendell Berry, *What Are People For?* (San Francisco: North Point Press, 1990), 180, 187.
5. On the universality of friendship (if it can be doubted) see Aristotle, *Nicomachean Ethics*, 1172a.

(those Brothers Grimm, for instance) and the nationalist and patriotic movements to which they gave rise argue in terms of race or national community. So dissolvent has the fluidity and money-grubbing of modern capitalism proved, that the modern citizen is perpetually in danger of forgetting the organic national body of which he is a part. Modern citizens share no past, their identities do not resonate in the chords of memory. They are atomized masses of equal individuals held together—to the extent they *are* held together—only by the force and sway of laws. The romantic position counters that they can hold themselves together by an *internal* desire rather than external coercion only if they know the truths that all of them hold in common; and those truths cannot be mere maxims, which are abstract, "portable," and in some sense placeless. The truth of a national community may be manifested by traditions and customs, but it is founded on narrative, myth, or story. When we all hold the same stories in our heads and hearts, this account runs, we shall share in something more profound than an abstract moral and legal consensus; we shall take on roles in an epic of blood.[6]

As Berry has fiercely argued, mass culture and the modern marketplace, which reduce the freedom of the human mind outside of the workday to a menu of preferences and consumer choices, cause us to lose interest in, and to forget how to tell and hear, the stories that reduce and even overcome all loneliness. The triumph of the administered state, with its exclusive love of efficiency and an elaborate but mechanical bureaucratic rationality, scours the surface of society to rid it of stories and remolds that surface according to its own geometrical principles. If postmodernity were the era in which "master" narratives disappear, it is entirely at the behest of the master. This much we see. And so, it has been the endeavor of the conservative, since the days of Swift, Burke, Wordsworth, and Coleridge, to fight in defense of reality as having, in essence, a narrative or dramatic structure. Tradition and story are our exclusive means of access to the truth about ourselves and God's creation, they tell us. The entirely abstract components of modern rationalism are, conversely, a source of untruth whose lies possess a frightening and vulgar efficacy. As we shall observe in the chapters that follow, at its extreme, this conserva-

6. This is a theory of romanticism in general, of course, not restricted to Germany. See, for instance, Maurice Barrès, *Les Déracinés* (Paris: Union Générale d'Editions, 1986).

tive romanticism elevates the tales of the *volk* to oracles of truth and regards discursive reason with suspicion. But, in the main, it perceives that
story-form can reveal form in the classical sense of essence, the intelligible
reality of being, and, therefore, seeks to preserve it as a way of knowing.

The modern structuralists and phenomenologists—in diverse, sometimes overlapping, ways—nuanced such accounts, and gave them the appearance of philosophic rigor by suggesting we could analyze without destroying stories. Rational abstraction is founded on narrative and always
returns to it dialectically, some tell us. Others go farther and insist upon
the archetypal forms of human experience as existing and repeating themselves independent of conscious human reason.[7]

From quite a different foundation, Alasdair MacIntyre's magnificent te-
tralogy, beginning with *After Virtue*, instructs us that ethical thinking, and
indeed all reasoning, is teleological in nature. When our reason sets to work,
it is always thinking in terms of a *telos*, an end, a purpose; practical reason
always envisions a kind of story about how someone discovers and "gets to"
the purpose for which he was made.[8] If one cannot think about what the
story of a good man's life looks like, the telling leading to an imagined vision
of that life-form, if one cannot imagine the flourishing, happy man whose
image is not just that of a person but that of his life, then one can hardly begin to ask the ethical questions about good and evil that confront us daily in
our own life stories.[9] MacIntyre shows us, in other words, that the antithesis
that critics and advocates of modernity both produce—an irreconcilable
distinction between reason and imagination, or abstraction and story—is a
false one. We all live and think within a particular story that, when reflected
upon, appears as a life. We live in communities with cultures that become
visible as history. And our history is not a series of events securely in the
past, but the movement that gives rise to tradition, that is, to language and
habits of thought adequate to our experience, all of which together makes
our reasoning possible.

---

7. This perspective developed from a negative critique in James Frazer's *The Golden Bough*,
and in other works of the Cambridge ritualists, to a largely positive one in the writings of Joseph Campbell. For a specifically literary rather than psychoanalytic or anthropological vision
of story-form as archetypal, see Northrop Frye, *Anatomy of Criticism* (Princeton, N.J.: Princeton
University Press, 1957), 131–239.

8. Alasdair MacIntyre, *After Virtue*, 226–27.

9. MacIntyre, *After Virtue*, 58–59. Cf. Balthasar, *The Glory of the Lord* 1:27–28.

Thus, to the extent that modernity elects in favor of abstract reason over narrative, the modern person would seem to deprive himself of the capacity for self-reflection. He may try to speculate abstractly regarding the nature and validity of the ethical principles and customs with which he lives, but he will at best produce bad arguments to justify them. Eventually, he shall conclude they must be irrational expressions of his will about which there can be no argument, only force of passion.[10] MacIntyre thereby suggests that the romantics and other discontented critics of modernity are at once all too modern and yet bearers of an ancient truth. They cannot explain why this man or that should feel compelled to learn the stories of the tribe, as it were, and yet they understand something invaluable lies hidden there. French counter-revolutionary traditionalism, for instance, found itself in the impossible position of formulating compelling arguments for obedience to tradition as such, even as tradition was taken as that which defied all rational scrutiny.[11] That way leads relativism; relativism is the liquidation of every story. Had they understood tradition as primarily that which bears intellectual and story forms together and across time, giving them integrity but never enclosing them in opacity, such traditionalists would have been both better defenders of tradition and more truly in contact with the ancient traditions of narrative reasoning they, at heart, wanted to protect.

Marcel Detienne has proposed that the relation between the *logos* of reason and the *mythos* of story is even closer than MacIntyre indicates. For the ancient Greeks, Detienne tells us, they are effectively the same. *Mythopoesis*, story-telling, is simply the reasoning of a primarily oral culture; abstract reasoning always takes place within the immediate occasion of a story, and so the being from which an idea is actually *abstracted* always remains present. *Logos* comes into being only once written culture develops. At that moment, the rehearsal of a particular story ceases to be the immediate and evident context for reflection on an idea. The idea will still be an abstraction—that is, it will be abstracted by its discussants from an increasingly distant, eventually forgotten, narrative occasion—but it will float free as a text, as if created from nothing. This liberation of the abstract idea, as MacIntyre

10. MacIntyre, *After Virtue*, 11–12.
11. See Christopher Olaf Blum, ed., *Critics of the Enlightenment* (Wilmington, Del.: ISI Books, 2004), ix; also Robert Spaemann, "Der Irrtum des Traditionalisten. Zur Soziologisierung der Gottesidee im 19. Jahrhundert," *Wort und Wahrheit* 8 (1953): 493–98.

would imply, may quickly become the cause of its death—but before the idea itself finally dies, reason itself will have ceased in its proper operation.

Detienne here reminds us of a difficult truth. It is not the rational content of abstract reasoning that is deadening and that has caused rational, philosophic, and (more recently) scientific discourses to appear like the soul-killing munitions of a deracinated and meaningless modern age. Rather, when an idea or a discourse becomes entirely abstract—when *logos* so fully comes into its own being that it completely extricates itself from *mythos*—it loses its identity as an idea. In a word, it ceases to be rational.

Here is the theme that guides the inquiry of the following chapters, and so I should rephrase it with greater precision: an idea can never in itself *become* irrational, for nothing we do can fully erase the *mythos* that gave it birth. Our discussions, or talk about ideas, our use of them—these may become irrational. In abandoning story, we lose the ability to reason about erstwhile rational propositions. So do we lose, as the romantics understood, the ability to know ourselves. We lose a sense of living in community, of being political animals; for that sense is of the commingling of intellects, not of the mere brushing together of bodies.[12] More devastating even than these great losses, we lose the ability to live as rational animals. It is no coincidence that the modern age came into its own in those few decades where the liberator of the abstract idea, Descartes, and the great theorist of society and politics as artificial rather than natural, Hobbes, crossed paths—and spoke at cross purposes. They were inaugurating an age in which communion and communication no longer seemed natural and soon enough would seem impossible.

The inherent narrative basis of reality and reason, then, is something that remains in effect regardless of our own arguments about it or discussions of it. We may well argue about the importance and moral authority of this story or that one, or the specific truth content showing forth from a story's possible forms, but we never escape the condition of *mythos*. Burke was correct to equate the modern scene with the tragic stage, and to follow Shakespeare more boldly (and less cynically) in hinting that all the world is a stage.

The following chapters seek to measure the dimensions of that stage.

12. Hannah Arendt, *The Human Condition* (Chicago: The University of Chicago Press, 1958), 24–27. Cf. Maritain, *Art and Scholasticism and the Frontiers of Poetry*, 32–33.

First, we shall consider the role of narrative as mother of all the fine arts: contrary to certain quintessentially modern aesthetic theories, narrative is the ineluctable foundation for every art form, and so we err in our efforts to think of aesthetic form as something standing apart from story-form, or to reduce story-form to one species among others within the genus of the aesthetic. When we think poetically, our mind always refers back to *poiesis* as story-telling. In "Novel, Myth, Reality: An Anatomy of Make-Believe," however, I consider some of the problematic understandings of narrative to which this may give rise. While it is appropriate to recover a sense of narrative as grounding the intellectual virtues of reason and art alike, we would stop short of a full understanding of these things if we concluded that one found its final realization in discursive demonstrations and the other in the structure or form of a narrative. Both these intellectual forms drive beyond themselves to an encounter with the true form of the real: being. In argument and story-telling, as in aesthetics, we must always conclude in seeing the form.

These considerations serve as prefaces to the sustained line of inquiry pursued in "Retelling the Story of Reason." There, I seek to provide an extended, if still essayistic, argument for the intrinsic connection of *mythos* and *logos*, and to indicate how this revision of reason and narrative may issue in a richer encounter with being as truth. *The Vision of the Soul* comes to a conclusion, then, with two chapters. The first explores the negative consequences for truth and human beings alike in an age that dislocates *logos* from *mythos*. The second, "Still Interested in the Truth," seeks to provide a vision of the intellectual life that integrates the themes of our three studies: the passionate pursuit of the good, the comprehensive vision of beauty as an encounter with the full dimensions of reality, and the natural ordination of human persons as pilgrims, as living out a story, to the pursuit of the truth that shows forth in beauty's splendor. It is one main purpose of this book to help conserve the rich, indeed blindingly brilliant, vision of reality as intrinsically loaded with truth, goodness, and beauty that the West may rightly pride itself for articulating. But the other is to invite others to embrace that tradition, to defend it, and, finally, to order their lives around its vision. And so, it will be appropriate to conclude our study with an account of the passionate pursuit of truth—both how it has been undertaken at different times, and how it may be renewed in our day.

TWELVE

Mnemosyne

MOTHER OF THE ARTS

So successful was the advent of modernist poetic, musical, and visual art in disrupting the critical vocabulary by which we describe them
that we have all but lost the means to account for how art actually works.
So blinding was its revolutionary blast that we have sometimes failed to
distinguish the various courses these arts took during the modernist period; moreover, we have often assumed modern art effected more radical
changes than it did, as if it put the aesthetic upon an entirely new basis.
Abstraction in painting, dissonance and atonality in music, and free verse
in poetry stand of a piece, historically, insofar as they denote the striking
features of modernist art, but their evident formal differences signify very
different relations to what I shall argue is the exemplar in which all art
participates and from which it can never escape—narrative.

Most critics of modernism have long contended that its works followed
other trends in modern intellectual life in the sacrifice of narrative in favor
of some kind of rarified (abstracted) formalism: form becomes content to
the extent that the work of art comes to be *about* its own form and nothing else. But what has been less fully appreciated is that such sacrifice was
imperfect at best. Modernist artworks, especially at the thought-silencing
extremes of abstraction, have themselves become characters *in* the story of
art, no more "liberated" from the conditions of time and narrative than
their predecessors. It is the burden of this chapter to show this to be the

244

case: to show modernism as, at most, adding a new inflection to the historical role of narrative in art, and thus to indicate why it is now appropriate to return to a classical understanding of the fine arts as *poiesis*, the making of plots. Mnemosyne, goddess of memory and source therefore of all story, has always been and remains the mother of the muses.

In the first two decades of the twentieth century, the visual, musical, and poetic arts each suffered related but distinct revolutions. Arnold Schoenberg introduced atonality, or serialism, as a new musical vocabulary to replace melody. Much less radically, Igor Stravinsky composed several ballets with clashing, dissonant tones. Visual artists, including Pablo Picasso and Wyndham Lewis, experimented with cubist and other techniques that attempted to give striking representational form to qualities abstracted from the lush profusion of everyday appearance. Such literal abstraction would soon lead to "abstraction," that is, to painting and sculpture of pure form that ceased to imitate or represent in any obvious way forms found in nature. Finally, beginning with the late work of the French symbolist, Stéphane Mallarmé, but only becoming a trend with the British and American Imagists, poets partly abandoned the formal practices of versification to experiment in so-called *vers libre* as a belated expression of the modern consensus that lyric rather than epic was poetry's most distinctive mode.

These three revolts share in a violation of long established conventions of melody, representation, and prosody; they asserted the integrity of the artwork as a reality standing apart from qualities of proportion, unity, and agreeability. But beyond this, their meaning and consequences are very various indeed. Atonality arose from a tension between felt emotion and musical vocabulary: melody frustrated Schoenberg's desire to express particular feelings, and so he deconstructed tonality and recombined its building blocks to suit them. As the more moderate dissonance of Stravinsky suggests, such a revolt in a certain sense made more, rather than less, evident the reliance of music upon narrative. Schoenberg's atonality derived from a romantic autobiography of the heart and nerves. Stravinsky's dissonance actually continued the developments of Wagner's *leitmotiv* to subordinate sound itself to the action and character-developing impetus of the opera and ballet. The appreciation of early modernist writers such as T. S. Eliot and W. B. Yeats for Stravinsky's *Rite of Spring* derived largely from his music's docility in conforming to a narrative of enduring, ritualized cycles. Disruptive formal techniques highlighted a narrative form that departed from the melodramatic tales that had served as stock material for traditional opera and ballet, thus making possible the modern representation of the tragic nature of historical existence. Melodramas may tell "immortal" tales of tragic love, but ritual and repetition demonstrate that apparent change is epiphenomenal to permanent patterns or archetypes. As a wheel, history is infinite, but every civilization endures for only one of its turns and concludes where it began.

Free verse served a related purpose for poetry. The first significant instances, found in the imagist poems of T. E. Hulme, H. D., and Ezra Pound, dispensed with versification (save the residual and mostly meaninglessly staggered line-break) as one means of increasing the density and intensity of poetic language. On the one hand, this intensification was intended to exclude essential aspects of narrative, such as exposition, plot, and development. On the other, the resultant lyrical fragments represented piercing, isolated moments of observation and emotion that become intelligible only if one provides for them a character's voice and dramatic context. When such practices were just getting off the ground, Pound confided to William Carlos Williams that he thought of his poems as the most fevered morsels broken off from dramatic monologues.[1] The radicalization of free verse in Eliot's *The Waste Land* and Pound's *Cantos* did nothing to further this; indeed, the patterns of fragments both works set before the reader allow for one to construct a clear, ritualized, and circular cycle of narratives akin to that of Stravinsky's *Rites*. No doubt, a circular and ritualized narrative is distinct from a linear one insofar as the linear emphasizes, as Aristotle argued, the temporal causality of the unexpected, whereas the circular foregrounds significance through repetitions unlinked from temporal causes—but, in either case, narrative remains.

The odd-man-out among the modern arts, therefore, may be the visual forms. The early modes of abstraction, such as cubism, at most lessened the usual dependence on narrative as a source of subject matter for representation.[2] In retrospect, however, it seems clear that early abstraction

---

1. Ezra Pound, *Selected Letters, 1907–1941* (New York: New Directions, 1971), 3.
2. I understand that some art historians would not include cubism as abstraction, because

only set the stage for a radicalization that would seek to sever visual form *tout court* from any narrative origin, and that this radicalization would become the main tradition of late modernist visual art. By the 1950s, poetry's fragmentation had made its narrative contents almost unintelligible (see, for instance, the work of Charles Olson), but narrative nevertheless perdured.[3] In contrast, the abstract expressionism of the same period, as exemplified by Jackson Pollock, Mark Rothko, Barnett Newman, Willem de Kooning, seems—but *only* seems—to have escaped all trace of representation much less reference to a narrative beyond itself.

One may grant readily that no modernist art "escaped" narrative, and that the visual arts made only an apparent escape, but demur that such an escape has little to do with the heart of the matter. What, then, did these different modernists attempt? The answer, in a word, is "silence." To the extent that modernist poets followed after the French symbolists, they sought not merely to break powerful emotion away from its occasion, but to break poetic language away from discourse, from "prose." The hard-boiled reticence of the best imagist poetry tries to convey strong emotion sensuously embodied, but entirely independent of any actual body bound to live on among the quotidian movements of a turning world. It takes a formal difference—verse and prose—and makes it an ontological one: prose speaks of time tables and railway schedules, poetry simply exists, like an overpowering and atemporal feeling. By "atemporal" they intended both feeling that did not derive from any chronicle or story and feeling that did not die away, but possessed a kind of independent permanence: it was "news that stays news," in Pound's characteristic phrase.[4]

The antecedence to pure abstraction in the visual arts came, perhaps inevitably, through the shepherding of the critic. The essays of T. E. Hulme propose that modern poetry must be a phenomenon keeping pace

---

it remains representational. However, I would contend that cubism is more truly abstract than nonrepresentational painting; it represents certain attributes found in nature, but abstracted and therefore conceptually clarified from their natural condition.

3. A counterexample suggesting the absence of narrative in modernist writing would be the works of Gertrude Stein. I think it significant that the most influential of English-language modernists, Eliot and Pound, thought her work signaled something other than the future of art: the end of civilization.

4. Ezra Pound, *The ABC of Reading* (New York: New Directions, 1960), 29. Cf. Timothy Steele, *Missing Measures* (Fayetteville: The University of Arkansas Press, 1990), 89–107.

with the advertising age—quick, short, and evanescent—but, in contrast, modern visual art will take on a classical, fossilized hardness.[5] Hulme's critique of humanism based on a novel understanding of original sin led him to argue that human beings were inexorably bound to the unstable and ever-passing realm of biological life; no permanence or perfection could there be had.[6] Modern sculpture, with its severe geometries, would serve as a sane reminder that the true realm of being, of the permanent, is that of religion and ideas. Reality is cut off from, discontinuous with, the slushy organisms of the life-world (the realm of becoming, as readers of Plato would call it). The partial-abstraction of such sculpture revealed, in other words, the permanent lines of reality set beyond hope of human attainment, and so rebuked any human person who would aspire to make himself perfect.[7] Its harsh and permanent lines arose within the artwork and disrupted the fluidity of the everyday as a severe revelation of the absolute. In brief, human life is short, ideas are permanent, and only sculpture crafted according to what Hulme dubbed the "classicist" sensibility mediated between these realities. Hence, the stiff forms found in the work of the ancient Egyptians, archaic Greeks, and, in Hulme's day, Mr. Jacob Epstein, all expressed this modern "classical" attitude because of their tempering of sensuous natural detail into the mathematical simplicities Hulme identified with permanence.[8] The ambition was not to abstract visual art from narrative directly, but rather to abstract it from the temporal conditions that make narrative possible.

---

5. Hulme's "A Lecture on Modern Poetry" advocates for the quick shelf-life of modern poetry, arguing that poets need no longer quest after formal perfection, but only a general rough-cut effect. Hulme argues that, in this cobbled, rather than well-chiseled, appearance, modern poetry resembles sculpture, rather than in any affectation of stone-set permanence. See *The Collected Writings of T. E. Hulme* (Oxford: Clarendon Press, 1994), 56. It is worth noting that the apparent contradiction in his theories (Why is modern poetry fleeting, when modern art in general has the endurance of stone?) stems in part from the swift development of his thinking over a stormy, truncated career. Nonetheless, Hulme's work is more important for how it was read historically—without any knowledge of his intellectual development—than how it might be read thanks to superb and careful recent scholarship.

6. We considered Hulme's account of modernism above, in defining Maritain's account of art and beauty.

7. Hulme's metaphysics of discontinuity is fully expressed in "A Notebook," in *Collected Writings*, 419–56.

8. See Hulme's most influential essay, "Romanticism and Classicism," in *Collected Writings*, 59–73.

During the same period, Clive Bell would advance an even more severe and ultimately more influential theory, in *Art*:

For a discussion of aesthetics, it need be agreed only that forms arranged and combined according to certain unknown and mysterious laws do move us in a particular way, and that it is the business of an artist to so combine and arrange them that they shall move us. These moving combinations and arrangements I have called … "Significant Form."[9]

Aesthetics as a philosophy itself becomes abstract and thus narrowed—so much so that the concepts of representation or imitation (*mimesis*), according to Bell, no longer have a place in it. An object represented cannot be the reality signified in an artwork, because form qualifies as significant only insofar as its elements immanently and independently move us to have a distinctly aesthetic experience. Hulme's classicism sought to limit the appearance of time's effects in the artwork; Bell eviscerates the artwork of every sort of content. Form alone remains to signify in its place. The effect of French symbolism and modern art as Hulme and Bell understood it was to silence the natural act of interpretation that begins with, and extends beyond, narrative content. Modernist lyric poetry achieved this through concentration, the simplifying and unifying of the meaning of a poem on a single emotional effect; hence, Pound's famous "In a station of the metro":

> The apparition of these faces in the crowd;
> Petals on a wet, black bough.[10]

But the aesthetics of Bell enforces a much greater, more absolute silence. One can say nothing about the content of a painting that is not essentially a distortion of the painting *qua* painting. Form is significant, but what does is signify? What does it say? It says itself, its own presence, like breath without words.

Despite some real similarities, developments in the theory of visual art are incommensurable with contemporaneous changes in the practice of music and poetry. Experiments in atonality and dissonance were readily

9. Clive Bell, *Art* (London: Chatto Windus, 1914), 11.
10. Ezra Pound, *Personae* (New York: New Directions, 1990), 111.

adaptable to the opera, ballet, and, eventually, the film score; they indeed contributed to the highlighting of character and narrative in those genres and, contrary to intention, made serious music less of an autonomous art form. The loss of real versification in poetry literally transformed it, and made certain kinds of narrative, such as the epic, harder to realize, and others harder to distinguish from the novel, but it did nothing to uproot the foundation of the lyric poem's content in a narrative "back-story." Indeed, Pound early wondered if a long imagist poem would be possible, not because imagistic free verse lacked narrative, but because its narratives were concentrated and tended to break apart into formally distinct moments of intensity. His *Cantos* nevertheless constitutes, in a manner of speaking, a long imagist poem; it does not lack for narrative, but fragments, truncates, and rearranges narrative elements in large patterns that defy easy comprehension.

This is not the place to speculate on why Pound undertook such an absorbing and doomed project, but it is worth noting that to understand the *Cantos* one must reconstruct and assume a narrative behind them. Everyone agrees with Pound, after all, that it is a poem *about* history. The unfortunate fate of professional exegetes of the poem has been the mere filling in of gaps in the stories to make the work more intelligible, rather than in engaging the finer points of interpretation. And so, again, only the pure abstraction of visual art seems to dispense with narrative origins altogether during the modernist period.

And yet, we must acknowledge to what these modernist projects eventually led. Serialism in music had always the potential to rarify itself until the symphony seemed to lose all trace of *expressing* a narrative. Painting and sculpture's movement toward abstraction continued unabated, until the rise of conceptual art in the 1960s and the lapse of serious formal experimentation thereafter. The later course of poetry is even more remarkable. Free verse did little to the narrative content of the art that lyric poetry in general had not always done, and most free verse poems published today are sweet-and-sour little stories of personal experience. Only when self-described avant-garde and "L=A=N=G=U=A=G=E" poets began to explore the subversion of language itself did formal practices seriously impinge upon this content. Such poets used collage and fragmentation to disrupt the formation of words into language, in hopes of escaping the "capitalist" and "colonial" "prison house" of—not *rational*, but—discourse *per se*. These poets have between them only two tropes according to which they order words: the representation of debased commercialized language and the liberated language of nonsense. Thus, Charles Bernstein's *Rough Trades* counterpoints grotesque modifications of cliché with isolated words. The cliché:

> It's like having
> our own baby. It's
> so cute & cuddly.
> It's better than
> yours
> because we're puppets
> too.

The words:

> Lose track of where seven Moabite
> everything the stove as agent you
> devolved and basically are
> spunk in a minute reprobated[11]

One sees that such truncations do not smoothly continue the concentrated narrative fragment of early free verse. And yet, one can hold up these writings of Bernstein's as "poetry" only if one has a sense of the story of their descent from the free verse of modernism. Their claim to belonging to the genre at all subsists tenuously in the pages of literary history rather than on the pages in which the "poems" appear.

The devolutions of such poetry are frequently attributed to a much earlier revolution than the modernist ones. Namely, as writers from Walter Pater to Erich Heller, Frank Kermode, and Timothy Steele have observed, the changing formal character of poetry was a consequence of poetry's losing its status as the highest of the fine arts, to be replaced by music. Pater celebrated the supposition that all art aspired to the "condition of music." Heller, Kermode, and Steele decried this as a perversion of hierarchy, though only the first saw it occurring as early as the seventeenth

---

11. Charles Bernstein, *Rough Trades* (Los Angeles: Sun and Moon Classics, 1991), 54, 58. Cf. Wilson, *The Fortunes of Poetry in an Age of Unmaking*, 179–89.

century.[12] But the very word "poetry" is a historical marker denoting the privileged status traditionally given to verse over all other art forms. *Poiesis*, to the Greeks, meant making in general, the making of fine art in particular, and the making of plots in verse above all.[13] Verse narrative seemed to be *the* exemplary form of fine art.

The careful ranking of different art forms may strike the contemporary intellect—haunted as it is with spirits of relativism, democracy, and materialism—as absurd. What could it possibly mean to judge the comparative rank, for instance, of history painting over portraiture? Of epic over satire or lyric? A great deal, actually, but nothing so much as this: poetry was historically the highest of the arts not because of its formal properties (versification) in themselves, but because it was measured *and* linguistic. It was therefore capable of bearing narrative unmistakably and primarily with only so much formal artifice as was necessary to make the language memorable and, so, suitable for public recitation. To elevate music was specifically to refuse the primacy of a narrative that could be heard and remembered in common. After the fashion of Bell's positing of significant form, theories of poetry and the other arts as "aspiring" to the condition of music most clearly means the escape from discursive, or discussible, content in favor of rarified sensuous experience. In practice, it means the attempt to sever one art or another from narrative.

No such escape is possible, however, and for several reasons. The French phenomenologist Paul Ricoeur has argued convincingly that time and narrative alike are the very condition of human life. Like the admirer of Hulme's statues, or the maniac in Platonic ecstasy, a person may seek to escape these conditions, but will inevitably fall back into them. Ricoeur suggests something even more profound, however: not merely that we cannot escape the conditions but that we cannot think outside of them. Thought and life alike resolve themselves in narrative terms.[14] We might punctuate this phenomenological claim with an "ideological" one. Fredric Jameson has argued in Marxist terms that narratives may be false but they

---

12. See Walter Pater, *The Renaissance* (1873), Erich Heller, *The Disinherited Mind* (1952), Frank Kermode, *The Romantic Image* (1957), and Steele, *Missing Measures* (1990).

13. Jacques Maritain considers further implications of these acceptations in *The Situation of Poetry*, 37. Cf. Wilson, *The Fortunes of Poetry in an Age of Unmaking*, 211–19.

14. See Paul Ricoeur, *Time and Narrative* (Chicago: University of Chicago Press, 1983).

are no less ineluctable.[15] As we noted above, he has insisted, against the pretensions of some varieties of postmodern thought, that to speak of an end to "master narratives" is itself to articulate a narrative. Such a labyrinthine claim, in which narrative's necessity is acknowledged but not its truth, seems inadequate on metaphysical and practical (artistic) grounds.

As we considered in the first part of this book, the metaphysical error of these otherwise rich claims lies in their locating the "categorical imperative" to narrate within the subjectivity of the person rather than in the nature of reality as such. But we are forced to think in terms of time not because of some condition of our consciousness, but because time is a reality in which we exist. We can, after all, think in terms of non-temporal forms and even in terms that would not make any sense were we to conceive them temporally. We generally understand the effects of justice, for instance, in temporal, sensuous images; but we do not understand the term "justice" itself in that way. Our mind routinely rises above its temporal, concrete condition even though it does so *in* time. Time is not, therefore, coextensive with reality, but it clearly is coextensive with bodily existence. As such, to know reality as we experience it (and this includes our *experience* of non-temporal, abstract ideas) is to come to a knowledge of time. And the inevitable reality of everything in time is a beginning and an end. This finitude of things makes them intrinsically dramatic; when we account for this drama, we give birth to narrative, and when we come to see the total form of a narrative we have a story.

Human life is a story, not because human beings think in terms of time, but because every human life has a birth and a death and a continuous series of events that affect that identical life in between. Hulme's theory of visual art reluctantly applauded the way in which artworks could allow temporally bound, finite persons to contemplate eternal truths. He appreciated that this contemplation from within time of what lies outside of time (by way of an artwork that "disrupts" time by entering it) in no way compromised the truth or reality of embodied temporal life, but only put into question its relative worth, its goodness. Every such attempt to contemplate eternity does not awaken us to our existence in a prison

15. More precisely, he insists that we cannot escape "periodizing" history and that such periods are not concepts but narratives. See Frederic Jameson, *A Singular Modernity* (London: Verso, 2002), 94.

of self-deception, as if time and narrative were hallucinogenic. It rather makes clear to us that so determinant is time of the shape of the reality we experience that everything—absolutely everything—in our knowledge has, either essentially or accidentally, as one cause of the perception of its metaphysical form (its being), a narrative form, a story (a *poiesis* that is above all a *telos*).

The anonymous medieval play, *Everyman*, expresses this elegantly. The play begins with God, eternal act beyond all time, stating the full truth about creation and the human condition; his words are in themselves un-conditioned by temporality, though, of course, his audience in merry old England could only hear them in time. God then sends a being who is the consummate marker of finitude, and so also of the temporal condition, to visit Everyman. It is Death who comes, and comes to remind Everyman of the truth about his own finite nature. In scrutinizing himself in terms of his death, Everyman sets about tracing the arc of his life, from birth to death, and discerning what properly belongs to it, filling up the space in between. By staring into the temporality of death, Everyman discerns the essential, timeless form of a properly lived human life: a form that is itself one of God's eternal ideas, but which we come to perceive and understand only within our temporal circumstances.[16] The absolutely finite and the absolutely eternal condition human life; they define its form as essentially temporal. The play as a whole indicates that this form can be perceived only through its enactment as a story. Human life must be dramatized to be seen in its innermost reality.

This metaphysical argument expresses itself practically in the nature of art in general, not just in a didactic work like *Everyman*. Until some ambiguous but definitely modern moment, *poiesis* explicitly meant the making of fine art, and the making of fine art meant the reification of nar-rative. Every work of art represents a plot, even if it does not represent the complete plot. Narratives are ideal forms, exemplars, that take on flesh in art. Hence, one may see a painting, read a poem, or hear an opera about the wanderings of Odysseus or the anger of Achilles; each work is a con-crete realization of the archetype. This is the case even with symphonic music, where the composer may at first seem not to be working from some

16. *Everyman* (Mineola, N.Y.: Dover Publications, 1995).

narrative. If one thinks of such music as the expression of an emotion or mood, one may quickly discern that the music, because of the feeling on which it is modeled, originates in some kind of story. For, while it is an unhappy fact of life that feelings often come to exist in us unprompted by any satisfactory cause, we can know a feeling is uncaused only by way of its *non sequitur* status within the narrative of human experience.[17] If, on the other hand, one argues as many modernists did (and did perceptively) that music expresses, not the emotions *per se* of a narrative, but the order of an often impassioned logic, one still ends with the same conclusion. Because of our temporally bound (discursive) way of reasoning, we are in particularly advantageous position to observe how the movements of logic have themselves a narrative form. Order is always the ordering of parts, and those parts—which may include simply the tones of a score—serve as well as anything for characters. St. Augustine wrote of the *distentio* intrinsic to created time and human thought alike.[18] Because, finally, music is inextricably temporal, it seems the exquisite medium for a particular kind of narrative, that of the intellect discovering the necessary order of contingent things and developing that order.[19]

The modern revolutions therefore did not cast off narrative as an archetype in preference for music, though that is almost surely what many modern artists thought they were doing. Some of them, rather, radically shifted the position of narrative in relation to the art work. Goya's painting of Christ cleansing the temple clearly derives from and represents an

17. This seemingly minor point was at issue in one of the most compelling, if little noticed, debates of modernist literary theory. Following the poetic theory of George Santayana, T. S. Eliot, in "Tradition and the Individual Talent" and in "Hamlet and His Problems," proposed that feeling or emotion is the raw (non-aesthetic) stuff that is molded into the objective materials of poetry. As is well known, Eliot did not mean that poetry expressed emotion, but rather that emotion counted as the mental object on which the artist works to make something else; see Eliot, *Selected Essays*, 8–11, 124–25. Yvor Winters would organize his entire critical theory as a negative response to Eliot's. A poem, as all life, begins in a scenario (a character, a plot, an event), which constitutes a *motive*. A poem depicts (however minimally) this motive, this story, and gives with it a complex of feeling. The best poems will be those that properly calibrate motive and feeling, but the latter is always a response to the former, of judgment to story; see Winters, *In Defense of Reason*, 363–70, 462–69.

18. Augustine, *The Confessions*, XI.23.30.

19. This is in fact the perception of *beauty*, according to von Balthasar: the self-interpreting disclosure of the full reality of things—above all of Christian revelation; see Hans Urs von Balthasar, *Love Alone Is Credible*, trans. D. C. Schindler (San Francisco: Ignatius Press, 2004), 52–55.

irreducible moment of a story from the Gospel. The narrative is internal to the work, informing it.[20] A Mark Rothko canvas, because of its abstraction, clearly lacks such an internal narrative. But to see the canvas, that is, to have any experience of it at all, requires one to come to it with a certain story already in mind. That Rothko and other abstract expressionists developed sophisticated rationales about the meaning of their paintings means that we might even approach the canvases not only with *any* story in mind, but with the correct story. The reader cries foul immediately: "this is the intentional fallacy. There is no ontological basis for such a narrative interpretation to be found *in* the painting itself."[21] That is partially true and accounts for both the extreme limitation of nonrepresentational art and its appearance of opacity and inadequacy to much of its audience.[22] But narrative has not vanished; it has merely become *exogenous*.

Most artworks take the elements, above all characters, of a narrative as objects for representation *in* the work. Abstraction renders the individual artwork a character within a larger narrative—one that informs, gives shape to, the work, but one to which much of the work's audience may have no ready access. In the same way that a single stray phrase may connote an entire tragedy (e.g., "To be or not to be …") a single abstract painting may connote a sprawling, complex, and meaningful narrative. It does this by its very nature. But in making that narrative exogenous to the art work—attached to it, but not assimilated within it—modern art surrenders most of its variety and interest. Rather than bringing into vivid and ordered reification the stories perpetually fleeing all around us, the artworks of exogenous narrative merely play a supporting role in those stories. But, again, we cannot talk about them, we cannot even see them, unless we approach them as we might the character of Hamlet upon the stage: a story swells behind him and before him no matter how still, for the moment, he appears.[23]

20. I owe the examples discussed here, and the seed of this chapter, to Alasdair MacIntyre's lecture, "What Makes a Painting a Religious Painting?" (presented at the Fall Conference of the Notre Dame Center for Ethics and Culture, Notre Dame, Ind., November 18–20, 2004).

21. See W. K. Wimsatt Jr., "The Intentional Fallacy," in *The Verbal Icon* (New York: Noonday Press, 1958), 3–18.

22. Algis Valiunas's fine essay, "The Spirit of Abstract Art," explores the narrative rationales that inform the works of the abstract expressionists, underlining their importance for interpretation and their inadequacy to make the paintings themselves interesting (*First Things* 159, January 2006, 28–33).

23. Eliot seems to have been working through these premises in "The Love Song of J. Alfred

If modern art sought with a spirit of rebellion to escape narrative but succeeded only in rendering it exogenous, we should not cling to its tattered battle flag. Exogenous narratives in artworks are intrinsically less comprehensible and indeed less interesting than internal ones. The techniques of atonality, free verse, and abstraction that to varying degrees led to this "turning out" of narrative have done their work of making visible by experiment what the tradition has known and passed on by myth from antiquity. They are radical not in making possible the "new" in art, but in curtailing its depth and variety. Moreover, they increasingly seem not, as was Hulme's statuary, a medium between the temporal and the eternal, but more like obstacles between the human person's desire to understand his own existence and the narratives that alone make such understanding possible. If works of art are to help us reason about the human condition and the nature of reality as human beings experience it, they will have to resume their role as the artifacts in which, and through which, we reason about stories. On this there remains much more to be said, but first we must offer a caution on the limits of narrative's comprehension.

Prufrock," which is an experiment of sorts both in how radically separated from "motive" a series of associative images representing feelings can be and still work as a unified poem, but also at what remove a character may stand from the story of his own life, being inserted, as it were, as an extra in the story of another, such as Prince Hamlet (Eliot, *Complete Poems and Plays*, 7).

THIRTEEN

Novel, Myth, Reality

AN ANATOMY OF MAKE-BELIEVE

In the last chapter, I contended that all art depends upon narrative. Even those modernist works, such as nonrepresentational painting, that seem most to escape the gravity of story-telling end up simply rendering the narrative exogenous but no less essential. I concluded by urging artists and writers to appreciate what such modernist experiments help reveal about the nature of art, but also to return to formal practices that better respect Mnemosyne as the mother of the arts and, in turn, better respect the form of the story as an essential means to understanding the human condition. In this recommendation, I am hardly alone.

Several years ago, novelist Lev Grossman argued in the pages of the *Wall Street Journal* that the modernist eschewal of plot is going to disappear with the inevitability that only a convergence of several causes could ensure.[1] While his observations are sometimes glib, and his explanations a little easy, they capture a number of significant truths about our cultural moment. In recent years, a culture of instant and spectacular entertainment coupled with a marketplace eager to satisfy, indeed to exacerbate, has made difficult art seem not worth the trouble. These tendencies meet little resistance from those quarters that once shunned the productions of mass

---

1. Lev Grossman, "Good Books Don't Have to Be Hard," *The Wall Street Journal*, August 28, 2009.

culture, now that institutions of education have bought into the idea that artistic achievement is a matter of taste and taste is ineluctably relative, and museums have become fora, not for the display of cultural achievement, but for the redress of various historical wrongs of "under-representation."

To this familiar postmodern pathology we add a more encouraging, if harder to measure, element of the "postmodern" sensibility: an increasing sense among scholars and lay persons alike of the inherent story-form of human life and even of reality as a whole, and a consciousness that a base, gossipy *curiositas* is not necessarily opposed to that more dignified desire for study (*studiasitas*) characteristic of liberal education, but in fact provides its antecedent and foundation.[2] The desire to eavesdrop or to pause before a traffic accident is but the inchoate form of Aristotle's observations that all "men by nature desire to know" and take particular delight in all manner of acts of imitation.[3] While lust is a perversion of *eros*, its movements are a first revelation of love's power, which lacks only its condign object and proper measure. As it is in romantic love, so also with the love of learning.

Many modernist artworks themselves depended on the intuition that reality is a cosmos or a creation, that is, something intelligible because of an antecedent Intellect; these works' difficulty typically expressed the consensus that, given the horrors of the Great War, the total-order of the real did not dwell on the surface of things but required labor to perceive.[4] It was only a matter of time before that sense of shellshock faded, however, and the surfaces of things began to shine again, as they already seem to in F. Scott Fitzgerald's *The Great Gatsby*. We have, further, already mentioned the kind of resignation to narrative, one that is epistemological even when it is not ontological, as in the criticism of Frederic Jameson.

Grossman thus gives us a smart and provocative first assessment of how the contemporary novel should look, how it *will* look, and why. Good stories are coming back, whether on the kiddy train that brought us Harry Potter or on the A-train that will bring more intellectually mature and satisfying plots to literary novels. The market will make it so, he

2. In this, our age faces the same questions that confronted St. Augustine, as he sought to adapt his pagan understanding of narrative to the new conditions of the Christian sensibility.

3. Aristotle, *Metaphysics*, 980a25 and *Poetics*, 1448b.

4. On this point, Eliot was the great spokesman; see Eliot, *Selected Essays*, 248–49.

takes glee in declaring, but the market would seem to be, in a reversal of Marxism, epiphenomenal to a deeper need at the heart of man today no less than at the heart of Achilles in the *Iliad*, to know stories and to know himself by means of stories.[5] I would like to pursue two reflections in response to Grossman's thesis, one that returns to my own life as a student and young writer, and another that pursues and sets a limit on the theoretical account of narrative begun in the previous two chapters.

I began this book by recounting my experience as an undergraduate amid the listless, relativistic, and nihilistic quadrangles of Ann Arbor, and probably gave the impression that it was only through solitary trips to the art museum or in the deeper solitude of my scholar's cell in East Quad that I found some permanent goodness and beauty despite all. But this is not quite the whole story. In those days, I was fortunate enough to spend most of my time around novelists and aspirant novelists. I was one of them. We were a voluble bunch and quick to devise strategies to get through college with an education and, better still, a solid apprenticeship in our chosen art. We had only to cultivate a small circle of disdain and to choose our professors from among the old humanists and the senior novelists on the faculty to receive an initiation into the writer's life that still held art and beauty as things to be prized and treated with diffidence and seriousness.

If there was anything on which we all agreed it was that the natural and halcyon form of the novel was that perfected by the Victorians. What we prized in modernist and contemporary authors—and this came to much— was their ear for voice, for dialogue. But for the broad architectonic of prose fiction, we knew the true masters were somewhat older. If the novel is to survive as an attractive and vital art, it will always gravitate back to the form that the Victorians gave it. Supposed evidence to the contrary proves this insofar as one can read a modern novel properly (take Joyce's *Ulysses* or any novel by Woolf here) only if one reads it with the Victorians in mind. If one does not feel, while blinking one's way through *To the Lighthouse* (or the whole lot of Woolf's novels), the tension of Victorian convention being bucked by modernist insouciance, Victorian mores being at once embraced, gutted, and tweaked, one simply has not read the book.

In personal support of the inevitability of the Victorian novel with its

5. Davis, *The Poetry of Philosophy*, xvii.

dense, winding plots and thick, well-etched, and morally significant characters, I also note that my little group of writers had a philosophy about fiction, one that I called the Intelligent Bar principle. The test of a story was this: if you cannot imagine going into the most intelligent of bars in the most intelligent of cities and sitting down with the most intelligent of tipplers and telling him a given story over a pint, then that story should *not* be told. (The formulation had to be negative, because I had read Ezra Pound's "A Few Don'ts by an Imagiste" and so presumed all manifestos were.) Because we lived in Ann Arbor, Michigan, we were all convinced that the environment was conducive to verifying this theory. For there were many bars and many people who thought themselves very smart. Once more, I was among them.

Beyond my little group, and very much in the air in those days, was also another principle that I would, in retrospect, call one of experimental realism. The universalization of fiction-writing as an academic subject in the previous few decades had created a condition wherein the typical aspirant writer was continuously coming into contact with contemporary American realist authors as well as with the clumsy, often abominable, attempts at story writing of one's coevals. Such frequent encounters with works of prose fiction that were at once so various in quality and so similar in literary convention naturally led one to generalize about the essence of story writing. What strikes me, in retrospect, as novel about these generalizations was not where they overlapped with more ancient notions of literary form, imitation, and decorum (such as those of Aristotle's supposed "three unities"), but where they specifically arose from the current climate of academic instruction. While there was always to be found the occasional writer of "postmodern" "metafiction," in those years just after the death of Raymond Carver, most of us understood him, Hemmingway, and Chekov as having helped establish the horizon of what constituted a serious work of fiction. Within that horizon, as in any world, there were natural laws that must be observed, and whose structure could be established and verified. One would frequently hear, for instance, the injunction that an author must not be cruel to his character. This was not an act of charity, but a piece of artisanal advice, if a dubious one compared to most of the others we tossed around. In most ages, critics and authors will assume a certain law of "verisimilitude" in art. But in ours, whether a character or plot was believable took on an especially formal quality. One could insert a character into a scene and determine what—and what not—it was plausible for him to think, to feel, and to do. Thus the horizon of realism made it possible to experiment not so much *with* stories as *within* them to arrive at something like a firm knowledge of how a plot or a character could or could not be realized. These laws governing fiction were not taken to be merely fictional but rather to constitute those points where the necessities of reality became visible as necessities of the inventive imagination. They enabled us to perceive how human lives unfold in thought and event. The truth value of fiction was, as Aristotle had of course first affirmed, something like history but more philosophical than history.[6] For history dealt in the facticity of events, while fiction dealt in their *possibility*, and to know what events are possible, one must have a sense of the inner necessities that govern them. The Intelligent Bar principle in a sense made possible this second one of experimental realism. A good story—a story worth telling—conformed to certain rules that in turn made possible a deepening of one's understanding of the possible forms a real story, that is, the story of a real life, could take.

Grossman retails a familiar history in explaining the turn against well-made plots in the modern novel, a history that would seem, at first blush, to militate against this principle of experimental realism. A Victorian age flush and confident in inevitable material and moral progress was also an age that saw the neat, ingenious, and edifying plots of, say, the novels of Charles Dickens as condign to its lived experience. With the First World War, the robust moral imagination and confidence in human progress of the Victorians came crashing down. In the aftermath of the Somme, the only art form that could adequately express reality was one that bore the lineaments of bombed-out landscapes, senseless furies of trench warfare, and empty jingoistic rhetoric.[7] The modern arts, of which T. S. Eliot's *The Waste Land* is the great example, bore witness to a social "panorama of futility and anarchy" by means of an ostensibly anarchical art—one that insisted that, if there were an order to history, it would not give itself to us in either the moral linearity of the novel or the triumphalist linearity

---

6. Aristotle, *Poetics*, 1051b.

7. See Vincent Sherry, *The Great War and the Language of Modernism* (New York: Oxford University Press, 2003).

of "whig" history.[8] Indeed, for Eliot, the novel was not expressive of the form of reality, was not even a form, but merely a normative voicing of the sensibility—the moral prejudices—belonging to a particular class during a particular age. The novel, he writes in defense of Joyce's *Ulysses*, "instead of being a form, was simply the expression of an age which had not sufficiently lost all form to feel the need of something stricter."[9] A Victorian reader could trust a Dickens novel to tell him the truth about human experience only because that reader would find the present social order beyond question, a time that would surely be surpassed only by a future even more *eminently* Victorian.

Grossman reinforces these claims of Eliot's, and not without reason. Eliot was an astute critic indeed regarding every species of secular humanism that attempted to link material and moral progress as the inevitable course of history. But, as there is in the critical writings of Woolf and Pound, in Eliot here, there is a trace of the adolescent in rebellion against the parent, in which the young critic is so intent on differentiating his coevals from the older generation that he loses sight of their immense similarities. We should query a little. The nineteenth century was the great age of the novel *not only* because the form had reached a sufficient stage of maturity that its natural and ineluctable conventions had been limned and tested and become sufficiently known as just those qualities necessary for the kind of beast the novel, by its nature, wanted to become. This was certainly the case, but does not sufficiently explain the achievement and centrality of the novel to the Victorian age. Eliot and Grossman too easily assume what we might call an unaltered reflection of the Victorian age as a whole in what they take to be the formal complacencies of the Victorian novel.

If we peer through the looking glass, however, we see that during the previous several decades, political revolution, urbanization, intellectual specialization, and industrialization had put it seemed all received traditions and truths into question. Life in the Victorian world can better be characterized as traumatic and vertiginous than as complacent and graced with equipoise. Its apparently easy pieties were hard won, its real

8. T. S. Eliot, *Selected Prose*, ed. Frank Kermode (New York: Farrar, Straus and Giroux, 1975), 177.

9. Eliot, *Selected Prose*, 177.

banalities sugared over anxieties about unprecedented historical turns.[10] The confident pronouncements of inevitable historical progress may have sounded bold and bluff, but it was indeed an effort analogous to Eliot and Joyce's: a strict rhetorical form indeed, attempting to hold a moment of doubt and anxiety together by means of an affirmation of hope. Philosophy and theology had fallen into decline more than two centuries earlier, and continued their precipitation into abstraction, incoherence, partiality, and irrelevance at an ever faster pace while the lived reality of the average person continued to spin all things like a centrifuge. The genius of Lord Tennyson's *In Memoriam* was not so much to capture in a sustained, companionable, and sincere voice the feelings of grief for an age confident in the singular worth of human life and the authority of sentiment, but rather to assert these things explicitly in the context of worry about what modern science seemed to tell us about our natures and the reliability of emotion. Tennyson concludes one lyric in the sequence thus:

> ... but what am I?
> An infant crying in the night
> An infant crying for the light!
> And with no language but a cry.[11]

He speaks justly. Nature may be red in tooth and claw, but what articulate voice could answer that brute fact? The decay of Christian belief and, above all, its intellectual systems had left him without a vocabulary to speak with confidence about the true meaning of the human yearning and suffering that nevertheless continued. The masterly elegance of his voice's music becomes a substitute for what was really needed—a compelling language that could understand the present age and show to it that there was indeed a "light" that transcended it and that offered rest to its yearning.

In a word, the Victorians were a very anxious people who were ill equipped to grapple with the sources of that anxiety, in part because the great intellectual tools first chiseled out by the Greeks and wielded with authority by the Schoolmen had fallen into contempt and desuetude, and

---

10. See T. J. Jackson Lears, *No Place of Grace: Antimodernism and the Transformation of American Culture, 1880–1920* (Chicago: University of Chicago Press, 1994).

11. Alfred Tennyson, *Tennyson: A Selected Edition*, ed. Christopher Ricks (Harlow, England: Longman, 2007), 396.

in part because the sheer rate of change in material conditions in that society would have created a disruption in even the most formidable intellectual culture. When historical change comes rapidly enough, it often
feels more singular than it is, and every resource of wisdom from the past
comes to appear as an archaism if not an absurdity. So it did seem to the
Victorians. Even the great mind of John Henry Newman was compromised in its achievement by the necessity of attending to the flux and confusion of his day. His books of *Essays* are of permanent importance, but
the absence of model and guide, the unevenness of their form, and their
improvisatory arguments and vocabulary, suggest the restless work of an
author scrambling for resources to meet the demands of his contemporaries', and of his own, rationality.[12]

The combination of spiraling social change, inadequately limber intellectual institutions in the Church and University, and—last of all—cheap
print, made the times auspicious for a kind of intellectual revolution.
Newman departed for Rome, but for the majority, the novelist became
the conscience, the moral inquisitor, of his age. The pious abstractions of
Protestant Christianity, the wild eschata of philosophical idealism, and the
anemic, bloodless abstractions of modern positivism were evidently too removed from any kind of human life to offer it sound guidance; but Victorian life was changing from day to day with each new Latin-named invention and each new biological or geological theory (also, inevitably, named
in Latin). But novels tell stories, and even the most remote story (think
of Scott's *Ivanhoe*) is more concrete than the bromides of *laissez-faire*, inevitable material progress, and Evangelical moral uplift, and indeed may be
thought of as the genre of change par excellence.

The dynamism of a novel's plot reassures us that historical change may
be radical, but permanent moral truths endure as a context by which to
observe and evaluate it. If the world were pure flux, one could not piece

12. This should not be taken as a criticism of Newman's work, but it does suggest his continuity with Burke, the romantics, and other post-revolutionary critics of modernity. In many,
perhaps most, of his writings, including *The Idea of the University* (Notre Dame, Ind.: University
of Notre Dame Press, 1982), we see clearly Newman's consciousness that he must rally an army to
fight a war for which it had been unprepared, and that, in consequence, he may be left to fight
alone. The *Essays* are, of course, *An Essay on the Development of Christian Doctrine* (Notre Dame,
Ind.: University of Notre Dame Press, 1979) and *An Essay in Aide of a Grammar of Assent* (Notre
Dame, Ind.: University of Notre Dame Press, 1989).

together something so complex yet steady as the form of a plot; if every new moment found no precedent in those that came before, we could, in Eliot's words, connect nothing with nothing.[13]

On the other hand, if the truth were as static as the eternal plane of abstractions, one would not have the continuous movement necessary for plot. Some austere and difficult form behind the screen of temporal experience would always put the value of that experience in doubt. Because a novel consists above all of plot and character—of persons and temporal events—it does not take a great leap of faith or a willful affirmation of banal optimism to believe in it as a reflection of reality. For the Victorians, plot in the novel provisionally closed the gap between truth and uncertainty, while character (the beautiful, the admirable, the dastardly, the fallen) closed another between contingency and the good. And, as we considered in an earlier chapter, because the novel as a work of the imagination requires so few other a priori beliefs, one does not have to have in place a firm grasp of the real world or any fixed structure of philosophy or theology in order to accept the truths—above all, the moral truths—that a novel might try to convey.

The novel was thus the exquisitely adapted form for the Victorian period. In an age when everything was aswim in the flux, and where old verities seemed at best weakly connected to the present objects of experience and at worst astringent bones of abstraction, the novel provided the certitude of story with the confident, if flexible and malleable, conclusiveness of moral judgment. The Victorians often feared they were losing everything, and so, they devoured their stories as a last source of moral and emotional authority. The characters in the novel reassured them that, in a world where material advancements were incontestable, and where men, women, and children were being shoved into work houses and squalid tenements, there might still be a place for the human person.

The devastation of the Great War, which Grossman rightly emphasizes, did not turn the world upside down. It simply made the story of British progress and patriotism look like a sham, and so snatched the last loose, floating boards from the clutching arms of an already adrift, storm-tossed, and drowning people. The novel was exposed as the consolation, the last

13. Eliot, *Complete Poems and Plays*, 46.

resort, of a bourgeoisie that was about to lose integrity and power. Contrary to Eliot's sharp critique, the novel *was* the form Victorians required to make life possible amid futility and anarchy; a true inversion of Joyce and Eliot's modernist "mythical" method, the novel-form concealed these things beneath a well ordered surface. Grossman clearly has the unanticipated and fragmented formal elements of modern art in mind when he describes the effects of the First World War: neat plots stitched like tea doilies were to be replaced by palimpsests and fugues, torn sheets and trauma, geometry amid the ruins. But modern art did not spring merely from an even more exaggerated sense of historical chaos than that which the Victorians suffered. It sprang also from two intuitions, each of which is continuous with, rather than a rejection of, the earlier rise of the novel.

First, the moderns understood the power of story and character as it had served their ancestors, and they understood this power to be more profound than the plot of a novel could of itself reveal. Dickens was not superannuated because he was fiction, but because his stories did not penetrate far enough (truly speaking, he was not superannuated at all; the modernist writers devoured Victorian novels and genre fiction—especially detective stories—with relish; they just did not often write such things themselves). As such, the budding Victorian study of folklore and sentimental attachment to classical myths as poetically agreeable blossomed into a new cultural obsession with uncovering archetypes and prototypes: the origins of art in recurrent cultic ritual and the form of art in the mythic forms of the cosmos. Lord Tennyson, for instance, wrote an emotionally drenched tale of King Arthur in *Idylls of the King*; Eliot would savage that poem as mawkish and juvenile, even as he latched onto the form of at least one Arthurian tale—Percival's quest for the Holy Grail—as expressive of a ritualized, repeating sub-current of history. Since the surface details of human life were typified chiefly by their evanescence and mutability, what if there were forms beneath the surface of things that gave shape to the stories we all live? Since cultures vary radically in their sensible details, but repeat and repeat the same *formal* details across space and over time, what if they nonetheless were identical at some archetypal depth? James Frazer, in *The Golden Bough* (first published in 1890), was among the first to perceive that this continuity could not be attributed to any surface causality. In that study of primitive religions, he sought to explain why a priest must always be murdered by his successor, and introduces the "comparative method" to do so. He observes that

No one will probably deny that such a custom savours of a barbarous age, and, surviving into imperial times, stands out in striking isolation from the polished Italian society of the day, like a primaeval rock rising from a smooth-shaven lawn. It is the very rudeness and barbarity of the custom which allows us a hope of explaining it. For recent researches into the early history of man have revealed the essential similarity with which, under many superficial differences, the human mind has elaborated its first crude philosophy of life.[14]

Frazer's ambition was to provide the comprehensive genetic explanation that would demonstrate that the origin of each and every religion is to be found in a stability located not in divinity but in the nature of man. It was dissolvent of belief. But it was only a matter of time before the uncanny continuity of forms from culture to culture, people to people, began to look like a stable, eternal law written into the heart of history and, therefore (make of this what one will) a truth.

The age of mythology was upon us, and myth would take on an ever-more-loaded and potent cultural significance. No longer did myth mean the superstitions of primitive and naïve man; it connoted the archetypal forms that were the only possible source of meaning for human culture that could be known in such a way as to rival the physical sciences. Myth and archetype was the terrain where the truth about ourselves lies, impermeable to discursive reason, but apprehensible by means of aesthetic insight and verifiable by way of archival or field study.

This project had inevitably to fail because it did not go far enough. Mythic archetypes are a compromise for those who cannot entirely shut off their abstracting faculties, but who suspect anything that it not concrete. Aristotle critiqued the Platonic doctrine of the Forms because that doctrine did not explain the cause of anything; the same can be said about the modern fascination with archetypes.[15] One may experience a certain warm satisfaction in discovering that all men share in the narrative of the

---

14. James George Frazer, *The Golden Bough* (London: Oxford University Press, 1994), 12.

15. Aristotle, *Metaphysics*, 990b. It is clear that Aristotle simply does not wish to answer the same questions Plato answers with his theory of forms. For Aristotle, the line of inquiry is into causality, for Plato, it is into intelligibility. Plato's inquiry has to be completed before one can undertake Aristotle's.

quest or the "hanging god," but how do such elegant cultural rhymes explain anything? One thousand echoes do not make the argument of one live voice. On a speculative level they do not, and on a practical level they have alternately inspired a resigned relativism, a ritualistic quietism, or the bloody cults of race. Readers of Yeats and Seamus Heaney know this has made for abundant good poetry, but it has also made for some bad politics. If all human cultures share certain narratives, that is because they share something more permanent and profound as well—and that commonality may be discovered only at the level of metaphysics or, rather, philosophical theology.

Which leads us to the second intuition. The moderns saw the weakness of the Victorian dependence on the novel. When the reason reflects on experience, including the experience of reading a story, it rightly and inevitably rises by means of abstraction from contingent phenomena to necessary principles, if any there be. One cannot forever short-circuit this natural action of the intellect by saying that stories appeal only to emotion and that it is in the emotions alone that man may discover truth. The Victorians relied on such platitudes and despaired to see that it made possible unprecedented readerships for novels, poetry, and personal essays while the march of modern "reason" persisted in its efforts to dominate the world and to reduce all things—people included—to cash value or cannon fodder. If Victorian emotion was morally superior to reason, it was also trampled under its boots.

And so, in the wake of the Great War, intellectuals frequently abandoned or denigrated the novel in their efforts to restore true philosophy—metaphysics—to the canons of thought. The writings of T. S. Eliot and Jacques Maritain present to us a vivid and gnawing sense that unless one can grapple honestly with the question "What is real?" one may survive in the elegiac dreams of Tennyson, but not in any true world. Such writers, as it were, rejected the sentimental sociology of the novel for the anthropology of ritual, but only as a way to pass on to patterns of truth still more necessary. Popular manuals on Thomas Aquinas, published eventually in cheap paperback editions, took their place alongside novels in bookstalls. The quest for the real was the quest for Being, for the nature of things—and that quest required more than a good sense of dramatic form (although that was neither lacking nor unimportant). It required an unrelenting drive of the intellect to encounter existence and essence—and their identity and source in Being Itself, which everyone calls God.

Modernist art was often realist in the Victorian sense of providing unvarnished, naturalistic details; but, beneath these grubby surfaces, it was realist also in its insistence upon metaphysical realism, on the meaningful reality of Being that holds everything in existence despite the superficies of chaos. Modernism marks the Return to the Real, but not the realism of Nietzsche, Darwin, and Freud. Rather, it strives toward a return to the realism of Thomas Aquinas.[16]

Although the age of popular neo-Thomism began to wane with the Second World War and was annihilated by the Second Vatican Council, its residue has prepared us for the return of the novel as Grossman describes it. On the one hand, the ontological imperative of Thomism was instrumental in the rise of postmodern continental philosophy, which takes being seriously enough to declare all our statements about it an illusion. We are trapped in a "prison house" of language and cultural constructs outside of which we can know nothing. Such postmodernism is merely a radicalization of the anxieties the Victorians knew so well and sought to overcome by means of plot, character, emotion, and moral judgment; it is "radical" because it resists the efforts of others to return to the real, to restore metaphysics, even as it senses the irresistible drive to fundamental ontology St. Thomas symbolizes for the modern age. We all agree that what is real is what *is*. Much postmodern thought simply dwells on the urgency or yearning for being while refusing all paths that would attain it, out of fear that the yearning is more beautiful than the thing itself.

More constructively, and on the other hand, the rise of philosophical realism in the last century lay a brilliant foundation for us to conclude as a matter of reason what the Victorians could only tremulously affirm as a matter of feeling: if the world of beings is intelligible to us, it is so because it was created from nothing by Being Itself; our receptive intelligences participate in the creative intelligence of God analogously to the way our ears participate in the life of the person who chats with us at the local pub. We make sense of the world because the world is a great ontic repository of "logic." As such, our most hard-headed investigations of the world begin to arrive at the truth *not* when we cut through all the anthropomor-

16. Jacques Maritain, *Oeuvres Complètes* (Fribourg: Éditions Universitaires, 1984), 3:363.

phic projections of our consciousness (our sensible and ethical categories) and get to the cold gravel and hot protoplasm of geologic time and biological evolution. Rather, we arrive at truth when we begin to sense the formal principles of the world as created, as intelligently authored by he who is outside of it, beyond it, and eternally before it.

When we can affirm this as a philosophical point, we begin to understand why all persons like stories, and why stories seem to bear laws within themselves that art may violate but never ignore. We like them because they tell us the truth about ourselves. They show us the form of our lives—the lives we live, and those one may. But, also and above all, they lead us down a path toward the Form-giver of All Things. The Victorians were right to put their faith in the sagacity of stories, and the mythological-archetypalists were right that there is a foundation that makes our knowledge of stories among the most profound knowledge we may attain. But we may trust in stories only because we can discern beyond them the Is Who Is; the form of a plot is one expression of the form that constitutes a thing in being, in reality. To put the matter in the pat paradox all great truths require: We pick up a tabloid scandal sheet or a bus station dime novel for much the same reason we go to Church; we are hoping to see God.

FOURTEEN

Retelling the Story of Reason

It is now time to weave together a number of threads we have followed in earlier parts of this book, and to define what they have to tell us on the role of narrative in human life—and particularly in the life of reason and its vocation to truth. As we have seen in discussing both Burke and Dante, venerable claims have been made in our tradition for the power of the poetic and literary imagination; but Burke's counter-revolutionary importance should also remind us that many of those claims have been compensatory for losses experienced elsewhere. Consider, for instance, the rise of the English department and of the study of national literatures more broadly, during the last two centuries, as one tenuous consolation prize for the loss of a sense of rootedness, tradition, and community; as a rear-guard defense against the encroachments of a utilitarian form of rationality; as a tower of ethereal refinement under siege by the weighty swell of mass politics, mass culture, and mass education while also deriving from it; and, of course, as a fanciful substitute for systematic theology and as an un-compelling substitute for traditional religious piety. This life—or afterlife—of the literary seems always to place it in tension with other disciplines, and yet it does not offer a knowledge commensurable to that of other disciplines. It is neither as quantitative and subject to control as the physical sciences nor as intellectually definitive and open to genuine encounter with truth as philosophy or theology. Like the literary conservatism we discussed earlier, literature departments occupy at once a prominent and tenuous place in the modern university. They are the last ubiquitous vestige of the university as a place of humane study.

Professors of literature have better succeeded in creating a space for their work than in defining its object. Most of them, however, would confess that object to be rightly understood in terms of *mythos* and *poiesis*, in terms of story and fiction- or form-making. By contrast, the Christian Platonist tradition of philosophic enquiry takes its formal objects to be the life of intellect, of the *nous* and *logos*, and the nature of being (*ens*). In the modern academy, as *may* have been the case in Plato's Academy, there subsists a notion that the fanciful dynamism of the literary and the unconditional stasis of the real constitute entirely distinct worlds. When, sometimes, this division gets overlooked—as, for instance, in the precincts of literary theory or phenomenology—we usually encounter, not a reconciliation, but a fire sale, an exodus from one terrain to another. Either arguments about truth, about our intellectual grasp of being, get bracketed as discussions of imaginative possibility (as we considered in Part II), or literary artifice gets taken as an exemplar of human experience, and so philosophy becomes merely a critique of the fictional worlds we inexorably inhabit. I hope to argue that this particular disciplinary divide between the literary and the philosophic, as it presently appears, stems more from a disenchantment with reason—what D. C. Schindler, following Plato, bemoans as "misology"—rather than from a confidence in its capacities, comprehensiveness, or right conduct.[1] The trespassing of disciplinary boundaries is necessary, because truth is one, but as it is usually practiced, this trespassing amounts to a denial of truth outright. As the previous chapters have proposed, we need to establish a more systematic and compelling account of the relation of narrative to reality and reason than is currently on offer, and for two reasons. We will discover a richer conception of truth than that usually available in our age; and we will, in consequence, discover that the story of reason, the story of the *life* of reason, is more compelling than it typically appears.

I have already argued that the Greeks were right when they declared Mnemosyne the mother of the Muses: memory is the foundation of art,

---

1. D. C. Schindler, *Plato's Critique of Impure Reason* (Washington, D.C.: The Catholic University of America Press, 2008), 11–21. Plato, *Phaedo*, 89d–90d.

and so all art, whatever its critics' claims to the contrary, is ineluctably narrative in nature. In Part II and in the last chapter, I tried to establish the ontological foundations of art and beauty, suggesting that the aesthetic is rooted in being and that, consequently, the act of reading does not reach its apotheosis in the encounter with archetypal stories or myths but in the same place that the life of reason finds its end, in the real, as we understand it in terms of being, truth, goodness, and beauty. That is, I have claimed that narrative is the condition of possibility for art, and yet I have also insisted that it is not the end—the *telos*—of art in itself or as understood in the context of a full human life. Rather, we are always drawn, even by fiction, toward beauty and truth, toward what the Christian Platonist tradition holds up as a full encounter with reality.

We are prepared, then, to undertake a new investigation, one that takes us back to an ancient distinction and reevaluates it. For many readers, no doubt, another foray into what Plato called the "ancient quarrel" between poetry and philosophy, between *mythos* and *logos*, between story and reason, may have an antique rather than an auspicious ring to it.[2] Much of this book has sought to help readers overcome the modern suspicion that art and literature are manifestations of ideology and that any defense of their status as reasonable would accomplish little other than to root them more deeply in a violent project of "enlightenment." So also has it sought to resist the vision of the life of reason, of *logos*, as many people now understand it: one that has been so reinterpreted and subdivided into a particular mode of rarified logical analysis and into the nominal source of a wide-spread, utilitarian, and thoughtless drive for technological progress, that we can scarcely see any longer where the luster would lie in acknowledging some propinquity between these things and stories.

In brief, our age may be sufficiently disenchanted with reason not to find much salience in questioning the relation of *logos* to *mythos*. My contention, however, is that the rise of the literary-as-compensation that continues to haunt the study of literature, and this disenchantment with reason, which informs so much of professional philosophy and everyday life, are phenomena with a common cause.[3] While *mythos* and *logos* are verifi-

2. Plato, *Republic*, 607b.
3. This apposition of philosophy and everyday life is not an opposition. Cf. John Paul II, *Fides et Ratio*, par. 3.

ably distinct, we should understand *logos* as a particular moment within the context of *mythos*. When we reason, we reason *about* stories—when we reason, we reason *in* stories; when we examine the life of the intellect, we find it is a biography, a life-story. Insofar as we fail in this, we fail to be rational. The refusal of these propositions has historically resulted, first, in a withering of what qualifies as rational and, second, in a dispensing with the idea of reason as something of central importance to human life. My hope is that an account of human reason tied to the act of human story-telling might serve to restore our confidence in these things and our desire for the intellectual life as the realization of the truly human life. To resituate truth alongside the good and the beautiful as the destination of our human pilgrimage will bring this study to its proper conclusion.

To that end, I shall undertake four reflections. First, I ask, what are the chief assumptions the inhabitants of the modern age have made about myths? What myth do we tell ourselves about *mythos*? Second, how did Plato, to whom the first use of the word "mythology" is attributed, deploy and discuss *mythos*?[4] This will lead us to a third inquiry: does Plato, in practice, make the rigid division, familiar to our age, between *mythos* and *logos*, or does he relate them in a more complex manner? Further, what basis can we articulate for doubting this division, not only in Plato, but in truth? What might this imply, in brief, for our understanding of what it means to be rational? I shall offer three responses to these questions, all of which seek to justify my assertion that human reason's great capacity to know the real is grounded in, and contingent upon, the telling of stories. Fourth, and finally, I shall draw from the preceding reflections four theses I believe to follow from them, and which I propose as a basis for reforming our understanding of the relationship between narrative, reason, and the intellectual life.

Modern Myths regarding *Mythos* and *Logos*

When we turn to examine the modern world's understanding of myth and reason, we observe at least one universal phenomenon, that "a myth is perceived by every reader in the whole world as being a myth," as the

4. See Marcel Detienne, *The Creation of Mythology*, trans. Margaret Cook (Chicago: University of Chicago Press, 1986), 81.

276 REASON, NARRATIVE, AND TRUTH

anthropologist Claude Lévi-Strauss once asserted.[5] If this is true, we all presume that there is a historical object or phenomenon called myth and that, therefore, by means of myth-ology, the study of that object, we may arrive at an abstract theory of it. The universal assent ends there, however, and varied further distinctions commence in the form of understanding myth as outside of, and in relation to, modern rationality. Myth is to the primitive, prehistorical, and savage world what the rational is to our own. It is superstition, chthonic, rooted in the earth and the animal, in primeval mists and darkness, whereas reason stands forth, or rather, shines down from a temperate heaven like a light perfectly calibrated to the human eye and worthy not of its reflection but only its manipulation.

When we see that our age is smattered with superstitions and myths of its own, we make the further judgment that myths are rooted in ignorance, in the pre- or non-rational mechanisms of human life as animal, and so we may expect to find their traces anywhere that reason has not yet asserted itself. Myth is the location where forces and desires that cannot be controlled, or at least have not yet been brought under administration, persist as namable and animate. Conversely, reason comes to be understood *not* simply as the state that transcends thoughtless materiality, but as the power where force and desire become subject to human manipulation. As Karl Barth once observed, Enlightenment reason is precisely that conception of man and universe that recognizes all things outside of man as prime matter, existing effectively as potency awaiting actualization by the human mind; human reason becomes the disembodied, placeless, sovereign might that gives the raw plaster of the world form and meaning. It accomplishes this, therefore, not in an act of understanding but of forming, making; of subduing, dominating.[6] What is rational in such a scheme? We know only that which we control. What lies beyond our power's grasp is, for the present, unknowable; as such, it must not yet be formed, it must not yet be intelligible. And so, superstitions and myths appear, as they inevitably do, only as the undeliberated articulations of what is in reality inarticulate, as studies of and in the darkness: spiritual apparitions of what is "in fact" but crude matter.[7]

5. Quoted in Detienne, *The Creation of Mythology*, 1.

6. Barth, *Protestant Theology in the Nineteenth Century*, 23–24.

7. Cf. Ratzinger, *Introduction to Christianity*, 59, 61. Blaise Pascal writes, in his early-modern

Myth, in the analysis of the modern age, becomes our ancestral other, conceived before human reason learned how to control. As such, it constitutes our prehistory, the vague and fanciful accounts of the world, formulated by men when mankind was more nature than culture, more earth than light, more ape than angel, more witchdoctor than M.D. And here, modern reason conceives what is, indeed, a myth of its own. Myth may account for that which is spatially outside the perimeter of human domination, but it also represents that ancient moment, growing ever more distant, from which human reason emerged. As such, we may shut it safely in the past as that which we have surpassed, but we may also return to it like a rich quarry filled with fossils—fossils that turn out to be coded and enigmatic images of our own consciousness.

Modern reason claims an absolute privilege over the category of those things it declares to be alien and uncontrollable myths: the power either to shut the door on myth as a lamentable reminder of our irrational origins, or to bring it into the field of reason as a dense, cryptic specimen subject to our investigation. When this happens, myth experiences an afterlife of explanation, which the theologian John Milbank has helpfully catalogued. We moderns have accounted for the "supposed mythical delusion" in myriad ways, he writes. Auguste Comte deemed myth "proto-science"; Edward Tylor called it "language without abstraction"; Max Müller, the "deceit of metaphor"; it was "the trace of the subconscious" according to Freud; the "detritus of an archaic humanity which confused subject and object," claimed Lucien Lévy-Bruhl; whereas Claude Lévi-Strauss would elevate it to the "rational classification and grasping of contradictions in concrete terms."[8] Milbank can stop there only because he restricts himself to those modern thinkers who offer accounts of myth *per se*; he would have to extend his list considerably if he wished to include the many others who have sought to account for religion in terms of myth and myth in

---

anthropology, that one of the many obstacles to mankind's understanding the infinite universe in which it finds itself is a tendency to "speak of material things in spiritual terms" consequent to man's own spiritual and corporeal nature, which is disproportionate (i.e., poorly adjusted) to everything in and outside itself (*Pensées*, §21). In calling mankind to humility within this land of unlikeness, Pascal unfortunately ratifies the subjugation of Creation-as-inert-matter to the assertions of the human intellect-as-dynamic-will proposed by his contemporary and rival, Descartes.

8. John Milbank, "Fictioning Things: Gift and Narrative," *Religion and Literature* 37, no. 3 (Autumn 2005): 11.

terms of religion, and so have launched a whole other flotilla of speculative definitions.[9]

In sum, modern culture tends to deem myth an isolatable and identifiable *genus*, with origins in a primitive past, whose significance for our age ranges from its service as a reminder of our primeval ignorance to its revelation of knowledge about ourselves in concrete, non-conceptual terms now—at last—subject to human reason as the occasion of abstract speculation. Myths must be either explained away as the occupations of a barbarous people or patronized as the deep-structures of the human psyche awaiting our superior interpretive capacities to unlock their secrets. In every instance, *mythos* is a phenomenon temporally and objectively apart from modern reason and on which *logos* may autonomously turn its gaze whether in admiration or scorn.

Plato's Practice and Discussion of *Mythos*

As Marcel Detienne has observed, the coining of the term "mythology," which assigns individual myths to a formal category, belongs to Plato.[10] In his dialogues, he frequently has Socrates or other speakers relate "tales," "stories," or myths, but not in a fashion that obviously lends itself to a systematized explanation. In *Protagoras*, for instance, Socrates, arguing against the sophist Protagoras's claims to teach men virtue, begins by providing anecdotal accounts of contemporary Athenians from Pericles to Alcibiades that show the contrary. To this, Protagoras replies by telling a story that "would be more pleasant" than "developing an argument."[11] From this alone, we can recognize a generic distinction between *mythos* and *logos*. But Protagoras proceeds from the telling of his story to arguing more abstractly against the objections Socrates has raised—all in one, uninterrupted speech. After he finishes, Socrates observes,

9. One thinks, perhaps first, of James George Frazer, philosopher of religion Ludwig Feuerbach (see Barth, *Protestant Theology*, 520–26), and such modern poets and literary critics as John Crowe Ransom, in *God without Thunder*, and W. B. Yeats, in, among other works, "The Celtic Element in Literature," in *The Collected Works of W. B. Yeats*, vol. 4, *Early Essays*, ed. George Bornstein and Richard J. Finneran (New York: Scribner, 2007), 128–38.

10. Schindler, in *Plato's Critique of Impure Reason*, cites Plato explicitly distinguishing *mythos* from *logos* in *Gorgias* 523a, *Phaedrus* 61b, and *Protagoras* 324c; his study also directed me to several of the passages I discuss below.

11. Plato, *Protagoras*, 320c.

I was entranced and just looked at him for a long time as if he were going to say more. I was still eager to listen.... Now, you could hear a speech similar to this from Pericles or some other competent orator if you happened to be present when one of them was speaking on this subject. But try asking one of them something, and they will be as unable to answer your question or to ask one of their own as a book would be.[12]

In response to queries, the orator always produces "another long-distance speech," rather than an answer, Socrates tells us.[13] The absence of interruption, the seamless polish of rhetoric, distinguishes speech and story from discursive argument not because of its content, but because its smooth surfaces, as it were, are possible only by being a type of language whose surface repels interrogation and conceals the absence of understanding. What supposedly distinguishes Protagoras from Socrates is not the telling of stories—both of them tell stories—but rather Socrates's willingness and capacity to answer questions. This difference becomes more important in principle even if we concede that Protagoras argues quite well in fact; Socrates perceives distinct kinds of language that we might otherwise be tempted to gloss over or elide. An orator, like a book, possesses a complete, integrated artifice of words, but not an understanding of the truth. The philosopher knows what is true and can refer to that knowledge freely in order to speak and answer questions about it; the intellectual distinction-in-relation between knowledge and speech allows speech to remain subject to knowledge, whereas the speech of the orator is without relation: it has nothing beyond or behind it.

This association of oratory with writing and books occurs also at the end of the *Phaedrus*. There, Socrates tells a myth of the Egyptian god Theuth, the inventor of writing, who promises that writing will prove "a potion for memory and for wisdom."[14] The Egyptian king Thamus counters that writing will introduce forgetfulness, because it can provide only "the appearance of wisdom" not "its reality."[15] A book, like a vividly painted portrait, may seem as if it can speak the truth it knows, but "if you question anything that has been said because you want to learn more, it continues to signify just that very same thing forever."[16] Only the person

12. Plato, *Protagoras*, 328d–329a.
13. Plato, *Protagoras*, 329b.
14. Plato, *Phaedrus*, 274e.
15. Plato, *Phaedrus*, 275a.
16. Plato, *Phaedrus*, 275d–e.

who understands can answer questions by reference to the truth present to his soul, says Socrates; and Phaedrus, that greedy lover of speeches, at last knows the truth about his love through Socrates's dialectical provocations: "the living, breathing discourse of the man who knows" reveals this man's possession of knowledge, whereas "the written one can be fairly called the image" of that knowledge.[17] Stories and speeches by themselves are mere images or appearances and not the reality of truth. Argumentative reasoning as *dialectic*, in contrast, constitutes the activity of knowledge, the turning about and examining of truth really present to the knowing soul. Socrates's critique of writing, oratory, and stories, here, lies not in their mendacious appearance, as if they were opposed to the truth discoverable by reason. Rather, they are distinct from reason because they can at best remind the one who knows already of that which he knows: this is the function of *images*, and so myth is chiefly an image or, as we shall see, an imitation of what it, in itself, is not.[18]

The identity of myth, story, or poetry as imitation Plato takes up at length in the *Republic*. Imitations as images may have seemed to be passive materials lacking knowledge in the *Protagoras*; they take on a positive potency in serving to remind the active reason of one who already knows, in the *Phaedrus*; but in the *Republic*, imitation, specifically in the form of *mythos*, plays a more active and troubling role. The long discourses on the nature and style of poetry in the dialogue derive from Socrates's and Glaucon's concern with the education of guardians to protect the ideal city they invent and furnish in the dialogue as a whole. How does one produce guardians capable of defending the city, who will love justice and other virtues, and who will shun all indecent behavior? How, to get to the heart of Plato's real concern, should the soul be cultivated so that it lives according to reason, virtue, and justice? By education. And that comprises chiefly music, poetry, and gymnastics. Music and gymnastics are of great importance, but their pedagogical functions are easily described because unambiguous.[19] Poetry, on the other hand, requires an astringent exami-

17. Plato, *Phaedrus*, 276a.
18. Plato, *Phaedrus*, 275a.
19. The kind of education—aesthetic education, or the perception of form—we discussed in Part II corresponds directly to music, in Plato's account. It and gymnastics cultivate the body and soul after the fashion of habituation discussed in Aristotle's *Nicomachean Ethics*, making

nation—all the more so because the education it provides occurs not in a formal or controlled context but in the cradle, in the home, at the hands of nursemaids, old women, and old men.

Socrates tells Glaucon that education in poetry consists, initially, of the telling of false stories to children. The stories are "false, on the whole, though they have some truth in them," Socrates says—and his claim has two evident senses in the context of the dialogue.[20] Most clearly, he means that the stories are full of salacious and scandalous detail about gods and humans—imitations of violence, lust, and cowardice common enough in themselves but blasphemous to attribute to the gods. From such details the young must be sheltered. But more importantly, Socrates intends that the stories excised of these undesirable elements and told to children remain literally false, but contain some true element, namely, the presumptive image or pattern of the virtues. This indicates the approach to education taken in the *early* books of the *Republic* (we shall see that the approach changes in the later books). It teaches the "young and tender," because their "souls are most malleable" and so will take "on any pattern one wishes to impress" on them.[21]

Because of this malleability, first youth is the time for the firmest and most effective education; but also because of it, poetic education is dangerous. Shall we, asks Socrates, "carelessly allow the children to hear any old stories, told by just anyone, and to take beliefs into their souls that are for the most part opposite to the ones we think they should hold when they are grown up?"[22] Socrates presumes that the tales of old men and women will form the souls of children and he has no intention, in these first books, of eliminating that role in his effort to "purify" the city.[23] He recognizes, however, that this kind of education consists not of the mind's initiation into the paths of dialectic and reason, but of the soul's being

---

body limber for action and mind limber for perception and understanding. This is education as self-formation. Poetry becomes a focus here, as we shall see, chiefly in terms of its material content rather than its formal function. It is problematic because the substance of poetry (story-content) predominates over its own formal elements (the pattern of the plot, but also the pattern of the virtues modeled in the story) and indeed substantial content may undermine the possible formal benefits. Hence, we see Plato grappling with what it means for Mnemosyne (memory-as-story-material) to be the mother of the Muses (the specific art-forms).

20. Plato, *Republic*, 377a.   21. Plato, *Republic*, 377a–b.
22. Plato, *Republic*, 377b.   23. Plato, *Republic*, 399e.

sculpted into a certain form independent of and prior to the coming-into-being of reason within it. He hopes the old women of the city will agree to tell only the approved and "purified" myths. Further, because all images contribute to the pattern of the soul, the works of all craftsmen, not just those of the poets (of all *makers*), must strike the eyes of the young "like a breeze that brings health from a good place, leading them unwittingly, from childhood on, to resemblance, friendship, and harmony with the beauty of reason."[24] The formation of the young in virtue lies so far outside of reason that they are to conform to it "unwittingly"; its purpose is not to teach them reason itself, but to pattern their souls in such a way that they resemble and are, again, in "harmony with the beauty of reason" prior to their having reason's beauty itself. Thus, Plato bequeaths to modernity the notion of stories, or *mythos*, as a pre-logical, image-restricted participation in, rather than a comprehension of, the reality of things.

He also passes on to us a theory of story-telling as self-fashioning and as a social medium influencing us long before we know how to judge properly. The stories that old women tell, rocking infants by the hearth, unchastened, pose a danger to the city; but, once purified and harnessed, they remain the source of education in *images* and patterns of good things, prior to the attainment of the age of reason. One cannot avoid the chthonic and dark powers that Socrates recognizes at work here and seems, at least initially, incapable of eliminating. He would have understood immediately the infamous Robert Kee documentary on Irish history, *The Green Flag*, in which

an old Irishwoman appears, seated in her living room, telling the tale of Ireland's centuries-long oppression by the British. Immediately after her tale, there follows a cut to a violent explosion. We then cut to Robert Kee himself, seated in a book-lined study and equipped, unlike the old woman, with a large book.[25]

Plato may have found this large book a pretentious symbol of sophistry and rhetoric, but he would affirm the sense of *mythos* as antedating authoritative reason and wielding a power of explosive potential directed exclusively by images, precisely because images are in themselves indifferent to the true or false, good or evil.

24. Plato, *Republic*, 401c–d.

25. David Lloyd, *Ireland after History* (Notre Dame, Ind.: University of Notre Dame Press, 1999), 53.

Socrates suggests reason is founded historically, or diachronically, on story-telling, so that tales come first and reason later. But, strikingly, there is a synchronic priority of *mythos* to *logos* implied, as well, which would belie any project to conceive a purified reason that may proclaim itself entirely self-grounding, independent of any foundation beyond itself.[26] Images are themselves the patterns of the virtues that first form the soul, and that soul—precisely as the soul that has received its present form through seeing and hearing myths—will seek to attain those virtues in reality by the power of reason. The soul would not—or *may* not—pursue reason and virtue if it were not *even in adulthood* instinct with their patterns. Plato gives us a conception of sensibility, habit or connaturality of the will, and taste that leads the soul to pursue its true good even though it has only the image, not the reality of it, within. The educated youth will

object to what is shameful, hating it while he's still young and unable to grasp the reason, but, having been educated in this way, he will welcome the reason when it comes and recognize it easily because of its kinship with himself.[27]

The images conveyed by *mythos* are to be deepened, more fully possessed, rather than rejected or surpassed. But, lest we think these images themselves good, we are reminded that it is by artifice, falsehood, and manipulation that the mind is so stimulated—and not, again, by reason. So Socrates himself will conceive a "noble lie," in the form of a myth to induce his fancied guardians to defend the city with their lives and to rule it justly and without envy or tyranny.[28] This account of *mythos*, in the early books of the *Republic*, culminates in Socrates's frustration that he cannot make men now—that is, those who already possess reason—to believe the useful lie; their souls have already been shaped—or rather, misshaped—by other images.[29]

---

26. Cf. John Paul II, *Fides et Ratio*, par. 91.

27. Plato, *Republic*, 402a. Socrates also says that anyone properly educated in music and poetry, "will sense it acutely when something has been omitted from a thing and when it hasn't been finely crafted or finely made by nature. And since he has the right distastes, he'll praise fine things, be pleased by them, receive them from his soul, and, being nurtured by them, become fine and good" (Plato, *Republic*, 401e). Aesthetic education—becoming perceptive of the proportions of form—is prior to, contemporary with, and in some way determinative of reason's judgments.

28. Plato, *Republic*, 414b–e.

29. Plato, *Republic*, 415d.

In the final book of the *Republic*, Socrates returns to the subject of poetry and *mythos*, wondering whether they might have to purify the city of imitations and images entirely. *We* shall return to analyze *this* return further on, in the context of the work of D. C. Schindler, but here, I wish merely to observe what Socrates explicitly says regarding poetry. Having arrived at an understanding, in Book VI, that what "gives truth of the things known and the power to know to the knower is the form of the good," in the later parts of the *Republic*, Socrates seeks to re-examine other matters in light of this knowledge.[30] And so, he observes that imitative poetry "is likely to distort the thought of anyone who hears it, unless he has the knowledge of what it is really like, as a drug to counter it."[31] This is not a new suggestion, of course. "Distorting" the soul into a pattern in harmony with the good was the social function of stories in the first place, and was intended to be the eventual cause of a person's pursuing what is genuinely good and virtuous rather than something unworthy; to leave the formation of souls (education) to mere chance was the only alternative to forming them on sanitized myths.

But Socrates, conscious of the anger he might provoke among playwrights, goes on to define poets as those who can imitate all things only because they have real knowledge of none of them.[32] This is a rebuke of poets and their stories, but also reveals precisely what Socrates found *useful* about these things in the first place: they pattern the soul at a point when reason cannot. The risk inherent to this very utility is that the pattern, as we observed already, does not dissolve when the child becomes an adult and attains to virtue and reason. It remains present as the habitual drive toward these things—or, crucially, toward others less desirable. Further, if poetry urges the soul to the pursuit of the good, the patterned soul in adulthood continues to glance backward with relish to that pre-rational education in the matronly lap of story. This fact partly explains Socrates's ambivalence in discussing the matter; "the love of this sort of poetry," he says, "has been implanted in us by the upbringing we have received."[33] Note the term "implanted." The soul is but pre-rational soil made fruitful from without by the implanting of seeds of myths; to be taught requires

30. Plato, *Republic*, 508d–e. See below, but also Schindler, *Plato's Critique*, 105–22,
31. Plato, *Republic*, 595b.   32. Plato, *Republic*, 601b.
33. Plato, *Republic*, 607e.

a kind of passivity before, and subjection to, images.[34] This is not merely Socrates's vision of how to rear docile and virtuous guardians for his ideal city. In the section of the *Phaedrus* we examined earlier, Socrates takes up this image of planting as the act not only of those dangerous chatterboxes, the old crones, but of the true philosopher who would convey not images of the true but the true itself.[35] He tells Phaedrus,

> The dialectician chooses a proper soul and plants and sows within it discourse accompanied by knowledge—discourse capable of helping itself as well as the man who planted it, which is not barren but produces a seed from which more discourse grows in the character of others. Such discourse makes the seed forever immortal and renders the man who has it as happy as any human being can be.[36]

All education amounts to "being planted." Myth and stories remain powerless in themselves to give knowledge, but they prepare the soil for the further sowing of discourses, which in turn generate the true knowledge that, joined to and pollinating reason, remains forever fruitful. As Diotima instructs Socrates, in the *Symposium*, perpetual engendering partially describes the condition of true human happiness.[37]

The *Republic* itself never explicitly settles whether myth-telling is a *necessary* moment in education or a menace that should be banned from the city; rather than proceeding to dramatize a discourse in defense of poetry, Plato has Socrates outline the criteria of such a discourse and then let the matter drop. He drops it, however, in order to tell the tale of Er, who journeys through the morally ordered corridors of the afterlife and back to bring news to mortals that they are right to pursue justice above all things in this life.[38] Myth almost literally has the last word in the dialogue; after relating the story, Socrates speaks for only a short paragraph

---

34. The education of souls provides much difficulty in Plato, one presumes, precisely because the soul is by its nature active; in education an agent is treated as a patient. That it should be passive under any circumstances is at once troubling—the soul can be "distorted" or malformed by others—and promising—the philosopher can propose a method for how souls may become fully active and rational conforming to a good pattern and, above all, ordered to the good.

35. For "chatterboxes," see Detienne, *The Creation of Mythology*, 131, and Aristotle, *Nicomachean Ethics*, 117b34.

36. Plato, *Phaedrus*, 276e–277a.

37. Plato, *Symposium*, 205a (on happiness as possessing the good forever), 206e–207a (on "engendering in beauty" as a means of "immortality" and happiness). As we argued in Part I, this is the conception of goodness and happiness in the Christian Platonist tradition more generally.

38. Plato, *Republic*, 614b–621b.

more: and not to interpret the myth but to enjoin us to adhere to its example—its image—as well as that of himself, if we would "do well and be happy."[39] Thus, even in the *Republic*, where discussion of myth seems always to locate it in a position prior to dialectic—that activity par excellence of reason—in practice, story-telling remains contemporary and continuous, though not identical, with reasoning.

We should advert once more to the *Symposium*. Perhaps none other of Plato's dialogues so evidently seeks to confuse us regarding whether it is sowing discourse or myth. The entirety of the dialogue is spoken by Apollodorus, Socrates's faithful but frustrated disciple during his last years, to an anonymous stranger who has queried him regarding his master. Apollodorus's subject is a drinking party Socrates had attended at the home of the tragedian, Agathon, many years earlier; but Apollodorus did not himself witness the speeches or events of the party after which the friend is asking. He has it from Aristodemus, and has related the events previously to Glaucon, one of Socrates's interlocutors in the *Republic*. As Joseph Pieper once remarked, it seems plausible that neither Glaucon nor the anonymous friend are interested in the events for worthy intellectual reasons. They come in search of gossip—perhaps regarding the drunken and vainglorious general, and "ignored" lover of Socrates, Alcibiades— rather than in hopes of gaining the wisdom that Apollodorus is mad to acquire.[40] Plato provides us characters, then, whose position relative to the narrative Apollodorus has heard and now retells must be understood in terms not of their propinquity to it but of their intention in listening in the first place. As such, the core of the *Symposium* does not come to us as an instance of fruitful dialectical reasoning (*logos*) but provocatively as a story (*mythos*) capable of being heard and interpreted in multiple ways, some admirable and some frivolous.

Within Apollodorus's tale, the abundance of narrative detail sometimes proves more informative about the meaning of the six (or seven) speeches on love delivered at the drinking party than is the content of the

39. Plato, *Republic*, 621c–d. See Schindler, *Plato's Critique*, 325, whose discussion of the *Republic* I follow here.

40. Joseph Pieper, *Leisure, the Basis of Culture*, trans. Gerald Malsbary (South Bend, Ind.: St. Augustine's Press, 1998), 72. David K. O'Connor convincingly argues, in his notes to *The Symposium* (79–80), that we are intended to presume the friend and Glaucon are interested merely in gossip and not in being "planted" with those discourses that are accompanied by truth.

speeches themselves.[41] For instance, the plausibility of the physician Eryx-imachus's speech is undermined largely by the circumstantial instances of sententious pedantry he exhibits outside of it. His avuncular advice, to those present who are hung-over from the previous night's excess, not to drink to excess again, and his taking the place of—and giving medical advice to—Aristophanes, on account of the latter's hiccups, together couch his speech in buffoonery.[42] He thus loses authority, even though his speech's discussion of love as a principle of universal harmony anticipates Socrates's own absolute claims about the *telos* of love as engendering in eternal beauty and in conformity with what is most real (which fruitful-ness constitutes the movement of the *cosmos*).[43] That is, Plato encases the enduring, true element in Eryximachus's talk with frivolities, so that we initially dismiss it all out of hand. Similarly, the hiccups of Aristophanes put in scare-quotes the authority of the comic myth he relates of ancient human beings as giant billiard balls split in half by a Zeus jealous of hu-man ambition but covetous of human worship; men become, according to Aristophanes, halved-beings who, in love, go ever in search of their missing half and whose *telos*, whose purpose in life, is intimate whole-ness.[44] The dialogue frequently suggests that this personal coupling is the most widely accepted definition of love, and so Aristophanes gives, under the guise of a silly tale, the most superficially plausible account of love in the *Symposium*. Furthermore, his emphasis on love as leading to fulfill-ment will be appropriated and modified by Socrates, as are diverse ele-ments of all the speeches preliminary to his own. And yet, Aristophanes's ridiculous presence and presentation undermine what might otherwise appear as "old fashioned" common sense.[45]

Socrates, in the story, begins his own speech by insisting he cannot

41. David K. O'Connor's *Plato's Bedroom: Ancient Wisdom and Modern Love* (South Bend, Ind.: St. Augustine's Press, 2015) illustrates in rich detail how dense the narrative and dramatic el-ements of the dialogue are and the ways in which story-forms in-form and trans-form the explicit content of the dialogue.

42. Plato, *Symposium*, 176d, 185d–e.   43. Plato, *Symposium*, 206b.

44. Plato, *Symposium*, 189a, 189e–190a.

45. Later in the dialogue, Diotima implicitly rejects Aristophanes's account in her revelation to Socrates (Plato, *Symposium*, 205e). In my experience of teaching the *Symposium*, students con-sistently grow impatient with the work precisely in the middle of Aristophanes's speech; Plato has made a conception of love most modern persons take for granted appear unbelievable, thus plowing the soil to accept a more enduring seed.

follow the fine but false rhetoric of the other speakers, and he proceeds to engage Agathon in dialectic to set forth the fundamentals of his definition of love.[46] Having established that love is intrinsically relational and that it signifies the desire for good and beautiful things, Socrates abandons dialectic and enters into a speech in which he tells the story of his encounter with the Mantinean priestess, Diotima. In the story, she engages *him* in dialectic just as he had Agathon, but she also tells a myth of Love as the child of Poverty and Resource.[47]

Diotima then, speaking "in the manner of a perfect Sophist," initiates Socrates into the mystery of *eros* as the desire that leads the reason from the appreciation of beautiful bodies on to ideas, until the soul enters into the vision of eternal Beauty Itself—in whose intellectual sea the human person may give birth in mind and body to great words and deeds that make possible the immortality Diotima teaches is necessary for human happiness.[48] Dialectical reasoning, therefore, occurs in the *Symposium* only at two transitional moments and probably in order to suggest that what follows such rational exchange is to be taken seriously as an extension or completion of it even as what actually follows upon *logos* is a further articulation of *mythos*. As in the *Republic*, the "implanted" image appears not just at the beginning of discourse as an object for subsequent interpretation, but at the "matured" end—a practice for which the author provides no explicit explanation. We are left wondering to what extent Plato's dialogues constitute the love of wisdom and to what extent they provide merely the pedagogical image of that love. What is more, we are provoked to ask whether Plato ever gives us reason to believe that reason could function outside the context of story-telling.

Three Hypotheses on the Reconciliation of *Mythos* and *Logos*

Having considered some of Plato's discussions and representations of myths in his philosophical dialogues, we may profitably seek to explain the ambivalence with which they are treated.[49] But I would like to triple

46. Plato, *Symposium*, 201b–c.   47. Plato, *Symposium*, 203d.
48. Plato, *Symposium*, 208c.
49. The discussions of myth cited here have been limited to those in which the relation of

this task of interpretation with a historical and a theoretical question. From what we have seen, might we conclude that stories serve more than a pre-rational function in Plato's philosophy? And that, therefore, we would be unjust to make the sort of longstanding and absolute divisions between rational and mythical man, which I described as typically modern, and for which Plato has been consistently held responsible? If we can answer these questions in the affirmative, can we also arrive at a satisfactory account of reason that overcomes or at least complicates these divisions and in some way "reintegrates" *mythos* and *logos*? I shall approach these questions by three distinct avenues guided, respectively, by the work of D. C. Schindler, Marcel Detienne, and Jacques Maritain.

D. C. Schindler's recent study of the *Republic* answers the first two of these questions decisively. Readers have long noted Plato's radical distinction between the true being of the eternal, unchanging forms and the world of appearance, which lacks in being because of its endless flux.[50] Nietzsche identified this division as the invention of "truth" and the beginning of the West's decline; Martha Nussbaum has more recently argued for the more common opinion that this dualism should be understood as part of a Platonic quest for "purity."[51] Schindler contests these claims, observing that the understanding of this division both as absolute and as scornful of appearances may be a venerable account of Platonism, but if it is the one we choose to accept, then we must also conclude that Plato is no Platonist.[52]

Schindler reads the *Republic* as tracing a journey vividly manifested in the allegory of the cave. The philosopher, by the soul's power of reason, escapes the realm of mere appearances, rises to the intelligibility of the eternal forms, and continues on until he arrives at the good beyond intelligibility and appearance alike. The end of reason is therefore the good itself, and Plato describes the nature of the good as "good in itself *and* good in

---

mythos to *logos* seems most at stake in the dialogue. For a compelling theory of myths in Plato, see Joseph Pieper, *The Platonic Myths*, trans. Dan Farrelly (South Bend, Ind.: St. Augustine's Press, 2010).

50. The more frequent formulation is that Plato distinguishes "being and becoming," but Schindler's account, focused on the *Republic*, refers to "being and appearance" throughout in order to underscore that dialogue's concern with the relation of *images* to the real rather than of the contingent to the necessary.

51. Schindler, *Plato's Critique*, 285–86.

52. Schindler, *Plato's Critique*, 288.

its effects," as "absolute (good in itself) *and* relative (good for us)."[53] The good is beyond appearances, but it is also beyond the being of the eternal forms—and since the forms are intelligibility, the good is at once the end of reason and beyond things known. The good is beyond everything, because it is the cause of everything, and so in its simplicity and primacy it leads us to a surprising conclusion: "By virtue of the twofold nature of goodness, things in themselves are good not only in themselves, but also in their relations; that is, in their appearances and images."[54] The ascent of the reason to the good therefore achieves not only a vision of the "invisible" ground of intelligibility; it achieves an apprehension of the Good Itself that also allows one to perceive the goodness of its effects. Although the stripping away of appearances is necessary as one stage in the philosophical ascent toward being, the philosopher's reason can now embrace "truth as a whole": the good and everything that proceeds from the good, including the visible parts of that whole; appearances can be restored.[55]

Having risen in thought to the absolute, the philosopher does not experience a remote species of "eternal indwelling" with it, permanently apart from a transcended mankind; he, rather, suffused with knowledge of the good, returns to the cave of appearances.[56] He sees the good of the absolute and that of the relative which is the good's effect; he is able to return to and know the goodness of appearances and the truth they manifest for the *first time*.[57] Thus, the understanding of images dramatically differs before and after the ascent to the good. Before, "images all possess a certain opacity," but after the return to the world of appearances, the philosopher can know relative images "to be a transcendent manifestation of reality. The good that was *beyond* it turns out *therefore* to be present within it."[58]

53. Schindler, *Plato's Critique*, 37.   54. Schindler, *Plato's Critique*, 137.
55. Schindler, *Plato's Critique*, 307.

56. The felicity between Platonism and Christian soteriology, recognized since the first Christian centuries, becomes even more pronounced in this reading of Plato, which eliminates the purifying tendencies of neo-Platonism, such as those found in Plotinus (*Enneads*, V.5.12). With the end of reason as the good rather than the one, Plato suggests that the elimination of all number, all multiplication, in favor of simple unity is not included in the good: the good's multiplicity of effects are themselves good. Just so, the Johannine soteriology suggests eternal indwelling as the *telos* of the saved human person (Jn 15:9, 17:3), but manifests this salvation in the subsequent love of neighbor (Jn 13:34, 15:18), while Plato's philosopher ascends to the good and—like Er—returns to tell the tale and save souls for the life of justice and reason.

57. Schindler, *Plato's Critique*, 309.
58. Schindler, *Plato's Critique*, 309–310.

Schindler provides an example of this transformed perspective on images by referring to the "noble lie" mentioned above; in doing so, he reveals much about the function of myths in Plato as a whole. In the early books of the *Republic*, Socrates has not yet shown forth the good, and so, while his extended discussion of stories and imitations *aims* toward that good, and while he hopes stories will help others so aim, he nonetheless still lacks the perspective that *knows* it as a whole. Images, here, serve as practical and imperfect means by which one tries to reach the good, but their very admixture of truth and falsehood indicates that their makers—in this case, poets—do not know the good toward which they nonetheless gesture.[59] But *after*—including in the closing book of the *Republic*—the philosopher knows the good: the images he encounters upon returning to the realm of appearances are transformed in significance. In brief, he knows the reality of which they are images, and *as images* they manifest (make present) that reality to the knowing mind even though they do not possess it.

As testimony to the unity on this point of the Platonic corpus as a whole, we even see such transformations occur across, not just within, dialogues. Early in the *Republic*, for instance, Socrates tells us that poets, despite the multiplicity of imitations they can produce, can only imitate a small number of things well. The same poet, for instance, cannot write both comedy and tragedy.[60] But at end of the *Symposium*—a dialogue whose action takes place *after* the *Republic*—we hear a different story. By this point in the dialogue, it has become clear that Socrates himself is an image of the good, of love, and so of one who engenders in Beauty Itself.[61] Aristodemus tells Apollodorus, and he, in turn, tells us that, in the early hours of the morning, Socrates is still awake and arguing that the same man may write both tragedy and comedy.[62] We might extrapolate: a poet who is *just* a poet cannot; a good man *should* be able to do so; and the

---

59. Language as gesture would of course acquire a distinguished pedigree in the works of Christian Platonist theology and in some instances of contemporary analytic philosophy, in which the pre-good use of images corresponds more precisely to the apophatic language of theology (in faith) than does that of the philosopher "returned." For the Christian, that post-return language could be found only in sacrament or in eternal life. Cf. Pseudo-Dionysius, *Mystical Theology*, in *The Complete Works*, trans. Colm Luibheid (New York: Paulist Press, 1987), 1025A–B. See also Herbert McCabe, "The Logic of Mysticism," in *God Still Matters* (London: Continuum, 2005), 13–28, n.b. 21–22.

60. Plato, *Republic*, 345a.   61. Cf. Schindler, *Plato's Critique*, 179–87.
62. Plato, *Symposium*, 223d.

philosopher, who knows the whole of things through the good, indeed *can* write in these opposite modes and, by implication, in any. What the poet achieves by haphazard imitation, the philosopher accomplishes with all-encompassing knowledge. Hence, Plato, the "invisible" philosopher behind the nested stories of the *Symposium*, in fact does write in both modes.[63] He is, in reality, the author of Aristophanes's comic myth and of Alcibiades's speech about Socrates, which testifies to Alcibiades as a tragic figure fated to abandon his love of Socrates for other, self-destructive, ambitions. Plato can make the images of all things because he knows their forms just as they truly are.

Plato does not just grudgingly allow that appearances are *relatively* good within the absolute economy of the good itself. Nor has he, therefore, contrived a late excuse to allow imitative poets to remain in the city despite his better judgment. Rather, the appearances of myths take on a new, positive function. As Schindler notes, in the *Phaedrus*, Socrates pokes fun at those who seek "to distill a conceptual insight from myths rather than simply" believe them.[64] These hermeneutists will be at their business forever, because the complexity of myths is endless. This infinite density of meaning serves to remind the philosopher of the simple totality of the good in a way that discursive speech, including that of dialectical reasoning, could not. Myths may serve as a point of departure for reasoning; but, for the philosopher, they come to manifest meaning and goodness in ways that cannot be exhausted in language.[65] Finite images manifest an infinity; the philosopher may see the world in a grain of sand, as William Blake proclaimed, and attest to the picture that is worth more than a thousand words, as the cliché would have it. He will, above all, understand it to be in the order of things that the *logos* should become flesh and dwell among us.

This surprising development of the image from *imitation* to *manifestation* was hardly a forgotten episode within the larger Platonic tradition. In the neo-Platonist *Enneads* V.8, Plotinus will return to the Egyptian in-

63. Cf. Schindler, *Plato's Critique*, 224–25.

64. Schindler, *Plato's Critique*, 319.

65. Schindler concludes, "The rationalist assumption that meaning can be exhaustively reduced to discursive accounts of meaning—so that the whole of the meaning of a thing would be strictly equal to the sum of statements made about it—will necessarily undermine itself because the need for explanation goes on to infinity" (*Plato's Critique*, 320).

vention of writing and the inscribing of myth, which Plato introduced in the *Phaedrus*, to argue that

Egyptian hieroglyphics suggest, much as an art work might, the lack of discursiveness in the intelligible world, showing forth how the Ideas are not propositional truths, but Beings (*onta*) ... [and] that Ideas may be envisaged as *agalmata*, each bodying forth in a species of translucence the inner wealth of its ontic truth and beauty.[66]

Modern readers may have missed Plato's canny preservation of appearance and reality, myth and reason, within the economy of the Good, but his ancient disciples did not.[67]

Without erasing the distinction between story and reason, Schindler argues that myth does not merely fill gaps "where there is not knowledge." It is "the foundation of all knowledge whatsoever" and is included within the penumbra of dialectic.[68] Plato may give us reason to believe that myth alternately refracts and reflects truth, but in theory and practice he suggests that the rational soul and argumentative reasoning alike require myth.

If this were where Plato left things, then the Myth of Er would stand out as the great exemplar of myths in Plato. It is a story that brings to a halt all dialectic and in one sense at least transcends it. For, by Schinder's account, it would seem to make manifest, for the philosopher who knows the good, everything that might be discovered about the life of justice, could dialectic just continue forever. It is certainly the case that Er's tale provides us an image of justice and its effects. It is hard to imagine that the relationship of *mythos* and *logos* could be any closer: *mythos* remains distinct from *logos*, but it is not only the concrete image of reason's truth, but the container, or rather, the *incarnation*, the formal-material unity, of it.

---

66. Quoted in Robert J. O'Connell, SJ, *Art and the Christian Intelligence in St. Augustine* (Cambridge, Mass.: Harvard University Press, 1978), 46.

67. As we have already seen, and shall further develop below, Jacques Maritain would recover this ancient position in terms of form and beauty, which, as a transcendental property of being, is convertible with truth. He explicitly resists one evident conclusion of this Platonic and neo-Platonic idea, however: images can manifest the full knowledge of the philosopher and so are not the exclusive property of the fine artist, as Maritain so often suggests, as when he says "Metaphysics snatches at the spiritual in an idea, by the most abstract intellection; poetry reaches it in the flesh, by the very point of the sense sharpened through intelligence" (Jacques Maritain, *Art and Scholasticism and The Frontiers of Poetry*, 128).

68. Schindler, *Plato's Critique*, 319, 321–22.

Other moments in Plato's dialogues, however, suggest that even this may leave the distinction seeming greater than it really is.

In Socrates's deathbed argument regarding the immortality of the soul and the consequent importance of virtue, in the *Phaedo*, Plato provides an intricate description of the topography of the underworld akin to that given in the Myth of Er. This account begins with the familiar language of myth. "We are told," Socrates says at the outset, that after "each person dies," his soul is judged and then guided to the underworld.[69] He then objects to the playwright Aeschylus's description of the path to Hades as one—and does so on rational grounds: if the path were one or simple "there would be no need of guides."[70] The basis of this deduction? He tells us, "I base this judgment on the sacred rites and customs here."[71] Myth, therefore, provides the condition, context, and subject, for a certain act of reasoning. But, by Socrates's own admission, the results of this reasoning would seem to hold true only *if* the sacred rites, *if* the myths that precede reason, are themselves true. By the end of his description of the afterlife, however, Socrates is prepared to make a claim much more bold:

No sensible man would insist that these things are as I have described them, but I think it is fitting for a man to risk the belief—for the risk is a noble one—that this, or something like this, is true about our souls and their dwelling places, since the soul is evidently immortal, and a man should repeat this to himself as if it were an incantation, which is why I have been prolonging my tale.[72]

The details of the afterlife Socrates has provided are not themselves rational conclusions on which to insist. And yet, they follow as likely or probable truths, as "incantatory" prolongations of a truth for which, Socrates has already argued, we do have a strong rational foundation—the immortality of the soul. Everything Socrates tells us here constitutes a speculative elaboration of truths known by reason, and therefore constitute, at the least, probable consequences of those truths.

Similar language appears in the great myth that constitutes the *Timaeus*—the dialogue, perhaps not incidentally, that immediately follows the *Republic*. As Timaeus prepares to give an elaborate description, or story, of the creation or the fashioning of the cosmos, he pauses to qualify

69. Plato, *Phaedo*, 107e.
71. Plato, *Phaedo*, 108a.
70. Plato, *Phaedo*, 108a.
72. Plato, *Phaedo*, 114d.

the precise kind of speech on which he has just embarked.[73] An account, that is to say, a demonstration of *logos*, regarding what is "stable and fixed" will itself be "stable and unshifting."[74] But the account he is about to give regards not being, but becoming, and so must necessarily lack that kind of apodictic clarity and permanence. He will offer "accounts of what is a likeness," and so the account itself will be only "likely," and not "completely and perfectly accurate."[75] These likely stories are founded on necessary truths, just as becoming is founded on the principle of being. But, once more, they seem to be prolongations of truth that become less certain and more "likely" as they proceed from the eternal and necessary in the direction of the unlikely or impossible. The criterion for accepting such "accounts" is that they be "no less likely than any" others on offer.[76] The *Timaeus* makes explicit what has remained, at best, a possibility in the *Phaedo*. Myths and discursive arguments are both "accounts." This much we know insofar as an argument is often called a rational account, and (to anticipate our next hypothesis), we traditionally argue for the authority of some stories by saying they offer "the true account," to distinguish them from those others in the world to be dismissed as fiction or rumor. *Mythos* and *logos* are kinds of accounts. Or, rather, myths constitute a particular species—the *likely* species—within the genus of *logos*, even as *logos* unfolds within *mythos*. A kind of circumincession occurs here akin to the enfolding of truth and goodness within beauty that we discussed in Part II.

If myths can incarnate or contain rational truth, the genus of rational truth may also contain myth as a particular specification of itself. This does not leave us back where we started, early in the *Republic*, where myths comprise an amalgam of truth and falsehood. For that would entail that some further act of reasoning may superintend the myth from above and finally divide the true from the false. Myths, rather, are likely accounts, *within and among which* we may argue, as Socrates, in the *Phaedo*, argues with Aeschylus regarding the path to Hades. Because they are founded on rational truths (*logos*) outside themselves, it is possible to stand apart from and analyze myths. But this will not, and need not, always be the case, because the myth itself constitutes a kind of argument for its own possible truth. This point is set in particular relief in still another analogue

73. Plato, *Timaeus*, 28b.
75. Plato, *Timaeus*, 29c.

74. Plato, *Timaeus*, 29b.
76. Plato, *Timaeus*, 29c.

to the Myth of Er. In the *Gorgias*, Socrates makes a compelling case for the importance of virtue, because the "naked" soul will, after its death, be brought before the judgment of Minos, Rhadamanthus, and Aeacus.[77] Socrates is little less detailed here than he is in the tale of Er or in the *Phaedo* on the moral topography of the afterlife. What does differ is how he prefaces these details. In his effort to convince the Sophist Callicles of the importance of virtue, he says, "I'm willing to give you an account," showing that what he has said is true.[78] He continues, "Give ear ... to a very fine account. You'll think that it's a mere tale, I believe, although I think it's an account, for what I'm about to say I will tell you as true."[79] As we shall see just below, when we turn to Detienne's thought on myth, it is possible to interpret a passage like this exclusively as asserting the difference between mere tales (*mythos*) and true accounts (*logos*). But such a conclusion is not obvious. Socrates seems to be saying, once more, that there is a mode of discourse distinct in form from dialectic, but which may arrive at truth just as dialectic does. This is sufficiently the case, that a certain kind of *mythos*, of story-telling, can constitute a true account. A myth may not only bear within it the infinite depths of truth, it may also bring us to the perception of that truth as well as discursive reasoning does, but by different means.

Let us now pursue these questions from a slightly different angle. Marcel Detienne's writings call into question the dualism of *mythos* and *logos* even more radically than does Schindler's interpretation of Plato, and gives us a deeper historical basis for the interpretations I have just offered of Plato's use of myths. Detienne's monograph, *The Creation of Myth*, provides a genealogy of the word and idea of *mythos* that traces them back to a surprising origin. According to Detienne, *logos* and *mythos* were once synonyms: they both meant speech.[80] Over time, *mythos* acquired varied connotations: the speech of men in rebellion whom a tyrant had deprived of their power to speak as citizens, initially, but, with the emergence of written history in ancient Athens, myth comes to serve as a derisive term for hearsay and rumor, for every kind of speech that does not meet a particular historian's criterion of plausibility.[81] Myth is not a particular kind

77. Plato, *Gorgias*, 524a.
79. Plato, *Gorgias*, 523a.
81. Detienne, *The Creation of Myth*, 45, 51.

78. Plato, *Gorgias*, 522e.
80. Cf. Pieper, *The Platonic Myths*, 5–7.

or genre of story—it is simply marginal speech and, through the influence of the *writings* of the ancient historians, it comes to be associated with any kind of orality, with oral tradition, and so, finally, with unreliable, senile, or feminine chatter, in distinction from written language.[82]

Mythology as a concept comes into being much later—at that moment when spoken stories—whether called *logos* or *mythos*—first come to be written down; in its new stasis as text, the story, once told, becomes a corpse subject to dissection and re-dissection. For Plato and, centuries later, for modern scholars, to speak of "mythology," therefore, does not mean to refer to the tales told by an oral culture, but to gesture toward such stories as already pinned down as writing, assumed to have a common genesis in primitive orality, and now rendered passive for second-order rational examination.[83] *Mythos* appears not as the necessary foundation, but as the possible prey, of *logos*.

Detienne's aim seems to be entirely nominalist in nature; he wishes to dissolve the supposedly intelligible category of mythology and to put to rest the endless speculations, especially those of modern structuralist anthropologists, on the essential (or trans-cultural) form or function of the tales it is supposed to include. The ever-increasing multitude of theories regarding what myths are—the proliferation of mytho-logies—appears explicable as a series of impossible attempts to assign a common essence to heterogeneous phenomena. Perhaps, he concludes, we should stop pretending that everyone recognizes a myth when he sees one. One detects also a cunning irrationalism in Detienne's project: what has been called myth must be liberated from an ongoing series of highly ideological criteria of what constitutes legitimate speech and rational knowledge. Accepting neither of these tendencies, I would propose an interpretation of the genealogy he provides that helps us to recover the aboriginal identity of *mythos* and *logos*.

As Milbank has argued, Detienne's research primarily reveals that *mythos* and *logos* taken as synonyms encompass the "entire world of oral narrative reasoning."[84] In an oral culture, human beings tell stories. They contest and interpret those stories not in a second-order moment of reflection or commentary on an established, neutral text—a moment that

---

82. Detienne, *The Creation of Myth*, 61.
84. Milbank, "Fictioning Things," 11.

83. Detienne, *The Creation of Myth*, 81.

is alone to be called an act of reason. Rather, they do so by retelling, re-conceiving, and re-thematizing in their own way the stories they have heard. Thus, one does not need to depart the terrain of a myth in order to enter into rational discourse about it; that discourse takes place in and gives shape to the story as told and retold, and even the most discursive digression can be included within its bounds. The judgment made by the ancient historians that myths are unstable and unreliable, and thus should be dismissed as mere "rumor," testifies to stories' existence as vital media of intellectual exchange rather than as failed bodies of fact. What they saw as unreliable instances of unreason may indeed have been the traces of the contestation of rational arguments: one version of a story answering another. Recall, again, Socrates's correction of Aeschylus *within* his story as one peculiarly obvious late example of this *kind* of arguing.

While we, in our minutely specialized intellectual culture, might insist on *logos* as an act distinct from *mythos*, a differently inflected kind of speech, in an oral culture, we would have to locate that act as one taking place within the context of a story. When stories get written down, their form loses its flexibility, but loses also the appearance of reason. The words acquire a certain opacity that requires an inflow of interpretive knowledge for them to take on luminous life once more. Because a written text can be cut off entirely from the context and intention of its author, this opacity is routinely exacerbated. We really do have to know of what the text is an image if we are to discover its *logos*, its founding rationality. Far from wanting in reason in themselves, the words of oral tradition come to appear as deprived of rationality only in the condition of being written down. Written language does not, therefore, establish reason but risks cutting us off from it. As Plato observes in his discussion of writing in the *Phaedrus*, writing (as rhetoric or *mythos*) truly severed from its origin in the reason of its author itself ceases to be rational.[85] Similarly, were *logos* to attempt to cut itself off entirely from the *mythos*, the lived stories that occasion its questions, arguments, and conclusions, then it too would be deprived of rationality.

This should lead us to reinterpret that central act of discursive reasoning: abstraction. The process of abstraction by way of which we seek to

---

85. Plato, *Phaedrus*, 275d–e.

formulate rational statements as unconditionally true (i.e., as true regardless of concrete contingencies), should not be taken as grounds for thinking such statements may leave behind the narrative conditions that led to
their formulation in the first place. As Maritain frequently argues, the intelligible universes to which the sciences gain access through abstraction,
and which are constituted as "universes of laws and necessary relations"
are absolutely immanent to the "universe of existence" with its "individuals and events," "contingency and chance," and "irreversible flux" of singulars.[86] While our discursive reason could get nowhere regarding essences
without abstracting from the existent, its movement is in fact an entering
into the intellectual or spiritual infinity present everywhere within existent being. As I shall propose below, the universe of existences remains always implicitly present as part of the truth of abstract statements, and not
only as their first occasions, but also as part of the reality they describe.
We may distinguish between reasoning and story-telling, but not as isolated or opposed activities. They coexist much as hearing (aurality) and
speaking (orality) do in an oral culture, and as text and interpretation do
in written culture, as modes of speech that engage one another and even
enter into one another. In brief, *logos* may sometimes be understood as
the interpretation emerging from the *mythos* present to it. There would be
no reasoning that is not about stories, and none that does not take place
within stories, if only through the "editing" or revision, or between the
lines, or at the margins. *Logos* turns out to be marginal *legitimate* speech,
on this criterion: a gloss on a reality whose existential fullness might be
designated the universe of *mythos*. If abstraction is to be thought of as a rational act within this universe, then the familiar distinction between the
abstract and the concrete will have to be revisited, as it will be in the next
chapter.

A third hypothesis replies to a possible objection to the one I have just
concluded. One might say that story-telling and argumentative reasoning
are irreducibly distinct. Stories conform to *poiesis*, to the making of plots,
as Aristotle said, and reasoning conforms to the rules of logic.[87] I would
not want to contest the validity of systematic logic, and my claims thus far

86. Maritain, *The Degrees of Knowledge*, 145.
87. Aristotle, *Poetics*, 1450a15.

have been in the interest of exploring and defending the comprehensive intellectualism essential to the Christian Platonist tradition. However, it would amount to a narrow sense of intellectualism—that is, a familiar breed of modern rationalism—to pretend that *logos* is reducible to the term "logic" rather than to "reason," or that it must be understood as independent of a higher function of the mind: what we discussed above as the *nous, intellectus*, wisdom, or "intellect."[88] According to Socrates, the philosopher, the lover of wisdom, lives the life of reason; philosophers are those "who love the sight of truth."[89] To recall the passage from St. Augustine we discussed earlier, the young Platonized Christian convert would personify Reason and have her define herself in a similar manner:

Reason who speaks with you promises to let you see God with your mind as the sun is seen with the eye. The mind has, as it were, eyes of its own, analogous to the soul's senses. The certain truths of the sciences are analogous to the objects which the sun's rays make visible, such as the earth and earthly things. And it is God himself who illumines all.[90]

The intellect is the vision of the mind—or the soul, as we might say, if again, *pace* early Augustine, we take the eyes to be bodily senses—and while we see different objects with different degrees of clarity and certainty, everything that falls under the mind's gaze falls under that of the intellect.[91] Note that here, as always, it is the vision of God that Augustine's reason seeks—a vision he continuously reminds us can never be properly articulated in concepts and which, however intimately encountered, remains mysterious and a cause of wonder precisely because it can be seen only refracted through concepts like "light" and "happiness."[92]

What the intellect sees is the being or form of things. A formula of logic, or of discursive reason more generally, could at most be one sort

88. For discussion of the broad and narrow senses of intellectualism, see "Intellectualism" in Pierre Rousselot, *Essays on Love and Knowledge*, trans. Andrew Tallon, Pol Vandevelde, and Alan Vincelette (Milwaukee, Wisc.: Marquette University Press, 2008), 225–49.

89. Plato, *Republic*, 375e.

90. Augustine, *Earlier Writings*, 30.

91. At least in his early writings, Augustine followed Plotinus in believing that only the mind operated as active agent in the intellectual creature's sense perceptions, thus the traditional five senses are proper to the soul rather than to the body. Cf. O'Connell, *Art and the Christian Intelligence*, 73.

92. See Augustine, *The Confessions*, X.26, 29, 31.

of posterior definition of the form that has been seen—known—by the rational soul, whose vision amounts to a participation in the *intellectus* or *logos* of all things. The Scholastics understood an essence to be the definition of a species, but they did not, for all that, reduce the reality of the essence to the definition itself. If they did, logic would be our only means of seeing truth, and it has a very nearsighted vision that has to blink constantly as it moves from one part of a thing to another. When the soul sees, it penetrates with intensity into the fundamental intelligibility of reality that proceeds from the Second Person of the Trinity. Form is the unit that renders being intelligible (it is what the mind *sees*); precisely because intellectual vision is the perception of form, it transcends any one particular methodology suited to a particular kind of being.[93]

If the intellect sees all truths, regardless of the method of apprehension, it must see stories among them. But, more strongly, I would propose that to perceive a story *qua* story, as opposed to viewing it as a mere chronicle or a narrative, implies that one has not just encountered a sequence of events whose causal and meaningful connections remain opaque. When we see things and events drawn together into a coherent form, we know them as a story, as something that can be understood and analyzed—in which items can be included and from which others can be excluded with a certain rationality grounded in the criterion of "plot." We have noted already that, while even the most skeptical postmodern would acknowledge that reality has a narrative appearance, our age is rife with such persons' resisting the proposition that to know a narrative form properly entails seeing it as a story and as a reality. They would say, rather, that story is an ideological projection onto, an epiphenomenon of, the undifferentiated chronology of the real. Even when such figures affirm the necessity of reading a story *into* reality, they relativize it as a necessary subjective act or projection, and so refuse the possibility that a story might really be the form—or rather the real relation of a great number of forms taken together.[94] This resis-

93. Maritain's most striking and intense account of intellection occurs not in his works on the philosophy of knowledge, but in that early book on art and beauty we discussed above. See Maritain, *Art and Scholasticism and the Frontiers of Poetry*, 24–25, 32–33.

94. Hayden White offers the classic articulation of this position in "Interpretation in History," *New Literary History* 4, no. 2 (Winter 1973): 281–314; in *Metahistory* (Baltimore: Johns Hopkins University Press, 1973); and in the more recent selection of essays, *The Fiction of Narrative*, ed. Robert Doran (Baltimore: Johns Hopkins University Press, 2010).

tance derives directly from a fundamental suspicion of the human reason's capacity for truth, which must either be affirmed as being realized only in some particular "scientific" methodology or be dismissed outright. Thus, in recent decades, story-telling and reason have often been attacked together, however implicitly; I would suggest they must be defended together, as well, if they are to be defended at all.

Here we arrive at a path we cannot follow to its end; whether one concurs with Plato that the final cause of reason is the good, or qualifies, with Aristotle and St. Thomas Aquinas, that the mind is ordered first to being, one accepts that it is ontological form that the mind most properly knows: to repeat, being is the currency in which the reason and intellect trade.[95] Thus, there would be something myopic to any account of reason that restricted its perception to individual forms or essences, excluding the perception of those relations that subsist *within* forms as their integrity, and *among* different beings or modes of being as intentions and proportions, and across time as causes.[96] We could know very little indeed if we could not grasp the modes of being that relations take.[97] It is precisely the apprehension of these things that we argued Aquinas understood as the *visio* of beauty, which must be understood as a kind, or kinds, of proportion. Proportions are relations. Beauty is that relation which may be summarized as "the true perceived as good."[98] There is something, in brief,

95. Aquinas writes in *De Veritate* 1.1, "that which the intellect first conceives as, in a way, the most evident, and to which it reduces all its concepts, is being. Consequently, all the other conceptions of the intellect are had by addition to being," quoted in Kevin E. O'Reilly, *Aesthetic Perception: A Thomistic Perspective*, 103. Cf. *Summa Theologica*, I.5.2, where Aquinas affirms the priority of being to the good in intellectual perception.

96. I here advocate the realist conception of intentional being more fully articulated in Jacques Maritain's "Sign and Symbol," in *Ransoming the Time*, trans. Harry Lorin Binsse (New York: Charles Scribner's Sons, 1941), 217–54.

97. To offer a brief list on the modes of being relations might take: we have relations that are second intentions, which exist in the mind of the knower only; first intentions, which include real relations (Joseph Bobik, *Aquinas on Being and Essence: A Translation and Interpretation* [Notre Dame, Ind.: University of Notre Dame Press, 1965], 17–18); and the substantial relations instanced in the persons of the Trinity (Aquinas, *Summa Theologica*, I.40.3). As Pope Benedict has argued, the Trinity's substantial relationality reveals relations as a mode of being equal to that of substance (Ratzinger, *Introduction to Christianity*, 184). This is the metaphysical lesson implicit in the Old Testament, where God and man are revealed to man entirely by their relations—the being for and from another (cf. Ratzinger, *Introduction to Christianity*, 234, and Balthasar, *The Glory of the Lord*, 1:381–82).

98. O'Reilly, *Aesthetic Perception*, 110.

consummately rational about the perception of stories we hear and also those we apprehend in seeing the form of our experience.

Maritain once proposed that plot was one form among many in the dramatic genres of art. This is compelling so far as it goes, but it also seems a narrow conception derived from Maritain's desire to secure the orientation of artistic creativity as ontological (as ordered to being) rather than merely imitative of a certain kind of being: of action, as represented in plot.[99] His project is largely my own, here, and yet it would seem more just not to subordinate plot as but one more kind of essential form within art and metaphysics. We now have good reason to say, rather, that plot-form, or story, is one kind of form necessarily present and awaiting perception in all human experience, because it is *the* form of that experience. When we know our lives, we understand them as story; the essential form of human life is a story-form, and to know ourselves is just to perceive that form. Because we do not breathe or walk outside a story, it is inconceivable that we could satisfactorily reason about ourselves or anything in our experience without also and always reasoning about stories. We might suggest, then, that the beginning of all our reasoning lies in understanding the story in which we dwell: that of our own lives, which is always the site on which and in which our *logos* sets to work.[100]

99. He means this in the hylomorphic sense that form combines with matter to constitute a material being. See Maritain, *Creative Intuition in Art and Poetry*, 356–57. No doubt, in the changeless eternity of the divine mind, plot might be just one form among others, but for the human mind it is nearly as ubiquitous to knowledge as the very idea of being. This observation becomes all the more vital when one considers the Scriptural bases for our knowledge of God in faith, for it is largely by means of a story, the story of love given, betrayed, forgiven, and returned immeasurably, that the Scriptures teach Christians to understand, not God himself, but their role in his Providence. Maritain's prototype for artistic creation, however, was the timeless vision of the painter or lyric poet, and so he saw story as secondary and inessential to artworks in general, however necessary it might be to certain genres of art.

100. Von Balthasar argues for the "indissolubility of form" in every act of knowing and proceeds to claim that every element in a life is to be "subsumed by the form of man" (*Glory of the Lord*, 1:26). He illustrates his larger point by claiming, "to be Christian is precisely a form" (*Glory of the Lord*, 1:28), so that we see the identity between the meaning and integrity of a life with its form. We go beyond this claim only to affirm that the form of human life is a story-form. For von Balthasar, the perceptibility of the life-form seems to be moralized; the good life will be one with form, the poor life will be one lacking in form. This is the case also in the work of Wendell Berry; see his "Quantity vs. Form," in *The Way of Ignorance and Other Essays* (Emeryville, Calif.: Shoemaker and Hoard, 2005), 81–90. And while it follows that a poor life will be lacking in form precisely because it is lacking in being and ontological goodness, it is also the case that every life

One possible objection to the notion of story as the *form* of a human life is that form constitutes an essence, and essences are universal, whereas individual lives are no less singular than the individuals who live them. But, as our discussion of Aristotle's *Poetics* in Part II indicates, this is not truly the case. It is precisely in its realization as story that a human life acquires a universality transcendent of all material singularity—without leaving any of that singularity behind. For, while I may live only once, my story may live on in the memory of others, in the telling, and retelling. This capacity to be repeated *as story* is what made honor and glory so attractive for the ancient Greeks and many another civilization: it is one way in which the contingent and finite person can approximate the eternity and necessity of pure intellect, pure form.[101] In a story, every particular detail is "eternized," given a permanent significance in filling out the enduring form of the whole. Maritain's conception of plot as a formal abstraction helps explain this capacity for universality and permanence, while it also accounts for the freedom and individuality that constitute this or that particular telling of a story. What it does not address—and this seems to be the whole point—is the way in which the "substantial relation" of a plot, a life-story, is comprehensive rather than comprehended. How would we abstract the *plot* from the life of someone? We could not; the plot is the form that constitutes that life. To perceive that plot as a story is to attain to the most comprehensive and profound knowledge one may have about a life—containing all its aspects.

Aristotle reasons about human life and defines human happiness only by proposing the happy-life as a form: "a certain sort of being-at-work of the soul in accordance with virtue" with all "the other good things" that are necessary to it present, including a good beginning and a good end.[102] When he recalls the words of Solon—"Call no man happy until he is dead"—he does so specifically to propose that we cannot judge a human life happy until we can perceive its full form, its full story, including its death.[103]

---

has form insofar as it has being; an evil or unhappy human life may be judged not just in terms of the relative absence of form but also in respect of the form it does have.

101. See Aristotle, *De Anima*, 415a, and Plato, *Symposium*, 206b.

102. Aristotle, *Nicomachean Ethics*, 1100a.

103. Aristotle, *Nicomachean Ethics*, 1100a.

One might think that this would have given Aristotle a greater respect for history than his well-known comment in the *Poetics* (discussed in Part II) seems to indicate.[104] After all, Herodotus, in the *Histories*, depicts Solon as offering a reflection on just this phrase in his own account of human happiness to Croesus of Lydia. Solon is there shown to be an experienced traveler of the world, a historian—much like Herodotus—who has seen the habits and customs of different peoples, who has itemized their peculiarities, and who is thus in a position to judge among them. He is able to show Croesus the form of others whom he judges to be happier than Croesus himself. When the king reacts in disbelief that Solon does not judge *him* the happiest of men, Solon at last offers an abstract definition of the form of the happy life. The decisive closing of the form closes his definition:

Now, if a man thus favoured dies as he has lived, he will be just the one you are looking for: the only sort of person who deserves to be called happy. But mark this: until he is dead, keep the word "happy" in reserve. Till then, he is not happy, but only lucky ... whoever has the greatest number of the good things I have mentioned, and keeps them to the end, and dies a peaceful death, that man, my lord Croesus, deserves in my opinion to be called happy.[105]

So far, in fact, the historian and the philosopher are identical—so much so that the historian sounds like a philosopher indeed. They depart not in this formal inquiry but in how the inquiry is to be conducted, what the life-form should contain, and the end at which the good life-form aims. Herodotus and Solon suggest that inquiry is purely a matter of the knowledge gained through wide experience; it is merely empirical, we would now say. The contents of the form would seem to be primarily practical, with noble or heroic deeds, including on the occasion of one's death, being the most important elements in a happy life. And happiness as the end at which one aims is finally to be understood as the attainment of "glory" that can be remembered—made immortal—above all through the lasting record of the historian.[106]

104. Aristotle, *Poetics*, 1051b5–10

105. Herodotus, *The Histories*, trans. Aubrey de Sélincourt (Harmondsworth, U.K.: Penguin Books, 1972), 53.

106. Herodotus, *The Histories*, 41. M. I. Finley's translation is helpful on this point: "These are the researches of Herodotus of Halicarnassus, which he publishes in the hope of thereby pre-

Empirical research takes a central place in Aristotle's account of the various branches of learning, as well. The intellectual virtue of "knowledge" or reasoning (*logos*) is what allows one to make demonstrations with the elements encountered in experience, rising up from contingent particulars to what is necessary and universal.[107] This is the virtue Solon demonstrates himself as having in Herodotus's narrative. Aristotle proceeds to argue, however, that knowledge must be complemented by "intellect" or understanding (*nous*) about the first principles, "the source of what is known."[108] Only these two virtues together make possible the still greater virtue of wisdom, which directs knowledge and intellect toward "the things that are most honorable."[109] Aristotle therefore thinks wisdom, rather than a kind of wide-ranging reason, is the virtue that guides true inquiry. So also is it the greatest of the intellectual virtues in human life, as opposed to Herodotus's implicit endorsement of "practical judgment" as the highest, because it is the intellectual virtue that is won by age and experience and whose sole purpose is to guide human action.[110] Finally, Aristotle departs from Herodotus in affirming that the life of wisdom, the contemplative life, is the most perfect human life. While it is one that may earn one glory, it is a good in itself far greater than the glory that may incidentally accrue.[111]

We see from this digression that the historian and the philosopher give us largely incompatible accounts of human life and happiness. Herodotus claims Solon the wise as an advocate for far-flung practical knowledge aimed at glory as the most perfect form of human life. Aristotle with some rhetorical difficulty seeks to refine Solon's views so that they support the contemplative life as the perfect form.[112] Between them there is a radical breach, one which I would characterize as the Christian Platonist tradition establishing its superiority to other possible, competing traditions in western thought.[113] But what both Herodotus and Aristotle have in common

serving from decay the remembrance of what men have done, and of preventing the great and wonderful actions of the Greeks and barbarians from losing their due meed of glory," in *The Portable Greek Historians* (New York: Penguin Books, 1977), 29.

107. Aristotle, *Nicomachean Ethics*, 1139b.   108. Aristotle, *Nicomachean Ethics*, 1141a.
109. Aristotle, *Nicomachean Ethics*, 1141b.   110. Aristotle, *Nicomachean Ethics*, 1142a
111. Aristotle, *Nicomachean Ethics*, 1178b.   112. Aristotle, *Nicomachean Ethics*, 1179a.
113. See Alasdair MacIntyre, *Whose Justice? Which Rationality?* (Notre Dame, Ind.: University of Notre Dame Press, 1988), 64–70.

is a clear sense that knowledge is of the form, and that knowledge about human life and judgment about happiness are necessarily to be made in reference to the life-form. Because human life has a story-form, their dispute can be understood as about both the "shape" or content of the form—those individual details that take on universal significance—and the way we arrive at knowledge of it all. But story is in each case essential to their account of reasoning about human life.

The modern attempts by René Descartes to set up a new criterion of true reason as self-grounded certainty and, later, by David Hume to cordon off the rational from human experience, can be understood as tortured attempts to reason without the use of fictional and real myths. They want to see the truth, but they do not want to see life as having a form that is its true story. Both of them insisted on a criterion of rational certitude akin to that Augustine provides in *The Soliloquies*: clear, distinct perception.[114] But each of them silently dismisses the unsystematic nature of vision and intellectual vision alike in order to establish the criterion of seeing as that of the clarity of the things established *by particular methods*, and not as the native act of the seeing mind. Descartes and Hume, in different ways, sought to reduce the sight of reason to one of its possible methods or means, so that not all the vision of the soul any longer counts as sight. Thus, they bequeath to the contemporary skeptic the gnawing response to every proposition, "But *how* do you know?" Method narrows intellectual vision to the smallest of apertures.[115] Their principled exclu-

---

114. See René Descartes, *Meditations on First Philosophy*, 41, 46; and David Hume, *An Enquiry Concerning Human Understanding* (Indianapolis: Hackett Publishing, 1993), 15, 19, 40.

115. This is the dominant historical account of Hume in relation to Descartes and reflects the light in which he was understood by such figures as Jeremy Bentham and John Henry Newman. However, in recent years, Donald Livingston has made a fascinating effort to recover Hume as a traditionalist and a conservative, as suspicious of the pretentions of modern philosophical reasoning and as deferential to Christian pieties as was Jonathan Swift or Edmund Burke. Certainly, this possibility merits serious consideration, when we observe the extended references to Hume's historical writing in the French ultramontane traditionalist, Joseph de Maistre—see Maistre, *Considerations sur la France*, in *Oeuvres Complètes*, vol. 1. (Lyon: Librairies Générale Catholique et Classique, 1891). For Livingston's account of Hume, see "David Hume and the Conservative Tradition," *The Intercollegiate Review* 44, no. 2 (Fall 2009): 30–41; and the comprehensive *Philosophical Melancholy and Delirium* (Chicago: University of Chicago Press, 1998). Granting the interesting case Livingston makes for Hume as a conservative negating ideology and a traditionalist heaping scorn on the pretensions of pure reason and deferring to rite, religion, and cult, several questions remain open: (a) whether the Hume of revisionist history or the

sion of the idea of final causality (*telos*) in philosophy strikes a note distinctly modern, insofar as they could not imagine objects on the horizon, including on the temporal horizons of life stories, as admissible in human reason. In doing so, they were asking the reason to set aside those forms it perceives most intimately, routinely, and anxiously to think on foundations much thinner: only those clear and distinct ideas present to the reason at the moment (synchronically) could be rational; all that indicated the diachronic, from narrative and tradition to revelation received from *elsewhere* was disallowed for various reasons.[116]

Perhaps the best known and most richly exemplary text that gives full

---

Hume of his readership should be *our* Hume; (b) whether Hume's critique of modern philosophy and rationalism, in saving him from accusations of rationalism, does not simply make him an English antecedent to the problematic strain of counter-Enlightenment traditionalism more frequently found in France—cf. Blum, ed., *Critics of the Enlightenment*; and (c) whether Hume's insistence upon the rationality of his claims could ever be reconciled with the second insight of the Christian Platonist tradition, with its vision of *ratio*/*logos* as a mere participation in *intellectus*/*nous* suitable for composite rational animals.

116. We shall return to this briefly below, but it is worth noting that Descartes's method is to establish rational certainty only on the basis of what is now and necessarily in the mind; while he forbids arguments from final causes explicitly only in natural philosophy (Descartes, *Meditations on First Philosophy*, 37), they have in fact been excluded entirely from his method of all true philosophy. If the exclusion of *telos* is always fundamentally an exclusion of thinking in terms of stories, then the "curious" revenge story wreaks for its exclusion comes at the end of the *Meditations*. There, "memory" is suddenly called back from exile to vouch with certainty that Descartes wakes rather than sleeps and can know the difference (58). The "experimental" narrative Descartes gives us in the *Meditations* compares intriguingly with those of Augustine in *Confessions*: if both authors give similar ontological proofs for the existence of God, Augustine's is grounded as much in the absence as the presence of God in the soul witnessed in his life story, whereas Descartes, having refused the admissibility of all experience except that of the disembodied thought present (as in, without prior history) in the *Meditations*, finds himself asking us to take on his authority alone a matter on which his entire philosophy depends: the origin and clear presence of the idea of God in his mind.

Hume, of course, excludes everything in human knowledge from complete rationality, because the first cause of everything we know cannot be demonstrated (*Enquiry Concerning Human Understanding*, 28–29). Hume's argument that custom derived from sense experience is the great guide to human life obviously makes a place for story-telling—but that place, like all customary knowledge, lies forever outside of the criterion of reason he shares with Descartes (a conclusion he nonetheless affirms as reasonable). Thus, Hume notes the marked harmony of custom and habit that preserves human life in lieu of the slow and almost useless operations of reason. This harmony gives cause to those "who delight in the discovery and contemplation of *final causes*." They may "have here ample subject to employ their wonder and admiration" (*Enquiry Concerning Human Understanding*, 36). But all such contemplation can be only so much "religious hypothesis" or poetic speculation. It can never *require* anything of us, as the use of reason, or the giving of sound reasons, clearly does (cf. Schindler, *Plato's Critique of Impure Reason*, 1).

reign to reason as the vision of the soul and takes *mythos* as the foundation and condition of reasoning is Augustine's *Confessions*. Fashioning a textual Matryoshka doll, Augustine couches his record of his life's memories and the story of his conversion within discursive reflection on the nature of the soul in its longing for God. Further, he couches within the narratives extended arguments on the particular matters to which his life's story draws notice—from the nature of literature and education to the death of a friend, from the metaphysics of good and evil to the character and capacity of the memory. One cannot call that volume a memoir or an autobiography, or a philosophical or theological treatise—nor can one chop it into sections under these rubrics, unless one would mince even individual paragraphs. The *mythos* and *logos* are tessellated through the work without becoming merely confused; discursive reflection routinely interrupts and frustrates the movement of the narrative, lest we take delight in it merely as a story (a delight whose goodness St. Augustine doubts insofar as it derives from mere *curiositas* rather than the virtue of *studiositas* or the *caritas* of the Christian for the drama of sin and redemption in the saved soul). Prayer, moreover, interrupts narrative and discourse alike in order to remind us that the *final cause* of Augustine's life and the life of his book is praise for the gift of eternal life in God—an ontic stasis and indivisible unity to which myth and discursive reasoning both lead, but at whose gates they remain, though the intellect itself proceeds.[117] The book rises up to incantatory prayers, at times, to reveal that, as a whole, in its perfection, it *is* prayer.

At such moments in his *Confessions*, we begin to conceive how reason, as the vision of the soul, finds completion and clarity, rather than redundancy or frustration, by means of the infused light of faith.[118] Augustine seems to have chosen this form of composition in response to the same concerns about images Plato introduces in the *Republic*.[119] It may indeed better put into practice these theories of *mythos* we have inferred from

117. Cf. Augustine, *Confessions*, IX.24–25 and X.38.

118. See Pierre Rousselot, *The Eyes of Faith*, trans. Joseph Donceel (New York: Fordham University Press, 1990), where he contends that the light of faith "does not provide us with new objects for knowing … but it accounts for our perceiving the connection, making the synthesis, giving the assent" (28). As such, the eyes of faith are merely the eyes of reason granted proper illumination or full intellectual vision—as the passage cited from Augustine suggests.

119. Augustine, *Confessions*, III.2–4.

the Platonic dialogues than do the dialogues themselves. The "distend-ed" condition of time, for Augustine, makes possible human reason and story-telling alike; they cleave to one another, they are both "accounts," and so they both lead to an eternal unity that absolutely transcends them.[120] As such, *mythos* and *logos* subsist together in the realm of creation and merge with all things else in the realm of the divine wisdom, the *intellectus* of "Heaven's Heaven." And so, the *Confessions* provides both an example of the rich interplay of story and reasoning that we have tried to uncover in Plato and a model for how the life of reason as a story might be undertaken now—in this age as skeptical and superstitious as was Augustine's—if we should wish once more to be rational.

Four Theses on the Interdependence of *Mythos* and *Logos*

Having offered several reasons to question any easy separation of story-telling and reasoning, I would sketch four theses on the implications their interrelation might have for contemporary thought. I do so with the intention of drawing tentative conclusions rather than of introducing new arguments to be fully pursued here.

First, I would recall my discussion of the real story-form of human life and experience. Contemporary philosophers and cultural theorists do not hesitate to affirm the historically conditioned nature of all truth claims. To propose that all reasoning arises within a particular temporal and cultural milieu and that this milieu inevitably informs that reasoning is not simply uncontroversial—it is the daily bread of academic critics and undergraduate relativists alike. However, this affirmation almost invari-ably occurs in arguments for historicism—the contention that all ideas are mere expressions of their historical moment and do not transcend that moment to express permanent truth.[121] Furthermore, it generally serves as a critique of reason itself: if all our reasoning is determined by forces

---

120. "I see, therefore, that time is a kind of strain or tension. But do I really see it? Or only seem to see? You will show me, O Light, O Truth" (*Confessions*, XI.23.30). Light and Truth are one for Augustine, and are without the "strain" of (fallen) created being, of which time is the fundamental condition.

121. See, for instance, Erich Auerbach, *Scenes from the Drama of European Literature* (New York: Meridian, 1959), 184.

outside of reason—historically contingent forms of power are the typical external informants—then reason is at best epiphenomenal and at worst a mask of something else. But, as the work of Alasdair MacIntyre has shown with astonishing care and depth, this is far from a necessary conclusion. To confess that *logos* is conditioned need not lead to its renunciation in favor of a "hermeneutics of suspicion," but rather should lead us to understand it in light of those conditions. Our reason is grounded in the particularities of narrative and as such is informed by it as an interpretation is normally informed by the text to which it is a gloss. But to understand the story of one's reasoning entails more than merely a confession of the contingency of one's historical position; it suggests that the foundation of reasoning is itself an intelligible reality—a form built of other forms, called a story. We are excited to the activity of discursive reasoning precisely because the ontological realm in which we exist is already so intelligible—is already informed and ready to be thought. History as story therefore does not relativize reason but gives it the depths and resources that it requires if it is to function.

Second, if narrative is the ground of reason, it should also be admissible *into* reason; they should display a certain kind of compenetration or even circumincession. The portions of Platonic dialogues we examined demonstrate this in practice, as does the *Confessions*. Narrative elements often move arguments along, fill in portions of arguments, as do the hiccups of Aristophanes, or constitute arguments unto themselves. The challenge Plato poses is to integrate such elements into philosophy without reducing them to the function of examples; the speech of Diotima or Timeaus does not furnish an example for arguments presented elsewhere, nor does the myth of Er at the conclusion of the *Republic* merely illustrate the desirability of virtue in this life demonstrated by argument earlier. Rather, however exemplary in their own right, all three serve as distinct arguments in favor of the positions the dialogues advocate and add to the content of those positions. We require an account of argumentation that can understand the typical constituents of story-telling—the authorial claims of tradition and revelation, rite and scripture, for instance—in terms other than those of logical fallacy, weak argument, or the exemplary, or anecdotal.

Third, if ontological form is the principle of intelligibility (the perception of truth) in the Christian Platonist tradition, so also is it the principle of beauty, and the principle of the good. If we can affirm that formal logic delineates the rules of discursive reasoning as that reasoning seeks the true, and if we can affirm that the perception of form understood in terms of beauty operates according to some other analogous process (as I proposed in noting the logic of "plot" in narrative and the logic of proportion in aesthetic form more generally), then we should seek for a third term beyond the formal perception of truth and the formal perception of beauty. These come readily to hand: intellect and being. Indeed, St. Thomas tells us that all intellectual acts ultimately resolve into the same power insofar as they find their end in the same "objective aspect ... of being and truth."[122]

Far from proposing, therefore, a "narrative logic" that stands in absolute contradistinction from traditional logic, I suggest that a reunion of *mythos* and *logos*—one that does not collapse one into the other—makes more visible the dependence of human intellection on form. Or rather, it reveals in a new way that the intellect's natural pursuit of being may proceed by multiple routes. The most adequate account of intellection will be that which encompasses the greatest diversity of forms—that "drinks being," in Maritain's phrase, both wide and deep. As St. Augustine suggests in Book X of the *Confessions*, the arrival of the intellect at the elusive uncreated reality of God proceeds by an interwoven variety of means, the culmination of which is the intellectual vision of Being Itself. Precisely because the advent of phenomenological and hermeneutic approaches to philosophy have made compelling arguments for admitting narrative into philosophy in terms of the event or the dialectic, it is important to underscore this dimension of my argument: the recovery of story-telling should not compel us to discover a new lexicon in philosophy, but to recover that which made the metaphysics of the Greeks and of the Schoolmen possible. Story-telling is not an alternative to the study of the real, including the study of metaphysics, but a dimension of it.

Fourth, the most palpable consequence of reintegrating story-telling and reason is that we may discover the intellectual life to be a singularly compelling, a particularly excellent, form of story. Socrates, in Plato's dialogues, serves not simply as the mouth-piece for true ideas, but as the embodiment of them in a complete human life. Separating *logos* from *mythos*

122. Aquinas, *Summa Theologica*, I.79.9.

in principle has practical consequences for how we relate human reason to human nature and to human life as it is or ought to be lived. Restoring story-telling to the life of reason reminds us that reasoning is itself part of a story in which the rational animal is a protagonist. Reason occurs not at a second-order remove from life, abstracted from the life-form, but is one integral action within life that leads ultimately—the example of St. Augustine proposes—to a consummate life-form, the life of pure contemplation. Thought loses the utilitarian character it has gained in modernity and, in becoming a way of living, of being, becomes a proper end (*telos*).

I have tried to account for the longstanding severance between *mythos* and *logos*, to provide three reasons to call it into question, and to offer four theses on how their reunion might enrich contemporary thought. In the next chapter, I shall consider the consequence in our day of severing reason from story-telling. In the one that follows, we shall take stock of all we have seen in this book in order not only to conserve but to renew and nourish our understanding of the reality of truth, goodness, and beauty, that we may recover our sense of the dignity of the intellectual life proper to all heirs of the perennial, Christian Platonist tradition.

FIFTEEN

The Consequences of Our Forgetting

Let us begin with a distillation of the long argument we have been pursuing. I have contended that modern thought routinely sets *logos* (reason) in opposition to *mythos* (story-telling), and favors *logos* as authoritative and true. This habit breeds an unhappy myth of its own: mankind was once subject to the vague powers of hearsay, superstition, and old wives' tales, but has emerged triumphant from such antiquated miasma into the knowing precisions of a rational age. While such a myth gained traction in the modern age, particularly during the Enlightenment, its basic form dates back to Plato. Or rather, it dates back to a certain reading of Plato. My essay called that reading into question, returning to some of Plato's best-known statements on the "ancient quarrel" between poetry and philosophy, in order to show that, for Plato, stories serve as the condition of possibility for reasoning, and *mythos* naturally and properly interweaves with *logos* in our efforts to approach truth. While Plato certainly distinguishes between the two, his writing provides us ample reason to acknowledge that distinction as subsisting within a natural unity. If Plato is to be believed, the philosopher must reason both *in* stories and *through* them, so that sound reasoning might itself be understood as a kind of story-telling, and story-telling a foundation for, and species of, reasoning.

I built upon this account of Plato to advance three arguments in favor of a modern reunion of *mythos* and *logos*. Plato himself provides resources for such a reunion, but so does the classicist and theorist of myth, Marcel Detienne. In a loose reading of Detienne, we might say that the modern separation between *logos* and *mythos* has its origin in the methodologies of the classical Greek historians. If we can get behind this division, which Detienne critiques as an ideological contingency rather than a necessary typology, we shall find that *logos* and *mythos* were once synonymous. By Detienne's account, *pace* Herodotus and his descendants, we have further reason to believe that story-telling is a kind of reasoning, reasoning is a kind of story-telling, and that the prototype of this union is found in an oral culture, where the telling and re-telling of stories serve as a dominant mode of oral reasoning; its use of retelling as interpretation, commentary, and contestation qualifies as a kind of argument that comes to appear, in the age of writing, as mere incoherence. Finally, I considered the Christian Platonist tradition's understanding of man as an intellectual animal, whose intellect is by nature ordered to the knowledge of being. In its highest function, the intellect *sees* the form of beings: as Plato and the Greeks understood, when the truth is fully present to us, it no longer hides within a mere "image" or lingers as extended discursive definition, but shows forth as a form. If stories are incontestably "forms" in the sense of having a certain perceptible shape, as Maritain proposes, then to see the form of a story may well be yet another instance of rational vision: to see the form of a story entails an intellectual vision that bypasses the plodding methods of discursive logic but is nonetheless rational, indeed supremely so. The form of a story may emerge from contingent events, but the form itself is universal no less than any other form. It is already universal, Aristotle indicates, in the mind of the living actor who sees the form his life may take prior to its realization in history. Further, its universality is instanced by the telling and retelling—the accounting—of a life story. For the form—the essential, intelligible meaning—of a human life is always a story-form. We reached this conclusion only after noting, however, that all human reasoning essentially depends upon and emerges from the existence of narrative. And so, however much stories may be a universal form, and story-telling a kind of reasoning, all human reason stands in an ineluctable relation to narrative.

These ideas from Plato, Detienne, and Maritain argue for a reunion of *logos* and *mythos*, and culminate in the four theses with which I concluded the last chapter. Each of these propose some positive consequences that might result from it. First, rejoining *mythos* and *logos* would further the recognition that all reason is conditioned by the narrative in which it takes place, even as it reinforces rather than dissolves the integrity of reason. Such dissolution in some strands of postmodern thought has resulted in a fashionable historicism among contemporary persons that is intrinsically anti-intellectual. I counter that we must deepen and widen our conception of reason to include its narrative conditions and elements. Second, narrative should be admissible as a fundamental part of reasoning, and so we must find a way to articulate that admission in terms other than that of the mere gratuitous example. *Logos* and *mythos* are both species of "accounts." Third, by admitting *mythos* and *logos* as distinct modes of rational inquiry, we relativize both, but only in order to foreground the ultimate terms of all knowing: the intellect that *sees* and the form as truth *seen*. How the reason arrives at the form of truth is a mere matter of method, but it is the vision of truth made present in the soul that truly matters. The vision of the soul is the good of the intellect and the condition that makes evident beauty as the architectonic principle of reality. It is, in consequence, our entrance into the fullness of truth. Fourth, the intellectual life should itself be understood as a particularly excellent form of life-story. Having excised story-telling from philosophy, we have sacrificed on the altar of logical method the fifth great insight of the Christian Platonist tradition, to wit, of the philosopher as human being and of the philosophical or intellectual life as the best way of life for the human being.

Having established the reasons for and enrichments of a reintegration of *mythos* and *logos*, in this chapter, I would like to outline some consequences of our forgetting their near identity. I begin by recalling the rather "literary" revenge *mythos* has taken on *logos*, a revenge we have already discussed in terms of conservatism as a distinctly literary historical movement. As soon as modern philosophy excluded story-telling from its methodological city, that very human practice reasserted itself precisely as an irrational or alogical way of knowing. While there are historical instances of this reassertion of story-telling's (or poetry's) claim to truth dating back to the age of Plato and appearing in the poets of the Italian renaissance, in Shakespeare, Pascal, and elsewhere, we see it most forcefully in the romanticism inaugurated by Burke's *Reflections*. There, in a trope typical to his century, and which we have mentioned in another context, abstract "metaphysics" gets unfavorably contrasted with the concrete, morally-binding realities Burke believed we could know only by means of the lived drama of social life. What Kirk would theorize as the "moral imagination," Burke understood as a refusal of abstract ratiocination and as an emersion of the *humane* sentiments in the dramatic forms of human events, which are *informed* with meaning through the weight of ancestry and posterity. While I have argued that the mature Burke does not reduce moral knowledge to the feelings, but rather seeks a new vocabulary to recover the Christian Platonic understanding of the centrality of beauty to reality, it is nonetheless true that his early aesthetic treatise would lead us to just such an anti-intellectualist conclusion; and this was the conclusion embraced by many of those he influenced.[1] In such an understanding, truth becomes dramatic to the exclusion of abstract discourse. Truth comes to subsist in the ghetto of the heart, while rationality carries the field by becoming a bloody yet bloodless automaton.[2] Such a literary revenge of story-telling seems destined to find its image in Burke's historical reputation: that of the prophetic cry of a sensibility largely ignored by the mechanics of a confident modern rationalism and utilitarianism. *Mythos* claims to have comprehension of a kind of truth to which reason has no access, but, to the extent such claims are entertained, they are kept to the margins, sometimes lamented, more frequently ignored.

More than thirty years ago, MacIntyre made clear a related consequence of the divorce of *logos* and *mythos*, in *After Virtue*. He contended that all ethical arguments become incommensurable and so interminable unless they can occur in the context of a community's reflections on the nature of the human *telos*, that is, on the form of the achieved good life for man. To draw speculative pictures of what a good human life looks like requires being able to talk in terms of stories; and, indeed, the "raw data" prerequisite to such speculation about possible good lives consists not

1. See Burke, *Reflections on the Revolution in France*, 241–44. Cf. Kirk, *Redeeming the Time*, 69–73. Burke's rhetoric on this point derives most obviously from Swift (see Burke, *Reflections*, 301) and should be taken as conclusive regarding his thoughts on the capacities of human reason. However, it is precisely his rhetoric that furnishes a position that emerges in romanticism and after as an anti-intellectual voluntarism that idolizes either deference to tradition or the power of the imagination as emergent from feeling, instinct, or emotion.

2. Cf. Pascal, *Pensées*, §277.

of the atomized events of a human life or of abstract propositions about moral right, but rather of formed accounts of entire lives. We need the capacity to interpret human life as a story in order to ask meaningfully how we ought to live. And while we retain this capacity ineluctably in virtue of human life's natural, finite story form, MacIntyre rightly notes that modern ethics since Hume has refused the admissibility of narrative to rational argument.[3] The criteria we actually follow in determining how to live has perversely been excluded from that formal philosophical discipline dedicated to living well. Because of this, a modern person may *be* moral, but he can no longer account for himself ethically.

This ethical impasse relates directly to an intellectual one—another consequence. In the ancient world, philosophy was a way of life, just as the religious life has been in the Christian era.[4] It was natural that so much of philosophy should be concerned with, and should appear in the form of, stories in order to represent what the life of a philosopher properly looks like. Because man was seen to be a rational animal, his true happiness could be experienced only by those with the capacity to dedicate themselves to the cultivation of the intellect as a good in itself. The life of the philosopher was that of a man drawn by his own love toward the lasting intellectual fulfillment that, sustained, alone constitutes human happiness. The quest to come to a vision of the good, and the life of contemplation made possible thereafter, was not measurable in terms of its hard, exacting method but only in terms of the kind of joy it made possible.[5] To advert once more to Plato, we may say that while it is easy to distinguish the philosophy of Socrates from the character and story of Socrates, one misunderstands the nature of the dialogues in doing so. They are bound together as idea and manifestation, premise and demonstration, theory and practice.

3. See MacIntyre, *After Virtue*, 56–58, on Hume and the problem of modern ethics. See MacIntyre, *After Virtue*, 124, on the story-form of human life. MacIntyre's virtue theory may reject Hume's skeptical epistemology, but it also seeks to meet that epistemology on its own terms, so that MacIntyre, from a certain perspective, stands within the ethical tradition Hume initiated and corrects its deficiencies. From another perspective, of course, MacIntyre tells us that the Enlightenment project to which Hume belonged failed, and its failure opens up room for a renewal of the Aristotelian and Thomist tradition to which MacIntyre explicitly claims to belong (MacIntyre, *After Virtue*, x).

4. Cf. Hadot, *What Is Ancient Philosophy?*
5. Cf. Pieper, *Leisure, the Basis of Culture*, 32–33.

Those inevitable founding voices of modern philosophy, Descartes and Hume, expressly sought a philosophic method that cut it off from daily life. Philosophy's method required a self-seclusion of the reason from everyday assumptions and experience. For Descartes, the ambition was to establish a position of certainty regarding pure ideas. For Hume, philosophy served merely to explain and methodize the proceedings of customary behavior in civil society: it described what one already did in any case—changing nothing and certainly not qualifying in itself as a kind of *living*. The philosopher's life was no longer understood, therefore, as a particularly excellent type of human life, but rather became that of an abstracted commentator spinning *logos* apart from his own or others' lives.[6] It has been the practice of post-Cartesians to separate the philosophy of Descartes from the highly symbolic narrative dream from which it germinated. This is no doubt contrary to how the two related in Descartes' own experience, though it is in perfect continuity with the desiccated and abstract method he inaugurated.[7]

As we shall consider in our concluding chapter, if love and longing have always been associated with poetry, they *were* always associated with the life of philosophy as well; indeed, Socrates grasped both better than did Aristophanes.[8] To the extent that this association has been lost, we are no longer capable of sensing or even understanding why the ordering of the mind as a whole to being and the ordering of the reason to the true, good, and beautiful should be the *telos* of a well-lived human life. As such, universities have withered to mere husks, whose ivied and rocky piles have ceased to be intelligible to their occupants. Their cloisters were not constructed to set up a parallel zone of abstract methodology in which no one can breathe, but to make possible a kind of life elevated above necessity. In such an age, we can appreciate history's cruel sense of humor regarding the end of Descartes' life. The man who promised to give us dominion over nature was, to the extent he could deliver such dominion, revered, but for the most part came to be viewed as someone not quite human. He

6. Thus, Hume could contend that philosophical beliefs "are entirely indifferent to the peace of society and security of government" (Hume, *Enquiry Concerning Human Understanding*, 93).

7. See Jacques Maritain, *The Dream of Descartes*, trans. Mabelle L. Andison (New York: Philosophical Library, 1944), 15–16.

8. Plato, *Phaedrus*, 244a–245b.

would die thinking himself a dispeller of rational mysteries, but in fact as something like a court jester fated only to amuse a queen.

We arrive, then, at a further consequence: the shape of higher education has felt the impact of this hollowing out, of the rarifying of the life of the intellect to the occupation of intermittently useful fools. Our administrators, faculty, and students see that the intellectual "function" seems to have as its form an exacting and abstract method removed from the happiness proper to human life. As Hobbes argued, our felicity is whatever we happen to like, and reason serves only to help us get it.[9] Disenchanted with this species of reason, recognizing its servility but unable to see an alternative, since the middle of the last century, many of us have been complicit in efforts to make educational institutions—if not the intellectual life—"relevant." Rather than critiquing abstract rationalism for its failure to animate the drama of intellect and the joy of contemplation known in the past, those in positions of authority set up the facile dualism of abstraction and concretion; they seek to remodel the life of the university on concrete action to the exclusion of what they now view as the fearful loneliness of thought.

Freeing the soul for the contemplation of the highest realities is deemed not enough, is not even possible; philosophy, theology, and literature must now serve the most crudely political ends. Increasingly, we see students called to "social awareness," exhorted to "effect social change" by engaging in charitable service as part of or as the total content of their course work. We no longer tolerate a place where these activities might be acknowledged as important, but secondary, elements of a good life; an imperative to ease the material human estate blots out the possibility of an end beyond it and superior to it. We fear to offend the "less mentally-abled" by proposing that the life of contemplation might be superior to the practical life, since contemplation is the point of contact between the human soul and the divine.[10] Instead of thought, we have information sessions: course work in the humanities becomes a positivist form of history and sociology intended to excite indignation and lead to "service," the raising of funds in a charitable campaign, or, at least, the hand-wringing of "white guilt."[11] In Maritain's

9. Hobbes, *Leviathan*, 6.53.

10. Maritain, *The Person and the Common Good*, 25.

11. See Paul Gottfried, *Multiculturalism and the Politics of Guilt: Toward a Secular Theocracy* (Columbia: University of Missouri Press, 2002).

words, the University now seeks to enhance the lives of material individuals but at the expense of denying them the expansion and spiritualization that would make them more fully human persons.[12] It is no longer clear why an intellectual or scholar belongs in the university, but administrators become increasingly essential to manage the social good of "diversity," while scientific researchers seek to extend our lives and increase our domination over nature.

At most contemporary American Catholic universities, the Catholic "mission" of the institution is most in evidence just at those practical points on which liberal society in general has already reached a consensus: the distribution of recycling bins, the use of the buzzwords "green" and "sustainability," hospitality to the disabled, and—within hygienic limits—corporal works of mercy for the poor. In their proper place, I would strongly approve of nearly all these initiatives. If they serve, however, as a substitute for the intellectual tradition to which Catholic universities are scions, then they have at their root a set of ideas that we willfully keep ourselves too busy and diverted to contemplate. This relentless hum of good will serves to distract us from the fact that we no longer believe in the capacities of human reason to know the truth; we no longer believe the truth could be anything greater than the crude, intractable matter we seek to control in the name of bodily comfort; we begin to suspect, as it were, that if silence should fall upon our mind and our hearts for a moment, we might awaken to discover the world and ourselves are alike devoid of meaning.[13] One seldom hears, against this restless and evasive nihilism, an authoritative voice raised to echo Aquinas that the ultimate end of human life is our contemplative knowledge of and intellectual assimilation to God:

Since all creatures, even those devoid of understanding, are ordered to God as to an ultimate end, all achieve this end to the extent that they participate somewhat in His likeness. Intellectual creatures attain it in a more special way, that is, through their proper operation of understanding Him. Hence, this must be the end of the intellectual creature, namely, to understand God.[14]

To the contrary, contemporary universities absolutize change. Human life is viewed as in a double sense endless: without a ground of meaning to

---

12. Maritain, *The Person and the Common Good*, 55, 62.
13. Pascal is the great psychologist on this point. See Pascal, *Pensées*, §139.
14. Aquinas, *Summa Contra Gentiles*, 3.25.

give it purpose and therefore without the prospect of a final state, a true happiness, where it may enjoy peace and freedom (the sixth insight of the Christian Platonist tradition). Aristotle would have judged both these conclusions as "bad" and absurd.[15]

I am aware that the world is not dying from an excess of charitable works, though many of those works may themselves be dead to the real spirit of *caritas*.[16] In the West, at least, we see our intellectual and spiritual emptiness compensated for less by self-giving than by consumption.[17] In particular, we fixate upon the creation and commoditization of new technologies for, I think, a very curious reason, and one apposite to our subject. The narrative of "unstoppable" material progress, of technological advancements that will relieve us of the burdens of mortality, the labors of survival, the contingent determinism of nature regarding our weight, sex, and the shape of our noses—this seems to be the one story still permitted public recognition as rational. The story of technology receives such deference just because we confuse the power it provides with reason; it *must* be good, it *must* be a testimony to some kind of human greatness; its fruits lie all around us. It provides a meaningful narrative to a society otherwise lacking, and it makes us think we are rational gods, when in fact we are superstitious slaves.[18] Why else would it happen that the mere suggestion that computers are not an unmixed good can excite wrath in the breasts of otherwise complacent and amiable, if sterile, persons?[19]

Here, contemporary higher education comes in for one more bit of opprobrium. Most humanities and social science courses preach this narrative of technological progress in such a way that it would seem the sum-

---

15. Aristotle, *Nicomachean Ethics*, 1106b.

16. See Benedict XVI, *God Is Love* (Washington, D.C.: United States Conference of Catholic Bishops, 2006), par. 19–21, 28; he notes that "It is time to reaffirm the importance of prayer in the face of the activism and growing secularism of many Christians engaged in charitable work" (par. 37). Cf. Benedict XVI, *Caritas in Veritate* (San Francisco: Ignatius Press, 2009): "I am aware of the ways in which charity has been and continues to be misconstrued and emptied of meaning, with the consequent risk of being misinterpreted, detached from ethical living, and, in any event, undervalued" (par. 2).

17. Kirk speaks of the contemporary West as a "consumption-society" (*The Conservative Mind*, 11), and we are all familiar with the term "consumer society" and the demotic redefinition of persons and citizens as "consumers" and "customers."

18. See Bruno Latour, *We Have Never Been Modern* (Cambridge, Mass.: Harvard University Press, 1993).

19. Berry, *What Are People For?*, 170–96.

mons to charitable service amounts to little more than helping those in poorer countries access the garden of technological delights in which we freely romp. Having said that, many other courses couch themselves as critical of western consumption and power; they generally do so exclusively in the form of *criticism*—that is, in the attempt to undermine the assumptions of our experience by exposing their manipulative ideological structures. Because this criticism always remains a strictly anti-western or anti-capitalist position that refuses to offer a more robust or dignified account of human life than that offered on every airwave and video screen, even the most savage criticisms of western technocratic and ideological lusts for domination wind up having an unintended consequence. They merely liberate their students from what little sense of ethical obligation or intellectual calling they are likely to have acquired within this generally amoral order, by calling it all a lie and a cheat.

In a word, the greatest ally of a society entirely organized in terms of exchange between corporations, state social services, and private consumers is the western Marxist tradition of culture critique. In claiming to expose the lines of power to criticism, they advance a vision of pure immanence, where nothing transcends the exercise of power and where, indeed, there is *nothing but* power and its relations. This can only prompt students to see no purpose to their lives beyond seeking a power of their own. This *de facto* alliance has overcome its *de jure* antagonism and become most comically evident in such things as the rise to institutional respectability of media and cultural studies. In the study of cartoons and soap operas, our students learn the most banal of lessons: the bottom line to all the claptrap regarding the true, the good, and the beautiful is the cliché that the "customer is always right." Life is a buying and selling of power; criticism merely lets us know, lest in our glee we have forgotten, just who is selling whom.

This singular public narrative of technological progress, power, and pleasure, however, is always the story we tell about other people, that thoughtless mob, and never ourselves. But we all need a story of our own. And so, our unsatisfactory condition gives rise to the proliferation of private narratives deprived of any ethical or rational force. To wit, the tales of the talking cure, unfolded on the psychologist's couch. The triumph of the therapeutic reveals at once the vanquishing *and* the vindication of human life as a story and human reason's dependence on story-telling. The thera-peutic narrative, to be sure, is rife with unfortunate elements. It presumes the total isolation of the feelings of the interior, subjective state from the objective conditions of nature and ethical discourse, so that psychological therapy becomes a stoic exercise in interior adjustment to inalterable and morally indifferent external conditions.[20] So, too, it despairs of such con-fessions having any purchase on reason, or reason any purchase on them. The patient's task is simply to state the raw feeling of experience, upon which reason operates only to make a diagnosis. This last, private refuge of story-telling not only robs it of ethical or rational force, but it has the effect of narrowing the *kinds* of stories we are capable of telling about our-selves.[21] As has been noted for decades, we find that our popular narra-tives conform to the stock fixtures of therapy: trauma, mourning, revenge (or "acting out"), and interior-adjustment. And yet, the very fact that hu-man beings feel compelled to tell these stories indicates not how trauma-tized we all actually are, but our need for the more varied conventions of story-telling that become available when story-telling itself is readmitted to the public realm as a source and basis of wisdom. This re-admittance, and not an increase in the number of psychologists, or the already-under-way switching of method from the "talking cure" to the prescription of psychotropic drugs and scrupulously managed social institutions, is the solution to the conditions modern psychology generally misdiagnoses.

The causes of the aforementioned phenomena are, no doubt, multiple and complex. My argument is not so crude as to suggest that the exile of *mythos* from *logos*, or rather, the abstraction of *logos* from the condition of its possibility, has alone been their progenitor. Other factors have helped misshape the modern university and sent untold millions in search of therapy. But surely there is a causal relation. I have tried primarily to make the case that our age misunderstands the nature of stories and of reason alike; that this misunderstanding has its roots in Plato, but that Plato himself gives us salient reasons to reject it. Further, I have tried to sug-

20. In recent years, however, our therapeutic morality has sought to manage interior states by managing the environment in which they function. Therapy began by denying the normative goodness of nature so that the feelings of the subject could be managed; now that the world (na-ture) has been deemed a matter of indifference, it can be reconfigured in various ways for the sake of helping the subject to feel better about himself.

21. See Philip Rieff, *The Triumph of the Therapeutic* (Wilmington, Del.: ISI Books, 2006).

gest that human experience detects instinctively the reliance of *logos* on *mythos*, even when it has lost the ability to recognize as much. Our predicament is that we have failed to take stories seriously enough for them to merit the attention of anyone besides our therapist. Plato's pedagogical theory of poetry has, in this regard, one further lesson to teach us. If we have formed our own pre-rational sensibilities on the irrelevance of stories to rational thought, and on the irrelevance of reasoning to the narrative form of human life, then we risk making ourselves unwittingly insensible to a reality on which our happiness fundamentally depends. Nothing could be more irrational than that. We have, therefore, not only a material interest in the knowledge that gives us power, but an essential interest in the pursuit of the truth that may inform and fulfill us. We must now consider that interest and why it has become so difficult for us to embrace.

SIXTEEN

Still Interested in the Truth

We began this study with the claim that conservatism should be viewed as the modern, settled disposition that perceives the form of politics, of culture, and of reality as an essentially aesthetic one. These things are ordered by and to beauty. The conservative is one who sees their forms, recognizes them as both good and true, and who therefore seeks to conserve and cultivate these orders in shifting, often hostile, circumstances. The tradition Burke inaugurated is distinctively modern, because it was formulated in response to the modern doxa forged during the Enlightenment, but it is also ancient and venerable, because it seeks to keep alive insights that are foundational to the West's Christian Platonist tradition and that constitute its genius.

Those who have read these arguments in favor of a genuine, universal good for human life, of a beauty comprehensive and encompassing of not only the fine arts but also reality as such, and of a truth to which we attain only through and with stories, will recognize immediately how much they shock the prejudices of modern thought in general. Modern intellectual prejudices begin, after all, with such a figure as Hobbes, who sought to reduce the spiritual and corporeal multiplicity of the cosmos to the simple quantities of matter and motion, and who, in the process, stripped the idea of goodness of anything but the most sub-rational, subjective, and facile meaning. It continues with the philosopher Kant who, in his effort to preserve the freedom of the spirit from the determinism of modern physics, makes a sacrifice of the being of beauty on the altar of physical science. And, from beginning to end, from Descartes to John Dewey, the modern mind has sought to reduce truth to simple, clear, and verifiable ideas, whether in the bloodless abstraction of a mathematical formula or in the blood-letting simplifications of utilitarianism. Most of us still think in these terms—even self-described conservatives.

Anyone who sees the impoverishment of reality wrought by modern intellectual tendencies, more often than not perceives at their heart a darkness that is the very inverse of the light of the sun perceived with much difficulty by Plato's philosopher in the *Republic*. Whereas Plato and the Christian Platonist tradition tell us that the reality of sense experience and the temporal world is either a veil over the true, super-luminous reality of the Good, or a mirror, a sign, a manifestation of that Good, the project of modern thinkers has been to welcome us into an abyss of disappointment. When we leave behind the veil of ignorance, our eyes see clearly not a real brilliance that fulfills and transcends them, but an empty dark that cannot answer our stare and whose one lesson is to teach us that we are just meat and all we ever took for truth, beauty, and goodness are the mere impulses of a will to power. To say that we are a "postmodern" people generally means only that we have awakened to this will to power and seen how it structures our perception of reality—including the reality of our own selves.

It is good to see through modernity, to see it for what it really is. But it strikes me as a rather partial and peculiar vision indeed that would conclude that, because the modern world wore a mask, and beneath that mask lay only a menacing skull, we should conclude power is the only reality. To say as much would be to accept the modern world's hollow pretensions to comprehensive and disenchanting rationality under the equally hollow pretense of claiming to have transcended them. Far more defensible—it has been the position taken in this book—to recover the essential goodness of the West's genius, the Christian Platonist tradition. Far more compelling to take seriously, to accept the real insights, given to us through our everyday and exceptional encounters with the beautiful. Far more logical to see that for one to say power is the only truth and to find that prospect shocking or saddening already bears within it the conclusion that truth is distinct from power and, indeed, means something altogether different. To do these things is to change not only an attitude here and there but how we understand ourselves and reality—and how we set about living in this world.

But there lies a last obstacle before us. Readers of Aristotle on the moral virtues will appreciate that to know what truth, goodness, and beauty are is not the same thing as to have one's life transformed by them.[1] We are accustomed to cloistering the speculative from the practical, the reason from the will, the imagined from the believed, the truth known from the good loved. In so doing, we fall prey to one more modern prejudice. If we can remove it, this study will have completed its work.

Despite the "postmodern" turn among intellectuals in our age, historians will still frequently recall the eighteenth century as a golden age of public philosophers and men of letters, of discussion and speculation, but also, significantly, of experimentation in the physical sciences and in the art of statecraft. As an age of enlightenment, it was an epoch of ideas, but one in which ideas had real consequences in action. Perhaps for this reason, the virtue its citizens held up for greatest praise appears nowhere in the *Ethics* of Aristotle or in the morality of any prior age—that of *disinterestedness*.

One finds the word frequently in private letters, public newspapers, and on crooked headstones in churchyards from the period. To judge without prejudice, to observe without inclination, to weigh the "facts" (another word clunking through the discourse of that century) without placing a thumb on the scale—this was a measure of greatness.

One seldom hears open nostalgia for that time of couplets and courts, cabinet wars and musket duels, periwigs and knickers. And yet, whenever we lament the "bias" of the media, the politicization of the classroom, the manipulation of science for political ends, we are in effect observing problems that the Enlightenment bequeathed to us, and we are implicitly longing for the solution to these ills that the Enlightenment recommended: the virtue of disinterest.

In the Victorian age, the English poet and social critic Matthew Arnold looked upon the all-consuming materialism of his contemporaries—their thoughtless dynamism of making, selling, and getting—and longed for a realm of disinterested contemplation. Could the English sustain a place in their lives, where the best that had been thought and said could be contemplated for its own sake, free of considerations for its market value? Arnold was no admirer of Enlightenment poetry, but he looked wanly upon the freedom of thought enjoyed by those who lived just on the far side of

---

1. Aristotle, *Nicomachean Ethics*, 1103b.

modern industrialization and commerce. So, also, the French philosopher Julien Benda, writing amid the nationalist fervors of the early twentieth century, denounced the "treason of the intellectuals," of those, that is, who deployed their academic positions to advance the nationalist agenda instead of cloistering themselves in the life of disinterested thought.

We all can distinguish between speculative thought—whose purpose is primarily to lead to new knowledge *within* the mind—and practical thinking, that engagement of the intellect in the doing or making of something *beyond* the mind. Precisely because these two so easily become entangled with one another, we can also understand why it might appear necessary to grant a particular freedom to intellectuals whose lives are spent in speculative pursuits. Most of us also understand that this freedom depends on the intellectual's commitment to engage in those pursuits in a disinterested manner, betraying his vocation neither for petty gain nor distorting what he learns and says to suit the preferences of his friends, the president of his employer, a large pharmaceutical company, or the righteous indignation of the broadcast news hour. Such privilege may appear all the more necessary in a climate where ideas shape the destiny of nations, as they certainly did in the eighteenth century; it may seem all the more precious in a time like ours, where the din of manipulative rhetoric in advertisements, political speeches, and in the mass media alike carries on almost unrelieved.

Disinterestedness practiced as a mode of intellectual engagement is necessary and precious. Yet, I cannot help thinking that the age that gave us this virtue misunderstood the nature of the intellectual life it was supposed to preserve. Moreover, it would seem that the contemporary politicized classroom is not so much a violation of the rule of "disinterestedness" as it is a woeful but natural extension of it.

"Intellectual," as we use it, is a relatively new word, conceived to describe those professors, public philosophers, and men of letters who live by and for the realm of thought. They are supposed to be experts in their fields, caretakers of methods and disciplines, but what chiefly distinguishes them is a commitment to no cause that would cloud otherwise clear— we say, "objective"—thinking. But where did this exceptional character come from?

If we look back beyond the eighteenth century, we come upon some familiar but paradoxically alien figures. Early in the Christian Platonist

tradition, in ancient Athens, we find the philosopher, the lover of wisdom, who sometimes appears foolish to the washer-women of his city, so
absorbed is he in contemplation. But this same fellow also appears great
and noble at times, as if his visible actions sought to conform to an invisible beauty. The dialogues of Plato tell us that the philosopher possessed
the virtue of temperance in regard to bodily pleasures, because he took far
greater pleasure, admixed with some pain, in the yearning for truth, goodness, and beauty. He brooked no occupation that kept him from staring
into the heart of light that was the Good—a light he relished though it
blinded, and which humbled him even as it raised him up above himself
and inspired in him the most noble of deeds. Socrates, after all, was not
just a snub-nosed street-talker, but a great warrior whom foreign cavalry
dared not to attack. Such was the harbinger of the first academy.

The figure Socrates cut was like the statue of a god, the sight of whom
commands a response—not one of servile adoration, but nonetheless one
of ecstasy and love. In his seventh letter, Plato gives us a sense of what an
encounter with the philosopher should look like. The philosopher should
make clear "with how many difficulties" the intellectual life "is beset, and
how much labor it involves."[2] This hard work might seem to require a set-
ting aside of passion, a neutralization of one's interests and even one's happiness for the sake of some good that needs to be done. But no, that is not
the purpose of his speech at all:

> For anyone who hears this, who is a true lover of wisdom, with the divine quality
> that makes him akin to it and worthy of pursuing it, thinks that he has heard of
> a marvelous quest that he must at once enter upon with all earnestness, or life is
> not worth living; and from that time forth he pushes himself and urges on his
> leader without ceasing, until he has reached the end of the journey or has become
> capable of doing without a guide and finding the way himself.[3]

The rational discipline of the philosopher is not one undertaken in spite
of, and at a remove from, one's desires. It is the discipline that makes possible their warm pursuit, the practice that spares the lover from ever having to part from his beloved—wisdom.

In the medieval world we find characters not much removed from

2. Plato, *Letters*, 340c.
3. Plato, *Letters*, 340c.

the Greek philosopher. The medieval monks, who passed their days literally cloistered in monasteries or only figuratively so in the first great
universities, did not *sacrifice* the life of pleasures to be found in the wider
world. Rather, like Socrates, they moved *beyond* those pleasures to bask
in the one joy they believed truly fitting for the rational human being. By
means of work and study they equipped themselves for the life of prayer;
but prayer was not an exercise in mindless piety, it was the highest activity of the human intellect bathing in the light of truth. Plato had always
stressed that the philosopher did not possess wisdom but *yearned* for it,
stared into it, knowing it could never become a mere possession trapped
by the human mind. Wisdom is always ecstatic: drawing us beyond ourselves into a reality that fulfills us. So also did the medievals yearn in the
thought-that-is-prayer for a light that is visible but blinding, a truth perfectly intelligible but ever incomprehensible. Academy, monastery, and
university alike were places where the most profound desires of the human spirit moved toward actualization, and where individual lives were
given form and beauty as they sought to conform to light and truth.

In these antecedents we may see the figure, like an outline, of the
modern disinterested intellectual—but it is a hollow outline indeed, akin
to those traced at a crime scene. The philosophers and monks set out on
a journey with a real destination, and their lives could be called happy or
blessed because they advanced, by clear thought and a triumph over lesser
goods, toward the highest good imaginable. Their lives were truly human,
conducted not in scorn of self except insofar as that self proved refractory
to the hope of its own fulfillment.[4] They stepped beyond the mundane activities and concerns of this world so as to think and act the better within
it—and ever after.

With the rise of the "lay" intellectual during the Enlightenment period, we do not find a reconfiguration of the monk on secular lines, as
if the yearning for truth could be better conducted without the chaste
burden of the monastery. Rather, we find the old forms continuing but
without a clear sense of the purpose for which they had been designed.
The triumph over worldly pleasure was re-described as mere "disinterestedness," but disinterestedness *for* what? "For the life of thought," was the

4. Ponticus, *The Praktikos and Chapters on Prayer*, 60.

reply. The thinking *of* what? "Of speculative rather than practical ideas, of sophisticated and free rather than prudent and servile ideas." No further answer was forthcoming.

The modern intellectual engages in thought without end, for all purpose would be denounced as agenda or ideology. Restless before this convergence of freedom and uselessness, his occupation takes a critical turn and becomes the mere dissecting of all the interested buzz of the world of practical action. As we considered in the last chapter, because it lacks a sense of where thought might find fulfillment, the intellectual realm becomes not a place above the mundane world, but a parallel zone of criticism, where the beliefs of others may enter only to be seen through. The intellectual life reduces itself to functional nihilism, diverting itself from despair only by means of attacking the latest ideology voiced at the lip of its sibylline jug. Thus, the persistence of the intellectual life after its entrance into a state of decadence—the loss of all object or purpose—helped bequeath to us the problem of liberalism and culture with which this book began. To be cultured, to be intellectual, came to entail the dissolving of cultural authority and the suspicion of truth as a counterfeit good.

This eviscerated condition of the modern intellectual can hardly be dismissed as a mere moral perversion or weakness of chin, of course. Those contemporary thinkers who still see their vocation as in continuity with the tradition of medieval contemplatives and ancient philosophers have provided us a wide variety of compelling accounts to explain the missteps taken in modernity that led to the nihilistic dead-end so evident in our age. One common argument holds that the emergence of late-medieval nominalism convinced many persons that ideas were but names imposed upon an infinitely diverse reality, and so the world itself began to appear unintelligible.[5] What mattered, then, was not the discovery of truth in the cosmos, but the imposition of human will upon "raw" nature. This rise of nominalism was but one manifestation of a broader tendency to divide ever more rigidly the realm of nature and grace, so that nature, that is, the created world, came to include only the "facts" of things as inert and present entities, and the realm of grace, wherein the meaning, purpose, and essence of things was supposed to repose (meaning to be itself has to be *given*, after all; we do not know how "to make" our own meaning), stood

5. Richard Weaver, *Ideas Have Consequences* (Chicago: University of Chicago Press, 1984), 3.

in an at-best-tenuous relation to such "facts." This division occurred not only—as talk of "grace" might suggest—in Reformation theology, but in nearly every branch of learning.[6]

In the seventeenth century, we witness an increasing vision of nature as dead and meaningless fact, and a consequent privileging of the rational ideas present in the human mind as the only plausible source of meaning to be found in reality—and the human mind took on an uncanny, anomalous appearance, an alien spirit floating amid the great masses of dead matter. This is what led Descartes to constrain what could be affirmed as rational to that which conformed to the model of mathematical abstraction: any idea lacking the clarity of an equation could not be so affirmed. Because such clear ideas were not present in the world as such, but only in the human mind, Descartes felt at liberty to give an account of the world as a mere mechanism, as a place that has nothing to do with us as humans, but which we might freely exploit as the "masters and possessors of nature."[7] Pascal, a mathematician like Descartes, similarly contended that neither nature nor anything external to the human being's fallen interior condition could justify belief in the meaning or purpose of human life. While man could look in upon his evident wretchedness and sense, amidst it, a trace of fallen greatness, the remnant touch of God, it would avail him nothing to look out into the world. Because of his spiritual element, man could not see the simple matter of the universe as it was; for he was bound to project spiritual qualities where none were to be found. And, while the infinites of space and time were an imprint of God as true infinity, that told one nothing—for infinities are to be found *everywhere* in Pascal's vision, and merely remind us of the inadequacies and emptiness to be found within the soul.[8]

Such doubt over the "graced" intelligibility of nature, and such reliance on the clarity of mathematical ideas and the exclusively "interior" reality of human thought, had two marked effects. Man came increasingly to doubt the capacities of human reason to reach beyond the bounds of

---

6. See Brad S. Gregory, *The Unintended Reformation* (Cambridge, Mass.: Harvard University Press, 2012).

7. René Descartes, *Discourse on Method and Meditations on First Philosophy*, trans. Donald A. Cress (Indianapolis: Hackett, 1998), 35. Cf. Descartes, *The World and Other Writings*, trans. Stephen Gaukroger (Cambridge: Cambridge University Press, 1998).

8. Pascal, *Pensées*, §72, §242.

his own "subjectivity." He came to think that he knew with certainty only himself and those ideas clear and present in himself. Reason could no longer stretch beyond those bounds to a confident knowledge of nature, and it certainly could not over-stretch itself to the tenuous apprehension of the divine. Man became what he never had been before, an anxious alien spirit whose intelligence could find no echo, no answer, in the abyss of space enveloping him.

With the model of mathematical reasoning as the exclusive standard for what qualified as rational, thinkers after Descartes began to insist that only that which could be logically demonstrated could be affirmed as true according to reason, and they also took the methods of mathematics as the model for how reason worked. Though the ancient Pythagoreans had also privileged number as the highest reality, the resemblance with Cartesian thought ended there. Rather than being understood as an ascent of the infinitely capacious human intellect up to a faint taste of the highest good, the life of reason came to be associated with the hard slog of calling into question every idea and determining whether its truth could be methodically demonstrated. The intellectual life ceased to be a pilgrimage toward happiness and turned into an expert procedure whose end was simply the "rational" affirmation of what one already thought one knew—that one's body existed, for instance.

The supposed alienation of meaning and purpose from nature, the subsequent restriction of reason's grasp to the immanent and reduction of its nature to mere method, bore fruit in the culture of the eighteenth century. There, man found himself standing before two blocked roads. By pure intellectual ascent, he could no longer seek after God. Moreover, the natural world gave him no alternative pathway: it was no longer read as God's "book of nature," but as a mere inert quantum, infinitely various but empty of intelligible meaning. If it were to be "read," we would have to imprint the words there first. As we noted above, Karl Barth argued that this sense of inward and outward frustration hardly led Enlightenment man to despair. Rather, he reconstituted the older vision of nature as the created expression of the Divine Intellect on immanent terms. The human mind, which alone gave birth to ideas, was the source of all intelligible form in reality. The natural world was raw life, crude matter, awaiting the impress of the human mind. Man's task was to remake the natural world according to the forms and orders he himself invented. The test of an idea's truth became whether it could be imposed upon nature.

Man, as a creature in God's universe capable of rising above himself by means of the intellect to the contemplation of a truth he could never command or control, disappeared. Now, only that was rational which could be made or done. The conception of reason as a guide to the experience of truth fell to a model of reason as that which could dominate nature by means of experiment—by measurable, repeatable results.

If reason was, on these terms, exclusively practical, to what purpose did the Enlightenment preserve, even in the diminished form of "disinterestedness," the fifth Christian Platonist insight that man's dignity lay chiefly in his speculative intellect, which alone could pass beyond the instrumental doings and makings of this world to the permanent things of truth, goodness, and beauty? What were truth, goodness, and beauty, in any case, if they could not be harnessed by reason to beget by the force of our will new forms and inventions on nature's crude matter?

Over the course of two centuries, the disinterested intellectual served as a reminder that the criterion of truth and goodness was not simply whether something was possible—whether something *could be done*. His social function, as it were, was to serve as a check on action. His learned penury was supposed to beg the ambitious entrepreneur to pause and take thought.

But, by and large, the contemporary academic accepts this instrumental understanding of reason and so is in no position to encourage anyone to stop and think. Following Marx, he believes speculation to be a drug and truth to be found in practice, in doing, alone. His privileged role of engaging in "disinterested" speculation therefore appears to him as a largely empty and humiliating one. And so, he spends his intellectual labor in critique of the wider, "useful" world, exposing how the claims to progress, efficiency, rationality, and utility so typical as moral justifications for activities of state, corporation, or individual in our time, are mere masks upon the clenched jaw of man's will to power. Here, again, is the awkward "postmodern" position of the intellectual.

Is there any place one can look in the contemporary world to find the contemplative life still lived as it once was? Of course the world is still full of monks: Matthew Arnold's poem, "Stanzas from the Grand Chartreuse," speaks of the Carthusian monks, whose monastery he visited on his honeymoon in 1852, as the last of a dying breed. The 2005 documentary film *Into Great Silence* makes it a matter of public record that the Carthusians pray on, though Arnold has long since gone under the earth.

For many modern persons, however, the love of truth and the life of yearning for it have found most compelling and familiar expression in the works of the poets. William Wordsworth and Samuel Taylor Coleridge in the nineteenth century, and, to a lesser extent, W. B. Yeats and T. S. Eliot in the twentieth, captured in their writings the yearning for and basking in intimations of light and truth. Such poets' lives are almost one with their work, precisely because the truth they sought to manifest in language was also the truth they lived for, and so it gave form to how they actually lived. As we have discussed, the relative marginality of poetry in the modern world, its evident "uselessness" but also its natural function as an aesthetic expression or formal distillation of the form of a full human life, has made it a necessary oasis for those who wish to discover the riches of the intellectual life but stand hesitant before the claims to rational truth found in the ancients and medievals. Here we encounter yet again what it would mean for conservatism to be a literary movement: literature keeps alive what modernity has sought to extinguish but cannot, despite itself, live without. We find, also, why the conception of the fine arts as imaginative, as holding a suspension of disbelief and an opening onto possibility, is one important, though finally unsatisfactory, account of the role beauty should play in human life.

The skeptical W. B. Yeats did not think "belief" something to be talked of in a time like ours, and so absorbed his desire for divine truth and moral goodness within the winding stair of poetry. He deemed himself "very religious" precisely because he had founded his life upon an imaginative vision that refused to be tethered to the instrumental rationality of the modern world.[9] In a more affecting case, the young T. S. Eliot gave up his study of philosophy in despair, seeing its pursuits as a negligible compromise between art and science. He committed himself to the life of "*real* art."[10] Within a decade, however, the profound reflections in which

9. W. B. Yeats, *Autobiographies*, ed. William H. O'Donnell and Douglas N. Archibald. (New York: Macmillan, 1999), 115.

10. T. S. Eliot, *The Letters of T. S. Eliot*, vol. 1, *1898–1922*, rev. ed., ed. Valerie Eliot and Hugh Haughton (London: Faber and Faber, 2009), 81.

poetry had involved him led from "skepticism" to baptism in the Angli-
can Church, and in later life, Eliot would understand that his recourse
to poetry had been thrust upon him by a conception of philosophy that
refused its proper openness to the divine.[11] Poetry made it possible for
Eliot to seek order in aesthetic form; aesthetic form led him to a vision of
historical order; historical order, he took for an intimation of the divine
beauty; and this divine beauty, he finally recognized, was the sovereign
goodness and truth of the universe. The work of the imagination led him
to a renewed confidence in human reason, but also to the completion of
reason in faith. With that, he took his distinguished place as a conservative member of the Christian Platonist tradition.

Having said this, we must bear in mind that most contemporary artists have succumbed to the same critical and ideological hollowness as did
philosophers and other intellectuals before them. Poets like Eliot and Yeats
become all the more important for being the rarer. Unsatisfactory though
it may be for such poets of the imagination to become the residual tokens
of the quest for truth, a case like Eliot's encourages us to recall our discussion of *logos* and *mythos*. Plato himself, in the *Republic*, says that poetry—
that is, storytelling—is the seed that grows into the life of reason and virtue. Today's lyrical tatters may be rewoven as tomorrow's hope. What many
persons dare attempt today only on the stage of make-believe, they may, on
some future occasion, undertake as the real pilgrimage toward light and
truth.

It has been the ambition of this book to provide a few threads for that
reweaving. We have taken stock of our present moment and tried to offer
as an alternative to that penury a vision of the West's Christian Platonist
tradition as a good in itself and as an authoritative account of reality as
good and of the good of human life. Central to that good is the splendor
of Beauty itself, and so we have sought to provide an account of beauty
at the heart of this book. But goodness and beauty cannot stand alone.
And so, we concluded with an account of truth that re-grounds it in narrative and, in particular, in the story-form of human life. About this truth
we cannot be disinterested. For it involves us all and involves everything

11. T. S. Eliot, Introduction in Joseph Pieper, *Leisure, the Basis of Culture* (London: Faber
and Faber, 1952), 14–15.

within us, body and soul, intellect and will. We are erotically drawn to truth, and truth is itself being's—reality's—sign that it is erotically drawn to us, that it gives itself to us not as a possession to be mastered but as a word to be known. Against a modern vision of the world that generally seems dead to wonder and hungry for power only because it has hope of nothing better, we offer those supreme, indeed divine, useless properties of reality: truth, goodness, beauty. This book seeks to conserve them, to keep them alive for some of its readers, and perhaps to reawaken the natural yearning—the irresistible interest—for them that is always at least germinally present in the human spirit and, above all, is woven into the ordered fabric of the cosmos itself. I hope this book will help its readers to dwell more richly and joyfully in the order, the beautiful form, that was created in love by the *Logos* of God to be the one, true reality intended for the vision of our souls.

BIBLIOGRAPHY

Abrams, M. H. *The Mirror and the Lamp*. Oxford: Oxford University Press, 1953.

———. *Natural Supernaturalism*. New York: W. W. Norton: 1973.

Adorno, Theodor W. "A Social Critique of Radio Music." *The Kenyon Review* 7, no. 2 (Spring 1945): 208–17.

———. "Theses upon Art and Religion Today." *The Kenyon Review* 7, no. 4 (Autumn 1945): 677–82.

———. "Spengler after the Decline." *Prisms*. Cambridge, Mass.: The MIT Press, 1982.

———. *Aesthetic Theory*. Translated by Robert Hullot-Kentor. Minneapolis: University of Minnesota Press, 1997. First published 1970.

———. *The Adorno Reader*. Edited by Brian O'Connor. Oxford: Blackwell Publishers, 2000.

Adorno, Theodor W., and Max Horkheimer. *Dialectic of Enlightenment*. London: Verso, 1979. First published 1944.

Aertsen, Jan A. "Beauty in the Middle Ages: A Forgotten Transcendental?" *Medieval Philosophy and Theology* 1 (1991): 68–97.

Arendt, Hannah. *The Human Condition*. Chicago: The University of Chicago Press, 1958.

Aristotle. *The Complete Works of Aristotle*. Edited by Jonathan Barnes. 2 vols. Princeton, N.J.: Princeton University Press, 1984.

Arnold, Matthew. *The Collected Works of Matthew Arnold*. Vol. 11. London: MacMillan and Co., 1903–1904.

———. *Culture and Anarchy and Other Writings*. Cambridge: Cambridge University Press, 1993.

Auerbach, Erich. *Scenes from the Drama of European Literature*. New York: Meridian, 1959.

Augustine. *Earlier Writings*. Translated by John H. S. Burleigh. Philadelphia: The Westminster Press, 1953.

———. *The Trinity*. Translated by Edmund Hill, OP. Hyde Park, N.Y.: New City Press, 1991.

————. *The Confessions*. Translated by Maria Boulding, OSB. Hyde Park, N.Y.: New
    City Press, 1997.

Babbitt, Irving. *Literature and the American College*. Washington, D.C.: National
    Humanities Institute, 1986.

Balthasar, Hans Urs von. *The Glory of the Lord: A Theological Aesthetics*. Translated by
    Erasmo Leiva-Merikakis. San Francisco: Ignatius Press, 1982.

————. *Love Alone Is Credible*. Translated by D. C. Schindler. San Francisco: Igna-
    tius Press, 2004.

Barrès, Maurice. *Les Déracinés*. Paris: Union Générale d'Editions, 1986.

Barth, Karl. *Protestant Theology in the Nineteenth Century*. Translated by Brian Coz-
    ens and John Bowden. Grand Rapids, Mich.: William B. Eerdmans Publishing
    Company, 2002.

Beer, Jeremy. "By the Book." *The American Conservative* 8, no. 9 (May 4, 2009):
    19–20.

Bell, Clive. *Art*. London: Chatto Windus, 1914.

Benedict XVI. *God Is Love*. Washington, D.C.: United States Conference of Catholic
    Bishops, 2006.

————. *Caritas in Veritate*. San Francisco: Ignatius Press, 2009.

Bernstein, Charles. *Rough Trades*. Los Angeles: Sun and Moon Classics, 1991.

Bernstein, J. M. "'The dead speaking of stones and stars': Adorno's *Aesthetic Theory*."
    In *The Cambridge Companion to Critical Theory*, edited by Fred Rush, 139–64.
    Cambridge: Cambridge University Press, 2004.

Berry, Wendell. *What Are People For?* San Francisco: North Point Press, 1990.

————. *The Way of Ignorance and Other Essays*. Emeryville, Calif.: Shoemaker and
    Hoard, 2005.

Blum, Christopher Olaf, ed. *Critics of the Enlightenment*. Wilmington, Del.:
    ISI Books, 2004.

Bobik, Joseph. *Aquinas on Being and Essence: A Translation and Interpretation*. Notre
    Dame, Ind.: University of Notre Dame Press, 1965.

Boccaccio, Giovanni. *Life of Dante*. Translated by Philip Wicksteed. Richmond,
    U.K.: Oneworld Classics, 2009.

Bonaventure. *The Soul's Journey to God, The Tree of Life, The Life of St. Francis*. Trans-
    lated by Ewert Cousins. New York: Paulist Press, 1978.

Brague, Rémi. *Eccentric Culture: A Theory of Western Civilization*. Translated by
    Samuel Lester. South Bend, Ind.: St. Augustine's Press, 2002.

————. *The Wisdom of the World*. Translated by Teresa Lavender Fagan. Chicago:
    University of Chicago Press, 2003.

————. "Necessity of the Good." *First Things* 250 (February 2015): 47–52.

Brooks, David "The Organization Kid." *The Atlantic Monthly* 287 (April 2001):
    40–54.

Burke, Edmund. *A Philosophical Enquiry into the Sublime and the Beautiful and*

Other Pre-Revolutionary Writings. Edited by David Womersley. London: Penguin Books, 1998. First published 1757.

————. *Reflections on the Revolution in France*. Edited by J. C. D. Clark. Stanford, Calif.: Stanford University Press, 2001. First published 1790.

Carroll, William. "Illusions of Unity? Mind, Value, and Nature," *Public Discourse* (www.thepublicdiscourse.com), September 23, 2013.

Cassian, John. *Conferences*. Translated by Colm Luibheid. New York: Paulist Press, 1985.

Chesterton, G. K. *Collected Works*. Vol. 1, *Orthodoxy, Heretics, Blatchford Controversies*. San Francisco: Ignatius, 1986.

The Cloud of Unknowing. Mahwah, N.J.: Paulist Press, 1981.

Coleridge, Samuel Taylor. *The Major Works*. Oxford: Oxford University Press, 1985.

Cowley, Malcolm. *A Second Flowering*. New York: Viking Press, 1976.

Crary, Jonathan. *24/7: Late Capitalism and the Ends of Sleep*. London: Verso, 2013.

Dante Alighieri. *The Literary Criticism of Dante Alighieri*. Edited by Robert S. Haller. Lincoln: University of Nebraska Press, 1973.

————. *The Divine Comedy*. Translated by Allen Mandelbaum. New York: Everyman's Library, 1995.

Darwin, Charles. *Autobiography*. New York: W. W. Norton, 2005.

Davis, Michael. *The Poetry of Philosophy*. South Bend, Ind.: St. Augustine's Press, 1999.

Deneen, Patrick J. "Counterfeiting Conservatism." *The American Conservative* 9, no. 4 (April 2010): 16–18.

Dermer, Scott B. "Augustine and the Virtue of *Studiositas*." (Unpublished paper), http://wesley.nnu.edu/fileadmin/imported_site/wts/44_annual_meeting/papers/Scott%20Dermer%20-%20Augustine_and_the_Virtue_of_Studiositas_3_1_09.pdf

Descartes, René. *Meditations on First Philosophy*. Translated by Donald A. Cress. Indianapolis: Hackett, 1993.

————. *Discourse on Method and Meditations on First Philosophy*. Translated by Donald A. Cress. Indianapolis: Hackett, 1998.

————. *The World and Other Writings*. Translated by Stephen Gaukroger. Cambridge: Cambridge University Press, 1998.

Detienne, Marcel. *The Creation of Mythology*. Translated by Margaret Cook. Chicago: University of Chicago Press, 1986.

Donoghue, Denis. *Speaking of Beauty*. New Haven, Conn.: Yale University Press, 2003.

Dreher, Rod. *Crunchy Cons*. New York: Crown Forum, 2006.

Dreyfuss, Hubert, and Sean Dorrance Kelly. *All Things Shining*. New York: Free Press, 2011.

Dupré, Louis. *Passage to Modernity: An Essay in the Hermeneutics of Nature and Culture*. New Haven, Conn.: Yale University Press, 1993.

————. *The Enlightenment and the Intellectual Foundations of Modern Culture* (New Haven, Conn.: Yale University Press, 2004.

Eagleton, Terry. *After Theory*. New York: Basic Books, 2003.

Eco, Umberto. *The Aesthetics of Thomas Aquinas*. Translated by Hugh Bredin. Cambridge, Mass.: Harvard University Press, 1988. (First published 1956)

————. *Art and Beauty in the Middle Ages*. Translated by Hugh Bredin. New Haven, Conn.: Yale University Press, 2002. (First published 1959)

Edmundson, Mark. *Why Read?* New York: Bloomsbury, 2005.

Eliot, T. S. *Selected Essays 1917–1932*. New York: Harcourt, Brace and Company, 1932.

————. *Essays Ancient and Modern*. New York: Harcourt, Brace and Company, 1936.

————. Introduction to *Leisure, The Basis of Culture*, by Joseph Pieper. Translated by Alexander Dru. London: Faber and Faber, 1952.

————. *To Criticize the Critic and Other Writings*. New York: Farrar, Straus and Giroux, 1965.

————. *Selected Prose*. Edited by Frank Kermode. New York: Farrar, Straus and Giroux, 1975.

————. *Christianity and Culture*. San Diego: Harcourt, Brace and Company, 1976.

————. *Complete Poems and Plays 1909–1950*. New York: Harcourt, Brace and Company, 1980.

————. *The Letters*. Vol. 1, *1898–1922*. Revised Edition. Edited by Valerie Eliot and Hugh Haughton. London: Faber and Faber, 2009.

————. *The Letters*. Vol. 2, *1923–1925*. Edited by Valerie Eliot and Hugh Haughton. London: Faber and Faber, 2009.

Everyman. Mineola, N.Y.: Dover Publications, 1995.

Finley, M. I., ed. *The Portable Greek Historians*. New York: Penguin Books, 1977.

Frazer, James George. *The Golden Bough*. London: Oxford University Press, 1994.

Frye, Northrop. *Anatomy of Criticism*. Princeton, N.J.: Princeton University Press, 1957.

Fukuyama, Francis. *The End of History and the Last Man*. New York: Avon Books, 1992.

Gilson, Etienne. *Études sur le rôle de la pensée médiévale dans la formation du système cartésien*. Paris: Vrin, 1930.

————. *The Spirit of Mediaeval Philosophy*. Translated by A. H. C. Downes. Notre Dame, Ind.: University of Notre Dame Press, 1991.

Godwin, William. *Caleb Williams*. London: Penguin, 2005.

Gottfried, Paul. *Multiculturalism and the Politics of Guilt: Toward a Secular Theocracy*. Columbia: University of Missouri Press, 2002.

Gracia, Jorge J. E. "The Transcendentals in the Middle Ages: An Introduction." *Topoi* 11, no. 2 (September 1992): 113–20.

Gregory, Brad S. *The Unintended Reformation*. Cambridge, Mass.: Harvard University Press, 2012.

Grossman, Lev. "Good Books Don't Have to Be Hard." *The Wall Street Journal*, August 28, 2009.

Hadot, Pierre. *What Is Ancient Philosophy?* Translated by Michael Chase. Cambridge, Mass.: Harvard University Press, 2002.

Hanke, John W. *Maritain's Ontology of the Work of Art.* The Hague: Martinus Nijhoff, 1973.

Hart, Kevin. "Contemplation: Beyond and Behind." *Sophia* 48 (2009): 435–59.

Hazlitt, William. *The Spirit of the Age or Contemporary Portraits.* London: Henry Colburn, 1825.

Henrie, Mark C. "Why Go to College?" *The Canon* (Spring 2008): 24–35.

Herodotus. *The Histories.* Translated by Aubrey de Sélincourt. Harmondsworth, U.K.: Penguin Books, 1972.

Hobbes, Thomas. *Leviathan.* Indianapolis: Hackett, 1994.

Hopkins, Gerard Manley. *The Major Works.* Oxford: Oxford University Press, 2009.

Howard, Claud. *Coleridge's Idealism: A Study of Its Relationship to Kant and to the Cambridge Platonists.* Boston: R. G. Badger, 1924.

Hulme, T. E. *Speculations.* London: Routledge and Kegan Paul, 1987.

———. *The Collected Writings of T. E. Hulme.* Oxford: Clarendon Press, 1994.

Hume, David. *An Enquiry Concerning Human Understanding.* Indianapolis: Hackett Publishing, 1993.

Ignatius of Loyola. *Spiritual Exercises and Selected Works.* New York: Paulist Press, 1991.

Jameson, Fredric. *Postmodernism, or, the Cultural Logic of Late Capitalism.* Durham, N.C.: Duke University Press, 2001.

———. *A Singular Modernity.* London: Verso, 2002.

Jay, Martin. *Marxism and Totality.* Berkeley: University of California Press, 1984.

John Paul II. *Laborem Exercens.* Encyclical Letter. September 14, 1981.

———. *Ut Unum Sint.* Encyclical Letter. May 25, 1995.

———. *Fides et Ratio.* Encyclical Letter. September 14, 1998.

Jenkins, Iredell. "The Postulate of an Impoverished Reality." *The Journal of Philosophy* 39, no. 20 (September 24, 1942): 533–47.

Joyce, James. *The Portable Joyce.* New York: Penguin Books, 1975.

Julian of Norwich. *Showings.* Translated by Edmund Colledge, OSA. Mahwah, N.J.: Paulist Press, 1978.

Kalb, James. *The Tyranny of Liberalism.* Wilmington, Del.: ISI Books, 2008.

Kant, Immanuel. *Religion within the Limits of Reason Alone.* Translated by Theodore M. Greene and Hoyt H. Hudson. New York: Harper Torchbooks, 1960.

———. *Critique of Judgment.* Translated by Werner S. Pluhar. Indianapolis: Hackett Publishing, 1987.

———. *The Critique of Pure Reason.* Translated by Paul Guyer and Allen W. Wood. Cambridge: Cambridge University Press, 2007.

Keats, John. *Complete Poems and Selected Letters*. New York: The Modern Library, 2001.

Kerr, Fergus. *After Aquinas: Versions of Thomism*. Oxford: Blackwell Publishing, 2002.

Kinsella, Thomas. *Collected Poems*. Winston-Salem, N.C.: Wake Forest University Press, 2006.

Kirk, Russell. *The Sword of Imagination*. Grand Rapids, Mich.: Eerdmans, 1995.

———. *Redeeming the Time*. Wilmington, Del.: ISI Books, 1999.

———. *The Conservative Mind: From Burke to Eliot*. 7th ed. Washington, D.C.: Regnery Publishing, 2001. First published 1953 by H. Regnery as *The Conservative Mind: From Burke to Santayana*.

———. *Eliot and His Age*. Wilmington, Del.: ISI Books, 2008. First published 1971 by Random House.

———. *Prospects for Conservatives*. n.p: Imaginative Conservative Books, 2013.

Latour, Bruno. *We Have Never Been Modern*. Cambridge, Mass.: Harvard University Press, 1993.

Lawler, Peter Augustine. *Aliens in America*. Wilmington, Del.: ISI Books, 2002.

Lears, T. J. Jackson. *No Place of Grace: Antimodernism and the Transformation of American Culture, 1880–1920*. Chicago: University of Chicago Press, 1994.

Livingston, Donald W. *Philosophical Melancholy and Delirium*. Chicago: University of Chicago Press, 1998.

———. "David Hume and the Conservative Tradition." *The Intercollegiate Review* 44, no. 2 (Fall 2009): 30–41.

Lloyd, David. *Ireland After History*. Notre Dame, Ind.: University of Notre Dame Press, 1999.

Loy, Mina. *Lost Lunar Baedeker*. Edited by Roger L. Conover. New York: Farrar, Straus and Giroux, 1996.

Lubac, Henri de. *The Mystery of the Supernatural*. New York: Herder and Herder, 1998.

Lucretius. *On the Nature of Things*. Translated by Anthony Esolen. Baltimore: The Johns Hopkins University Press, 1995.

Lyotard, Jean-François. *The Postmodern Condition: A Report on Knowledge*. Minneapolis: University of Minnesota Press, 2002.

MacIntyre, Alasdair. *Whose Justice? Which Rationality?* Notre Dame, Ind.: University of Notre Dame Press, 1988.

———. "What Makes a Painting a Religious Painting?" Paper presented at the Fall Conference of the Notre Dame Center for Ethics and Culture, Notre Dame, Ind., November 18–20, 2004.

———. *After Virtue*. 3rd ed. Notre Dame, Ind.: University of Notre Dame Press, 2007.

———. *God, Philosophy, Universities*. Lanham, Md.: Rowman and Littlefield Publishers, 2009.

Maistre, Joseph de. *Oeuvres Complètes*. Vol. 1. Lyon: Librairies Générale Catholique et Classique, 1891.

Maritain, Jacques. *A Preface to Metaphysics: Seven Lectures on Being*. New York: Sheed and Ward, 1940.

———. *Ransoming the Time*. Translated by Harry Lorin Binsse. New York: Charles Scribner's Sons, 1941.

———. *The Dream of Descartes*. Translated by Mabelle L. Andison. New York: Philosophical Library, 1944.

———. *Creative Intuition in Art and Poetry*. New York: Pantheon Books, 1953.

———. *The Situation of Poetry*. New York: Philosophical Library, 1955.

———. *Art and Scholasticism and the Frontiers of Poetry*. Translated by Joseph W. Evans. Notre Dame, Ind.: University of Notre Dame Press, 1962.

———. *The Degrees of Knowledge*. Translated by Gerald B. Phelan. Notre Dame, Ind.: University of Notre Dame Press, 1995.

———. *The Collected Works of Jacques Maritain*. Vol. 11, *Integral Humanism, Freedom in the Modern World, and A Letter on Independence*. Edited by Otto Bird. Translated by Otto Bird, Joseph Evans, and Richard O'Sullivan, KC. Notre Dame, Ind.: University of Notre Dame Press, 1996.

———. *The Person and the Common Good*. Translated by John J. Fitzgerald. Notre Dame, Ind.: University of Notre Dame Press, 2006.

Maritain, Jacques, and Raïssa Maritain. *Oeuvres Complètes*. 17 vols. Fribourg: Éditions Universitaires, 1984.

Marx, Karl. *Early Political Writings*. Edited by Joseph O'Malley. Cambridge: Cambridge University Press, 1994.

McCabe, Herbert. *God Still Matters*. London: Continuum, 2005.

McCarthy, Conor. "Seamus Deane: Between Burke and Adorno." *The Yearbook of English Studies* 35 (2005): 232–48.

McGinn, Bernard. *The Foundations of Mysticism*. New York: Crossroad, 1991.

Milbank, John. "Fictioning Things: Gift and Narrative." *Religion and Literature* 37, no. 3 (Autumn 2005): 1–35.

Miles, Margaret. "The Eye of the Body and the Eye of the Mind in Saint Augustine's *De trinitate* and *Confessions*." *The Journal of Religion* 63, no. 2 (April 1983): 125–42.

Newman, John Henry. *An Essay on the Development of Christian Doctrine*. Notre Dame, Ind.: University of Notre Dame Press, 1979.

———. *The Idea of the University*. Notre Dame, Ind.: University of Notre Dame Press, 1982.

———. *An Essay in Aide of a Grammar of Assent*. Notre Dame, Ind.: University of Notre Dame Press, 1989.

———. *Discourses Addressed to Mixed Congregations*. Notre Dame, Ind.: University of Notre Dame Press, 2002.

Nietzsche, Friedrich. *The Works.* 5 vols. Translated by Anonymous. New York: The Tudor Publishing Company, 1931.

O'Connell, Robert J., SJ. *Art and the Christian Intelligence in St. Augustine.* Cambridge, Mass.: Harvard University Press, 1978.

O'Connor, David K., ed., *The Symposium of Plato: The Shelley Translation.* Translated by P. B. Shelley. South Bend, Ind.: St. Augustine's Press, 2002.

———. *Plato's Bedroom: Ancient Wisdom and Modern Love.* South Bend, Ind.: St. Augustine's Press, 2015.

O'Reilly, Kevin E. *Aesthetic Perception: A Thomistic Perspective.* Dublin: Four Courts Press, 2007.

Pascal, Blaise, *Pensées.* Translated by W. F. Trotter. Mineola, N.Y.: Dover Publications, Inc., 2003.

Pauken, Tom. *Bringing America Home.* Rockford, Ill.: Chronicles Press, 2010.

Pieper, Joseph. *Faith, Hope, Love.* San Francisco: Ignatius Press, 1997.

———. *Leisure, the Basis of Culture.* Translated by Gerald Malsbary. South Bend, Ind.: St. Augustine's Press, 1998.

———. *The Platonic Myths.* Translated by Dan Farrelly. South Bend, Ind.: St. Augustine's Press, 2010.

Pinker, Steven. "Evolutionary Psychology and the Blank Slate." In *What Scientists Think*, by Jeremy Stangroom, 23–36. London: Routledge, 2005.

Plato. *Complete Works.* Edited by John M. Cooper. Indianapolis: Hackett Publishing Company, 1997.

———. *Phaedrus.* Translated by Stephen Scully. Newburyport, Mass.: Focus Publishing, 2003.

Plotinus. *The Enneads.* Translated by Stephen MacKenna. London: Penguin Books, 1991.

Ponticus, Evagrius. *The Praktikos and Chapters on Prayer.* Translated by John Eudes. Kalamazoo, Mich.: Cistercian Publications, 1981.

Pound, Ezra. *The ABC of Reading.* New York: New Directions, 1960.

———. *Selected Letters, 1907–1941.* New York: New Directions, 1971.

———. *Personae.* New York: New Directions, 1990.

Pseudo-Dionysius. *The Complete Works.* Translated by Colm Luibheid. New York: Paulist Press, 1987.

Rahme, Mary. "Coleridge's Concept of Symbolism." *Studies in English Literature, 1500–1900* 9, no. 4 (Autumn 1969): 619–32.

Ransom, John Crowe. *God without Thunder.* London: Gerald Howe Ltd., 1931.

Ratzinger, Joseph. *Introduction to Christianity.* Translated by J. R. Foster. San Francisco: Ignatius Books, 2004.

Raubicheck, Walter. "Jacques Maritain, T. S. Eliot, and the Romantics." *Renascence* 46, no. 1 (Fall 1993): 71–79.

Reno, R. R. "A Philosophy for the Powerful." *First Things* 219 (Janurary 2012): 3–6.

Richard of St. Victor. *The Twelve Patriarchs, The Mystical Ark, Book Three of the Trinity*. Translated by Grover A. Zinn. New York: Paulist Press, 1979.

Richards, I. A. *Principles of Literary Criticism*. New York: Harcourt Brace, 1934.

Ricoeur, Paul. *Time and Narrative*. Chicago: University of Chicago Press, 1983.

Rieff, Philip. *The Triumph of the Therapeutic*. Wilmington, Del.: ISI Books, 2006.

Rigolio, Alberto. "Aristotle's 'Poetics' in Syriac and Arabic Translations: Readings of Tragedy," *Khristianskii Vostok* 6 (2013): 141–43.

Rousselot, Pierre. *The Eyes of Faith*. Translated by Joseph Donceel. New York: Fordham University Press, 1990.

———. *Intelligence: Sense of Being, Faculty of God*. Translated by Andrew Tallon. Milwaukee, Wisc.: Marquette University Press, 1999.

———. *Essays on Love and Knowledge*. Translated by Andrew Tallon, Pol Vandevelde, and Alan Vincelette. Milwaukee, Wisc.: Marquette University Press, 2008.

Rowland, Tracey. *Ratzinger's Faith*. Oxford: Oxford University Press, 2008.

Ruddick, Lisa. "When Nothing Is Cool." In *The Future of Scholarly Writing*, edited by Angelika Bammer and Joerres Boetcher, 71–85. New York: Palgrave Macmillan, 2015.

Russello, Gerald. *The Postmodern Imagination of Russell Kirk*. Columbia: University of Missouri Press, 2007.

Ryn, Claes G. "Allan Bloom and Straussian Alienation." *Humanitas* 25, no. 1–2 (2012): 5–19.

Sachs, Joe. Introduction to *Nicomachean Ethics*, by Aristotle. Translated by Joe Sachs. Newburyport, Mass.: Focus Editions, 2002.

Santayana, George. *Three Philosophical Poets*. Cambridge, Mass.: Harvard University Press, 1922.

———. *The Essential Santayana*. Edited by Martin A. Coleman. Bloomington: Indiana University Press, 2009.

Schiller, Friedrich. *On the Aesthetic Education of Man*. Translated by Reginald Snell. Mineola, N.Y.: Dover Publications, 2004.

———. *Essays*. Edited by Walter Hinderer and Daniel O. Dahlstrom New York: Continuum, 2005.

Schindler, D. C. *Plato's Critique of Impure Reason*. Washington, D.C.: The Catholic University of America Press, 2008.

———. *The Catholicity of Reason*. Grand Rapids, Mich.: Eerdmans, 2013.

Schloesser, Stephen. *Jazz Age Catholicism: Mystic Modernism in Postwar Paris, 1919–1933*. Toronto: University of Toronto Press, 2005.

Schumacher, E. F. *A Guide for the Perplexed*. New York: HarperCollins, 1977.

Shannon, Christopher. *A World Made Safe for Differences*. Lanham, Md.: Rowman and Littlefield Publishers, 2001.

Shelley, Percy Bysshe. *Selected Poetry and Prose*. New York: Rinehart, 1956.

———. *The Selected Prose and Poetry*. Ware, U.K.: Wordsworth Editions Limited, 2002.

Sherry, Vincent. *The Great War and the Language of Modernism*. New York: Oxford University Press, 2003.

Shiffman, Mark. "Shaping the Language of Inquiry: Aristotle's Transformation of the Meanings of *Thaumaston*." *Epoché* 10, no. 1 (Fall 2005): 21–36.

Singer, Irving. *George Santayana, Literary Philosopher*. New Haven, Conn.: Yale University Press, 2000.

Spaemann, Robert. "Der Irrtum des Traditionalisten. Zur Soziologisierung der Gottesidee im 19. Jahrhundert," *Wort und Wahrheit* 8 (1953): 493–98.

Starr, Kevin. *The Lost World: American Catholic Non-Fiction at Midcentury*. Bismarck, N.D.: Wiseblood Books, 2016.

Steele, Timothy. *Missing Measures*. Fayetteville: The University of Arkansas Press, 1990.

Tennyson, Alfred. *Tennyson: A Selected Edition*. Edited by Christopher Ricks. Harlow, England: Longman, 2007.

Theile, Verena, and Linda Tredennick, eds. *New Formalisms and Literary Theory*. Basingstoke, U.K.: Palgrave Macmillan, 2013.

Thomas Aquinas. *Summa Theologica*. Translated by the Fathers of the English Dominican Province. Allen, Tex.: Christian Classics, 1981.

———. *Selected Writings*. Edited by Ralph McInerny. London: Penguin Books, 1998.

———. *Summa Contra Gentiles*. Translated by Vernon J. Bourke et al. 5 Volumes. Notre Dame, Ind.: University of Notre Dame Press, 2002.

Trapani, John G., Jr. *Poetry, Beauty, and Contemplation: The Complete Aesthetics of Jacques Maritain*. Washington, D.C.: The Catholic University of America Press, 2011.

Valiuna, Algis. "The Spirit of Abstract Art." *First Things* 159 (January 2006): 28–33.

Viladesau, Richard. *Theological Aesthetics*. New York: Oxford University Press, 1999.

Virgil. *The Aeneid*. Translated by Allen Mandelbaum. New York: Bantam Dell, 2004.

Weatherby, Harold L. *The Keen Delight: The Christian Poet in the Modern World*. Athens: University of Georgia Press, 1975.

Weaver, Richard. *Ideas Have Consequences*. Chicago: University of Chicago Press, 1984.

Weigel, George. *Witness to Hope*. New York: Cliff Street Books, 1999.

Weil, Simone. *The Need for Roots*. Translated by Arthur Wills. London: Routledge Classics, 2007.

Williams, Raymond. *Culture and Society*. New York: Harper and Row, 1966.

Wilson, James Matthew. "Louis MacNeice's Struggle with Aristotelian Ethics." *New Hibernia Review* 10, no. 4 (Winter 2006): 53–70.

———. "Representing the Limits of Judgment: Yvor Winters, Emily Dickinson and Religious Experience." *Christianity and Literature* 56, no. 3 (Spring 2007): 397–422.

———. "Style and Substance: T. S. Eliot, Jacques Maritain, and Neo-Thomism." *Religion and Literature* 42, no. 3 (Autumn 2010): 49–81.

———. "Socrates in Hell: Hecht, Humanism, and the Holocaust," *Renascence* 63, no. 2 (Winter 2011): 147–68.

———. *Timothy Steele: A Critical Introduction*. West Chester, Penn.: Story Line Press, 2012.

———. "Conservative Critics of the Bourgeoisie." *Modern Age* 55, no. 3 (Summer 2013): 14–26.

———. "The Splendor of Form," *Dappled Things* 8, no. 1 (Candlemas 2013): 43–55.

———. "An 'Organ for a Frenchified Doctrine': Jacques Maritain and *The Criterion*'s Neo-Thomism." In *T. S. Eliot and Christian Tradition*, ed. Benjamin J. Lockerd, 99–117. Lanham, Md.: Rowman and Littlefield / Fairleigh Dickinson University Press, 2014.

———. "Ancient Beauty, Modern Verse: Romanticism and Classicism from Plato to T. S. Eliot and the New Formalism." *Renascence* 67, no. 1 (Winter 2015): 3–40.

———. *The Fortunes of Poetry in an Age of Unmaking*. Bismarck, N.D.: Wiseblood Books, 2015.

———. "John Paul II's 'Letter to Artists' and the Force of Beauty." *Logos: A Journal of Catholic Thought and Culture* 18, no. 1 (Winter 2015): 46–70.

Wimsatt, W. K., Jr. "The Intentional Fallacy." In *The Verbal Icon*, 3–18. New York: Noonday Press, 1958).

Winters, Yvor. *The Collected Poetry of Yvor Winters*. Edited by Donald Davie. Chicago: The Swallow Press, 1978.

———. *In Defense of Reason*. Athens: Ohio University Press/Swallow Press, 1987.

White, Hayden. "Interpretation in History." *New Literary History* 4, no. 2 (Winter 1973): 281–314.

———. *Metahistory*. Baltimore: Johns Hopkins University Press, 1973.

———. *The Fiction of Narrative*. Edited by Robert Doran. Baltimore: Johns Hopkins University Press, 2010.

Wollstonecraft, Mary. *A Vindication of the Rights of Men and A Vindication of the Rights of Woman*. Edited by Sylvana Tomaselli. Cambridge: Cambridge University Press, 1995.

Yeats, W. B. *Autobiographies*. Edited by William H. O'Donnell and Douglas N. Archibald. New York: Macmillan, 1999.

———. "The Celtic Element in Literature." Chapter 12 in *The Collected Works of W. B. Yeats*. Vol. 4, *Early Essays*. Edited by George Bornstein and Richard J. Finneran. New York: Scribner, 2007.

Yezzi, David. "The Unrealists' Return." *The New Criterion* 24, no. 8 (April 2006): 24–27.

INDEX

Abstraction: in thought, 12, 83, 126, 149, 191, 192, 203, 215–16, 240–41, 264–66, 269, 277, 298–99, 304, 320, 324, 327

Accounts, 294–295, 310. *See also* Logos; Mythos

Adorno, Theodor W., 31, 136, 137, 155–75, 204, 206

Apology (Plato), 68, 108

Appearance, 16, 54, 57, 82, 99, 140, 158–60, 168, 170, 172, 174, 192, 215, 220, 223, 240, 245, 248n5, 256, 279–80, 289, 293, 298, 301, 333

Aquinas, Thomas, 15, 28, 92, 102, 136, 146, 148, 178–79, 269, 270, 302; on act, 95n134, 96; on art, 180, 184–88, 191; on beauty, 15, 31, 82n76, 193–204, 211, 215–25, 302; on being, 312; on contemplation, 96–97, 321; on God, 74; on intellect, 75–76, 79, 84, 88; on man, 79

Aristotle, 127, 143, 147, 152, 184, 203, 261, 280n19, 322, 328; on beauty, 86, 122–23, 230–31; on causality, 80, 131; on contemplation, 79, 89–90, 304; on form, 16, 178n2, 184, 217, 268, 308, 315; on God, 74, 96; on happiness, 46, 89, 95; on intellect and knowledge, 75–78, 83, 259, 302, 306; on imitation and poetry, 204–6, 221, 246, 262, 299, 304–5, 315; on the noble, 121–22; on wonder, 55–62. *See also Nicomachean Ethics*

Arnold, Matthew, 70n17, 145, 152, 187, 328, 335–36

Augustine, 64n1, 74n29, 77–79, 80n67, 81, 82n74, 84, 87, 96, 97, 105, 107, 143, 146,

147–49, 198, 216n13, 225, 255, 259, 300, 307, 308n116, 309–10, 312–13. *See also Confessions*

Balthasar, Hans Urs von, 16n16, 85, 85n86, 93n123, 122n9, 240n9, 255n19, 302n97, 303n100

Barth, Karl, 61n49, 276, 278, 334

Beauty: as perfection, 85, 187, 204, 210, 223–225, 228, 248; as property of being, 30, 31, 33, 98, 137, 149, 154, 161, 168, 193–94, 200, 204, 206, 210, 211, 214n8, 219n23, 223–25, 228–29, 293n67

Berry, Wendell, 134, 238–39, 303n100, 322n19

Bouguereau, William-Adophe, 215, 220n26

Brague, Remi, 21n35, 59n42, 87n97, 105n176, 107n183

Burke, Edmund: 8, 10, 11, 22, 25, 27–28, 29, 125–29, 132, 133, 135, 136, 151, 190, 239, 272, 316, 326; on aesthetics, 11–16, 19, 126, 128–29, 193, 196–197, 224–25, 231, 232; on culture, 17, 26; on the moral imagination, 31, 124, 242, 317

Canons of conservatism, 2, 10–11, 17–21, 26, 31

Catholicism, 2, 9, 10, 69n16, 147, 148, 150, 162, 177n1, 178, 183n13, 321

Chesterton, G. K., 2, 27, 28, 135

Christian Platonism, 16–22, 26–29, 63–97, 100, 102–9

Clarity, 194, 196, 198–200, 203, 209, 210, 211–14, 217, 218–20. *See also* Splendor

The Vision of the Soul: Truth, Goodness, and Beauty in the Western Tradition was designed in Adobe Garamond and composed by Kachergis Book Design of Pittsboro, North Carolina. It was printed on 60-pound Natures Natural and bound by Thomson-Shore of Dexter, Michigan.